Perspectives in Psychological Experimentation: Toward the Year 2000

In honor of Professor
Gustav A. Lienert's
60th birthday

PERSPECTIVES IN PSYCHOLOGICAL EXPERIMENTATION:
Toward the Year 2000

Edited by

VIKTOR SARRIS
*University of Frankfurt,
West Germany*

ALLEN PARDUCCI
*University of California,
Los Angeles*

LAWRENCE ERLBAUM ASSOCIATES, PUBLISHERS
1984   Hillsdale, New Jersey   London

Lawrence Erlbaum Associates, Inc., Publishers
365 Broadway
Hillsdale, New Jersey 07642

Library of Congress Cataloging in Publication Data
Main entry under title:

Perspectives in psychological experimentation.

  Bibliography: p.
  Includes index.
  1. Psychology, Experimental.   I. Sarris, Viktor.
II. Parducci, Allen.   [DNLM: 1. Psychology,
Experimental—Congresses.   2. Research—Congresses.
3. Psychology—Trends—Congresses.   BF 76.5 P467 1981]
BF181.P45   150'.724   83-16380
ISBN 0-89859-273-9

Printed in the United States of America
10 9 8 7 6 5 4 3 2 1

Contents

Foreword   **xi**

Preface   **xiii**

1. **The Experimental Approach: Dead End or Via Regia of
   Psychology**   **1**
   Allen Parducci and Viktor Sarris

   The Experimental Dream   *1*
   Dead End to the Dream?   *2*
   Continuing Incompatabilities   *6*
   References   *13*

   PART I: HISTORICAL DEVELOPMENT AND GENERAL METHODOLOGY

2. **The Experimental Method in Nineteenth- and Twentieth-
   Century Psychology**   **17**
   Michael Wertheimer

   References   *25*

3. **Experimentation and the Myth of the Incorrigible**   **27**
   Kenneth J. Gergen

   Positivist-Empiricist Metatheory: The Erosion of
      Confidence   *29*
   Experimental Science and the Problem of Phenomenal
      Instability   *31*
   Meaning Systems and Scientific Metatheory   *32*
   The Pseudo Objectivity of Behavioral Description   *34*
   Experimental Assumptions Revisited   *37*
   Experimentation in an Interpretive Science   *38*
   References   *41*

4. **Contemporary Aspects of Psychological Experimentation**   43
    Ruben Ardila

    The Experimental Method   *43*
    Experimentation in Psychology   *44*
    Social Research   *46*
    Vigor and Rigor   *46*
    Experimentation and Quasi-Experimentation   *47*
    The International Scene   *51*
    The Future of Psychology   *53*
    References   *54*

PART II: BASIC PROCESSES OF ANIMAL LEARNING AND MEMORY

5. **Learning in Man and Other Animals**   59
    M. E. Bitterman

    Vertebrate and Invertebrate Learning   *60*
    The Role of Reward in Instrumental Learning   *64*
    Future Prospects   *68*
    References   *68*

6. **Animal Memory—as Compared with Human Memory**   71
    Lajos Kardos

    Memory—A Neglected Issue in Animal Psychology   *71*
    Some Specific Characteristics of Memory in Animals   *72*
    Problems in Maze Learning: Some Further Evidence for
        Specific Visual Memory in Animals   *80*
    Concluding Remarks   *84*
    Summary   *85*
    References   *85*

7. **The Future Study of Learning and Memory from a Psychobiological Perspective**   87
    Norman E. Spear

    Trends in the Study of Motivational Influences on Learning
        and Memory: A Brief Note   *88*
    Categories of Learning and Memory   *89*
    Summary   *100*
    References   *101*

PART III: PERCEPTUAL AND COGNITIVE PSYCHOLOGY

8. **The Construction and Limitation of Consciousness**   109
        George Mandler

    The Functions of Consciousness   *110*
    The Schema as a Building Block of Consciousness   *111*
    The Construction of Conscious Experience   *112*
    The Limitation of Conscious Experience   *115*
    Future Directions   *123*
    References   *124*

9. **Perceptual and Mnemonic Functions: A Psychological
    Paradigm**   127
        Damián Kováč

    Psychic Regulation and Methodological Integration   *128*
    Recent Research   *129*
    Perception and Memory in an Interfunctional
        Context   *130*
    Where Do We Go From Here?   *133*
    References   *134*

10. **Perceptual and Judgmental Relativity**   135
        Allen Parducci

    Adaptation-Level Theory   *135*
    Range-Frequency Theory   *138*
    Implications of Range-Frequency Theory   *142*
    Future Research on Judgmental Relativity   *144*
    The Future of Experimental Psychology   *147*
    References   *148*

11. **Perceptual Processings of Words and Drawings**   151
        Paul Fraisse

    Iconic Storage   *153*
    Encoding Storage   *154*
    The Organization of Response(s)   *158*
    References   *162*

12. **Studies in Text Comprehension: Toward a Model for
    Learning from Reading**   165
        Walter Kintsch and Eileen Kintsch

    Framework for a Model for Text Comprehension   *166*
    How the Model works   *168*

Competence of the Model   *172*
Future Applications   *174*
References   *175*

PART IV: DIFFERENTIAL, SOCIAL, AND DEVELOPMENTAL
          PSYCHOLOGY

13. **The Biology of Individual Differences**   **179**
     Hans Jürgen Eysenck

     References   *193*

14. **Biological Determination of Personality Dimensions**   **197**
     Jan Strelau

     Biological Determination of Personality Dimensions   *198*
     References   *208*

15. **The Situation in an Interactional Paradigm of
     Personality Research**   **211**
     David Magnusson

     Importance of the Situational Context in Behavior   *211*
     Theoretical Models and Their Implications   *213*
     Empirical Illustrations of the Role of Situations   *220*
     Age Differences in Situation Perception   *220*
     Interindividual Differences in Behavior   *224*
     Consequences of an Interactional Paradigm   *227*
     Concluding Recommendations   *230*
     References   *232*

16. **Perspectives in Human Motivational Psychology: A
     New Experimental Paradigm**   **235**
     Julius Kuhl and John W. Atkinson

     The Past: Three Theoretical Developments   *237*
     The Present: Two Experimental Paradigms   *244*
     The Future: A New Experimental Paradigm   *247*
     References   *250*

17. **Social Psychology: What it is, Where it Came From,
     and Where it is Headed**   **253**
     Philip G. Zimbardo

     Current and Projected Directions   *258*
     References   *265*

18. **From Traditional Factor Analysis to Structural—Causal
     Modeling in Developmental Research**   267
         John R. Nesselroade and Paul B. Baltes

     Introduction   *267*
     Some Factor Analysis History: Analysis Procedures versus
         Research Purposes   *268*
     Combinations of Data Analysis Procedures and Research
         Purposes   *271*
     Causal Modeling and Structural Analysis: Toward
         Convergence of Purpose and Data Analysis in
         Multivariate Developmental Explanation   *273*
     What Lies Ahead?   *284*
     References   *284*

PART V: CLINICAL AND APPLIED PSYCHOLOGY

19. **Information Processing in Psychopathology**   291
         *Mitchell L. Kietzman, Joseph Zubin, and Stuart
         Steinhauer*

     Visual Persistence   *294*
     Basic Questions   *296*
     Visual Persistence and Psychopathology: Illustrative
         Data   *301*
     Summary and Conclusions   *304*
     References   *307*

20. **Nonspecific Factors and Drug and Placebo Response
     in Psychiatry**   311
         Robert W. Downing and Karl Rickels

     Clinical versus Research Orientation in
         Psychopharmacology   *313*
     References   *320*

21. **New Approaches in Behavior Therapy Research**   323
         Johannes C. Brengelmann

     Introduction   *323*
     Broad-Spectrum Therapy   *324*
     Multicomponent Analysis as Used in the Treatment for
         Smoking   *327*
     Large-Scale Application in Prevention   *331*
     From Behavioral Psychiatry to Behavioral Medicine   *332*
     Expectations for the Future   *336*
     References   *339*

**22. Decision Analysis: A Nonpsychological
Psychotechnology**   **341**
Ward Edwards

What is a Decision Analysis?   *341*
The Research and Development Problems of Decision
    Analysis   *346*
Incompatibilities Between Scientific Psychology and
    Decision Analysis   *347*
What Might Psychology Be About in 20 Years?   *350*
References   *353*

**Epilogue: The Future of Experimental Psychology—
Toward the Year 2000**   **355**
Viktor Sarris and Allen Parducci

Author Index   359
Subject Index   367

Foreword

It was a beautiful and scientifically stimulating idea for the editors of this volume to assemble, toward the end of the twentieth century, leading experimental psychologists to discuss viewpoints and directions for psychological research. As I see it, the experimental approach has proven the most fertile source of development in psychology throughout its one-hundred year history. The experimental approach has been the most fertile in that it has yielded the highest value of research, both in the reliability and conclusiveness of its findings. The psychological experiment has indeed become the *via regia* for the pursuit of knowledge in our science.

A review of the great theoretical speculations in psychology makes clear that few have prevailed. The premature, all-inclusive concepts of personality dynamics, the numerous typologies and graphologies, the all too early, abstract, and global mathematical models, and the enthusiastic embracing of various philosophical systems for psychology—none have prevailed. In contrast, the paradigm of psychological experimentation has not only held its ground but has even systematically expanded.

Whether one views nineteenth-century psychophysics as already a part of experimental psychology or instead as a marginal aspect of sensory physiology, Ebbinghaus' (1885) *Über das Gedächtnis* (*On Memory*) was the crucial step towards experimental psychology. It was Ebbinghaus who introduced continuity into the progression of knowledge, a continuity that psychologists respect today and will, for good reasons, go on respecting in the future. Ebbinghaus stimulated the kind of research and problem solving that previously had lead to the great triumphs of the natural sciences during the eighteenth and nineteenth centuries. This approach to science became the model for many of the great experimental psychologists of the twentieth century.

In the course of its development, experimental psychology has become differentiated so that it now includes subject areas that seemed inaccessible to experimentation just a generation ago. The present volume gives impressive proof of this development. Consequently, it provides a fitting occasion for reporting a new recognition of the place of psychology among the natural sciences.

For almost two years, certain psychologists have conferred officially about the possibility of a worldwide representation of psychology in the Association of Natural Sciences. Up to now, psychology has been represented at the international level only among the social sciences. It has been the aim of the International Union of Psychological Science to become a full member of the International Council of Scientific Unions (ICSU), composed of the 18 most important natural sciences as well as the National Academies of Science of more than 70 nations. Many of these academies, including the British Royal Society, the Royal Academies of Sweden and the Netherlands, the Hungarian Academy, the American National Academy of Science, the German Research Foundation, the Academies of Science of the German Democratic Republic, the Philippines, Japan, and other countries, have declared their support for the affiliation of psychology with ICSU—and thereby for its recognition as a natural science.

On September 17, 1982, 71 academies of science and 17 international societies voted at Cambridge University to admit the International Union of Psychological Science as the nineteenth full member of ICSU. This action unites psychology with mathematics, chemistry, and (perhaps most important) with the three societies of the biological sciences and the International Society of Physiology.

This decision has far-reaching consequences. It makes possible for psychologists from various countries participation in the broad international research projects of our time: Earth and Space, Environment, Technologies and Society—to name only a few of the ICSU projects.

On each project, the effectiveness of psychology's contribution will depend on what substantive knowledge it has to contribute. Such knowledge will be acquired through the expansion of experimental methods and their application to the different fields of psychology. Thus we have strong indications that experimental psychology, toward the end of the twentieth century, is subject to new and powerful impulses for further development. It seems likely that these impulses will produce qualitative changes in the character of psychology, changes that will enhance its worldwide role in the twenty-first century.

Friedhart Klix
Humboldt University, Berlin, GDR

Preface

One response to questions about the *future* of psychology is to attempt an answer to another question: What have we learned from psychology's past? This book presents a collection of original papers by authorities with international reputations in various fields of psychology. Contributors were invited to appraise the past of their own research specialties, with an eye toward the future. The emphasis is upon the more scientific areas of psychological research.

The catalyst for this book was an international conference honoring Gustav A. Lienert, held at Bad Homburg, West Germany, in 1981. Some two dozen psychologists from both Western and Eastern Europe, North and South America, and representing fields as different as psychophysics is from clinical psychology, or animal memory from human decision making, described their research and argued the prospects for the future of experimental psychology. In spite of dramatic differences in viewpoint, communication was remarkably open and empathic. Disagreements were pursued in friendly give-and-take discussion. Most of the arguments found their way into this book where readers can confront the different viewpoints in more polished form.

The introductory chapter tries to summarize contemporary conflicts about how psychology should develop, classifying them with respect to enduring polarities. Questions are raised about the past success of experimental psychology and its future prospects. The three chapters of Part I examine experimental psychology from historical, philosophical, and methodological perspectives. Like the rest of the book, these chapters are written for research scholars, graduate students, and even those advanced undergraduates in psychology who are concerned about where experimental psychology is going.

The remaining chapters sample specific research areas. Part II examines substantive research on animal learning and memory—a mixture of genuinely comparative psychology, concerns with classical problems such as place learning, and attempts to bridge the usual separation between animal and human psychology. Part III continues the mixture of old and new. Its topics vary from classical perception and judgment to contemporary information-processing approaches in cognitive psychology. Though necessarily a limited sampling of this huge domain of research, the variety of problems and methods seems characteristic of contemporary research on cognition. Part IV leaves the traditional experimental laboratory to examine recent developments in motivation, personality, and social fields and in the biopsychology of individual differences. With its liberal mixture of correlational and experimental approaches, Part IV ends with a sober consideration of new techniques for drawing causal inferences from correlations. Part V samples the more research-oriented areas of applied psychology, including psychopharmacology, the psychopathology of perception, and different behavior therapies. The final chapter criticizes experimental psychology's aloofness from practical problems, and the Epilogue summarizes the grander dreams entertained by the 29 contributing authors for the future of scientific psychology.

ACKNOWLEDGMENTS

In addition to our fellow authors, as editors we wish particularly to thank M. E. Bitterman, Hans J. Eysenck, Walter Kintsch, and Norman E. Spear for their helpful comments and work on the style of some of the papers by contributors whose native language is not English.

The following list of reviewers of individual chapters includes highly respected experts in various research specialties: N. H. Anderson, W. F. Angermeier, M. E. Bitterman, Lilian Blöschl, J. Bredenkamp, J. Brengelmann, W. Butollo, R. Cohen, J. Delius, H. J. Eysenck, C. F. Graumann, J. P. Huston, K. J. Klauer, R. Kohnen, W. Krohne, J. Kuhl, J. R. Nesselroade, P. Netter, R. Pongratz, E.-R. Rey, Barbara A. Rosenberg, E. Scheerer. L. Schmidt, W. Traxel, D. Vaitl, F. E. Weinert, D. Wendt, Barbara Zoeke, and J. Zubin. We are grateful for these careful reviews which varied from brief comments to extended critiques. This review process provided a useful basis for feedback to the authors. We are also grateful to Yvonne Sturm and Gisa Stolze for help with the index.

Franz E. Weinert deserves special recognition as one of the promoters of the conference leading to this book, as do Paul E. Baltes, Hans J. Eysenck, John E. Nesselroade, and Michael Wertheimer who were especially helpful in their suggestions for bringing this book to publication.

Rudolph Kerscher, Secretary General of the Fritz Thyssen Foundation sponsored the conference, and the Werner Reimers Foundation provided space and facilities in the most beautiful surroundings. They have our gratitude.

Finally, we take pride that Friedhardt Klix, one of the most eminent East European representatives of modern experimental psychology and currently President of the International Union of Psychological Science (1980–1984), has provided the Foreword to this book.

A. P.
V. S.

1 The Experimental Approach: Dead End or Via Regia of Psychology?

Allen Parducci
University of California, Los Angeles, USA

Viktor Sarris
University of Frankfurt a.M., West Germany

THE EXPERIMENTAL DREAM

The psychological experiment is the basic research tool employed by most of the contributors to this book. With few exceptions, their faith in the experimental method remains firmly secure. Conceptually, the independent variation of different causal factors seems the ideal way to disentangle the natural confounding that otherwise makes arbitrary the choice between alternative explanations. This is the approach that has proven so useful in natural science, and it has also worked in psychology. Perhaps the most enduring examples have been in psychophysics where independent manipulation of simple physical stimuli elicits highly predictable responses, as described by the psychophysical laws of Weber and Fechner. Behavior is predictable when the experimental constraints are arranged with sufficient simplicity and control.

The crucial role of the experimental method is evident in its effects upon our thinking about the psychology of everyday life as well as upon the advancement of psychology as a science. In everyday life, the experimental approach provides a powerful prophylactic against the quackery, superstition, and prescientific thinking that characterizes the public scene in psychology. Within the scientific discipline itself, controlled experiments have falsified a host of plausible hypotheses, leading to better theories and a bedrock of empirical facts.

And yet, in spite of its century or more of vigorous development (see Boring, 1950, for the monumental but obviously limited history), the experimental dream has had rough going. Even if one were sophisticated enough not to have expected a simple linear development, the possibility of a spiral ascension might not have seemed unrealistic. Unfortunately, the spiral model of progress, as portrayed in

1

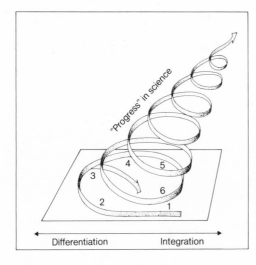

FIG. 1.1. The naive spiral model of scientific progress toward increased integration. Numbers refer to: (1) creating research issues, (2) generating testable hypotheses, (3) designing empirical tests, (4) collecting, (5) analyzing, and (6) drawing conclusions leading to new research hypotheses. Unshaded arrow from 3 back to 1 represents influence of available methods upon hypotheses. Modified from Sarris, 1982.

Fig. 1.1, leaves no room for the erratic ups and downs, the unfilled promises, and the revolutionary shifts in purpose that have characterized our history.

One hears so often that psychology is in a state of crisis. Psychologists are supposed to have lost faith in their discipline, whether that enterprise be conceived as basic or as applied science. Most of the chapters in this book give testimonial against this notion of a crisis, the authors evincing confidence in their own approaches and arguing for continued application of similar methods for dealing with the problems of psychology. Nevertheless, it seems appropriate to consider in this introductory chapter the particular concerns that divide scholars in their assessments of the progress and future of psychology. We take up these concerns first. Then, we discuss major differences in approach and objectives, particularly as represented by the chapters that follow.

DEAD END TO THE DREAM?

Substantive Failure?

A primary concern has been with the fruitfulness of efforts to apply the experimental method to the study of higher mental processes. Among the most negative of such assessments is the famous ending of Wittgenstein's *Philosophical Investigations:* ''The confusion and barrenness of psychology is not to be explained by calling it a young science—the existence of experimental methods makes us think we have the means of solving the problems that trouble us; though problems and methods pass one another by.'' (Wittgenstein, 1953).

A more recent appraisal, from an American philosopher, is equally negative. Searle (1982) states:

But couldn't there be . . . a science of human beings that was not introspective common-sense psychology but was not neurophysiology either? This has been the great dream of the human sciences in the twentieth century, but so far all of the efforts have been, in varying degrees, failures. The most spectacular failure was behaviorism, but in my intellectual lifetime I have lived through exaggerated hopes placed on and disappointed by games theory, cybernetics, information theory, generative grammar, structuralism, and Freudian psychology, among others. Indeed it has become something of a scandal of twentieth-century intellectual life that we lack a science of the human mind and human behavior, that the methods of the natural sciences have produced such meager results when applied to human beings [p. 3].

At the other extreme, we have the enthusiasm of contemporary cognitive psychologists, tasting the new freedom from behavioristic constraints. Taking the computerized processing of information as their model, they have directed their research to problems that would have seemed outside the pale of prescriptive behaviorism.

With the current popularity of cognitive approaches, experimental psychology seems to have come full circle. As a formal laboratory discipline, psychology started with Wundt's attempt to build a chemistry of mental elements. The promise was great, but substantive findings were sparse: only a third of a century later, the scientific community welcomed Watson's (1913) injunction that there could never be a psychological science based on introspection. The ability to condition and control the behavior of laboratory animals seemed to promise so much more, and theories of learning eventually came to dominate much of experimental psychology. This approach reached its apogee of popularity and methodological respectability with the work of Clark Hull (1952) who attempted to base a whole psychology on the association of stimulus and response by reinforcement. Early cognitive psychologists, such as Edward C. Tolman (1948), knew that this would not work for the intentional aspects of psychology. Attempts to make it work stretched the basic concepts to the point where it became clear that the theories were untestable (cf., Koch, 1954). Disenchantment replaced the dreams of a grand, all-embracing theory. ''Miniature systems'' became the stuff of the new, more realistic dreams. Mathematical models, such as *statistical learning theory* (Estes, 1960) and *signal detection theory* (Swets, Tanner, & Birdsall, 1961), achieved limited success in accounting for behavior in certain highly restricted experimental situations. But again, there was a disappointing lack of substantive development, and the more cognitive features of even the miniature system defied explanation (cf., Anderson, 1964). Nor were the expected generalizations across situations confirmed: theoretical concepts proved useful only with respect to the experimental paradigms for which they were developed. The difficulties seemed particularly egregious with respect to the *intentional* features of behavior. From many directions, this created a receptive climate for the information-processing approach. Although respectably be-havioristic in most of its methods, the current scene in psychological theory embraces mentalistic concepts like "images," "rehearsal," "storage," "re-trieval," "context," "strategies," "schemas," and the like. Its successess, some of which are described in the chapters that follow, are with specific situa-tions and problems. Some of these are of a verbal and very general character; others are more precise, using mathematical models and flow diagrams to specify particular cognitive processes and to relate them to observable conditions and responses. But, all in all, it seems that hypostatization of mental entities is once again in full flower. Are we not almost back where we began?

Hard vs. Soft Psychology

The notion of a crisis in psychology is not particularly new. In his historical monograph entitled *Krise der Psychologie,* Karl Bühler (1929) argued that the methods stemming from the three principle sources for psychology, viz., natural sciences, social sciences, and humanities, are at least partially incompatible. Where the influence of natural science steers psychology toward the study of behavior, social science encourages an emphasis on cultural environment and values, whereas the humanities direct attention to subjective experience. Bühler's argument is illustrated in Fig. 1.2.

If there is a crisis in contemporary psychology, it seems to be most serious for what Meehl (1978) has bluntly identified as the "softer" subfields: "I consider it unnecessary to persuade you that most so-called 'theories' in the soft areas of psychology (clinical, counseling, social, personality, community, and school psychology) are scientifically unimpressive and technologically worthless [p.

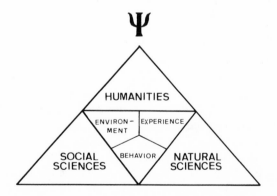

PSYCHOLOGY AS A SCIENCE (K. BÜHLER)

FIG. 1.2.   Bühler's triangular model of scientific psychology, as illustrated by Hofstatter (1977).

806].'' In distinguishing between ''hard'' and ''soft'' science, Meehl ascribes to the latter a long list of more detailed problems less clearly shared by those fields of psychology closest to physical and biological science, viz., physiological psychology, sensory perception, and psychophysics. Special problems for the softer areas are the questions of what is the stimulus, what is the response, what is the domain of application? Can theories in clinical and social psychology even be tested? The softer fields drift from theory to theory, not so much because of new evidence as because each new theory, in its turn, loses the novelty that had been its initial claim to attention.

The distinction between ''hard'' and ''soft'' areas of psychology raises questions about the boundary between them. On which side does the study of learning and memory fall—or, more reasonably, on which side does any particular study in cognitive psychology fall? And where should one locate motivation or the factor analytic research on intelligence and personality? The problems of the softer areas are shared, to some extent, by these fields; and one can raise disturbing questions about the explanatory usefulness of the theories developed in each of them.

Regarding Meehl's characterization of the technological state of the soft areas, the question of usefulness becomes most disturbing when considering the applied fields of psychology. After a half-century of experimental evaluations, it is still not clear whether traditional psychotherapies are beneficial. Recent positive claims, based on ''meta-analyses'' in which tests are performed on data compiled from hundreds of experiments (Smith & Glass, 1977), have not convinced the skeptics (e.g., Eysenck, 1978). The newer behavior therapies will have to run the same gauntlet. Successful applications of psychological concepts to social problems—whether in education, crime, or industrial relations—seem conspicuously lacking. The distinction between basic and applied concerns will be taken up later.

Standards vs. Anti-Intellectualism

When assessments are so discouraging, an obvious interpretation is that standards are too high. Perhaps psychology has promised too much or asked too much of itself. Perhaps it should be more satisfied with anything that gets it beyond common sense, with any signs of practical usefulness. The temptation to apply psychology to the complex world of everyday affairs may have encouraged a serious underestimation of the difficulties of the enterprise.

We have been writing as though the crisis within psychology were strictly an internal matter, a soul-searching by psychologists themselves. However, it seems clear that the field has also been under attack from without, and in a number of ways. Most generally, one can say that there has been a growth in anti-intellectualism (perhaps particularly rampant in North America and in Western Europe). This may be seen in the revived popularity of astrology, of unsubstantiated theories of nutrition, of creationism, of antiscientific attitudes in general. Science is often seen as a threat rather than as a benefactor.

Antiscientific sentiments have sometimes been encouraged by developments *within* the field of Psychology. For example, the idea of one human controlling another, as in certain projects based on operant conditioning, evokes fears of totalitarianism. The popularity of humanistic psychology, which was conceived (e.g., by Maslow, 1965) as a revolt against both behaviorism and psychoanalysis, opened the door to a philosophy of "anything goes." Feelings were exalted as more important than ideas. A rash of "pop" therapies appeared, each promising "a quick fix." None of these movements were rooted in the discipline of empirical research.

The question of a crisis in psychology is rarely addressed directly by the contributors to this volume. Nevertheless, their differences in approach often reflect different positions on basic dimensions of concern about the future of psychology. We shall now consider some of them in a general way, leaving their more detailed exposition to the separate contributors.

CONTINUING INCOMPATIBILITIES

Cognitive vs. S–R Psychology

The influence of contemporary cognitive psychology is reflected in the majority of the chapters of this book. Although Mandler's and the Kintsches' chapters are most clearly in the mainstream of this movement, those by Kardos, Kovač, Magnusson, Zimbardo, and Spear also make conspicuous use of the information-processing approach. Where there is a reluctance to be carried along (as in Bitterman's chapter), it is revealed more by use of traditional concepts than by direct opposition.

Perhaps it is too early to say whether cognitive psychology is mostly "old wine in new bottles" or whether it is a genuine revolution in psychological theory. In part, certainly, it is a rejection of the straightjacket imposed by reflexology and behaviorism. A lot must be going on between input and output. Where cognitive psychologists depart from the strictures of methodological behaviorism is in their readiness to speculate about intervening processes, in particular about the intentional aspects of mental phenomena. The behavioristic credo was that such speculation is unnecessary, that one can understand whatever is scientifically understandable by reducing all psychological notions to stimulus and response. Some of the great behavioristic theoreticians (especially Tolman) would have welcomed the information-processing explanations of contemporary cognitive psychology. Others (Watson, Hull, and Spence) would have been disturbed by the proliferation of hypothetical processes, fearing that it has gotten out of hand, that the mentalistic terminology is playing to our subjectivist sentiments without leading to general laws of psychology. Skinner, with his radical behaviorism, is perhaps the most extreme of contemporary holdouts.

Hardware vs. Software

The computer analogy employed by contemporary cognitive psychology concentrates on programs (software) that simulate the actual processing of information by humans. The other side of the analogy, the physical processes of the human brain (hardware), are typically of lesser interest. In this respect, cognitive psychology continues in the black-box tradition of learning theory. It is not that anyone denies the crucial importance of physiological mechanisms, of neuroscience, but rather that the program describing some cognitive process may be compatible with many different physical mechanisms, just as a computer program may be compatible with many different kinds of computer.

None of the chapters that follows takes a strict hardware approach. Nor is it clear when this should be the method of choice. However, a number of the contributors speculate about relationships between the psychological phenomena they are studying and physiological processes (e.g., Spear speculating that the work on neurotransmitters will rejuvenate the study of motivation; Bitterman that principles of learning are different for different species, depending upon evolutionary status; Kietzman, Zubin, and Steinhauer about where visual processes are localized in the nervous system and about how more of the psyche will be understood in terms of basic hardware).

Generalized Human Mind vs. Individual Differences

Many psychologists object to what they hold to be a naive attempt to discover nomothetic laws without regard to organismic factors or individual differences (Stern, 1901, 1911; cf., the chapters by Edwards, Eysenck, Magnusson, and Strelau). Presumably, even the most nomothetic of theorists would allow that the parameters of his models could reflect individual differences and that much of what he now attributes to experimental error (random factors) might eventually be explained in terms of organismic factors. Special experimental designs can incorporate tests for such factors and their interactions with experimental factors. Clear examples of how this may be accomplished are given by functional measurement (Anderson, 1981); in the procedures of functional measurement, each subject is exposed to all of the many experimental conditions (often different combinations of stimuli), and the scale values of the stimuli and sometimes their weights also are inferred separately for each subject.

In spite of this flexibility in experimental design, who can deny that traditional experimental psychology gives scant attention to individual differences? This seems due in part to the absence of sound theory about individual differences, in part to the absence of useful measures of the differences. And yet, the field of psychometrics must take a prominent place when one thinks of practical applications of psychology. The first great growth spurt of psychology was stimulated by mass testing of intelligence. Although tests of mental ability have continued to have the highest validity coefficients of any psychological measures, they remain desperately lacking in theoretical grounding (e.g., what is intelligence?). An interesting combination of the experimental and psychometric approaches is illustrated by Magnusson (Ch. 15) who shows how even the intelligence tests can yield an interaction between the individual test takers and different situations (types of items)—an approach similar to that taken by Mischel (1973) and Endler (1977). Although this example and the various other cognitive studies described by Magnussen are not experiments in the traditional sense, this mode of analysis illustrates how concern for organismic factors can assume a greater role in experimental psychology. Such is the case more generally when contemporary cognitive psychologists analyze component skills and work with them experimentally (e.g., Estes, 1978; Hunt, Lunneborg, & Lewis, 1975). However, it is not yet clear that this has advanced the practical application of psychometrics.

Eysenck makes a persuasive argument in Chapter 13 for the association between psychometric and physiological factors. It is interesting that controversy about the heritability of intelligence has produced the most acrimonious literature in the history of psychology. This is because it touches upon such sensitive political values. If Gergen is right about psychological research exemplifying social values (as he argues in Chapter 3), other theories should elicit similar levels of acrimony; that they do not may mean only that people cannot see how the research relates to their own values.

Experiments vs. Correlations

In the spirit of Quinn McNemar ("correlation is the instrument of the devil"), many experimental psychologists have regarded experiments that randomly assign subjects to systematically different conditions as the necessary prerequisite, or at least the royal road, to causal analysis. Correlations, at best, could be interesting sources of hypotheses that might then be tested experimentally. If the skeptic about laboratory experiments questions their ecological validity, the skeptic about correlations questions their interpretations.

The potential value of combining correlational and experimental approaches is now widely recognized, with particular emphasis by Cronbach (1957, 1975), Campbell and Stanley (1963), and Eysenck (1981). This position is illustrated by Fig. 1.3. In Chapter 4, Ardila discusses this combined approach and gives as an example his own large-scale correlational field study.

Chapter 18 by Nesselroade and Baltes represents a relatively recent and potentially powerful approach to correlational analysis, one that purports to wring appropriate causal inferences from nonexperimental data or from natural experi-

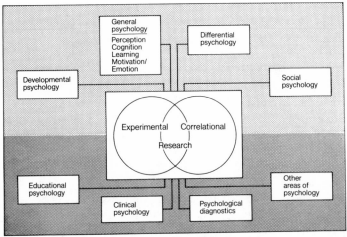

Experimental and correlational research in the different fields of psychology

FIG. 1.3.   Model for "experimental-correlational" research, suggested for all fields by Cronbach (1957, 1975). Overlapping circles represent differing emphases by "basic" (upper section) and "applied" fields (lower section). Modified from Sarris, 1983.

ments in which the conditions have not been systematically manipulated. These methods were first used in economics and sociology, but they are seeing increased application in psychology. If they prove useful, a whole range of problems will become open to causal analysis in a way that strict experimentalists previously thought impossible.

Other psychologists, such as Eysenck (Chapter 13), find it useful and even necessary to combine experimental and correlational research. This is a natural way of bringing the concern with individual differences into the laboratory. It is interesting to consider that if Eysenck had not segregated his subjects by extraversion vs. introversion, his main experimental effects would have been lost and incorrect conclusions would have seemed consistent with the data (cf., Cronbach, 1975).

Representative Design and Ecological Validity

A closely related concern is the sampling of environments (as well as subjects) for psychological research. Again, it is a problem of generalization. The model for much of experimental psychology has been the simple situation, taken by analogy from the development of classical mechanics: the solar system, a marble rolling down an inclined plane, a pendulum. Physicists do not try to predict the trajectories of leaves falling from trees. The appeal for ecological validity by means of representative design (Brunswik, 1956; Holzkamp, 1964; Petrinovich,

1979) is based on the belief that prediction is better when based on past experience with situations similar to the ones to which one wants to predict, as argued by Wertheimer (Ch. 2). In principle, simpler psychological experiments lack external validity or generalizability. The objection to representative design is that it is unlikely to reveal basic causal relationships, for these are obscured by the embarrassment of riches: too many conditions are varying so that the samples of the environment are unlikely to permit inferences about how the most important factors are operating (see Parducci, Ch. 10). The proof is in the eating, and both skeptics and believers in representative design can ask what triumphs the other approach has produced in psychology.

The desire for ecological validity, expressed in a number of the chapters, cannot be separated from the concern to make psychology more practical. Suppose that we could really achieve a respectable level of understanding about some miniature system (as appears to be the case in many areas of cognitive psychology): What reason is there to believe that this understanding would illuminate any practical domains or problems? The analogy to subsequent practical applications of classical mechanics does not satisfy those who believe in practical applications now.

Basic vs. Applied Psychology

But not all, not even most, of the contributors are concerned that psychology should become an applied science. Consider comparative psychology, taking Bitterman's Chapter 9 as an example. One finds there something of the old dream, Hull's dream and also Tolman's, of discovering through experimental studies of rats in mazes universal laws of behavior applying to all animal species, including man. Bitterman finds phylogenetic and ontogenetic differences in basic laws of learning. But these are of interest apart from any usefulness they might have in solving human problems. So too with many of the chapters by the European contributors to this book: Scientists continue to study psychological problems without apparent concern for practical applications. And when the concern is not with applications, the problems of generalizing the results, of ecological validity, seem much less pressing. Laboratory scientists can pursue a particular problem, such as how some species masters some particular type of problem, without worrying about whether their findings will generalize to other problems or other species. Those with this orientation to science may argue that premature worrying about ecological validity precludes substantive advances.

On the other hand, some contributors want scientific psychology to develop a more practical bent. Edwards (Ch. 22) is perhaps the most outspoken on this issue. His position is all the more striking in view of his own substantive contributions to basic research. In his own case, it is decision analysis that is the basis for practical applications. However, his position is much more general, arguing for greater concern for developing practical applications of psychology.

There do seem to be strong forces pushing even traditional areas of psychological research in practical directions. Granting agencies, particularly in the U.S., have recently been favoring "mission" research, projects designed to solve practical problems. This is not just in psychology: In medical research, the recent emphasis has been on projects specifically tied to diseases like cancer rather than on basic biological research. Many able research psychologists have shifted in this direction, in part to get funded but also perhaps believing that fundamental understanding may be a long time in coming while practical problems can be solved at an empirical level (see Table 1.1.)

Those pushing toward the practical end of the continuum believe that psychology either already has practical techniques to offer or else that it could with greater effort develop such techniques. Zimbardo (Ch. 17) obviously subscribes to this belief, as do Brengelmann (Ch. 21) and Eysenck (Ch. 13), at least with respect to behavior therapy. Bitterman (Ch. 5), Parducci (Ch. 10), and Wertheimer (Ch. 2) are more skeptical about what has already been accomplished, but

TABLE 1.1
Differences within Psychology
(modified from Bickman, 1981)

	Basic Research	Applied Research
Purpose and Goals	Knowledge	Problem Solving
	Relationships	Large Effects
	Causes	Predictions
	Theory	Program
	Development	Evaluation
Methodology	Internal Validity	External Validity
	Mono-method	Multiple Methods
	Experimental	Quasi-experimental
	High Precision	Low Precision
	Behavioral	Self Report
Environment	Laboratory	Field
	Not time-bound	Real Time
	Long-Duration Conception	Short-Duration Conception
	Self Initiated	Initiated by Sponsor
	Low Cost-Consciousness	High Cost-Consciousness
	Flexible	Inflexible
	Autonomous	Hierarchical
Researcher	Specialist	Generalist
	Solitary	Team Orientation
	Evaluations-Publications	Evaluation-Experience
	Average Social Skills	Special Social Skills

Wertheimer emphasizes that with a more practical orientation much more could be accomplished.

Skeptics would object that premature efforts to apply psychology have done more harm than good. A little knowledge may be a dangerous thing. By presuming to advance on methods developed over the millennia before psychology evolved as a separate discipline, we are only likely to make matters worse. Probably most psychologists working in traditional areas of basic research would line up with the skeptics while those working in applied areas would assert that psychology can already offer a great deal of practical value, e.g., Edwards and Brengelmann.

Psychology: One Discipline or Many?

Although the various contributors to this volume seemed able to communicate easily with each other at the conference that brought them together, one can well ask for how long psychology will continue to be a single discipline. What holds the different parts together? In academia, the glue may be provided by pragmatic administrative considerations: What university would countenance separate departments of physiological, clinical, personality, social, industrial, psychometric, comparative, perceptual, learning, thinking, and who knows how many other separate psychologies? And yet the primary concerns of clinical psychologists may have less in common with those of psychophysicists than sociologists have in common with economists, or linguists have with geographers. Sigmund Koch (in Wertheimer et al., 1978), while predicting the future disintegration of the field, has argued: "That psychology can be an integral discipline is the 19th-century myth that motivated its baptism as an independent science—a myth which can be shown to be exactly that both by a priori and empirico-historical considerations [p. 637]." Koch asserts that others' predictions of future integration is at variance with the recent trends toward greater modesty with respect to range of application of each separate theory.

Experimental Method: Deadlock or Royal Road?

Where do all these contemporary differences leave us with respect to the future of experimental psychology? None of the contributors question the potential usefulness of experimental methods. And yet, there is a good deal of impatience. Some would like to see a greater freedom from the traditional restrictions of experimental science. Others favor continued devotion to traditional procedures, even if this means a drawing back in the number and popularity of psychologists. Assessments of the success of experimental psychology depend on what standards are applied. Compared with the promissory notes that have shaped the popular view of the field, it has been a dismal failure: The human mind may be too complicated for successful experimental analysis; psychology is therefore in a crisis, and its most respected methods have reached a deadlock. But compared with more realistic standards, standards more typical of basic physical sciences, the various specific approaches described in these chapters have been surprisingly successful. Although the subject matter of psychology may seem frightfully complicated, the progress in such a remarkable variety of fields should encourage those who believe that the experimental method remains the royal road to understanding.

REFERENCES

Anderson, N. H. An evaluation of stimulus sampling theory: Comment on Prof. Estes' paper. In A. W. Melton (Ed.), *Categories of human learning*. New York: Academic Press, 1964.

Anderson, N. H. *Foundations of information integration theory*. New York: Academic Press, 1981.

Bickman, L. Some distinctions between basic and applied approaches. In L. Bickman (Ed.), *Applied social psychology annual*. Vol. 2. Beverly Hills, Calif.: Sage, 1981.

Boring, E. G. *A history of experimental psychology*. 2nd ed. New York: Appleton, 1950.

Brunswick, E. *Perception and the representative design of psychological experiments*. Berkeley: University of California Press, 1956.

Bühler, K. *Die krise der psychologie*. 2nd ed. Jena: G. Fischer, 1929.

Campbell, D. T., & Stanley, J. C. *Experimental and quasi-experimental designs for research*. Chicago: Rand McNally, 1963.

Cronbach, L. J. The two disciplines of scientific psychology. *American Psychologist*, 1957, *12*, 671–684.

Cronbach, L. J. Beyond the two disciplines of scientific psychology. *American Psychologist*, 1975, *30*, 116–127.

Endler, N. S. The role of person-by-situation interactions in personality theory. In D. Magnusson & N. S. Endler (Eds.), *Personality at the crossroads: Current issues in interactional psychology*. Hillsdale, N.J.: Lawrence Erlbaum Associates, 1977.

Estes, W. K. Learning theory and the new "mental chemistry," *Psychological Review*, 1960, *67*, 207–223.

Estes, W. K. The information processing approach to cognition: A confluence of metaphors and methods. In W. K. Estes (Ed.), *Handbook of learning and cognitive processes, Vol. 5: Human information processing*. Hillsdale, N.J.: Lawrence Erlbaum Associates, 1978.

Eysenck, H. J. An exercise in meta-silliness. *American Psychologist*. 1978, *33*, 517.

Eysenck, H. J. *A model for personality*. New York: Springer, 1981.

Hofstatter, P. R. *Psychologie*. Frankfurt/Main: Fischer, 1977.

Holzkamp, K. *Theorie und experiment in der psychologie*. Berlin: de Gruyter, 1964.

Hull, C. L. *A behavior system*. New Haven: Yale University Press, 1952.

Hunt, E. B., Lunneborg, C., & Lewis, J. What does it mean to be High verbal? *Cognitive Psychology*, 1975, *7*, 194–227.

Koch, S. Clark L. Hull. In S. Koch (Ed.), *Modern learning theory*. New York: Appleton-Century-Crofts, 1954.

Maslow, A. H. *Toward a psychology of being*. Princeton: Van Nostrand, 1962.

Meehl, P. E. Theoretical risks and tabular asterisks: Sir Karl, Sir Ronald, and the slow progress of soft psychology. *Journal of Consulting and Clinical Psychology*. 1978, *46*, 806–834.

Mischel, W. Toward a cognitive social learning reconceptualization of personality. *Psychological Review*, 1973, *80*, 252–283.

Petrinovich, L. Probabilistic functionalism: A conception of research method. *American Psychologist*, 1979, *34*, 373–390.

Sarris, V. *Methodologische grundlagen der experimentallen psychologie.* Berlin: de Gruyter, 1983.

Searle, J. The myth of the computer. *The New York Review of Books,* April 29, 1982, 29, 7, 3–6.

Smith, M. L., & Glass, G. V. Meta-analysis of psychotherapy outcome studies. *American Psychologist.* 1977, *32,* 752–760.

Stern, W. *Psychologie der individuellen differenzen.* Jena: G. Fischer, 1901.

Stern, W. *Die differentielle Psychologie in ihren methodologischen Grundlagen.* Leipzig: Barth, 1911.

Swets, J. A., Tanner, W. P., & Birdsall, T. G. Decision processes in perception. *Psychological Review,* 1961, *68,* 301–340.

Tolman, E. C. Cognitive maps in rats and men. *Psychological Review,* 1948, *55,* 189–208.

Watson, J. B. Psychology as a behaviorist views it. *Psychological Review,* 1913, *20,* 158–177.

Wertheimer, M., Barclay, A. G., Cook, S. W., Kiesler, C. A., Koch, S., Riegel, K. F., Rorer, L. G., Senders, V. L., Smith, M. B., & Sperling, S. Psychology and the future. *American Psychologist,* 1978, *33,* 631–647.

Wittgenstein, L. *Philosophical investigations.* New York: MacMillan, 1953.

HISTORICAL DEVELOPMENT AND GENERAL METHODOLOGY

"Optimism" and "pessimism"—such could be the titles, respectively, of the first two chapters of Part I. "Optimism," as represented by Michael Wertheimer, envisions a unifying progress within psychology, a progress toward a more enlightened application of experimental methods in each of its various fields. After a scholarly presentation of the history of experimental psychology, one that emphasizes the diversity of its beginnings, Wertheimer freely indulges in the kind of prospective ruminations that were encouraged by the organizers of this volume.

Wertheimer's optimism is expressed with respect to the future integration of psychology, a combining of nomethetic and ideographic approaches that will bring together the research strategies of experimental, correlational, and clinical psychology. He is also optimistic about the possibility of greater ecological validity for traditional experimental research. This is to be accomplished by a more serious concern with the taxonomy of the environment, the complex network of conditions under which the psychological phenomena in question occur. It is at this taxonomic stage that correlational techniques will illuminate the particular conditions most worthy of controlled experimentation. According to Wertheimer, this will permit psychology to escape its fate of seeming to learn more and more about less and less.

The pessimistic view of psychology, as represented by Kenneth Gergen's chapter, questions its very foundations. Drawing upon contemporary developments in the philosophy of science, Gergen argues against the notion of progress in the sense of uncovering the truth about psychological phenomena. His concrete illustrations are drawn primarily from his own field, social psychology; but he challenges the reader to decide whether the same difficulties do not apply to other domains of psychology. If Gergen's disheartening assessment is correct, what then can be the function of psychological experiments? Gergen's answer is that they "vivify the theoretical language," enhancing its utility. Is psychology as a science at best a purveyor of values?

In the third chapter of Part I, Ruben Ardila presents a much less-skeptical assessment of scientific psychology. Although accepting the conventional view of what the experimental method is about, Ardila's concerns tend to be more concrete and practical than those of the two preceding chapters. His own research is an example of capitalization upon natural experiments, cross-cultural differences in patterns of childrearing. His optimistic projections for the future envision continuations of present trends. Ardila's chapter also characterizes contemporary parochialisms of the international scene in psychology, with interesting insights into the pragmatic difficulties of Third World Psychologists.

2 The Experimental Method in Nineteenth- and Twentieth-Century Psychology

Michael Wertheimer
University of Colorado, Boulder, USA

A research psychologist wrote that he "attached on a dark background at the level of my eyes a small round piece of white paper, to serve as a [fixation point]; and meanwhile I attached another to my right, at a distance of about two feet, but a little lower than the first in order that [its image] would fall on the optic nerve of my right eye, while I [kept] the left closed. I stood facing the first paper and moved away little by little, always keeping my right eye fixed on the first; and when I was about ten feet away, the second paper, which was nearly four inches [in diameter], completely disappeared."

This elegantly simple experiment on the blind spot, although typical of work done in the late nineteenth and early twentieth century, was reported by Mariotte more than 300 years ago—in 1668, to be exact (1981, pp. 267–268). Wilhelm Wundt may have founded the world's first psychological institute only a little over a century ago, but the experimental method was used for psychological investigations long before his time. As Meischner (1978) documents, Wundt himself, referring to Ernst Heinrich Weber's dissertation of 1834, called Weber "the father of experimental psychology." Many others could be charged with this paternity during the eighteenth and nineteenth centuries, such as the Czech physiologist, Jan Evangelista Purkyně (Kruta, 1969); the Germans, Gustav Theodor Fechner or Hermann von Helmholtz; the British physicist, Charles Wheatstone; the American philosopher, Charles Sanders Peirce; the Frenchman, Pierre Bouguer, who measured the differential threshold for brightness in 1760; the Dutch physiologist, F. C. Donders; or even the American astronomer, David Rittenhouse (Hindle & Hindle, 1959), who in 1786 published some ingenious experiments on reversible relief. As Robinson (1981) points out, psychology was not a latecomer to this method: "psychology's adoption of an experimental outlook occurred at very nearly the same time as that outlook was shared generally by the community of sciences, and that time was the nineteenth century [p. 396]." Although Robert Grosseteste may be responsible for changing the Greek rational approach into the modern methods of experimental science around the turn of the twelfth to the thirteenth century (Crombie, 1953, pp. 10–11), it was not until well into the nineteenth century that natural scientists began to take this method for granted as the most powerful one for obtaining scientific knowledge. Yet by no means were all psychologists of the late nineteenth century convinced that the experimental method is an appropriate tool for psychological research (Tweney, 1981).

But Wundt, as Pongratz (1967) observed, recognized that: "like natural science, psychology too must obtain its findings through use of the experimental method. . . . Only the experiment can lead us . . . to natural laws, because only the experiment makes it possible to identify causes and effects [pp. 101–102]."

By late in the nineteenth century, Franz Brentano was to question whether the systematic experiment used by Wundt and his followers is really an appropriate strategy for a new science that has barely begun to explore the enormous realm of its subject matter. Rather than making meticulous determinations of the value of a dependent variable at many different settings of an independent variable and thus specifying in detail the form of the relationship between the two, Brentano suggested that it makes more sense to find out in the first place whether a particular independent variable has any major effect on a particular dependent one. Let us develop an inventory of the most significant causes of the most interesting effects, before we devote excessive attention to what may turn out to be only trivial functional relationships. Brentano's prescription that psychologists should perform crucial rather than systematic experiments was taken seriously by a few phenomenologists, by the Gestalt psychologists, and by several later experimenters (such as Kardos), who sought to design crucial experiments to help decide among competing theories of the same phenomenon.

The mainstream of experimental psychology, though, pursued the systematic strategy championed by Wundt. More than seven decades after Wundt's *Vorlesungen* were published, Woodworth wrote in his monumental *Experimental psychology* (1938) that "an experimenter . . . has several advantages over an observer who simply follows the course of events without exercising any control." Among other things, the

experimenter can systematically *vary* the conditions and note the concomitant variation in the results. If [one] follows the old standard "rule of one variable" [one] holds all the conditions constant except for [a single] factor. . . .

As regards the rule of one variable, it applies only to the independent variable, for there is no objection to observing a variety of effects of the one experimental factor. With careful planning two or three independent variables can sometimes be handled in a single experiment with economy of effort and with some chance of discovering the interaction of the two or more factors [p. 2].

Woodworth referred here to R. A. Fisher's *Statistical methods for research workers*, which was first published in 1925. Prior to Fisher's work, statistics played only a minor role in experimental psychology. The results of early experiments were typically presented discursively, or in raw tabular form with descriptive statistics no more sophisticated than a measure of central tendency and an occasional average deviation; and "the rule of one variable" was followed by the great majority of experimenters. Tests of the statistical significance of a difference, indeed inferential statistics of any kind, had not yet come to dominate the scene. But, in the 1930s (Glass, 1981), scholars from North America went to England to hear the word then being preached by Fisher. His methods had an enormous influence on later experimental design; among the ideas central to his strategy was the crossing of multiple orthogonal factors and the study of simple and complex interactions. Lindquist is a direct descendant of this line, and his 1953 text was the methodological Bible for experimental psychologists for many years.

By just pass the middle of the twentieth century, then, the sophistication with which data from psychological experiments were subjected to statistical scrutiny had increased substantially. The experimental method had also spread far beyond such traditional areas as sensation, perception, rote memory, motor learning, and attention. Wundt had initially reserved the method for study of "basic" psychological processes and was convinced that the far more interesting "higher mental processes"—the fascinating human products of custom, myth, and language—could never be studied experimentally; it was this conviction that led to his prodigious 10-volume *Völkerpsychologie*. But by the beginning of the second half of the twentieth century, the experimental method had already been applied to problem solving, complex learning, set in thinking, and even subtle phenomena in social psychology, motivation, and personality. Psycholinguistics, to which much of Wundt's *Völkerpsychologie* was devoted, was just beginning and was to flourish as a major focus of experimental research down to the present.

William James's (1890) celebrated two-volume *Principles of Psychology* provided a reasonably complete compendium of the then available findings of the fledgling science of experimental psychology. But the corpus of findings grew at a rapidly accelerating pace. The preface to Woodworth's 1938 *Experimental Psychology* contains a graph of the dates of publication, by decade, of all the works he cited in his text; projection of the trend of his curve to decades that are now history, such as the 1970s or even the 1960s, yields thousands, or tens of thousands, of publications during those decades. Because of the explosive growth of the published literature of experimental psychology, Woodworth's book may have been the culmination of the classic tradition in general experimental psychology. It took him 900 pages, even though he explicitly excluded consideration of individual differences, social psychology, child development, animal psychology, abnormal, educational, or applied psychology, physiology, or work and motivation (p. iv). Osgood (1953) was perhaps the last psychologist to attempt a single-handed overview of experimental psychology; Woodworth and Schlosberg issued a revision of Woodworth's text in 1954, using almost 1000 double-column pages; and the individual chapters of S. S. Stevens's massive and definitive *Handbook* of 1951, comprising 1400 small-print, double-column pages, were prepared by 34 specialists, providing tacit testimony that it had become impossible for any single individual to have simultaneously a detailed yet panoramic knowledge of all experimental psychology. By the middle of the twentieth century the literature had simply become too voluminous for such integrative efforts to be feasible. As W. K. Estes puts it in his retrospective review of Woodworth's 1938 "bible" (1981): "one is left wondering whether there is likely ever to be another Woodworth, capable of comprehending and interpreting the whole range of experimental psychology. The perennially losing battle to keep up with research output in even fairly restricted specialties is enough to convince most of us that the answer is surely no [p. 330]."

Meantime, three further developments have had profound effects on the course of experimental psychology: massive government and foundation funding of psychological research, rapid growth in computer technology, and a humanitarian backlash against treating people who participate in experiments as "subjects."

That psychology could be useful to society had been demonstrated early in this century in France with identification of children who were likely to have trouble in school, and in the United States during World War I with selection of recruits for military service and during World War II with applications of sensory psychology and principles of psychomotor performance to the design of complex systems. As a consequence, public funds were made available to help support further work, initially in directly applicable areas such as human engineering and training programs for learning to use sophisticated equipment. It was soon recognized that basic research is at least as likely as applied to yield information that can be used in solving practical problems, so public support was allocated to basic psychological research as well, much of it experimental. Especially during the 1950s, 1960s, and early 1970s, many millions of dollars were funneled annually to psychological research through such U.S. agencies as the Office of Education, the National Science Foundation, and the Office of Naval Research; and various other nations and private foundations added further sources of funding. This massive infusion contributed to the continued growth of research in virtually all areas of experimental psychology. The political climate in the mid-1970s began to reverse this trend, and recent political trends in the United States threaten to curtail such programs severely in that country in the near future. Nevertheless, experimental psychology enjoyed a quarter century of substantial public support—for training of new experimental psychologists as well as for targeted research.

Second, the burgeoning world computer industry has also had a vast impact upon experimental psychology. Modern high-speed computers have been instrumental in generating the new area of artificial intelligence and have played a central role in research on cognition and information processing. These effects have been in addition to changes in the mode of presentation of stimuli, which now are often displayed on computer consoles, in the automatic recording of a variety of aspects of subjects' responses, and especially in the design and analysis of sophisticated multivariate experiments—multivariate on both the independent and the dependent side.

The third revolutionary development, which took place mostly during the last decade, is at least indirectly related to the so-called "humanistic" viewpoints in psychology, in that it reasserts the dignity and inviolability of human beings. In the United States, concern with the welfare of subjects in scientific experiments led to their official redesignation as *participants,* and to the demise of experimental methods that may be viewed as ethically questionable. No potentially damaging procedures may be used, and no persons can participate in experiments without their informed consent. Although these new restrictions have radically changed the style of experimentation in newer areas of psychology such as personality and social psychology, their impact on research in the more traditional fields of general psychology has been less severe. They have, it is true, added substantially to the "red tape" involved in doing almost any psychological experiment on human beings, but one can only applaud this long-overdue correction of what had occasionally become intolerable practices. Scientific research must not be pursued at the expense of human beings, but to their benefit.

The organizers of this volume have asked us to make projections to the years 1985 and 2000. It is doubtful that the use of the experimental method in psychology will be very different in 3 years from what it is today, but 2 decades may produce major changes.

By the year 2000, the designs used in psychological experiments will probably be even more sophisticated than is typical today. Research is apt to be more problem centered and less computer centered than now, as the computer becomes less the tail that wags the dog of design, theoretical model, and statistical analysis. Fusion of humanistic and scientific concerns may lead to research that is devoted more to everyday, natural, phenomenologically salient processes than to the artificial setting of the laboratory; Brunswik's (1956) prescription that an experiment should be "ecologically valid" is, one hopes, likely to be honored more in the future than it is today. Related to this expectation is that the experimental method is apt to be combined much more systematically with other strategies, such as correlational design, and with greater reliance on naturalistic observation, phenomenology, unobtrusive measures, and the so-called clinical methods.

Second, the worldwide publication explosion in experimental psychology is going to require a more systematic procedure for integrating the findings in subareas of the field than that used for, say, the chapters of the *Annual Review of Psychology,* which are written by experts in the subfield, whose task it is subjectively to develop—somehow—an integrative overview of the hundreds of studies published during the preceding 2 or 3 years in their specialty. If techniques can be found for generating reasonably complete bibliographies of the experimental literature in specific subareas of psychology—and finding such techniques is not going to be easy—then methods such as the meta-analysis of Smith and Glass (Glass, McGaw, & Smith, 1981; Glass & Smith, 1979; Smith & Glass, 1977; see also Underwood, 1957) are likely to be widely applied in efforts to arrive at broad generalizations that do justice to the experimental results from many partially overlapping studies. These meta-analytic procedures are sophisticated, rational, and quantitative and appear promising for making sense out of what otherwise is a jumble of conflicting findings from experimental studies that ask similar questions about a particular phenomenon but ask these questions in somewhat different ways.

The prediction that future experiments will be integrated more closely with correlational and "clinical" studies emanates from the pleas of the followers of Brunswik and from concerns raised by humanistic psychologists. Consider the following quotations from an article by the Brunswikian, Lewis Petrinovich (1979): "The systematic experimental method separates the variables controlling behavior from the fabric in which they are embedded, and this destroys the pattern of correlations [among] variables as it exists in natural situations [p. 375]." Further, psychologists should study

> variables within a sample of the situations to which they are to be generalized [p. 382]. . . . To have a sufficient science of the behavior of organisms in their environment, the step must be taken to obtain representative samples of both subjects and environmental situations. . . . The most radical departure involved in the use of representative design is the emphasis on obtaining random samples of the ecology of the organism in order to study behavior in the natural . . . habitat of organisms [p. 383].

Humanistic writers have complained that experimental psychology is trivial and sterile, that it has little to contribute to an understanding of human beings *qua* human beings, indeed that it presents a far too mechanical, cause–effect, automatic—a far too degrading—picture of human nature. Furthermore, the typical laboratory experiment is inherently artificial; the behavior that is studied and the setting in which it is studied are both so unrepresentative of real human behavior in real human situations that its findings cannot be generalized in any meaningful way to real people. Perhaps the methodological prescription of representative design could satisfy both the experimentalist and the humanist: Psychological research would be more directly relevant to human conduct in the real world and, at the same time, remain precise and quantitatively sophisticated.

Experimental psychology in the past has generally been limited to investigations of processes "inside the individual," with relative disregard for the environment within which the individual lives and functions. Theorists as diverse as Kurt Lewin, with his "$B = f(P, E)$," J. R. Kantor, with his "interbehavioral psychology," and Egon Brunswik, with his emphasis on representative design, have urged that psychology be concerned with organism–environment *interaction*, because *all* behavior occurs in a context. Environments must therefore be systematically sampled if we are ever to be able to generalize the results of psychological research to settings other than those in which the research is performed (Scott & Wertheimer, 1962, 1981, Chapter 3).

It is impossible, though, to select a representative sample from an unspecified domain. Whereas it is relatively easy to delineate a population of organisms, or of people, from which a representative sample is to be drawn, no one (with a few rare exceptions, such as Barker & Wright, 1951) has attempted to record naturally occurring everyday behavior and the settings in which it occurs and, thus, to generate a taxonomy of real behavior in real situations. This, though, is the awesome consequence of taking seriously the humanist's—and the Brunswikian's—challenge to traditional experimental psychology and is absolutely necessary if the results of psychological research are ever to be truly relevant to real conduct in real settings.

We must, then, begin with a taxonomy of behavior in its real-life setting. Certain behaviors are, of course, more likely to occur in some situations than in others. Records of the frequency with which certain behaviors occur in different naturalistic situations can yield contingency tables that will provide information about natural correlations: Under what conditions do organisms do certain things? (This is akin to some of the procedures that have been used fruitfully in ethology and in biological studies of animal behavior.) Early findings should yield hypotheses about what leads to what, that is, causal theories that try to explain the observed contingencies.

Only after such correlational data are available, then, would it make sense to employ the powerful experimental method. Its epistemological function, of course, is to go beyond mere concomitance to identification of cause and effect (although Dr. Gergen's article in this volume attempts to persuade us that it cannot do so). In settings that are truly representative of the real world, in which behavior *B* appears to be associated with situation *S*, the experimenter can then manipulate aspects of situation *S* so as to determine which manipulations have what effects on behavior *B*. Take, as a classic example, Tinbergen's (1953) beautiful experiment in which he varied a range of visual attributes of a decoy fish placed before a male stickleback fish and found that what generates attack by the fish is not so much the size or shape of the decoy as the presence of a reddish color on the decoy's underside. The same paradigm, barring ethical problems, could theoretically be used to study not an attack by one fish on another, but aggression among teen-agers, affectional behavior in social communities, the development of competence in a foreign language, and conflicts among groups of politicians. First, select a behavior that is of inherent interest, then record its natural occurrence in a variety of settings, then manipulate potentially relevant situational variables in a real-life setting (or even in a carefully constructed analog in a laboratory!) to determine the causes of the behavior. Typically, one might conjecture, the determinants of the behaviors that most of us find interesting will not be single variables, or even a small number of variables, acting linearly and independently, but a complex of interacting nonlinear variables.

This methodological prescription may sound radical, and indeed it is. But some past experimental research has come close to this ideal, such as that of Fechner and Ebbinghaus. Psychophysics has proved to be generalizable to many real-life settings, and the principles that Ebbinghaus discovered have turned out to apply to the memorization of meaningless material of any kind—though it is to be hoped that committing nonsense to memory is ecologically not a frequent human endeavor. Unfortunately, only a fraction of the rest of the findings of experimental psychology to date is likely to prove comparably representative of the real conduct of real organisms in real settings.

Let me close with a few remarks in response to a request that the organizers of this volume made just a few weeks before the conference, in the last of their many conscientious communications, namely to speculate specifically about the five main foci in the program: basic processes of learning and memory, perceptual and cognitive psychology, personality and differential psychology, motivation and social psychology, and clinical psychology. How will these fields look in the year 2000? My answers are intentionally somewhat controversial or provocative, in the hope that this may help generate discussion.

First, though, let me repeat a general point that many of the other participants also make in their chapters (Nesselroade & Baltes, Kováč, Fraisse, Edwards, Hamilton, Brengelmann, Rickels, and Downing). Twenty years from now experimental psychology will be less purely nomothetic, and more a combination of the nomothetic and the idiographic—which I interpret to mean that there will be a much more genuine fusion of experimental, correlational, and clinical strategies than in today's fragmented psychology. Let us hope that the change will not be merely a continuation of what has been going on for decades: new terminology replacing old, new fads displacing old ones, without much genuine progress. Perhaps the time has come for a new version of the old French adage: plus ça change, *moins* c'est la même chose.

One implication for the study of *basic processes in learning and memory* is that experiments will not be limited to grossly unrepresentative laboratory oversimplifications of these processes, as has all too frequently been the case in the past. Ulric Neisser, among others, has pointed to the rich complexity of human learning and memory processes in real life. Kintsch, Spear, and others in this volume have voiced the same plea and have begun to make impressive progress along these lines.

A similar point holds for *perceptual and cognitive psychology,* which is already beginning to transcend the detailed study of nothing more than artificial, oversimplified, piecemeal analogs of genuine, ecologically ubiquitous, perceptual and cognitive phenomena (see, e.g., Parducci's chapter in this volume). The nomothetic–idiographic fusion is apt to affect this area no less than the area of learning and memory—indeed, the already quite blurred border, between learning and cognition, itself is likely to break down even further during the coming vigennium, as implied, among others, by Klix and by Mandler.

Personality and differential psychology have been struggling for decades, under the leadership of such pioneers as Eysenck, to become accepted as a legitimate part of scientific psychology. As the nomethetic–idiographic fusion continues to develop, this aspiration will inevitably come closer to consummation.

Motivation and social psychology have both had two uneasy houses within them. The biopsychologist in his laboratory, such as Bitterman or Angermeier, has had little interaction with the theorist about complex human motivation, such as Atkinson; and social psychology has long been split between the experimental manipulator (like Asch or Milgram) and the systematic assessor who studies huge correlation matrices. The coming fusion will inevitably reduce the rift within both of these fields.

Clinical psychology? With the exception of a few pioneer experimental psychopathologists like Zubin, it has traditionally been as far removed as anything can be from genuine experimental research. Perhaps as a manifestation of a kind of defense mechanism, many experimentalists have viewed clinical work with disdain, as not very far removed from charlatanism, voodoo, and mysticism; comparably, many clinicians have seen experimental psychologists as hopelessly lost in the compulsive study of irrelevant trivia. The coming nomothetic–idiographic fusion may produce a heuristic rapprochement between the experimentalist and the clinician. The two have an enormous amount to gain from meaningful cooperative endeavors, and so, in the years 1981, 1985, and 2000, do all human beings.

REFERENCES

Barker, R. G., & Wright, H. F. *One boy's day*. New York: Harper, 1951.

Bouguer, P. P. *Traité d'optique sur la gradation de la lumière*. Paris: Guerin & Delatour, 1760.

Brunswik, E. *Perception and the representative design of psychological experiments*. Berkeley: University of California Press, 1956.

Crombie, A. C. *Grosseteste and experimental science*. Oxford: Clarendon, 1953.

Estes, W. K. The bible is out. A retrospective review of R. S. Woodworth, *Experimental psychology*. New York: Holt, 1938. *Contemporary Psychology*, 1981, *26*, 327–330.

Fisher, R. A. *Statistical methods for research workers*. Edinburgh: Oliver & Boyd, 1925.

Glass, G. V. Personal communication, April 15, 1981, Boulder, Colorado.

Glass, G. V., McGaw, B., & Smith, M. L. *Meta-analysis in social research*. Beverly Hills, Calif.: Sage, 1981.

Glass, G. V., & Smith, M. L. Meta-analysis of research on the relationship of class size and achievement. *Educational Evaluation and Policy Analysis*, 1979, *1*, 2–16.

Hindle, B., & Hindle, H. M. David Rittenhouse and the illusion of reversible relief. *Isis*, 1959, *50*, 135–140.

James, W. *The principles of psychology* (2 vols). New York: Holt, 1890.

Kruta, V. J. E. Purkyně (*1787–1869*), physiologist: A short account of his contributions to the progress of physiology, with a bibliography of his works. Prague, Czechoslovakia: Academia, 1969.

Lindquist, E. F. *Design and analysis of experiments in psychology and education.* Boston: Houghton Mifflin, 1953.

Mariotte, E. Novvelle décovverte tovchant la veve, Paris, 1668. Translated by Richard Lewis Sahakian as The blind spot. In W. S. Sahakian (Ed.), *History of psychology: A sourcebook in systematic psychology* (Rev. ed.). Itasca, Ill.: Peacock, 1981.

Meischner, W. Ernst Heinrich Weber, "Vater der experimentellen Psychologie" (Wundt). *Zeitschrift für Psychologie,* 1978, *186,* 160–169.

Osgood, C. E. *Method and theory in experimental psychology.* New York: Oxford, 1953.

Petrinovich, L. Probabilistic functionalism: A conception of research method. *American Psychologist,* 1979, *34,* 373–390.

Pongratz, L. J. *Problemgeschichte der Psychologie.* Berne: Francke, 1967.

Robinson, D. N. *An intellectual history of psychology* (Rev. ed.). New York: Macmillan, 1981.

Scott, W. A., & Wertheimer, M. *Introduction to psychological research.* New York: Wiley, 1962.

Scott, W. A., & Wertheimer, M. *Introducción a la investigación en psicología.* Mexico City: Editorial el Manual Moderno, 1981.

Smith, M. L., & Glass, G. V. Meta-analysis of psychotherapy outcome studies. *American Psychologist,* 1977, *32,* 752–760.

Stevens, S. S. (Ed.). *Handbook of experimental psychology.* New York: Wiley, 1951.

Tinbergen, N. *Social behavior in animals.* New York: Wiley, 1953.

Tweney, R. D. The role of experiments in the history of psychology. Paper presented at the 1981 convention of the American Psychological Association, Los Angeles, Calif.

Underwood, B. J. Interference and forgetting. *Psychological Review,* 1957, *64,* 49–60.

Woodworth, R. S. *Experimental psychology.* New York: Holt, 1938.

Woodworth, R. S., & Schlosberg, H. *Experimental psychology* (Rev. ed.). New York: Holt, 1954.

3 Experimentation and the Myth of the Incorrigible

Kenneth J. Gergen
Swarthmore College, Swarthmore, Pennsylvania USA

During the past century psychologists have participated in what might be considered one of humankind's greatest intellectual adventures. They have, in J. L. Austin's (1962) terms, joined in the "pursuit of the incorrigible," or the "always true," a pursuit that has challenged thinkers from Heraclitus to the present. Perhaps the major stimulus for recent pursuits can be traced to philosophers of science who came to believe that it is possible to discern within the variegated activities of the natural sciences a common pattern of acquiring knowledge. As maintained, when those rules of knowledge acquisition were properly distilled, the resulting elixir would transform the character of human life. Natural scientists might employ such rules to determine what forms of inquiry were productive and thus accelerate manifold the impressive advances of the centuries preceding. And, within other spheres of inquiry, including the sociobehavioral sciences, the adoption of such rules would insure progress no less significant than the harnessing of electrical energy, the discovery of genetic transmission, or the smashing of the atom. In Bertrand Russell's (1956) terms, it was hoped that one day there would be a "mathematics of human behavior as precise as the mathematics of machines." I am speaking here, of course, of the positivist–empiricist movement toward a unified science, a movement generally committed to the belief that when properly employed theoretical language can act as a representation of the contours of nature and can be constrained through rigorous assessment of such contours. With steady increments in the objective certainty of theoretical language, humans might become the arbiters of their own destiny.

In large measure, it is this context of optimism that has served as the progenitor to the experimental tradition in psychology. Whereas positivist–empiricist philosophy demonstrated the possibility of utopian ends, it was the experimental

27

method in psychology that was to serve as the major means to such ends. It was the experiment that was to enable investigators to trace precise causal sequences among events, to assess magnitude and directionality of effects, to examine the effects of factors both in isolation and combination, and to rule between competing explanations for given phenomena. Over time, concern with this means to knowledge, its improvement and sustenance, has largely replaced the concern with ends. As Wertheimer demonstrates in the initial chapter of this volume, immense strides have been made in terms of experimental proficiency, control of extraneous variables, precision in manipulation and measurement, safeguards over subjects' welfare, and associated statistical procedures. Further, powerful institutional frameworks have developed to enhance both quality and quantity of experimental products. The major periodicals within psychology are largely dedicated to reporting experimental findings, and advancement in the discipline is largely based on one's capacity to contribute to the corpus of experimental literature. Rigorous experimental contributions thus serve as professional talismans, inviting good fortune and warding off the evil spirit of professional failure. However, far less attention has been given to the efficacy with which such means are enabling the discipline to achieve its estimable goals. Are its methods indeed moving the discipline toward objectively secure knowledge?

It is at least sobering to note that in this latter respect a number of prominent scientists, moved to review the advances in their domains, have shown considerable dismay. For example, as the editor of a seven-volume study of the state of psychological knowledge, Sigmund Koch (1971) has summarized: "consider the hundreds of theoretical formulations, rational equations and mathematical models of the learning process that have accrued; the thousands of research studies. And *now* consider that there is still no wide agreement, even at the crassest descriptive level, on the empirical conditions under which learning takes place [p. 693]." In the field of personality psychology, Lee Sechrest (1976) has compared the major issues of study over a 10-year period and asked: "Now why have the themes changed? If it were because issues have been resolved, because important phenomena are now so well understood that they no longer merit attention, it would be cause for encouragement—rejoicing perhaps. Alas, one cannot escape the conclusion that investigators ran out of steam, that issues were abandoned, and that problems were never resolved [p. 1]." Similarly, in reviewing the nearly 300 studies on individual versus group risk taking, Dorwin Cartwright (1973) concludes: "After 10 years of research (the) original problem remains unsolved. We still now know how the risk taking behavior of 'real-life' groups compares with that of individuals [p. 225]." And, finally, in cognitive psychology, Allen Newell (1973) has commented on the : "ever increasing pile of issues in cognitive psychology which we weary of or become diverted from but never really settle [p. 289]."

Of course, such discontent may be attributed to the still less than perfect methods at our disposal, to the lack of funding, to insufficiencies in investigatory ingenuity, and the like. As it is said, it is a young science and one should not anticipate great strides at this stage. Yet, such undaunted optimism might be difficult to sustain if a serious assessment were made of developments within the philosophy of science since the bold empiricist years of the 1930s. Such assessment indicates a full-scale deterioration of the metatheoretical launching pad from which experimental psychology was thrust into the world. A brief summary of developments proves useful at this juncture.

Positivist–Empiricist Metatheory: The Erosion of Confidence

First, no satisfactory account has been discovered within the positivist–empiricist domain for the emergence of theoretical insight, postulates, or hypotheses. As widely recognized, one cannot induce general principles from observation; scanning the world in itself produces no ideas or theories to test. In effect, the fundamental basis for what we take to be knowledge does not grow logically from the soil of nature itself (i.e., empirical observation) but from some other source. The grounds for suppositions about the world do not thus appear to be objective, but subjective. And if the initial grounds for scientific propositions are essentially subjective, some might even say mystical, what is the warrant for believing that the experiment will restore rationality and objectivity? For after all, what is revealed as fact by the experiment depends on one's framework of interpretation. It is precisely this framework for which the grounds remain elusive.

With the publication of Popper's *Logic of Scientific Discovery,* it also became apparent that the empirical confirmation of theory could not furnish the basis for a progressive science. The location of confirmations does not act as a significant crucible for a theoretical account. The most important question is whether a given theory can withstand attempts at falsification. Thus, it might be argued, the common attempt to furnish experimental verification in psychology could not itself yield an accumulation of knowledge. Yet, Quine (1953), along with Duhem (1906) long before, also cast significant doubt on the process of falsification. As argued, any theory contains a host of unstated, or auxiliary, assumptions. Whenever data are brought to light that appear to falsify the theory as manifest, the theorist can dip into the nether region of unstated assumptions for distinctions or rationale that can be used to extract the venom from the fangs of falsification. Theories in this sense are not vanquished through falsification but progressively elaborated. It is this fact that enables members of the Flat World Society, dedicated to sustaining a belief in the flatness of the Earth, to remain steadfast in spite of what "everybody knows" to be convincing evidence to the contrary.

Quine (1960) has also challenged another shibboleth of traditional empiricist metatheory in his examination of the indeterminacy of theoretical language.

Precisely what are the empirical referents for theoretical terms, asks Quine; in order to test a theory one should be able to specify unequivocally the range of particulars to which it applies. But, argues Quine, the relationship between theoretical terms and particulars is inherently cloudy. If I point to an object and say that if it falls into my classification of *desk,* for example, to precisely what aspects of the object am I referring? Do I necessarily mean its color, the length of the legs, the number of corners at its perimeter? If I removed a leg, would it continue to be a desk? If I burned it, would the embers also constitute a desk? Thus, to speak of desks does not tell the listener precisely about anything in particular.

The argument has further been made by Hanson (1958) and others that observation is inherently theory laden; that is, one cannot undertake the process of systematic observation without certain ground rules for what constitutes a phenomenon. Such ground rules ensure that the evaluation of a theory proceeds in ways that are already theoretically constrained or contaminated. In this way if theories determine what counts as data, competing theoretical accounts may be empirically incommensurable. The phenomena supporting one theory simply do not count as phenomena relevant for its potential competitors. Thus, for example, in psychology, one may be unable to make empirical comparisons between operant theory and phenomenological theory, as the former fails to recognize the "phenomenological field" as an entity and the latter may hold that "reinforcement contingencies" are irrelevant to action unless they are constituents of the phenomenological field. In this sense the theories are empirically incommensurable.

It is in this context of generalized discontent with traditional empiricist metatheory that the writings of both Kuhn (1962) and Feyerabend (1976) could flourish. As Kuhn argued from a historical perspective, theoretical shifts in the science do not represent steady accretions in knowledge. Theories have not come to represent with increasing fidelity the contours of nature. Rather, the shift from one theory to another approximates a Gestalt shift, in which the world is seen through differing theoretical lenses. On this account scientific knowledge does not accumulate through continued empirical work; theoretical shifts over the centuries are not improvements in degree but alterations in kind. To this, Feyerabend has added his diatribe against any codified methods of the kind proposed by his positivist–empiricist predecessors. For Feyerabend knowledge is best achieved by a form of theoretical and methodological anarchy. Even mysticism is to be given serious attention as a candidate for physical explanation. The works of both Kuhn and Feyerabend have been widely discussed and need no further amplification at this juncture. Both have proved vulnerable to wide-ranging criticism. However, of particular significance is the fact that their voices have been among the loudest on the contemporary scene. If positivist–empiricist philosophy continued to demand broad confidence, such audacious voices would be reduced to a murmer. The broad audiences that they command are thus salient indicators of the deteriorated condition of the metatheoretical base on which rests the experimental research tradition in psychology.

Yet, one might continue to reply, in spite of the pervasive criticism of the traditional views of scientific activity, and in spite of those nagging doubts arising within the discipline itself one might hold steadfast to the hope for progress through empirical test. After all, the wide-ranging disillusionment in philosophical circles has scarcely had a dampening effect on the physical sciences. Perhaps the early account of scientific progress was inaccurate or misguided; perhaps the next time around philosophers will get it right. In the meantime natural scientists have continued their efforts undaunted, and the result has been an impressive array of technological advances. Let the common faith not be shaken, it may be argued; if we but continue along the route of rigorous, critical probing of human activity, we may ultimately hope for results of more telling significance.

Experimental Science and the Problem of Phenomenal Instability

There are few who would care to play out the heroic role implied by these latter sentiments more than the present author. There is a certain existential enchantment in launching oneself into the open space of a groundless faith. Yet, several concerns that have emerged within my own work over the past decade militate against such blind commitment. These are not the primary concerns of philosophers of science more generally but ones that grow out of an appraisal of the specific problems encountered in studying human activity. It seems to me that there are certain peculiarities of our craft that, if not in kind, certainly in degree, separate most investigation within the sociobehavioral sciences from that undertaken in the natural science domains. Most of my thinking about these problems has emerged within the context of social psychological research devoted to such topics as aggression, moral behavior, emotion, attitude change, rule following, personal dispositions, and a host of cognitive processes relevant to human interaction. Thus, I am uncertain of the extent to which investigators in other domains will find the basis for my particular misgivings either interesting or applicable. However, in the interests of a more rounded appraisal of the future of experimental inquiry, it may prove valuable to voice these concerns in the present context. Let me confine myself to three variations on a single theme.

At the heart of my concerns lies the protean capacity of the human organism for continuous change. On the level of momentary action, one's body is in continuous motion; patterns of action are undergoing continuous alteration and seldom is precisely the same configuration ever repeated. To be sure, there are certain recurring patterns dictated by biological necessity. Patterns of inhalation, ingestion, and excretion, for example, must occur on a periodic and repetitive basis. However, beyond a handful of essential functions, biology seems to furnish the individual with the capacity for immense variability in action. Or to look at it in slightly different form, biology seems to place limits on human functioning, but within these limits there is latitude for infinite variation. Change also seems a paramount feature of life across periods of history. As Feyerabend (1976) (borrowing from Lenin) characterized it: "Accidents and conjectures, and curious juxtapositions of events are the very substance of history, and the complexity of human change and the unpredictable character of the ultimate consequences of any given act or decision of men its most conspicous feature [p. 17]." If such characterizations seem compelling, then the traditional belief that, when properly conducted, scientific research enables us to proceed ineluctably toward the truth is rendered problematic. One may seek to comprehend the past with increasing clarity and to grasp contemporary pattern in transition. However, regardless of methodological precision, one does not thereby accumulate knowledge in the traditional sense or increase one's capacity to predict and to control in the distant future.

As this line of argument was developed with relevance to the range of human activity, one is moved to question its generality. In what degree does it apply to the kinds of processes of interest to investigators in learning, cognition, developmental, and clinical psychology? No blanket judgments appear possible in this matter; the range of topics treated in these domains is immense, and study of historical alteration is limited only to a few specialized domains (e.g., concept of childhood, hysteric symptoms, madness). However, one may employ a broad rule of thumb that would furnish an approximate answer in each case: To the extent that any pattern of activity is not demanded by the structure of the nervous system, such activity may be considered historically situated. In this sense one's responses to reward and punishment, the simultaneous pairing of stimuli, backward masking of letters, white noise at 90 db's, insoluable problems, and the like would not seem the kinds of data on which transhistorical principles of behavior would be rested. One's possible range of responses in each case would seem limited only by the human imagination. From this perspective, empirical methods such as the experiment take on the character of historical markers (Gergen, 1973, 1978). Except in delimited cases, these methods primarily serve to inform us about various aspects of contemporary life. Whether the experiment is a particularly effective vehicle for furnishing such information may be considered moot. The essential problem is the extent to which it is fruitful to adopt a theory of knowledge based on the stability or reliability of events in confronting creatures whose activities demonstrate precious little of either.

Meaning Systems and Scientific Metatheory

Given this major theme of human change, let me embark on the first of two significant variations. The first has to do with what may be considered a second fundamental characteristic of the organism, namely that of symbol generation and manipulation, along with the associated capacity for employing these symbols in the process of communication. As it is usually argued, the vast share of human activity appears to rely on the manner in which people cognize, symbolize, or conceptualize the world. It is not the stimulus of another's bodily movements to which people respond, as it is generally argued, but the meaning or conceptualization of these movements (Collingwood, 1946; Schutz, 1962; Winch, 1958). The same movement of a hand rapidly moving toward one through space may thus be conceptualized, for example, as an act of aggression (a blow), a signal of comradeship (a slap on the back), a practical joke (an attempt at sudden surprise), or a sign of inept gregariousness. The response to the stimulus is not, thus, produced by the stimulus itself but by the particular meanings that the individual happens to assign to it. And, it would appear, people possess the capacity to generate multiple conceptualizations and to communicate these conceptualizations to others.[1]

To the extent that one accepts this characterization of human functioning, support is rendered to the initial argument posed previously; that is, to the degree that human conduct is based on processes of conceptualization or meaning systems, presently existing patterns of activity myst be seen as historically situated. They would appear to depend on the current confluence of meanings within the culture. To illustrate, consider the work of Seligman and his colleagues on learned helplessness (Abramson, Seligman, & Teasdale, 1978; Seligman, 1975). As maintained in this case, when people confront situations in which they believe themselves to be helpless or without control over their outcomes, they become depressed and inactive. Yet, to the extent that such patterns do exist, they would appear to depend on one's particular way of conceptualizing helplessness or lack of control. One might, for example, view such a situation as a rousing challenge to locate ways of regaining control, as just cause for retaliation against the agent of deprivation, as a welcomed opportunity for relaxation, or as an opportunity for much needed self-reflection in a world dominated by the pervasive search for control. Depression and inactivity as responses to helplessness or loss of control would not thus appear to be constituent parts of "human nature"; rather they would appear to rely on conventional meaning systems that are subject to all manner of alteration across time.

Yet the problems posed for the behavioral scientist by human capacities for symbolization and communication are even more problematic than suggested thus far. Traditional science is predicated on the assumption that scientific knowledge does not itself alter the phenomena of interest; observation of the planets does not alter their trajectory nor does knowing about antibiotics alter

---

[1]In the present volume the chapters by Mandler, Parducci, Fraisse, the Kintsches, Magnusson, and Zubin and his colleagues are all consistent with the view that conceptual systems are central in guiding human conduct. However, these authors have given less attention to the implications of this view for the empiricist philosophy of science to which the field is generally committed. One is precariously situated in adopting an empiricist theory of scientific conduct on the one hand and a rationalist theory of human action on the other. To accept the rationalist (cognitive) theoretical perspective contradicts central assumptions within the empiricist metatheory (Gergen, in press).

their effects on bacteria. It is not being argued in the present case that research on human action need necessarily alter its character; typically investigators attempt to rule out such effects in a variety of ways. However, what is essential in the present case is the possibility that the knowledge resulting from behavioral science inquiry at any given point may so affect the culture that further inquiry would not yield the same results at a later juncture; that is, the results of exploring a given pattern T_1 may so influence the culture that the pattern may not be located (or may be accentuated) at T_2. The rationale underlying this argument follows readily from the preceding suppositions regarding the symbolic basis of human activity. For, after all, the major products of the behavioral sciences are symbols. We offer to the society ways of comprehending human conduct or forms of understanding. As these forms are communicated to the culture, they carry the potential for alteration of human conduct. After immersion in Freudian theory, a parent can scarely remain unaffected in the treatment of children; after exposure to Schachter's labeling theory of emotions, one is not likely to view others' reports of their feelings with the same degree of credulity, and so on.

This is not to argue that psychological theories have had widespread impact thus far. There is good evidence that psychoanalytic theory has been absorbed into large segments of Western culture, as has behavior theory in substantial degree. However it is less important to assess the extent to which patterns of human conduct have been affected thus far as it is to realize that enlightenment effects are possible in principle. And, although one may envision assessing the systematic effects of behavioral science on patterns of conduct, this solution can only be of transient expedience. Such formulations themselves may become absorbed by the culture and affect it in ways that blunt their prognostic capacities. In effect, to the extent that scientists are investigating matters of critical concern to the society, and the society is open with respect to communication, then the scientist may continuously engage in a game of hide-and-seek with patterns of conduct.

The Pseudo Objectivity of Behavioral Description

Let us turn, then, to a second important variation on this major theme of human change. The particular concern in this case is with the capacity of scientitic language to stand in a referential or ostensive relationship with human behavior. As made abundantly clear within early positivist circles, in order for empirical evaluation of scientific theory to proceed, theoretical propositions must have linkages to publicly observable events. Unless key theoretical terms refer to or are defined by real-world referents, a theoretical proposition is neither open to verification nor falsification through empirical test. Given this view we may inquire into the capacity of behavioral descriptors to be linked to observables. In particular, to what extent can theoretical terms be used to designate a configuration that is continuously changing?

To appreciate the question more fully, consider first a stationary pattern such as an immobile, black box. Although subject to subatomic alteration, for most practical purposes the box remains stable and thus subject to the kind of verbal tagging that would enable one to say whether the box was present or absent. If the box were called Igor, for example, we could easily reach agreement with respect to whether Igor was present in the room or not. But let us complicate the picture. Consider Boris, Igor's slightly more sophisticated cousin. He possesses two levers, one moving vertically and the other horizontally at varying intervals. Such complexity creates considerable problems for anyone wishing to render a verbal account for Boris' activity. To describe Boris' momentary states would require a considerable increment in the number of descriptive terms and continuous alteration in their arrangement (e.g., "At 10:28:01 Lever A left, Lever B downward," "At 10:28:02 Lever A right, Lever B up"). But now let us consider Ivan, the most sophisticated mechanism of this genre. Ivan possesses six levers that move in three-directional space in varying speeds and at varying times, and seldom is the precise configuration of its parts repeated. For one concerned with referential terminology, surely this is "Ivan the Terrible." An infinite number of terms might be required to describe Ivan's actions and few would ever be repeated.

To communicate at all about Ivan one might thus abandon the task of developing a referential terminology and consider instead what Ivan is able to accomplish, that is, the goals or endpoints that Ivan's many, infinitely variegated actions seem to achieve. For example, using a wide variety of motions, Ivan seems to place alcohol into its orifices. Although we cannot refer to the movements themselves, we can develop a term that refers to this achievement, *alcohol consumption* (or "drinking," in the common vernacular). And, we see that in a variety of ways Ivan manages to destroy all machines that do not share its characteristics. We may refer to activities that achieve this end as *aggression*.

With the analogy fully transparent, we can press toward a conclusion. As ventured, because of the infinitely varying configurations of human action across time, the vast share of terminology used in speaking about such action possesses no observable referent; that is, terms such as drinking, aggressing, learning, remembering, understanding, and helping, do not refer to the specific displacement of the limbs, the particular sounds emanating from the organism, and the like. Rather, such terms are primarily used to speak about what the organism is trying or intending to achieve.

At this point the problem for a science of human activity becomes particularly onerous. Objective criteria for what one is attempting or intending to achieve are simply unavailable both to the scientist and to the actor. Thus in naming an occurrence one is thrown back on the cultural conventions for the interpretation of action. On these grounds any action (or interaction) can serve as an exemplar of an achievement if one's interpretive system is so arranged. Presence or absence of a so-called phenomenon depends principally on whether one can gain others' agreement on using a specific system of interpretation. There is no event outside the socially constructed event. To illustrate, there are a potential infinity of actions that may succeed in propelling food into one's mouth. As we have also seen, the term *eating* does not refer to an observable set of actions but to the result. Yet, what is the result in this particular case? It might equally be said to be "pleasure achieving," "life sustaining," "food wasting," "habit fulfilling," or "time wasting." What for one person is eating is for another pleasure seeking or time wasting. Which term applies does not depend on observation (as the observation is equal in all cases) but on one's capacity to sustain agreement within a social group. Without agreement with others that the individual's actions are "wasting time," the individual is not wasting time. Or, to bring the point closer to our concerns, it would appear that without language conventions that enable us to speak as if subjects are aggressing, perceiving, processing information, changing their attitudes, thinking, nurturing, learning, and the like, they are not doing any of these things.

The argument in this case is not collapsible into the banal conclusion that without languages to speak about phenomena there are no scientific propositions. Rather, at its extreme, it is to say that propositions about aggression, altruism, thinking, cognitive schema, depression, and the like cannot be verified or falsified by observation. Instead, the apparent validity of statements employing such terms depends on the acceptability of such statements within current conventions. Consider, for example, a typical experiment on aggression (Bandura, 1973). The measure of aggression consists of the number of times the subjects depress a button delivering shock to another person within a specified interval. The experimenter chooses to interpret pressing of the button as an achievement that he or she terms *aggression*. However, each subject in the experiment may bring to the situation a different interpretation of the same event. From their standpoint they are not engaging in an aggressive act; aggression is not their intention. What grants superiority then, to the investigator's interpretation? It is not the actions of subjects themselves, as the button depressions are objectively similar to all who are present. Rather, the investigator's advantage is derived from his or her control over the language of interpretation within the scientific community. It follows that whatever can be said about aggression does not derive from observation but from linguistic conventions about what aggression is and how it is related to other integers within the language.[2]

---

[2]To clarify within the context of the present volume, measures of mental performance, schemata, decision making, memory, association, motives, and the like (see chapters in this volume by Parducci, Fraisse, the Kintsches, Zubin and his colleagues, Atkinson & Kuhl, and Bitterman) do not typically furnish the kind of evidence that can constrain what may be said about the hypothetical constructs in question. Rather, the conventions of talking about the constructs in question determine what may be said about the measures. There are no data that would inform one that "schemata are triple spaced" or that "information storage is four dimensional" because such propositions are nonsensical within the commonly accepted vernacular. Concomitantly, there are no data that could be used to falsify the assumption that "people employ concepts to process information," as the conventions for talking about concepts are sufficiently flexible that virtually all observations may be understood in these terms.

Experimental Assumptions Revisited

The implications of this condensed array of arguments for an experimentally based science should be clear enough. However, by means of summary, let us briefly consider three traditional beliefs about the value of empirical work. First, it has often been maintained that empirical methods should be employed to establish the factual inventory from which objectively based theories might be developed. As reasoned, sound theories depend on a reliable repository of factual data. To quote one source (Shaw & Costanzo, 1970): "Modern social psychology has largely been empirical in nature, basing its propositions and conclusions upon observations in controlled situations. . . . As a result of the empirical approach, a considerable amount of data about social behavior has accumulated. To be useful, such data must be organized in a systematic way so that the meanings and implications of these data can be understood. Such systematic organization is the function of theory [p. 3]." Yet as we see from the preceding, no satisfactory account can be given of how one can move from observation to theory. What is before us at this moment in no way constrains or dictates the concepts or theories we must employ. Further, what emerges as data or fact in an experiment is not that which is observed but is typically a system of concepts built around the investigator's beliefs about subjects' purposes or goals. To be informed by a scientist that subjects exposed to intermittent blasts of white noise failed at complex problem solving is not to be furnished with a fact but with a single, purposefully coherent account among an infinity of alternatives. Any theoretical synthesis of the facts may thus be viewed as a synthesis of interpretive creations.

Second, it is traditionally argued that empirical methods and, particularly, the experiment enables the investigator to establish causal relationships among classes of entities. Yet, as we see from the historical perspective, a virtual infinity of possible relationships among entities is possible. Or to adopt behavioral language, virtually any designated stimulus pattern may precede any designated response. Such relationships do not appear fundamentally fixed but, rather, seem to depend on historically situated conceptions or symbol systems. Further, the science itself may contribute to the pattern of relationships among events. And, from our latter concern with the nonobjective character of descriptive language, we see that the particular function forms designated by the science are neither engendered nor constrained by experimental data. Empirical results do not inform us about what can be said about patterns of aggression, learning, motivation, cognition, and the like. Rather, our language practices concerning such matters determine what we can say with empirical results.

Finally, it is traditionally argued that the empirical methods, and chiefly the experiment, enable one to verify or to falsify general theories of action. However, given the continuous alteration of human activity, it should be possible in principle to establish some empirical grounds for sustaining virtually any reasonable hypothesis—along with its negation—as long as neither violates what we accept to be sensible. As long as there are means for making sense of certain forms of action, there may be people willing to engage in such actions. Further, because the conceptual significance of an action is not dictated by its observable characteristics, it should be possible, in principle, to sustain any given theoretical position across any array of observations and, conversely, to employ virtually any array of observations to sustain one's theory (Gergen, 1980). Should such contentions be doubted, one might consult first the history of psychology for examples of clear refutations of theory by experiment. Can any compelling exemplars be located? Even Freudian theory stands largely unscathed by over a half century of empirical assault. And, if empirical results seem to convince one of the validity of a given theory, a proper antedote is to expose another intelligence to the findings alone, shorn of theoretical interpretation. One typically elicits from this procedure a shocking range of alternative and undreampt realities.[3]

Are these dour conclusions to be construed as a valediction for experimentation? Not at all. From the present perspective it is not experimentation that is problematic but the particular rationale or metatheory underlying its implementation. The experiment is good or bad only with respect to some purpose, and, as the present arguments suggest, we may have been overly cavalier with respect to the traditional purposes to be served by this means. Thus, whether we should continue to celebrate the experiment (or any other empirical method) depends largely on whether we may develop an alternative conception of the science of more compelling character than heretofore. With benefit of hindsight, are there more legitimate goals that we might hope to achieve through empirical work? It is far beyond either my talents or time to offer a fully elaborated alternative at this juncture. However, if you will permit me the luxury of conjecture, I do feel that the intellectual seeds have been planted for such an alternative, and at least a sketchy account may be furnished of the bloom in full.[4]

Experimentation in an Interpretive Science

Let us first consider the character of theory. As we have seen, it is not promising to view theoretical work as a form of description, a reflection of ongoing behavioral events. Rather, it seems preferable to consider theory first and foremost as a system of language. This is to say that the chief product of the vast attempts at

---

[3]This is not to argue that one can never learn from an experiment. However, the process of learning is ill considered as a confrontation of theory and fact. Rather, it is a confrontation of interpretations. If one's experimental findings appear to violate one's theoretical commitments, it is not essential to reconsider the theory's validity. Instead, one is invited to open oneself to the range of alternative interpretations that can inevitably be made of an array of findings.

[4]Especially pertinent to the view of behavior science developed here are the contributions of Winch (1958), Taylor (1964), Gauld and Shotter (1977), Bauman (1978), Giddens (1976), and Gadamer (1960).

manipulation, control, assessment, and quantification are essentially word patterns. In this sense the behavioral sciences are similar to the humanities; both possess certain forms of linguistic expertise. It may further be argued that these forms of expertise are not fundamentally different from other skilled activities of the human being. Just as people learn to use their feet for dancing, their hands for sculpting, or their eyes for surveying the safety of their surroundings, people learn to do things with words.

Yet, unlike certain other human skills, linguistic proficiency cannot be evaluated outside the social sphere within which it is imbedded. One may learn to play a musical instrument in ways that give pleasure solely to oneself; however, linguistic expertise can only be determined within the framework of others' activities. The autistic production of sounds does not constitute language. To adopt Wittgenstein's (1963) metaphor, one may usefully view words as pieces in a game played with others. Each move has implications for one's outcomes in the game. In this sense, scientific theories of human activity are more like dance steps than they are mirrors, more akin to checkers than to cameras.

It is also important to realize that the game of language is far more profound in consequence than most others, primarily because of its manifold implications for the remainder of one's activities. Linguistic terms may be used as substitutes or symbols for virtually all other forms of activity. Thus, through language one may truncate other interpersonal processes of longer and more arduous duration. Through language one may furnish the kinds of signals that can motivate or instruct people to do anything from staging a play to staging a revolution. Or, one may verbally instruct a child about forms of desirable activity and thereby circumvent innumerable instances of mutual discomfort. In this sense language is one of the most powerful tools available in the social sphere; linguistic expertise within various language communities may vitally affect other activities within these communities.

From the present standpoint we see that the chief question confronting the theorist is not that of accuracy in description, but the function of selected theoretical language within the human arena; that is, one must ask what forms of activity a theoretical account is designed to sustain, create, or destroy. How is the linguistic account to be employed within the society and for what ends? Viewed in this light there is no distinction to be made between theory and praxis: Theoretical work constitutes a form of praxis (Gergen, 1982). Consequently, we see that questions of value are catapulted into a position of cardinal significance. If objective fidelity is obviated, and theory is viewed as a form of activity that may be employed in achieving various purposes, then the central criteria for evaluating theory are generated by questions of human purpose.

In this light we may usefully distinguish between two major classes of purpose for theoretical work, those that are *exterior* as opposed to *interior* to the discipline. In the former case theoretical language may serve ends that lie beyond the boundaries of the discipline itself. The theorist may sustain the hope that his or her theoretical language may ultimately come to influence the existing order. Marxist theory furnishes the most powerful example of the potential effects of scientific theory on human conduct. However, political science and economics both furnish many additional instances in which theory has been of broad exterior consequence. Theories in both realms have frequently been designed in such a way as to be absorbed by various interest groups. Theorists have furnished the theoretical rationale for all manner of political and economic policies of broad social consequence.

Yet, theory may also serve valuable functions interior to the discipline. As we have seen, theoretical languages are equivalent to many other activities with respect to the range of skills that may be acquired. Some theoretical languages are feats of daring magnificence, whereas others are rudely fashioned and barren of potential. In this respect one may compare the languages of the child and the adult in terms of the range of accomplishments that may be achieved. Languages possessing conditionals, or subjunctives, for example, may be considered superior to those without such possibilities. In this light, it is of fundamental significance for the discipline to support and sustain theoretical inquiry, the chief aim of which is to enhance the skills of the discipline more generally.

Within this linguistic framework we find invaluable functions to be played by empirical research. Theoretical language lies empty until one can comprehend its deployment in particular contexts. One may develop new forms of understanding or go on to expand and enrich behavioral, cognitive, phenomenological, or other existing languages of understanding. However, unless these developments and elaborations are accompanied by concrete instantiations, they float away into an atmosphere of indifference. Thus, empirical work serves to vivify the theoretical language, to enhance its significance and utility, and to furnish a guide for its coordination to ongoing activity. The experiment may play an especially valuable role in this respect. For the experiment, like an artist's canvas, furnishes the investigator with immense freedom within which to construct the illustration of most telling significance. Thus, for example, experiments on operant conditioning neither add to nor detract from the truth value of operant theory; such truth value is inherently indeterminant. However, relevant experiments have served as profoundly effective constructions of the world through the lens of operant theory. Once the theoretical lens has been employed in this way, one can scarcely doubt the broad applicability of the theory. The experiment does not thus contribute to the "truth value" of the theory. However, it does bring essential life to the dry bones of abstraction. The more rigorous and well-designed the experiment, the more powerful its capacity for vivification. As we see, then, theory and research must continue to proceed hand in hand. It is only their mutual goals that require reformulation. As argued in the present case, it is not to an incorrigible future that such efforts should be devoted but to a pragmatic grappling with a malleable present.

Conclusion

The deep and pervasive yearning for incorrigible truths has led in the present century to a virtual deification of methodology. It is this belief in truth through method that has also served as a hallmark of the behavioral movement in psychology. Yet, after a long and valiant struggle to vindicate this faith, it is becoming increasingly apparent—both within philosophy and psychology—that methods are not sacred but profane constructions. That which is derived from methods is fully dependent on the interpretive perspectives brought to bear. And whereas the greatest share of professional attention has been diverted to method, the range and potential of interpretive perspectives has languished. Theoretical work must cease to play handmaiden to methodology. Rather, it is an auspicious time for reversing the tide of history and placing theoretical work in the center of disciplinary activity. Methods may then serve the ancillary purpose for which they are so well devised.

ACKNOWLEDGMENTS

The writing of this chapter was facilitated by a grant from the National Science Foundation (No. 7809393). Special appreciation is also expressed to Professor Carl F. Graumann, Psychologisches Institut, Universität Heidelberg, for providing the facilities and the intellectual milieu in which the present concerns were nurtured.

REFERENCES

Abramson, L. Y., Seligman, M. E. P., & Teasdale, J. D. Learned helplessness in humans: Critique and reformulation. *Journal of Abnormal Psychology,* 1978, *87,* 49–74.

Austin, J. L. *Sense and sensibilia.* London: Oxford University Press, 1962.

Bandura, A. *Aggression: A social learning analysis.* Englewood Cliffs, N.J.: Prentice-Hall, 1973.

Bauman, Z. *Hermeneutics and social science.* New York: Columbia University Press, 1978.

Cartwright, D. Determinants of scientific progress: The case of research on the risky shift. *American Psychologist,* 1973, *28,* 222–231.

Collingwood, R. G. *The idea of history.* Oxford: Clarendon, 1946.

Duhem, P. *The aim and structure of physical theory* (Trans. by P. Wiener). Princeton: Princeton University Press, 1954 (originally published 1906).

Feyerabend, P. K. *Against method.* London: Humanities Press, 1976.

Gadamer, H. G. *Truth and method* (Originally published as *Wahrheit und Methode*). Tübingen: J. C. B. Mohr (Paul Siebeck), 1960.

Gauld, A., & Shotter, J. *Human action and its psychological investigation.* London: Routledge & Kegan Paul, 1977.

Gergen, K. J. Social psychology as history. *Journal of Personality and Social Psychology,* 1973, *26,* 309–320.

Gergen, K. J. Experimentation in social psychology: A reappraisal. *European Journal of Social Psychology,* 1978, *8,* 507–527.

Gergen, K. J. Toward theoretical audacity in social psychology. In R. Gilmour & S. Duck (Eds.), *The development of social psychology*. London: Academic Press, 1980.

Gergen, K. J. *Toward transformation in social knowledge*. New York: Springer-Verlag, 1982.

Gergen, K. J. Social psychology and the phoenix of unreality. In S. Koch & D. Leary (Eds.), *A century of psychology as a science*. New York: McGraw-Hill, in press.

Giddens, A. *New rules of sociological method*. New York: Basic Books, 1976.

Hanson, N. R. *Patterns of discovery*. Cambridge: University Press, 1958.

Koch, S. Reflections on the state of psychology. *Social Research*, 1971, *38*, 669–709.

Kuhn, T. S. *The structure of scientific revolution*. Chicago: University of Chicago Press, 1962.

Newell, A. You can't play 20 questions with nature and win. In W. G. Chase (Ed.), *Visual information processing*. New York: Academic Press, 1973.

Quine, W. V. *From a logical point of view*. Cambridge, Mass.: Harvard University Press, 1953.

Quine, W. V. *Word and object*. Cambridge: Technology Press of M.I.T., 1960.

Russell, B. *Our knowledge of the external world*. New York: Menton Books, 1956.

Schutz, A. *Collected papers* (Vol. 1). The Hague: Nijhoff, 1962.

Sechrest, L. Personality. In M. R. Rosenzweig & L. W. Porter (Eds.), *Annual Review of Psychology*, 1976, *27*.

Seligman, M. E. P. *Helplessness*. San Francisco: W. H. Freeman, 1975.

Shaw, M. E., & Costanzo, P. R. *Theories of social psychology*. New York: McGraw–Hill, 1970.

Taylor, C. *The explanation of behavior*. London: Routledge & Kegan Paul, 1964.

Winch, P. *The idea of a social science*. London: Routledge & Kegan Paul, 1958 (originally published in 1946).

Wittgenstein, L. *Philosophical investigations* (Trans. G. Anscombe). London: Macmillan, 1963.

4 Contemporary Aspects of Psychological Experimentation

Ruben Ardila
National University of Columbia, Bogotá, Columbia

The basic foundations of psychological research are analyzed from a systematic and historical point of view. The conceptual frame of reference of contemporary psychology—both in its biological and in its social end—is considered. Current criticisms to experimental methodology are presented and refuted. Experimental psychology has contributed to a better understanding of behavioral issues and has a number of applications. The research program carried out by the author on early learning and psychological development is presented as an example of cross-cultural investigation. An international perspective shows that social and political factors influence the main trends in research. The most important trends that will define the future of psychology are analyzed.

THE EXPERIMENTAL METHOD

Experimentation has been the method of choice for psychologists during the last century. Originally it was a method borrowed from more "mature" disciplines, particularly from physiology and physics. The method was successfully applied to several areas of psychology, mainly perception, learning, and the physiological bases of behavior.

In recent years experimentation in psychology has enlarged considerably and included many fields not previously covered, among them cognition, personality, development, and social psychology. Experimental psychology today is very different from what Wundt conceived, and what he wanted. Complex processes are studied with experimental techniques and instrumentation (Sarris, 1967, 1968; Sarris, Heineken, & Peters, 1976; Sarris & Parducci, 1978). Current developments in mathematical psychology, in physiological psychology, in learning, in behavior genetics, and in the experimental analysis of behavior are very far from the mainstream of experimental psychology as Wundt wanted it to be. They are the mainstream of contemporary experimental psychology. The progress has been considerable. It seems to be the enlargement of a very important field of research and application that deals with one of the most difficult and varied entities of nature: behavior, both human and animal, and even experience and social processes.

On the other hand, a number of criticisms have been made against experimental psychology. It is supposed to be a discipline with no relation to real life that tries to copy the most developed sciences in order to gain prestige, that ignores social and political factors, and that is in a permanent state of crisis. Among the critical analyses of experimental psychology we could mention Braginsky and Braginsky's (1974) *Mainstream Psychology, a Critique;* Westland's (1978) *Current Crises of Psychology,* and others. A more balanced view is presented by Schultz (1970) in his book, *The Science of Psychology: Critical Reflections* (See also Germana, 1971).

The aim of this chapter is to analyze the experimental method in psychology, the areas in which it has been applied, the obstacles encountered, the criticisms presented against it, a way of refuting them, the current status of experimental psychology, the influence of social and political factors (both in the choice of problems and in the implications), and the probable future course of development of psychology. All this is presented in an international perspective given the experience of the author in different countries on both sides of the Atlantic Ocean.

EXPERIMENTATION IN PSYCHOLOGY

If we consider psychology as a reflection on human nature, it has existed practically since the beginning of history. In a modern sense, the founding of the Institute of Psychology and its laboratory in Leipzig in 1879 has been considered as the official date of birth of psychology. This means that psychology as a discipline and the use of the experimental method have been practically parallel. The use of the experimental method converted psychology into an "independent" field, different from philosophy. Psychology in its beginning was synonymous with experimental psychology.

The manipulation of independent variables and its influence on dependent variables has been the concern of psychologists during several decades. Problems of control, instrumentation, and generalization of results are issues discussed in all places in which experimental psychology is practiced (Ardila, 1971, 1977; Calfee, 1975; Díaz–Guerrero, 1980; Fraisse & Piaget, 1963–1967; Kling

& Riggs, 1971; Lauterbach & Sarris, 1980; Matheson, Bruce, & Beauchamp, 1970; Sidowski, 1966; Stevens, 1951; Underwood, 1966).

An experiment is a study in which the investigator manipulates one or several variables (independent) and measures other variables (dependent). This traditional definition comes from the natural sciences. In order to have an experiment, the investigator must control the situation: Vary the factors deliberately to create differences in the amount of the variable. To *measure* is not the same as to *experiment*. In many nonexperimental situations a good deal of control is obtained, and there is a good amount of precision in measurement. What distinguishes experimentation from nonexperimentation is the manipulation of variables.

In the traditional approach to experimental research, an experimental group is exposed to the assumed independent variable, whereas a control group is not; the two groups are later compared in terms of the assumed effect or dependent variable. However, today we have multivariable experimental psychology (Cattell, 1966), and we have also single-case experimental designs as used in operant conditioning (Hersen & Barlow, 1977).

The need for a control group comes from the necessity to make comparisons with the results obtained by the experimental group that will permit the investigator to eliminate alternative hypotheses. The results could be due to many different causes, and the control group—as similar to the experimental group as possible—shows whether the results are due to the manipulated variables or not.

In the multivariate experimental design we work with several variables and their interactions. In the single-case experimental designs, the subject is its own control. These innovations have enlarged considerably the scope of experimental research.

With the new advances in mathematics, experimentation has become more and more sophisticated. The articles published in the *Journal of Experimental Psychology* (in its four parts), *Quarterly Journal of Experimental Psychology, Acta Psychologica, Psychologie Francaise, Japanese Psychological Research,* and many other experimental journals are a proof of this. Different designs benefit from new advances in mathematics and in the use of instrumentation for recording variables. The modeling of psychological processes and the presentation of mathematical models has also advanced considerably, as found in journals such as the *Journal of Mathematical Psychology.*

Experimental psychology is not an area of psychology: It is a method applicable to all the fields of psychology (Ardila, 1968). At the present time it is applied only to some basic and applied areas, but in principle it could be used to solve problems in any branch of psychology. Historically our discipline has chosen the utilization of the experimental method, and probably it is only a matter of time before all psychology becomes experimental.

Of course, experimental psychology is not the only scientific psychology. Correlational psychology is also scientific, and many problems are best studied descriptively before correlational and experimental methods can be applied. For psychology, experimentation is still a goal, and it has been for 100 years. We have advanced considerably in this direction (Hearst, 1979).

SOCIAL RESEARCH

Social sciences, in the traditional sense, do not use the experimental method at all. Sociology, economics, and anthropology are not experimental sciences. Linguistics is an experimental discipline, at least in some of its approaches. Political science is not only a discipline that does not use experimentation but also is clearly not sympathetic to experimentation. In general, social sciences are not interested in the use of the experimental method and have a very narrow understanding of what experimentation is all about.

Psychology has been classified as a social science, as a natural science, and as a behavioral science. If we accept the first classification—as a social science—it could be considered as the only experimental social science. For many decades social psychology was a nonexperimental discipline. Wundt insisted that the psychology of peoples—his famous *Volkerpsychologie*—could not be experimental.

The rise of experimental social psychology is a relatively recent phenomenon. Although Murphy, Murphy, and Newcomb published their first *Experimental Social Psychology* in 1937, only several decades later did a real experimental social psychology come into existence.

Experimental social psychology uses the experimental method to investigate problems such as social perception, hostility, aggression, interpersonal attraction, attitude change, conformity, group pressure, interdependence in groups, and related phenomena. It is very much concerned with the value of experimentation, the difference between experimental studies and field studies, the "artificiality" of the experiments, the problem of generalization of results, the causal relationships that the investigators try to establish in social phenomena, and so forth.

The relevance crisis in psychology is related to the usefulness of the methodology and the results and raises philosophical and ideological issues. Not all social psychological research is experimental, and not all is applicable to the solution of contemporary problems.

VIGOR AND RIGOR

In the discussion between science and social relevance, a way of putting the situation is to talk about *vigor* and *rigor*. Experimental psychology emphasizes rigor, whereas traditional social psychology is more interested in vigor. An investigator must choose between vigor and rigor, in a matter of proportion: which percentage of rigor and which percentage of vigor. One selects the amount of vigor and the amount of rigor prefered. Apparently, the more rigor, the less vigor, and vice versa.

It is very difficult to have vigor and rigor at the same time. Some areas, however, have both. For instance, experimental social psychology is a very vigorous area, studied with very rigorous methods. The same could be said of behavior therapy. As another example our research project on patterns of child rearing in the Caribbean area is both vigorous and rigorous.

Patterns of child rearing, experimental social psychology, and behavior therapy are examples of areas of experimental psychology that are both vigorous and rigorous. It is not easy to have both. If we focus on control, we have more rigor and less vigor, although there is the hope of obtaining some vigorous applications in the future. The experimental analysis of behavior is an example of an area of experimental psychology that was "pure" science for many years and that today has given rise to a technology, the applied behavior analysis, with applications in the clinical, social, educational, and industrial areas (Ardila, 1974, 1979b). Nobody could see any possible applications in the experiments with rats in Skinner boxes, in the beginning of the 1940s and 1950s.

Even if a research area does not have any applications today or in the future, it could be valuable in itself. Applications and social relevance are not the criteria for science. The search for scientific laws and the understanding of the physical, biological, and behavioral world are important goals independent of any application, actual or potential.

EXPERIMENTATION AND QUASI-EXPERIMENTATION

If science follows a path that goes from observation to correlational studies and from there to experimentation, some areas of psychology are more developed than others. Theories, mathematical models, and higher-order concepts are found in all areas of psychology. However, experimentation is more common in the areas that are close to the biological end of psychology than in the more socially oriented ones.

The traditional experimental method presented in the classical books such as Woodworth and Schlosberg's (Kling & Riggs, 1971), Underwood's (1966), and Fraisse and Piaget's (1963–1967) has been complemented by many new techniques and approaches. Path analysis, quasi-experimentation, multivariate experimental psychology, and other methods and procedures have yielded important results and helped to solve several problems of design, data analysis, and interpretation. Methodology in psychology has evolved considerably in the last few years. One of the main trends is associated with Campbell and his quasi-experimental methods (Cook & Campbell, 1979).

In the areas of experimental social psychology a good deal of rigor and precision has been obtained by several investigators of very "vigorous" problems. As examples we could mention Schachter's (1959) work on the psychology of affiliation; Berkowitz's on altruism and helping behavior (Macaulay & Berkowitz, 1970); and Milgram's (1973) on obedience to authority. In all these works the strictest experimental methodology has been applied to the most relevant problems.

Our research project on patterns of child rearing has attempted to combine vigor and rigor in the treatment of a very relevant problem: the origins of human behavior, the biosocial foundations of "individuality," and "personality." Some methodological difficulties related to control of variables had to be solved. In general, cross-cultural psychology has to adapt the methods of psychological research to the problems under investigation; in some cases precision is sacrificed, although it does not have to be like that in all situations.

We are investigating the way in which parents raise their children in Colombia, Cuba, Puerto Rico, and Haiti. This project is designed to find the influence of several factors on child rearing and personality development, using the most modern sampling techniques and analysis of the data with the help of a computer. The areas we are studying are the following ones: feeding, father participation, hygiene habits, sexuality, gender roles, discipline, use of rewards, use of punishment, language development, independency and autonomy, relationships with peers, aggression toward the parents, aggression toward other children, expression of affection in the family, agreement between the parents, respect for property, moral rules, orientation toward the future, and similarity between child-rearing practices in this generation and in previous generations.

The 19 variables are related to socialization in the four countries. The influence of the United States in Puerto Rico, of the U.S.S.R. in Cuba, the traditional Spanish culture in Colombia, and the more "primitive," close to nature, culture in Haiti are considered relevant factors. In the long run we are interested in finding the influence of social, political, and cultural factors on behavioral development in Cuba, Puerto Rico, Haiti, and Colombia and a way of generalizing the data to other cultural frames of reference (Ardila, 1979a, 1981).

In the case of Colombia, some final results have been obtained. We compared patterns of child rearing in four social classes (upper class, middle class, low class, and rural class), and in four subcultures (Andean, Mountain, Neo-Hispanic, and Coast); the four subcultures include the large majority of the country and have been studied in detail from an anthropological viewpoint.

Tables 4.1, 4.2, 4.3, and 4.4 present the results concerning the Andean subculture (high class, middle class, low class, and rural class) in comparison with the other groups.

Data have been collected in the area of moral judgment and are being analyzed for intelligence and personality. In the other countries data collection is in process. In all cases native investigators do the interviews, apply the questionnaires, and adapt the materials to the language of the region, social class of the subjects, educational level, age, and so forth. We try to be as careful as possible concerning cultural bias and prejudices.

TABLE 4.1
Correlations Between Patterns of Child Rearing in the Andean Subculture, Lower
Social Class, with the Other Groups: ASM (Andean Subculture, Middle Class), ASH
(Andean Subculture, High Class), ASR (Andean Subculture, Rural Class), MSL
(Mountain Subculture, Low Class), HSL (Hispanic Subculture, Low Class), and CSL
(Coast Subculture, Low Class)

Variables	ASM	ASH	ASR	MSL	HSL	CSL
101 Feeding	.33	.17	.89	.06	.19	.03
102 Father collaboration	.00	.00	.46	.00	.72	.01
103 Hygiene habits	.05	.01	.00	.52	.44	.01
104 Sexuality	.03	.00	.28	.02	.03	.00
105 Gender roles	.18	.81	.39	.04	.19	.86
106 Discipline	.00	.00	.00	.00	.60	.00
107 Use of rewards	.00	.00	.03	.00	.32	.03
108 Use of punishment	.03	.00	.36	.20	.23	.02
109 Language development	.00	.00	.00	.00	.56	.00
110 Independency and autonomy	.74	.81	.88	.01	.59	.00
111 Relations with peers	.03	.87	.95	.03	.28	.36
112 Aggression toward parents	.75	.79	.51	.02	.27	.40
113 Aggression toward peers	.17	.34	.28	.94	.20	.81
114 Expression of affection	.00	.00	.15	.00	.64	.80
115 Agreement between parents	.00	.00	.07	.00	.97	.98
116 Respect for property	.10	.00	.15	.00	.40	.09
117 Moral rules	.00	.00	.10	.00	.24	.08
118 Orientation toward future	.51	.00	.10	.00	.71	.18
119 Similarity with previous generations	.00	.00	.53	.09	.92	.95

The analysis compares the 19 variables in the four social classes and in the different subcultures (four in the case of Colombia). We want to know, for instance, how rewards and punishments are used for socialization of children in the different social classes, in the different subcultures, and in the different countries. Cooperation and competition, moral rules, modeling, and cultural standards are to be understood in the proper context and not based on our personal prejudices.

Many difficulties are solved in this research project with proper design, adequate sampling techniques, standardization of tests and other measurement instruments, use of native investigators and native personnel for data collection, and—last but not the least—a sympathetic understanding of cultural differences and similarities.

TABLE 4.2
Correlations Between Patterns of Child Rearing in the Andean Subculture, Middle Social Class, with the Other Groups: ASH, ASR, MSL, HSL, CSL

Variables	ASH	ASR	MSL	HSL	CSL
101 Feeding	.02	.29	.00	.03	.00
102 Father collaboration	.07	.00	.02	.00	.02
103 Hygiene habits	.06	.00	.00	.34	.45
104 Sexuality	.08	.00	.90	.99	.67
105 Gender roles	.09	.02	.00	.90	.30
106 Discipline	.92	.00	.39	.00	.03
107 Use of rewards	.00	.00	.59	.00	.15
108 Use of punishment	.14	.00	.00	.50	.00
109 Language development	.73	.00	.61	.00	.05
110 Independency and autonomy	.93	.86	.01	.75	.00
111 Relations with peers	.03	.04	.96	.00	.29
112 Aggression toward parents	.57	.34	.05	.18	.28
113 Aggression toward peers	.67	.01	.17	.92	.11
114 Expression of affection	.90	.00	.20	.00	.00
115 Agreement between parents	.93	.14	.00	.01	.00
116 Respect for property	.27	.85	.40	.57	.81
117 Moral rules	.61	.00	.45	.00	.00
118 Orientation toward future	.00	.03	.00	.80	.51
119 Similarity with previous generations	.12	.00	.08	.00	.00

TABLE 4.3
Correlations Between Patterns of Child Rearing in the Andean Subculture, High Social Class, with the Other Groups: ASR, MSL, HSL, CSL

Variables	ASR	MSL	HSL	CSL
101 Feeding	.24	.59	.89	.38
102 Father collaboration	.00	.01	.00	.04
103 Hygiene habits	.00	.00	.17	.77
104 Sexuality	.00	.10	.10	.19
105 Gender roles	.49	.05	.09	.69
106 Discipline	.00	.44	.00	.04
107 Use of rewards	.00	.00	.00	.00
108 Use of punishment	.00	.00	.05	.00
109 Language development	.00	.85	.00	.02
110 Independency and autonomy	.93	.01	.72	.00
111 Relations with peers	.93	.03	.20	.41
112 Aggression toward parents	.69	.01	.39	.54
113 Aggression toward peers	.03	.36	.64	.25
114 Expression of affection	.00	.15	.00	.00
115 Agreement between parents	.10	.00	.00	.00
116 Respect for property	.19	.77	.10	.48
117 Moral rules	.00	.80	.00	.00
118 Orientation toward future	.00	.03	.00	.00
119 Similarity with previous generations	.00	.00	.00	.00

TABLE 4.4
Correlations Between Patterns of Child Rearing in the Andean Subculture, Rural
Class, with the Other Groups: MSL, HSL, CSL

Variables	MSL	HSL	CSL
101 Feeding	.10	.26	.06
102 Father collaboration	.00	.30	.00
103 Hygiene habits	.00	.00	.00
104 Sexuality	.00	.00	.00
105 Gender roles	.25	.03	.33
106 Discipline	.00	.00	.00
107 Use of rewards	.00	.34	.00
108 Use of punishment	.72	.04	.20
109 Language development	.00	.02	.00
110 Independence and autonomy	.01	.68	.00
111 Relations with peers	.04	.27	.41
112 Aggression toward parents	.00	.59	.78
113 Aggression toward peers	.23	.02	.43
114 Expression of affection	.00	.39	.24
115 Agreement between parents	.00	.14	.07
116 Respect for property	.29	.68	.68
117 Moral rules	.00	.76	.97
118 Orientation toward future	.00	.06	.00
119 Similarity with previous generations	.29	.52	.67

This research project in process is mentioned mainly as an example of an investigation that tries to work with relevant problems of contemporary society, using the techniques of the new quasi-experimental methodology in psychology. We still have a long way to go before understanding fully the influence of social and political factors in human development, but probably we are working along the right track.

THE INTERNATIONAL SCENE

In an international symposium such as this on perspectives in psychological experimentation, it is very important to point out some of the characteristics of international experimental psychology.

The fact is that psychology is to a large extent an Anglo–Saxon phenomenon, as we have indicated previously (Ardila, 1982b). As a discipline, psychology began in Germany, but later on the center passed to the United States and has remained there since. Today the most active centers of research in experimental psychology are in the United States, Canada, the Federal Republic of Germany, England, Japan, the Netherlands, and a few more countries. There are research centers in the developing world, particularly in Latin America, but the output does not compare favorably with the output of research in the United States and Western Europe.

Although other areas of science are more internationally oriented, psychology is not. The large majority of research is carried out in the United States, is written in English, and has the mark of the Anglo–Saxon culture.

Obviously, *science* is a universal enterprise, beyond the boundaries of cultures, including geography and ideology. The *results* of science could be used with different aims, but in general science as a social institution is "universal," in the best sense of the word: It searches for universal laws and has a methodology that is not directly dependent on culture. In an indirect way there are ideological influences, but in the main aspects science is a relatively culture-free institution.

In spite of this, scientific psychology has some narrow boundaries, geographically speaking. It is not due to the practical problem of lack proper funds for research. As a matter of fact, in many countries—including some of the Third World—there are appropriate funds for research that in some cases are not used. There is enough money but not enough good projects to be supported. The explanation lies in the lack of an appropriate research environment. Science is not a social value in many cultures; there are very few incentives for the investigators, few congresses, few journals, and few colleagues to which to talk about one's research.

In many countries psychology is thought of more as a part of the humanities than as part of the natural sciences. Experimental research particularly with animals is not considered "relevant" or "important." Animal models of psychological phenomena are supposed to be incomplete, because psychology is the science of "mind" and this attribute is considered exclusive to man.

In the international scene of contemporary psychology, there are some cultural trends. For instance, experimental research along the operant conditioning paradigm is more common in the United States, Japan, and Latin America than in Europe. Perception and psychophysics are cultivated in Germany. Work in progress in experimental social psychology exists in France and Belgium, as well as the United States. Psychophysiology and "defectology" are the favorite areas of Soviets investigators. Probably these trends will tend to disappear in the near future, because psychology will be a more unified discipline than it is today.

In the Third World, research is valued as something important but very costly considering its probable output in a short-time perspective. To do research is relevant but it is risky. Investigators are considered exotic people, who have to prove the usefulness of their work. Science is not a value in Latin America (Ardila, 1983a, 1982d), nor in the rest of the developing world.

The large majority of psychological research, as we have indicated previously, is culture-free. The work done in perception, learning, physiological psychology, and related areas does not have very much to do with ideology and politics. But the social areas, including personality and developmental psychology, are very much related to a specific culture. How much of the total variance is explained by general laws and how much by cultural relativism is something to be explained (Triandis, 1980). We are searching for universal laws, as it is the case in all sciences. The aim is to have a discipline beyond the limitations of culture, geography, and the social prejudices of our times.

THE FUTURE OF PSYCHOLOGY

The first century of experimental psychology and of psychology as an independent discipline has shown steady progress in many areas but has encountered obstacles and problems in others. The definition of the subject matter of psychology, that changed from the soul to the mind and finally to behavior, has implied important changes in methodology. A number of issues have arisen both in the biological and in the social areas of psychology.

Where do we go from here? Science has as one of its objectives the prediction of events and could try to predict its own development. This has not been easy, as Wertheimer, Barclay, Cook, Kiesler, Koch, Riegel, Rorer, Senders, Smith & Sperling (1978) have pointed out in the case of psychology. The future of psychology is a matter of concern to all of us who have worked in the development of psychology along the scientific path and who are interested in international issues and in social relevance.

I would like to present some ideas about the future of psychology, based on my own reflections during several years concerning this topic (Ardila, 1983b).

To begin with, it is important to remember that humanity faces three main dangers: overpopulation, lack of natural resources, and the possibility of a new world war. Overpopulation is a relative matter, and in reality there are not "too many people" in the world but too many in relation to the rate of development and the possibility of having a life of quality for everybody.

The lack of natural resources is a very contemporary problem that has preoccupied economists and social planners in the last decade. The possibility of a nuclear war is something that is always in the background and that changes with the policies of the big potencies, particularly the United States, the U.S.S.R. and China. Probably this danger is relatively remote, because in World War III there would be no winners, only losers.

If we are able to solve the problems of overpopulation, lack of natural resources, and escape from a new world war, science would have a future. Psychology is very dependent on our way of solving the preceding problems, although all disciplines are also dependent on these important social issues.

Extrapolating from the current situation we could say that the psychology of the near future will have the following characteristics:

1. More emphasis on science. Psychology in the near future will be more scientific, using the term in a broad sense. It is not true that we will stop being a scientific discipline and become a speculative discipline. The trend toward science will increase in the future.

2. More emphasis on social relevance. Psychology will leave its "ivory tower" and will work in socially important problems, without forgetting basic scientific issues.

3. Use of better mathematical models. In the future better mathematics will be used. Probably many behavioral problems could be understood with more appropriate mathematical models.

4. Work in complex problems. Psychology in the future will devote itself to problems such as cognition, ecology, conceptualization, behavioral development, and consciousness, problems that are recognized as important but have not been investigated until the last few years with the tools of experimental methodology.

5. More professionalization. Psychology has diversified and has become more and more specialized. Probably this trend will continue, both in the scientific and in the practical areas. However, psychology will maintain its identity and will not become several disciplines.

6. Integration of psychology and vanishing of the psychological "schools." Many of the systems of the past have disappeared as schools and probably this trend will continue. Psychology in the future will not be, however, an ecclectic discipline but a science with a unifying paradigm in the sense of Kuhn's (1970) analysis of scientific revolutions and the normal science.

One of the main possibilities for the near future would be an *experimental synthesis of behavior* that could function as a new paradigm for psychology, in Kuhn's sense, and replace the approaches and viewpoints of today. The experimental synthesis of behavior will be an outgrowth of the experimental analysis but will help to integrate many contributions of cognitive psychology and other areas.

These characteristics of psychology in the future are presented because a number of trends can be observed in present-day psychology. More emphasis on science, more emphasis on social relevance, use of better mathematical models, work in complex problems, more professionalization, and the integration of psychology and the vanishing of "schools" are trends already observed in present-day psychology. I think that they will define to a large extent what psychology is going to be in the year 2000.

REFERENCES

Ardila, R. En defensa del método experimental en psicología. *Revista de Psicología General y Aplicada* (Madrid), 1968, *23*, 689–724.
Ardila, R. *Psicología experimental*. Mexico: Trillas, 1971.

Ardila, R. (Ed.). *El análisis experimental del comportamiento.* Mexico: Trillas, 1974.

Ardila, R. *Investigaciones psicológicas.* Bogotá: Siglo XXI, 1977.

Ardila, R. *Los orígenes del comportamiento humano.* Barcelona:Fontanella, 1979. (a)

Ardila, R. *Walden tres.* Barcelona: CEAC, 1979. (b)

Ardila, R. *Pautas de crianza de los niños en Colombia.* Research project, sponsored by the Colombian Fund for the Support of Science (Colciencias), Bogotá, 1981.

Ardila, R. International psychology. *American Psychologist,* 1982, *37,* 323–329. (a)

Ardila, R. Psychology in Latin America today. *Annual Review of Psychology,* 1982, *33,* 103–122. (b)

Ardila, R. *La psicología en América Latina: pasado, presente y futuro.* Mexico: Trillas, 1983, in press. (a)

Ardila, R. *El futuro de la psicología.* Barranquilla, Colombia: Ediciones Pedagógicas Latinoamericanas, 1983. (b)

Braginsky, B. M., & Braginsky, D. D. *Mainstream psychology, a critique.* New York: Holt–Rinehart– Winston, 1974.

Calfee, R. C. *Human experimental psychology.* New York: Holt–Rinehart–Winston, 1975.

Cattell, R. B. (Ed.). *Handbook of multivariate experimental psychology.* Chicago: Rand McNally, 1966.

Cook, T. D., & Campbell, D. T. *Quasi-experimentation: Design and analysis issues for field settings.* Chicago: Rand McNally, 1979.

Díaz–Guerrero, R. *Lecturas para el curso de psicología experimental* (2nd. ed.). Mexico: Trillas, 1980.

Fraisse, P., & Piaget, J. (Eds.). *Traité de psychologie expérimentale* (9 vols). Paris: Presses Universitaires de France, 1963–1967.

Germana, J. *Contemporary experimental psychology: In flagrante delicto.* Monterey, Calif.: Brooks/Cole, 1971.

Hearst, E. (Ed.). *The first century of experimental psychology.* Hillsdale, N.J.: Lawrence Erlbaum Associates, 1979.

Hersen, M., & Barlow, D. H. *Single-case experimental design.* Oxford: Pergamon, 1977.

Kling, J. W., & Riggs, L. A. (Eds.). *Woodworth & Schlosberg's experimental psychology* (3rd. ed.). New York: Holt–Rinehart–Winston, 1971.

Kuhn, T. S. *The structure of scientific revolutions* (rev. ed.). Chicago: University of Chicago Press, 1970.

Lauterbach, W., & Sarris, V. (Eds.). *Beiträge zur psychologischen Bezugssystemforschung.* Bern: Hans Huber, 1980.

Macaulay, J., & Berkowitz, L. *Altruism and helping behavior.* New York: Academic Press, 1970.

Matheson, D. W., Bruce, R. L., & Beauchamp, K. L. *Introduction to experimental psychology.* New York: Holt–Rinehart–Winston, 1970.

Milgram, S. *Obedience to authority, an experimental view.* New York: Harper & Row, 1973.

Murphy, G., Murphy, L. B., & Newcomb, T. M. *Experimental social psychology.* New York: Harper & Row, 1937.

Sarris, V. Adaptation-level theory: Two critical experiments on Helson's weighted-average model. *American Journal of Psychology,* 1967, *80,* 331–344.

Sarris, V. Adaptation-level theory: Absolute or relative anchor effectiveness? *Psychonomic Science,* 1968, *13,* 307–308.

Sarris, V., Heineken, E., & Peters, H. Effect of stress on field dependence. *Perception and Psychophysics,* 1976, *43,* 121–122.

Sarris, V., & Parducci, A. Multiple anchoring of category rating scales. *Perception and Psychophysics,* 1978, *24,* 35–39.

Schachter, S. *Psychology of affiliation.* Stanford: Stanford University Press, 1959.

Schultz, D. P. (Ed.). *The science of psychology: Critical reflections.* Englewood Cliffs, N.J.: Prentice–Hall, 1970.

Sidowski, J. B. (Ed.). *Experimental methods and instrumentation in psychology.* New York: McGraw–Hill, 1966.

Stevens, S. S. (Ed.). *Handbook of experimental psychology.* New York: Wiley, 1951.

Triandis, H. C. (Ed.). *Handbook of cross-cultural psychology* (6 vols.). Boston: Allyn & Bacon, 1980.

Underwood, B. J. *Experimental psychology* (2nd. ed.). New York: Appleton–Century–Crofts, 1966.

Wertheimer, M., Barclay, A. G., Cook, S. W., Kiesler, C. A., Koch, S., Riegel, K. F., Rorer, L. G., Senders, V. L., Smith, M. B., & Sperling, S. E. Psychology and the future. *American Psychologist,* 1978, *33,* 631–647.

Westland, G. *Current crises of psychology.* London: Heinemann, 1978.

BASIC PROCESSES OF ANIMAL LEARNING AND MEMORY

The animal model of human behavior, so universally accepted 30 years ago (with the rat as the primary laboratory subject), has lost much of its grip on theoretical psychology. During the last two decades, animal and human studies have become progressively dissociated. The growth of cognitive psychology has turned attention to the more complex features of human information processing. This dissociation may have encouraged a higher level of methodological sophistication, both in animal and in human studies. But there also appears to be continuing efforts to bridge these two areas of research.

The three chapters constituting Part II reflect these recent trends. M. E. Bitterman's chapter reviews the main ideas that have guided his own comparative research. His work with honey bees and goldfish illustrates central issues of commonality versus evolutionary divergence in the mechanisms of learning and memory. Although comparative psychology is no longer one of the "hot" areas of psychology, Bitterman's sophisticated step-by-step approach should lead, as he predicts, to closer ties with the neurosciences (and one might expect, as does Bitterman, that neurophysiologists and biochemists will become better acquainted with the behavioral literature). Bitterman also expects a growing interaction with students of *human* learning. The concern will not be restricted to those processes shared with other animals but also to understanding which processes are unique to humans.

The chapter by Norman Spear boldly speculates about the links between animal and human mechanisms of learning and memory. It will be interesting to compare Spear's predictions with what actually happens in the next 20 years. For Spear, the basic question is whether it is useful to treat memory as a global capacity. His tentative answer is "no." That is why he favors analysis into separate, relatively independent systems. Spear predicts a further increase in studies dealing directly with learning and memory, paralleled by a decrease in studies of how motivation interacts with learning and memory. He also predicts that biopsychological research will make increasing use of human subjects—at the expense of the analogue research with animals favored by Bitterman. Spear links this research with both developmental and clinical–medical psychology. Although specifically citing the neuropeptides, he predicts significant advances relating other drugs and different brain structures to specific kinds of learning and memory.

Kardos' chapter strikes familiar historical chords, with its description of research on "place learning" and its emphasis on the role of visual memory in animal learning. Kardos' own basic research dates back to the 1920s and Gestalt concerns with human perception. His experiments distinguish between animal and human orientational behavior, but the net effect is to encourage hope for further integration in the future.

Taken as a group, these chapters question the assumption that animal psychology is dying. Indeed, they make a persuasive case for its underlying importance to the development of a biopsychology of the future.

5 Learning in Man and Other Animals

M. E. Bitterman
University of Hawaii, Honolulu, USA

There was a time not long ago when research in the tradition of Thorndike and Pavlov on the learning of nonhuman animals was a topic of central interest for psychologists, but hardly today. Contemporary students have little beyond the smattering of information about it provided by their glossy primers, and they care less. One reason, of course, is that psychology is more than ever anthropocentric in its concerns, and the work is thought to have little relevance for man; the brave hope, rekindled in every generation of psychologists since the turn of the century, that the great problems of human socialization and education and of psychopathology and psychotherapy will yield to a few simple principles of conditioning readily demonstrable in rats or pigeons seems on the way at last to being permanently dispelled. There is the impression too that the conditioning enterprise has been a failure even on its own terms—that years of effort have been wasted in fruitless controversy over rather meaningless questions. I argue here that this appraisal is incorrect—that reasonable questions have been asked, that a good deal of progress has been made in answering them, and that the work has considerable importance for understanding man, who leads the animals, in the words of Thorndike (1911), "not as a demigod from another planet, but as a king from the same race [p. 294]."

The main questions have been three, all closely interrelated and arising from the very earliest laboratory experiments. Thorndike set out to study the learning of chickens, dogs, cats, and monkeys under conditions in which they were required to do certain simple things in order to obtain food. He found no indication of the understanding attributed to these familiar animals by even the most disciplined of the anecdotalists (Romanes, 1882), only the more or less gradual formation of what he termed "practical" associations between sensory and

59

motor systems as a function in some degree of frequency of occurrence (the Law of Exercise) but as a function primarily of rewarding consequences (the Law of Effect). The two laws seemed to hold as well for the monkeys as for the simpler animals, although the monkeys showed a certain quantitative superiority (they learned more and learned more quickly), and Thorndike concluded that the laws probably hold also for man, where (he suggested) an even greater quantitative advance "conceals the real continuity of the process [p. 294]." There were immediate objections to every feature of Thorndike's hypothesis, and out of the ensuing discussion emerged the questions that structured subsequent research.

The first had to do with commonality *versus* evolutionary divergence of learning mechanisms. It stimulated numerous attempts to demonstrate that—even if the laws of association should prove to be the same in all animals—the intelligence at least of apes is not purely associative and reproductive but in some sense creative. Actually, the clearest evidence thus far of qualitative change in the course of evolution comes from work with simpler vertebrates. The second question, which had to do with the elements of association, prompted a variety of experiments designed to look for sensory–sensory (S–S) rather than the sensory–motor (S–R) associations postulated by Thorndike. One of them is the deceptively simple sensory-preconditioning experiment: After two neutral stimuli have been paired repeatedly, the animal is trained to make some new response to one of them, and then we ask whether the other stimulus will evoke the same response. Conceived originally by Thorndike himself, the experiment was not done properly for many years. The third question had to do with the role of reward in learning: Does reward strengthen association between stimulus and response as Thorndike and, later, Hull (1943) proposed, or does it enter into association with other stimuli, being learned about, remembered, anticipated, and serving in that way to influence behavior? The controversy was long and frustrating because there was much to be said for each side of each question. The answers (however unparsimonious) seem to be that there is far-reaching commonality of mechanism but also significant divergence, that both S–S and S–R associations are formed, and that reward both strengthens association and is learned about.

VERTEBRATE AND INVERTEBRATE LEARNING

It is important to emphasize that there is evidence of broad commonality, because some rather unlikely prophets armed with a few half-digested findings have in recent years been successfully promoting the belief that learning is a set of specialized adaptations about which we can make no general statements at all. Striking functional resemblances are found, not only among vertebrates of different classes but between vertebrates and invertebrates as well. Not all invertebrates seem to be capable of associative learning, although many questionable "demonstrations" of classical and instrumental conditioning in protozoans, co-elenterates, and echinoderms are to be found in the literature (Corning, Dyal, & Willows, 1973, 1975). As to the reality of associative learning in animals of the annelid superphylum—worms, molluscs, arthropods—there can, however, be no doubt at all, and evidence is accumulating that the resemblances between the performance of these animals and the performance of vertebrates in experiments designed originally for the study of learning in vertebrates are more than superficial, that they are products of common mechanisms evolved in remote common ancestors. For illustration, let me describe some of the work of my laboratory on appetitive conditioning in honeybees, although that may seem, in Germany, like carrying coals to Newcastle. The basic method was, of course, developed here for studying the sensory capacities of bees by von Frisch (1915), and in recent years it has been widely used for the study of their learning by investigators such as Randolf Menzel, Klaus Grossmann, and Bernhard Schnetter.

The vertebrate model for the experiments is provided by the work of Pavlov (1927) on salivary conditioning in dogs. The conditioned stimuli are colors and odors presented on a circular gray target that is a petri dish with small holes drilled in its cover. The target can be distinguished either with a disk of color or an odor from scented cotton wool in the dish, or both, or neither. The reinforcement is a drop of 40% sucrose solution in the center of the cover from which a pretrained bee comes repeatedly of its own accord to drink. The strength of conditioning is measured in terms of resistance to extinction. After several reinforced visits of the bee to the target, a drop of tap water is substituted for the drop of sucrose solution, and the number of contacts of the bee with the target in a fixed period (usually 10 min) is recorded; what the bee does when it finds the water is fly up immediately, return to the target, fly up again, and so forth, the rate of contact with the target systematically decreasing over time. Of the various control procedures that may be used to demonstrate association, the simplest is the discrimination procedure (Menzel, 1968). Suppose, for example, that in the course of training the animal is exposed on some occasions to a target with a yellow disk and a drop of sucrose, and on other occasions to a target with an orange disk and a drop of water. In a subsequent extinction test with two targets, one displaying a yellow disk, the other an orange disk, and both providing water, the bees show a strong preference for the yellow. Other animals, for which orange rather than yellow was reinforced in training, prefer orange in the test. In all these experiments, the stimuli are balanced (as were the colors in the example just given), and stringent precautions are taken routinely to control for the effects of irrelevant stimuli (such as those produced by the bees themselves).

On the basis of his early experiments, Pavlov concluded that a conditioned stimulus gradually acquires excitatory properties in a series of reinforced trials, that in unreinforced training a stimulus acquires competing inhibitory properties, that excitation and inhibition summate algebraically in the control of behavior, and that a compound stimulus acts in large measure as an algebraic sum of its components. The same conclusions are supported by the results of directly analogous experiments with bees (Couvillon & Bitterman, 1980). For example, summation of excitation was demonstrated in an experiment in which bees were given reinforced training with a yellow disk (Y) on some trials and a jasmine odor (J) on others, after which they were extinguished in a choice test with Y and J combined *versus* Y alone or J alone; the compound was significantly preferred to either of the components. An active process of inhibition was demonstrated in experiments of several different designs. In one of them, bees were trained to discriminate between Y and J, and then they were extinguished in a choice test with the negative stimulus *versus* the gray target alone (G), that is, without either Y or J; there was significantly less response to the negative stimulus (which in Pavlovian terms can be thought of as a sum of the negative stimulus and G) than to G (which must have developed some net excitatory strength on reinforced training trials). Algebraic summation of excitation and inhibition was demonstrated more directly in an experiment on what Pavlov called "conditioned inhibition." Bees were trained to discriminate Y (reinforced) from J (nonreinforced) and then extinguished in a choice test with Y and J in compound *versus* Y in compound with the novel odor of lemon (L); response to Y was suppressed significantly more by J than by L. In an experiment on the summation of inhibition, bees were given discriminative training in which G was reinforced, with Y unreinforced on some trials and J unreinforced on others; extinguished in a subsequent choice test, the animals responded less to Y and J in compound than either to Y alone or to J alone.

Pavlov was a bit disappointed perhaps to discover that a compound stimulus cannot be understood entirely as a sum of its components but seems to have certain unique properties derived from interaction of the components, and the same is true in bees (Couvillon & Bitterman, 1982). In one experiment with the colors O (orange) and Y and the odors J and L, the compound OJ was reinforced on some trials and the compound YL on others. Then there was an unreinforced choice test with the two training compounds along with the two new compounds (OL and YJ) that could be constructed by recombining the components. As may be seen in Fig. 5.1, which is plotted in terms of mean cumulative frequency of response to each pair, the previously reinforced compounds were preferred to the novel ones. Pavlov found another exception to the useful summation principle in the phenomenon he called "overshadowing"—a stimulus that can readily be conditioned by itself may acquire little excitatory value when conditioned in compound with another stimulus. Clear evidence of overshadowing is found also in honeybees. For example, after reinforced training with O, bees show a marked preference for O in an unreinforced choice test with O *versus* G but very little preference for O after reinforced training with O and J in compound; in the language of Pavlov, O is overshadowed by J. Although there has been a good deal of work on overshadowing in vertebrates, the phenomenon is not yet well understood. Loss of compound-unique properties may be a factor and so also

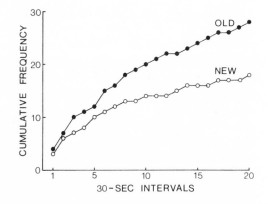

FIG. 5.1. Mean cumulative frequency of response in honeybees during an unreinforced choice test with two previously reinforced color–odor compounds (old) and two new compounds composed of the same components (Couvillon & Bitterman, 1982).

may be competition of the components for associative strength (Rescorla & Wagner, 1972) or for attention (Mackintosh, 1975).

The antithesis of overshadowing is "potentiation"—a stimulus actually may acquire greater associative strength when it is conditioned in compound with another than when it is conditioned separately (Durlach & Rescorla, 1980). This phenomenon, discovered only recently in vertebrates, appears in honeybees. In an unreinforced choice test with *J versus G,* there is a significantly greater preference for *J* after training with *OJ* than after training with *J* alone. One way to account for potentiation is on the assumption that the components of a compound are associated with each other during training with the compound. If, in the example given, a *J–O* association is formed in training with the compound, *J* will evoke *O* in the extinction test and the compound-unique properties conditioned in training with the compound will thereby be restored. There are other assumptions that have to be made to account for the fact that *O* is overshadowed by *J* but potentiates *J,* such as that there is a greater tendency in the compound training for the formation of a *J–O* than an *O–J* association; the phenomena are complex and no less so, apparently, in honeybees than in mammals. It is, however, perfectly clear now that within-compound association, which like potentiation has been discovered only recently in vertebrates (Rescorla & Cunningham, 1978) and which provides what is perhaps the clearest example of *S–S* association in vertebrates, is found also in honeybees. In the first stage of a representative experiment (Couvillon & Bitterman, 1982), bees had reinforced experience with one color–odor compound on some trials and with another color–odor compound on the remaining trials. In the second stage, the two odors were differentially reinforced in the absence of the colors. In the third stage, an unreinforced choice test with the two colors in the absence of the odors showed a clear preference for the color compounded in the first stage with the positive odor of the second stage. It should be evident that this sort of experiment is very much like sensory preconditioning in some respects and rather different in others.

Implications. Although the evolutionary relation between honeybees and vertebrates is extremely remote, such detailed resemblances in their performance point to the operation of common mechanisms of conditioning. To the extent that the various phenomena that have been described can be understood in terms of local synaptic events, the commonality hypothesis is supported by an essential identity of synaptic physiology in vertebrate and invertebrate nervous systems, although there are, of course, vast differences in neural organization. In any case, the implications of the hypothesis for human psychology are evident immediately; it must be thought rather improbable that there would be conditioning mechanisms common to all synaptic animals with the exception of man. The preoccupation now in work on human cognition is with capabilities superordinate to the acquisition of information and with purely functional models of those capabilities, but progress will almost certainly depend on the development of real-process models grounded in information about association that only experiments with nonhuman animals can supply. Apart from the better control of experimental conditions that is afforded, together with the vastly greater possibility of direct physiological intervention, work with simpler animals is essential because the powerful overlay of superordinate capabilities in man makes it difficult to isolate the associative processes for study (Ebbinghaus, 1885; Spence, 1966). For those who may not find the honeybee data entirely convincing, the same point may be made with respect to the commonality of associative mechanisms in vertebrates alone, although commonality with invertebrates is important for the prospect of neural analysis at the cellular level, which even in the simplest vertebrates is a forbidding task.

THE ROLE OF REWARD IN INSTRUMENTAL LEARNING

The fact that there seem to be associative mechanisms common to a wide range of animals does not mean, of course, that there has been no evolutionary divergence in learning. New levels of neural organization may bring new capacities for integrating primary associative products—even new modes of association that parallel the old in some respects—and it is difficult certainly to compare the achievements of man with those of even the most impressive of the other primates without the feeling that there has been a sharp qualitative advance, although to be able to characterize it in functional terms is another matter. In preparation for this difficult task, it may be useful to consider a divergence that seems to have occurred much earlier in the course of vertebrate evolution and that was discovered in comparative work on the role of reward in learning (Bitterman, 1975).

In the simplest instrumental learning experiment, which is schematized in Fig. 5.2, the occurrence of some defined response such as pressing a lever (R_1) in the presence of some stimulus (S_1) produces a reward such as food (S_2) to which

FIG. 5.2. Schematic diagram of hypothetical processes in instrumental learning. S_1, conditioned stimulus; R_1, conditioned response; S_2, reward; R_2, consummatory response; S_{R1}, proprioceptive feedback from R_1; a, association between S_1 and S_2; b, association between S_{R1} and S_2; c, association between S_1 and S_{R1}.

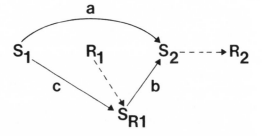

the animal makes a consummatory response (R_2). The result is an increase in the probability that S_1 will evoke R_1, and a good deal of thinking and research has been devoted to the question of why that should be so. The intuitive, so-called "cognitive" answer (Tolman, 1932) is that the animal remembers the food on the basis of an association (a) between S_1 and S_2, which are contiguous whenever the response occurs, and comes to expect that the response will produce the food on the basis of an association (b) between S_{R1} (the proprioceptive feedback from R_1) and S_2, which also are contiguous when the response occurs. Periodically it has been recognized and then forgotten that neither of these assumptions nor both combined will account for the change in behavior. Because S_2 evokes not R_1 but R_2, stimuli associated with S_2 may evoke R_2 but not some entirely different response. Furthermore, S_{R1}, which in the cognitive interpretation bears the burden of response selection, does not antedate R_1 but follows it. The animal may remember R_1 on the basis of an association (c) between S_1 and S_{R1}, which are contiguous whenever R_1 occurs, but so also should it remember all the other, unrewarded responses that occur on early trials, some with much greater frequency than R_1. Even if the memory of a response tends to evoke it, the selection of R_1 remains to be accounted for. A rather desperate recent assumption with little to recommend it is that the S_{R1}–S_2 association is "bidirectional"—S_1 evokes a representation of S_2, which then backwardly evokes a representation of R_1 (Mackintosh & Dickinson, 1979).

There is evidence enough in these experiments that S_2 may be expected, but it seems quite clear that the response produces the expectation (S_{R1}–S_2) rather than the expectation the response. In one kind of experiment (Kintsch & Witte, 1962; Williams, 1965), dogs are trained to press a lever (R_1) for food (S_2) on a fixed-ratio schedule of reinforcement, and, concurrently with lever pressing, salivation (R_2) is measured as an index of the expectation of food. An experienced subject begins to salivate only after having made a substantial number of presses. In my laboratory, a pigeon analog of this work gives the same results. The pecking key together with the aperture of the feeder are continuously illuminated, and insertion of the animal's head into the aperture (R_2) as well as pecking (R_1) are measured. An advantage of the technique is that the two responses are incompatible, which serves to put their temporal relation into clear perspective. The training program is such that only after 50 pecks at the key does insertion of the head into the aperture cause the grain tray to be elevated (for 4 sec); there is no other exteroceptive signal that the response requirement has been met. Experienced pigeons peck the key many times before trying the feeder and, after each feeding, peck the key many times again before trying the feeder again. If insertion of the head into the aperture of the feeder is taken as an index of the expectation of food, then it is the pecking that produces the expectation rather than the other way around. What then produces the pecking? Further evidence against an expectational explanation of instrumental responding comes from work on positive conditioned suppression. When a signal previously paired with food is presented, dogs that are lever pressing for food stop pressing and begin to salivate profusely (Konorski, 1967); rats stop pressing and investigate the aperture of the feeder (Karpicke, Christoph, Peterson, & Hearst, 1977). What then produces the lever pressing?

The answer provided by Thorndike's Law of Effect, restated later by Hull (1943) as the $S-R$-reinforcement principle, is that an association between S_1 and R_1 is established and strengthened by the reward. Once widely accepted, and even touted by the Hullians as sufficient to account for all conditioning, classical as well as instrumental, the principle fell into disrepute when at last it became clear that memory of reward does under certain circumstances play a role in instrumental performance. The most dramatic evidence comes from a line of experiments on incentive contrast beginning with the work of Elliott (1928). Rats that are trained only with small reward in a maze or runway perform moderately well, but rats shifted to small reward after training with large reward become disturbed, failing for a time to perform at the level of unshifted low-reward controls (negative contrast), and it seems reasonable to attribute the disturbance to discrepancy between the remembered large reward and the small reward actually encountered. The fact that rats extinguished after training with large reward show less persistence than rats trained with small reward can be understood as a special case of negative contrast (Gonzalez & Bitterman, 1969). Discrepancy between remembered reward and actually encountered reward accounts also for the finding in many experiments (Crespi, 1942) that rats trained with small reward and shifted to large reward perform better for a time than unshifted large-reward controls (positive contrast). Although there are different ideas as to how instrumental performance is modulated in these experiments— one interpretation relies on emotional responses to discrepancy that are conditioned to S_1 (Amsel, 1958)—there is no more reason to discard the $S-R$-reinforcement principle because it is insufficient to account for the modulation than to discard the principle of remembered reward because it is insufficient to account for selection of the modulated response. Both principles seem to be required.

The hypothesis that there are two mechanisms at work in these experiments at once suggests the possibility that they may have evolved at different times and, therefore, that animals may presently exist in which only one or the other of them is to be found. Results like those presented in Fig. 5.3 suggest that the goldfish is such an animal (Lowes & Bitterman, 1967). Four groups of goldfish were trained to strike a target for food in widely spaced trials (the intertrial interval was 24 hr). Two of the groups were trained with large reward and two with small reward, after which one of the large-reward groups was shifted to small reward and one of the small-reward groups was shifted to large. The preshift results are like those for rats, large reward producing better performance (lower latency of response) than small reward, but the postshift results are quite different: The shift from small to large reward improves performance, but there is no hint of contrast, either positive or negative. In goldfish, furthermore, the relation between amount of reward and resistance to extinction is not inverse as in rats but direct (Gonzalez, Potts, Pitcoff, & Bitterman, 1972). That the performance of goldfish in these experiments is not unique is demonstrated by analogous experiments with painted turtles, which perform like goldfish rather than like rats (Pert & Bitterman, 1970). As I have suggested elsewhere, if goldfish or turtles rather than rats had come to be the preferred subjects of analytical research on instrumental learning, the $S-R$-reinforcement principle would have much better standing today. The keen awareness of its insufficiency stemming from the discovery of incentive contrast in rats has tended to cloud the realization that no good way has yet been found to get along without it.

Implications.   The simplest interpretation of these results for goldfish and turtles is that $S-R$-reinforcement is the older of the two mechanisms assumed to operate in rats and that the modulation of instrumental responding by remembered reward (which is found also in pigeons) appeared for the first time in some crocodilian ancestor of birds and mammals. That the older mechanism was not simply replaced by a newer one can be argued on the ground that the $S-R$-

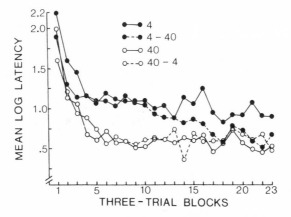

FIG. 5.3.   Mean latency of target striking in four groups of goldfish trained either with small (4 units) or large (40 units) reward from the outset and then (in a 2 × 2 design) either shifted or not to the alternative magnitude (Lowes & Bitterman, 1967).

reinforcement principle still seems required to account for selection of the re-warded response in birds and mammals. Evidence that the *S–R*-reinforcement mechanism has not been lost in mammals comes also from experiments with infant rats, which—like goldfish and turtles—fail to show incentive contrast (Stanton & Amsel, 1980). The postulated phylogenetic development seems then to be mirrored in ontogeny. An implication for human psychology is that the *S–R*-reinforcement mechanism is a general vertebrate mechanism that operates also in man and that the reinforcement theorists of the past have been misguided in their educational and psychotherapeutic prescriptions only in the exclusive importance they attached to it. The ontogenetic results suggest, of course, that the mechanism may play a central role in the learning of very young children and that for them at least Thorndikian curricula may be entirely appropriate. It would be useful to study the ontogeny of incentive contrast in human beings as Amsel and his students have done in rats.

FUTURE PROSPECTS

And what of the year 2000 to which we have been asked to look ahead? (The experimental study of animal intelligence, which got off to a somewhat late start, will only then be 100 years old.) Unfortunately, neither extrapolation from recent trends nor consideration of the present societal context generates much optimism as to what the scope of the enterprise will be. I believe, however, that a small group of specialists will carry on the work and that their progress will continue to be substantial, out of all proportion to their limited number and resources. The focus of the work—on the formation of associations and on the ways in which associations influence behavior—will remain much the same, although efficient computer techniques of parameter estimation will permit the theory to become more quantitative and its implications to be formulated and explored in greater detail. Interest in the mechanisms of association will grow rapidly, and there will be increasing contact with colleagues in neurophysiology and biochemistry, whose efforts to get at those mechanisms have thus far been hampered by lack of acquaintance with the behavioral literature (Horn, 1979). There will be genuine interaction as well with students of human learning, an interaction necessary for understanding not only the common processes but also any processes that may be unique for man.

REFERENCES

Amsel, A. The role of frustrative nonreward in noncontinuous reward situations. *Psychological Bulletin*, 1958, *55*, 102–119.

Bitterman, M. E. The comparative analysis of learning. *Science*, 1975, *188*, 699–709.

Corning, W. C., Dyal, J. A., & Willows, A. O. D. *Invertebrate Learning* (Vol. 1-3). New York: Plenum, 1973, 1975.

Couvillon, P. A., & Bitterman, M. E. Some phenomena of associative learning in honeybees. *Journal of Comparative and Physiological Psychology*, 1980, *94*, 875-885.

Couvillon, P. A., & Bitterman, M. E. Compound conditioning in honeybees. *Journal of Comparative and Physiological Psychology*, 1982, *96*, 192-199.

Crespi, L. P. Quantitative variation of incentive and performance in the white rat. *American Journal of Psychology*, 1942, *55*, 467-517.

Durlach, P. J., & Rescorla, R. A. Potentiation rather than overshadowing in flavor-aversion learning: An analysis in terms of within-compound associations. *Journal of Experimental Psychology: Animal Behavior Processes*, 1980, *6*, 175-187.

Ebbinghaus, H. *Über das Gedächtnis*. Leipzig: Duncker & Humblot, 1885.

Elliott, M. H. The effect of change of reward on the maze performance of rats. *University of California Publications in Psychology*, 1928, *4*, 19-30.

Frisch, K., von. Der Farbensinn und Formensinn der Bienen. *Zoologische Jahrbucher: Abteilung für allgemeine Zoologie und Physiologie der Tiere*, 1915, *35*, 1-182.

Gonzalez, R. C., & Bitterman, M. E. Spaced-trials partial reinforcement effect as a function of contrast. *Journal of Comparative and Physiological Psychology*, 1969, *67*, 94-103.

Gonzalez, R. C., Potts, A., Pitcoff, K., & Bitterman, M. E. Runway performance of goldfish as a function of complete and incomplete reduction of reward. *Psychonomic Science*, 1972, *27*, 305-307.

Horn, G. Preface to M. E. Bitterman, V. M. LoLordo, J. B. Overmier, & M. E. Rashotte, *Animal learning: Survey and analysis*. New York: Plenum, 1979.

Hull, C. L. *Principles of behavior*. New York: Appleton-Century-Crofts, 1943.

Karpicke, J., Christoph, G., Peterson, G., & Hearst, E. Signal location and positive versus negative conditioned suppression in the rat. *Journal of Experimental Psychology: Animal Behavior Processes*, 1977, *3*, 105-118.

Kintsch, W., & Witte, R. S. Concurrent conditioning of bar press and salivation responses. *Journal of Comparative and Physiological Psychology*, 1962, *55*, 963-968.

Konorski, J. *Integrative activity of the brain*. Chicago: University of Chicago Press, 1967.

Lowes, G., & Bitterman, M. E. Reward and learning in the goldfish. *Science*, 1967, *157*, 455-457.

Mackintosh, N. J. A theory of attention: Variations in the associability of stimuli with reinforcement. *Psychological Review*, 1975, *82*, 276-298.

Mackintosh, N. J., & Dickinson, A. Instrumental (type II) conditioning. In A. Dickinson & P. A. Boakes (Eds.), *Mechanisms of learning and motivation*. Hillsdale, N.J.: Lawrence Erlbaum Associates, 1979.

Menzel, R. Das Gedächtnis der Honigbiene für Spektralfarben: I. Kurzzeitiges und langzeitiges Behalten. *Zeitschrift für vergleichende Physiologie*, 1968, *60*, 82-102.

Pavlov, I. P. *Conditioned reflexes*. Oxford: Oxford University Press, 1927.

Pert, A., & Bitterman, M. E. Reward and learning in the turtle. *Learning and Motivation*, 1970, *1*, 121-128.

Rescorla, R. A., & Cunningham, C. L. Within-compound flavor associations. *Journal of Experimental Psychology: Animal Behavior Processes*, 1978, *4*, 267-275.

Rescorla, R. A., & Wagner, A. R. A theory of classical conditioning: Variations in the effectiveness of reinforcement and nonreinforcement. In A. H. Black & W. F. Prokasy (Eds.), *Classical conditioning (II): Current research and theory*. New York: Appleton-Century-Crofts, 1972.

Romanes, G. J. *Animal intelligence*. London: Kegan Paul, 1882.

Spence, K. W. Cognitive and drive factors in the extinction of the conditioned eye blink in human subjects. *Psychological Review*, 1966, *73*, 445-458.

Stanton, M., & Amsel, A. Adjustment to reward reduction (but no negative contrast) in rats 11, 14, and 16 days of age. *Journal of Comparative and Physiological Psychology*, 1980, *94*, 446-458.

Thorndike, E. L. *Animal intelligence. Experimental studies.* New York: Macmillan, 1911.

Tolman, E. C. *Purposive behavior in animals and men.* New York: D. Appleton–Century, 1932.

Williams, D. R. Classical conditioning and incentive motivation. In W. F. Prokasy (Ed.), *Classical conditioning: A symposium.* New York: Appleton–Century–Crofts, 1965.

6 Animal Memory—as Compared with Human Memory

Lajos Kardos
University of Budapest, Hungary

Zeno, the sophist, was eager to prove to Antisthenes, the cynic philosopher, that there can exist no motion. While listening, Antisthenes was pacing the room. Finally, Zeno asked him why he was walking up and down. He answered: I am refuting you.

MEMORY—A NEGLECTED ISSUE IN ANIMAL PSYCHOLOGY

Today we can state with certainty that one of the factors that has hampered fruitful research on learning and proper theoretical evaluation of experimental data was the neglect of mnemonic phenomena in animals. Until about the early sixties, little mention was made of memory in animal psychology. Learning and memory are so much intertwined in human psychology that one feels prompted to ask: Is it possible that research workers while investigating animal learning so assiduously have so rarely met with phenomena suggesting some sort of memory? In 1966, Russel said: "If the salient characteristic of learning is the modifcation of behavior through experience, then this can be achieved only by means of memory storage. In fact, the phenomena of memory and learning are inseparable . . . [p. 122]."

Now—as though to make up for the long neglect—the problem of animal memory is gradually coming to the fore of psychological research. Nevertheless the long omission may be one of the reasons why some theorists, who are prone

71

to think there is something basically wrong with the experimental method in psychology, often refer to the research on animal learning as a telling example. After almost a century of intensive experimental research, there is still no sufficiently wide agreement of opinions on the mechanisms underlying animal learning. There is still no clear decision on whether theories of the S–R type or those of S–S type or some combination of both are correct. This implies also a protracted indecision concerning the role of memory in animal learning. According to the S–R theories, no such assumption is necessary—unless one speaks of "stimulus-response memory," which is just a cover name for what has been called simply "retention" in conditioning theory and has nothing to do with genuine memory which we take to always involve the appearance of memory image; the latter is sometimes called "representational memory" (Ruggiero & Flagg, 1976).

The situation was characterized by Mackintosh in 1974 as follows: "The results of most experiments on instrumental learning can readily be analysed in S–R terms, i.e., supposing that the associations between the required response and the stimulus situation is strengthened by reinforcement." In this case, of course, no "representational memory" is involved. But Mackintosh adds: "However, they are equally consistent with the supposition that animals can learn to associate any events that occur together, including stimuli with other stimuli, stimuli with reinforcers, responses with stimuli and responses with reinforcers." Manifestations of such associations may already be conceived of as a sort of remembering. Yet it is interesting how the quotation continues: "When additional evidence is brought to bear on the question, the attempt to maintain the purity of S–R theory, i.e., to insist that all instrumental learning is based on the formation of stimulus–response connections, becomes increasingly more difficult [p. 221]." Now we shall call attention to such "additional evidence." We shall try to show that explanations by S–R connections or by other forms of association apply only to a peculiar form of animal memory that is rarely registered in man.

SOME SPECIFIC CHARACTERISTICS OF MEMORY IN ANIMALS

Before pointing out and analyzing the "additional evidence," we may raise the question: Suppose we are led to assume the existence of mnemonic reproduction in animals, what degree of "fidelity" of reproduction may be expected? If we regard animals as living beings on a lower level of development, as organisms of a lower degree of "perfection" than men, we may be tempted to assume that their mnemonic reproductions are less "perfect" than ours. Strange as it may seem, this would be a gross error. All we know of memory images suggests that the mnemonic reproduction of high fidelity—the "copy" or "photographic" image—is a more primitive form of memory. Eidetic images, as we know, come early, ontogenetically; hallucinations and dream images are of a regressive nature. Similarly, any mnemonic reproduction in animals may actually be closer to the original perception than it is in men.

Visual Memory Images of Special Localization

Now we describe and analyze that "additional evidence" we referred to earlier. First, we describe, very briefly, an experiment we made a number of years ago. Because the report on it was published only in Hungarian, psychologists in other countries could hardly have learned about it. However, the results seem worthy of attention.

The subjects (albino rats), from a short starting alley reached a choice point where they could turn either right or left. But both side alleys led to the same end-point, the entrance to a common alley (see Fig. 6.1, part A). There were two doors, one on the right wall, the other at the end of the common alley, each

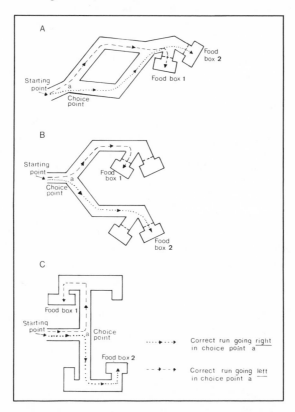

FIG. 6.1   Three mazes with food boxes (more and more separated, spatially).

leading into a food box (Doors I and II). If the subject had chosen the alley on the right, food could be found behind Door I (the other door being locked); if it had arrived there through the left-hand alley, it had to choose Door II (Door I being locked).

The reinforcement contingencies could be learned from the stimuli at the common end-point only in conjunction with the antecedent sequences of kines- thetic and other kinds of sensations. Animals were almost unable to master the reinforcement contingencies. Even after 200 trials, their accuracy was less than 80%. Through proper variations of the experimental setting, the cause of the very retarded learning could be established beyond doubt: *the pathways led to the same place*. When they led to separate end-points (see Fig. 6.1, part B), learning was much more rapid; in case of widely separated end-points (see Fig. 6.1, part C), learning was achieved in 3 to 5 trials. Without going into details, the results may be summarized as follows: Pathways leading from the same starting point to the same end point—or the correlated sequences of kinestetic and other kinds of sensations—are functionally equivalent; different responses can hardly become attached to the variants of such pathways, and there appears a tendency for any response that has got connected with one of the variants to become automatically associated with all the other variants. We have called this the "equivalence of equiterminal pathways" (Kardos & Barkóci, 1953).

A somewhat similar phenomenon had been pointed out by Hull (1934). He called the set of habits for traversing alternative pathways to the same end-point a "habit-family hierarchy." He assumed that different routes to the same goal are equivalent, in the sense that if one of them proves impassable the animal will choose another without additional learning. At the same time, the animal always prefers the shorter route. Obviously this has little to do with what we termed "equivalence of the equiterminal pathways." In fact, Hull's idea of habit-family hierarchy was an auxilliary hypothesis constructed to explain short-cut behavior.

Can we learn something more about the mechanism underlying the equiv- alence of equiterminal pathways—or about its significance in the life of the animal? Let us consider just those phenomena that Hull had in mind and tried to explain by his idea of habit-family hierarchy. From about 1930 on, the phe- nomena in question were repeatedly observed in experiments on maze learning and were referred to as "orientation towards the goal"—after Dashiell (1930), the first to study them systematically. For the sake of illustration, we describe one case of such orientation. In experiments on maze learning, it was invariably observed that the animal had extreme difficulty eliminating certain of the blind alleys. It kept turning into them, stubbornly as it were. These blind alleys were all oriented in the direction toward the goal. Thus, the animal behaved as if it oriented itself toward the goal—in spite of the fact that it did not see the goal and that entering the blind alley was never differentially reinforced. After Hull's attempt at an explanation—which was soon shown to be unsatisfactory—other ideas were advanced. Again we restrict ourselves to mentioning but one of them.

Some psychologists claimed that spatial orientation depends on "extra-maze cues," such as a lamp, a bright window, a dark corner, and the like which are visible from the interior of the maze. This claim was easy to test experimentally. In fact, the elimination of such cues caused some disturbance in orientation, but did not render it impossible. Later, the interest in the phenomena of orientation abated. The attention of psychologists was attracted to a more comprehensive problem which seemed to embrace that of orientation as well. Much theorizing and experimental work was, at that time, dedicated to the problem of "place learning." The results of many experiments were accounted for by declaring that the animal did not learn a sequence of movements but rather the place where the goal object was located; it learned place instead of movement. Having learned this, the animal simply goes to that place—taking any route at its disposal.

But the problem of spatial orientation is not really clarified by this statement. Let us look at the phenomenon from another angle. For the animal to be able to orient itself towards an object, it must localize the object. Localization is simple and clear in the perceptual situation: The animal sees the object *in a certain direction and at a certain distance from itself.* But what sort of localization may underly the animal's orientation when it stands, for instance, at the entrance of a blind alley and can in no way see the goal object?

There is a very definite condition for this mysterious orientation: *The animal must* a number of times (but at least once) *have gone from the entrance of the blind to the goal object* by some path permitted by the spatial arrangement of the maze. It is somehow with the aid of this journey, i.e., of the sequence of experiences during it, that the animal "knows" where, in what direction, and at what distance from itself the goal object is located. The difference from the perceptual situation is only that in the description the word "sees" is substituted by "knows." The latter expression is a sort of "unknown" in the definition, because the experience of "knowing" can hardly be supposed to exist in animals as it occurs in men. Tolman (1932) might have had the same idea in mind—but he generalized the "unknown"; he said that in the perceptual situation the animal "knows" by vision where the goal object is, in the maze situation the animal "knows" the same by remembering (perceptual cognition in the former case and "mnemonic" cognition in the latter). This is how the concept of "cognition" had become so central in his theoretical deliberations—thus starting the development of theoretical thought towards what is now known as cognitive psychology. Nevertheless, the expression "knowing" is, as we said, a sort of "unknown" in the formula, and we shall endeavor to specify it more concretely.

Men and many animals see everything localized, that is, at a certain place (in a certain direction and at a certain distance). The "place" of the object is perceived with the same immediacy as its color or size. The perception of place has its definite stimulus conditions just as does the perception of color or size. The place of an object (at point A) is given to the animal who is at point B by the light rays coming from the object and its environment. But sometimes no light rays can arrive at the animal's visual apparatus either because the object is screened off by other objects, or because there is no light. Yet the animal *can go* to the object, or near enough to catch sight of it; and by going to it, the animal can compute or construct objectively in what direction and at what distance the object at A is from point B. When it is back at point B, the animal then can "know" where, in what direction and at what distance, the object lies. Even so, the nature of this knowing remains a mystery.

Before attempting to unveil this mystery, we want to emphasize that the "computation" or "construction" by the central nervous system is nothing but a form of information processing. We humans can perform this sort of information processing only poorly, though the task is not alien to us. I do not know of any experimental inquiry into it; but surely there are people said to have "a good sense of orientation," who are able to tell with some precision where or in what direction an object is after having arrived at it in some roundabout way. But if men are not very good at this, they exhibit remarkable achievements in a quite analogous performance. A brief glance at an object is usually enough to recognize it, say, as a chair. But every normal person can recognize it as well in complete darkness by exploring its surface manually, i.e., by touch. Both form and size can be fairly well perceived haptically. In man, manipulatory behavior seems predominant whereas locomotion seems more predominant in animals (below the primates); through their mainly kinesthetic experiences during locomoation, animals seem capable of the same high-level achievements as are men with the aid of their haptic experiences during manipulatory operations. Humans just see where the object is; animals use other informational stimuli to the same end. By means of technical devices, we have brought this processing of information to an almost incredible level of perfection; but it is found already in primitive animals. In fact, seeing with moving eyes, or even the simple turning towards an object, serves a similar function. Our contention is simply that locomotion is just another means for picking up information.

Now we return to the question of what may the "knowing" acquired by such operational procedure actually consist? For the answer, we resort to the assumption: After having gone from point B to point A a number of times on any route, the animal may "remember" the object seen at point A; that is, a memory image of the object may emerge. That animals "remember," especially remember the reward, is accepted, tacitly or overtly, by an ever growing number of authors, whether it is termed an "internal stimulus state" (Capaldi, 1971) or simply as "memory" (Hulse, Fowler, & Honig, 1978; Spear, 1978; Spear & Miller, 1981). In fact the manifestation of every S–S association must involve the appearance of a memory image, in the form of a reproduction or a reconstruction of the sensory image. But we must add the following assumption: There is no "free-floating memory image" in animals (as, for instance, when I remember a friend while sitting in my room); *the animal's memory image is definitely localized.* The resemblance between original perception and memory image goes so far that the latter strictly preserves the localized character of the original perception. The animal "remembers" the object projected, as it were, on a definite place; it remembers the object in a way similar to how it sees it. *As it sees every object in a certain place, in a certain direction and at a certain distance from itself, so it remembers every object with a definite place character, in a certain direction and at a certain distance from itself.* This sort of egocentrically localized memory occurs only exceptionally in humans, as in the eidetic imagery by juveniles. The main characteristic of the eidetic image is its definite localization. Just on account of its resemblance to visual images, one generally speaks of "eidetic vision" instead of eidetic remembering, although it involves genuine memory images (and not, for instance, some sort of afterimages).

The use of the word "knowing" in the description of the animal's orientational behavior comes from a simile: The animal behaves as if it "knows" where the object is located. Another simile would do as well: The animal behaves as if it "sees" the goal object at a certain place. We think this is the better simile, or even that it is more than a simile. As we said before, the animal remembers, in a sense, in the same manner as it "sees." It seems more adequate to speak of the "mnemonic vision of animals, instead of their "remembering"—just as one does in the case of "eidetic vision."

Now we are in the position to answer our main question. When we say the animal, standing at point B, "knows" where the food is, we mean that the animal "sees" the food mnemonically at point A, in a certain direction and at a certain distance from itself. Or for those who are averse to the mentalistic overtone in analyzing animal behavior: The phrase "the animal knows" means that, in its central nervous system, events are occurring that are similar to those aroused when actually standing at point B and seeing the goal object at point A.

A plausible corollary to this theory is that the determination of the "place" of an object on the basis of information gained during antecedent locomotion (leading to the object) would be biologically senseless if the information gathered during locomotion on different routes to the object, i.e., on equiterminal pathways as we termed them, lent different place-characters to the object or the field-formation reached at the end of the journey. This corollary is not only plausible but also evident when one considers the results of the very first experiments on goal orientation, made by Dashiell (1930) using the "checkerboard maze." In this experiment, the rat could reach (and actually reached) the goal by many different routes—while maintaining the same direction of orientation. This phenomenon is a sort of *place constancy*. Securing the perception of invariant object properties (in our case, of the place) in the face of largely variable stimulus mediation is, though amazing, one of the routine functions of the nervous system.

This form of place constancy is at the base of what we described earlier as the equivalence of equiterminal pathways. Why could not rats learn to go to different doors, depending on whether they got to the same spot from the right or from the left? Our answer is that the part of the field they arrived at was perceived to be at the same place, regardless of which antecedent pathway had led to it. The next response (entering one of the doors) seems to have been determined entirely by the place, and not by the antecedent locomotor activity. Having performed their role in establishing the place, experiences gained on the pathways simply submerged.

Memory Based on Specifically Cued Retrieval Functions

We return again to the animal's memory. There is a vague point in our formulation of the problem. We said that in the animal at point B, the memory image of what it saw at point A is aroused. But we must ask: aroused by what? The most plausible answer is that the memory image is aroused by what the animal perceives at B, that is, *by the stimuli impinging upon it there.* These *situational stimuli* did not have this effect before the locomotor experience. In the traditional formulation, this owing to temporal contiguity—this time to close succession—associative connection between the situational stimuli and what was seen at A was localized on the basis of the pathway leading to it. This is a case of S–S association about the reality of which there is little doubt nowadays (see, for instance, Rescorla & Durlach, 1981).

Situational stimuli play an unusual role in evoking the memory image of the animal. An experiment with rats (Kardos & Radics, 1972) elucidates the point. The ground plan of the apparatus used can be seen in Fig. 6.2.

The animal starting from point I, arrived at the choice point V_o where it could turn to the right or to the left. Only the left alley was passable; the right alley was closed by barrier A_2 (barrier A_1 was not inserted). Only the box F_2 contained food, the others (F_1 and F_3) were empty. Thus the animals had to learn to turn to the left at V_o and to the right at V_1, then to enter F_2. The walls of the alleys were high enough to prevent an overview of the layout of the maze. Possible extra-maze cues were also eliminated. After the animals had learned the task (i.e., reached criterion), we supposed that the animals when they arrived at the choice

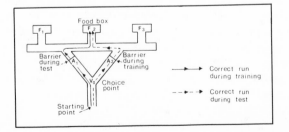

FIG. 6.2.   Maze for illustrating how animal memory is based on specifically-cued retrieval.

point V_o were already able to remember, that is, to "see" mnemonically, the goal object in F_2. Then the test trial followed: We closed the left alley by inserting barrier A_1 and opened the right alley by removing barrier A_2.

Our expectation was that the animals, having learned where the food was, would be well-oriented at V_2 and consequently turn left towards box F_2. But we were disappointed. The great majority of rats turned right as they had done at V_1 on the previous trials. Standing at V_2, they showed no sign of "knowing" where the food was. We varied the experiment in many ways, but the results remained essentially the same, seeming to contradict our ideas concerning goal orientation. Yet there was an easy explanation, provided we did not let ourselves be misled by our ingrained conception of human memory. We supposed that the animal standing at choice point V_o "sees" the food mnemonically in F_2. A precondition of this memory is that previously the animal got from point V_o to the box F_2 often enough. We can assume that the animal is able to "see" the food mnemonically in F_2 from all points of the pathway V_o–V_1–F_2—because from all of them it got to F_2 with equal frequency. Now we have to realize clearly that *the strictly localized memory image of the animal is evoked only and exclusively by situational stimuli at places from which it actually got to the goal object, by whatever route; the trip must have been made with sufficient frequency* so that the successive associations could have been formed. The trouble with our experiment is that *the animal never travelled from choice point V_2 to food box F_2*; so the stimulus situation in V_2 did not evoke any kind of memory to prompt it to go towards F_2. At V_2, the animal is in a sort of "mnemonic darkness" so that when travelling to any other point, however close, it cannot "hold" a localized memory image of the object. The antic philosopher, Seneca, might have been right when he stated that the horse might remember the road it had travelled before "but remembered nothing of it when in the stable afterwards [cited by Warden, 1927, p. 77)."

Concerning this point, a very sharp difference seems to exist between animal and human memory. Once we have seen an object anywhere, we are able to remember it independently of the place we stay at the moment. This is a characteristic of what we call "free recall." It seems then that the animal not only has no "free-floating memory images" in this sense but is incapable of "free recall." This reminds us of something that has been established in investigations of the so-called retrieval cues most efficient in human free recall. Tulving elaborated the "principle of encoding specificity" (Thomson & Tulving, 1970) which is described most appropriately by Postman (1972) as follows: "Information to be used in retrieval must be stored at the same time of input [p. 16]." In humans, this is, of course, but an efficient aid to a mnemonic retrieval, whereas *in animals it seems that only such "specifically cued retrieval" exists.* Thus, what is merely an auxiliary factor of memory in humans is for animals an absolute condition of memory. It is of some interest that in efforts at recall, even men fall back upon the primordial evoking mechanism, viz, associations formed at the time of original input.

2.3. Some Concluding Notes

In conclusion, we may briefly summarize the main differences between animal and human memory:

1. *The memory image in animals is always localized;* the animal sees everything in a certain place and it remembers everything as in a certain place.

2. *The visual image of animals serves simply as supplement to the visual field given at the moment;* it appears in a definite spatial relation to the momentary stimulation.

3. *Visual memory images in the animal are aroused only by the situation in which it finds itself at the moment;* thus, the memory image of the end box cannot be aroused independently of the place in which the animal happens to be.

4. *The memory image of the animal is as concrete as its percepts;* the animal cannot simply remember food or a barrier, but only food or barrier of a very definite form, color, and size.

5. *The memory image of the animal* is not an exact reproduction of the original percept; certain details may be missing, and there may be reduction in intensity; but it is *never simplified, schematized or reduced to selected details* (e.g., it cannot be compared to a map).

6. *The role of memory images in the determination and guidance of animal behavior is the same as that of perception;* the animal goes to the goal object seen mnemonically just as it goes to it when actually seen.

PROBLEMS IN MAZE LEARNING: SOME FURTHER EVIDENCE FOR SPECIFIC VISUAL MEMORY IN ANIMALS

We are aware that these theoretical propositions face a number of difficulties which they have to cope with. Rather than to discuss them here, we will describe a group of experiments that we regard as a sort of *experimentum crucis* for our theory of animal memory.

Maze Learning With Different Goal Objects at the Same Place

Almost half a century ago, Hull (1933) investigated the problem of what he termed "differential habituation to internal stimuli." The task required the animals (albino rats) to learn to turn right when thirsty, to turn left when hungry. Both turns led to the same goal box, but the appropriate incentive, water or food, was found there, depending on which way they had turned (see Fig. 6.3, part A).

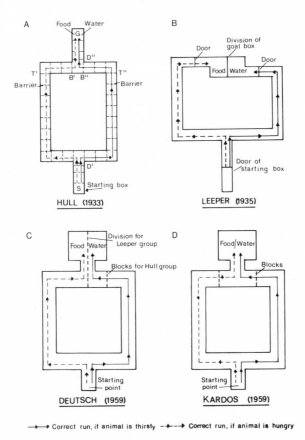

FIG. 6.3.   Four mazes from experiments illustrating the role of spatial separation.

The results of the experiment were astonishing: Even after thousand trials, the animals were unable to master the task completely, although they did show some improvement (Hull, 1933). There is no indication in Hull's reports of why he chose this spatial arrangement; possibly he just happened to have such an apparatus from another experiment. However, it was soon realized that the "strange" result might have something to do with the unusual feature of the apparatus.

Maze Learning With Different Goal Objects at Different Places

Two years later, Leeper (1935) did a series of experiments that differed from those of Hull only as regards the feature in question: The side alleys branching off from the choice point led to *different* places so that the goal objects, water and food, were also placed in different boxes (see Fig. 6.3, part B). Although the two places were near to each other, the animals mastered the task in this situation much more quickly and almost completely (Leeper, 1935).

But even after this very conclusive experiment, psychologists (Leeper himself included) did not see that the crucial condition was whether the goal objects were located at the same place. Confounding difference in the experimental arrangements obscured this condition. In Hull's (1933) experiment, the animal arrived at a barrier when it made the wrong choice and had to retrace its steps to get back to the choice point. In Leeper's (1935) experiment, there were no barriers; when the animal chose incorrectly, it arrived at the goal box with the irrelevant goal object, e.g., it found food though thirsty. In one of the goal boxes there was always water, and in the other always food. Leeper (1935) concluded (quite along the line of Tolman's teaching) that in his experiment the animals even learned when choosing wrong: They learned where the food was even when finding it while thirsty. He said: ". . . this one difference in the situation seems to make an enormous difference in the rate of mastery of the problem. It would seem, therefore, that the rats must learn almost as much from the incorrect responses as they do from the correct responses [p. 37]." This explanation found wide acceptance, and the problem seemed solved.

After twenty years or so—owing to new theoretical developments—the problem was brought up again. Leeper's explanation was easy to check experimentally. Hull's experiment was replicated by Deutsch (1959) but with a slight change: the elimination of barriers (see Fig. 6.3, part C). Unlike Hull's arrangement the animals got to the common end box independently of whether they chose correctly or incorrectly; but in case of a wrong choice they found the irrelevant goal object (e.g., water when hungry). This modification turned out to be of no significance. Learning was now just as slow as in Hull's original arrangement—although the animals could have learned from the incorrect choices in this arrangement, too (Deutsch, 1959; see also Fig. 6.4, part A). The results showed that the very retarded learning was due to the goal objects being *in the same place*. For the historian of science, it may be of interest that Deutsch's control experiment, in almost the same arrangement, was also performed by us and reported in Hungarian during the same year (without, of course, our knowing of his work). Our results were in full agreement with those of Deutsch (Kardos, 1959; see here Fig. 6.4, part B).

Yet our explanation was very different. It would take us too far afield to present Deutsch's ingenious theory about the structural basis of behavior. We restrict ourselves to showing that a crucial feature in his explanation is inconsistent with the data. According to Deutsch, the sequences of stimuli along both side alleys end up in a common phase, since the animals arrive at the same goal box. It is due to this common end phase ("the common link"—in the terminology of Deutsch) that the animal is eventually prompted with equal strength to choose either of the two side alleys, and so no differentiation can materialize. But the

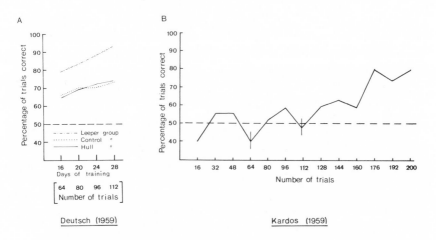

FIG. 6.4 Learning curves from Deutsch and from Kardos with control curves from Hull (1933) and Leeper (1935).

sequences of stimuli acting upon the animal while traversing both paths do not end in a common phase; when arriving through the one side alley, the animal sees and smells something quite different (food) than when it arrives there from the other side (water). Some difference is recognized by Deutsch (1964), too, when he says: "Owing to the construction of the maze the animal could see the goal box from a different angle, depending whether it was entering it from the left or from the right [p. 122]." But this is only a minor part of the difference as we described it; for *only the place where the animal arrives at, is the same,* and not the stimulus situation which awaits it there. Deutsch, however, does not so much as refer to the identity of the places being the main factor.

In contrast to this, it is just the identity of places which figures as the main point in our interpretation. The explanation offers itself almost as self-evident. Let us consider first the Leeper (1935) situation: We assume that after a number of trials the animal begins "remembering," that is, "seeing" the goal objects mnemonically in their respective places beside each other; just as what the animal sees at a certain place does not depend on whether it is hungry or thirsty, what it "sees" mnemonically in a certain place does not depend on its momentary state of need. Naturally, the hungry animal goes to the place (via the learned pathway) where it "sees" the food mnemonically. Thus, memory can control the animal's behavior correctly and efficiently, just as actual vision does. But consider what happens in Hull's (1934) situation: After a number of trials, the animal starts "remembering," that is, "seeing," the goal objects mnemonically. But how can it do it? When an animal's memory is strictly localized, how can two different objects (food and water) be remembered in the same place? Just as *the animal cannot see two different objects at the same place, it cannot "see" them mnemonically at the same place either.* It cannot remember them to be at the same place. It is a strange conclusion, considering our way of remembering; but it follows with logical rigor from what we have stated about the nature of animal memory.

A somewhat similar consideration arises in certain disturbances of binocular vision: As a result of strabism, different images are projected on corresponding points of the two retinas, and the person sees different things with his respective eyes. We know that this "double vision" is very disturbing for the proper control of visually-guided behavior. The person handles this problem by eventually suppressing the function of one of the eyes altogether, i.e., by resorting to monocular vision. The *"mnemonic double vision"* which we suppose to occur in the Hull situation may be just as disturbing. And again the organism may help itself by suppressing the disturbing factor, this time the mnemonic function. A sort of "mnemonic blindness" may develop. The animal chooses "blindly," as it were, and learning gradually reduces to S–R connections, without orientation, merely on the basis of reinforcement. One turn is conditioned to hunger, the other to thirst. Learning is retarded because this suppression of memory is presumably a slow and gradual process.

Because we consider the Hull–Leeper experiments so crucial for our interpretation, we recently replicated them carefully—confirming the results of the original experiments.

CONCLUDING REMARKS

In this chapter, I proceeded in a manner somewhat similar to Antisthenes (see the beginning anecdote). I described experiments that demonstrate one unique attribute of animal memory, its strict localization, an attribute that could have been uncovered only by the experimental method. I think we may have confidence in the experimental results, even if they still allow more than one way of interpretation; further experimentation may narrow down the range of theoretical possibilities, so that finally it would be reduced to a single interpretation.

I should not venture to predict what kind of concrete developments will be occurring at the next turn of the century, but I hope that by then psychologists will have succeeded in elaborating further the requirements of careful experimentation. I also hope that they will realize, more than they have done hitherto, the need for rigorous thinking (*"das strenge Denken"*—as German scientists called it). We need more rigor if we are to avoid the traps of figurative speech, the manipulative way of interpreting the data, and the incorrect use of concepts—to mention only the most important sources of error in the treatment of experimental findings. The danger of undisciplined thinking is much greater in psychology than in other sciences.

SUMMARY

Critics of psychology often refer to the apparent fruitlessness of experimental research in animal learning. Unfortunately, the role of memory in animal learning has for too long been either totally disregarded or at least misjudged. This chapter attempts to treat memory by carefully analyzing the results of some experiments on animal learning. In one of our older experiments, rats could arrive from the same starting point to the same end point by different routes ("equiterminal" pathways), pathways that were functionally equivalent. The results resemble those from experiments on animal locomotor learning. On the basis of theoretical considerations, we maintain that memory in animals has a strangely localized character. Animals do not have the "free-floating memory images" so common in men. What the animal remembers is as localized in space as what it sees or perceives. Another peculiarity of animal memory concerns the basic conditions of storage and retrieval. We referred to another of our experiments which suggests that in animals there exists a form of "specifically cued recall" known from the investigations of human memory. We ended by describing a group of classical experiments, recently replicated, that serve as an *experimentum crucis* for our theoretical interpretations.

REFERENCES

Capaldi, E. J. Memory and learning: A sequential viewpoint. In W. K. Honig & P. H. R. James (Eds.), *Animal memory*. New York: Academic Press, 1971.
Dashiell, J. F.   Direction orientation in maze running by the white rat. *Comparative Psychological Monograph*, 1930, *32*.
Deutsch, J. A. The Hull-Leeper drive discrimination situation: A control experiment. *Quarterly Journal of Experimental Psychology*, 1959, *11*, 155–163.
Deutsch, J. A. *The structural basis of behavior*. Cambridge: Cambridge University Press, 1964.
Hull, C. L. Differential habituation to internal stimuli in the albino rats. *Journal of Comparative Psychology*, 1933, *16*, 255–273.
Hull, C. L. The concept of habit-family hierarchy and maze learning. *Psychological Review*, 1934, *41*, 33–52.
Hulse, S. H., Fowler, H., & Honig, W. K. *Cognitive processes in animal behavior*. Hillsdale, New Jersey: Lawrence Erlbaum Associates, 1978.
Kardos, L. The role of the mnemonic field in the formation of connections between interoceptive stimuli and response. (In Hungarian). *Pszichológiai Tanulmányok* (Psychological Studies), 1959, *II*, 43–62.
Kardos, L. Visual memory in animals. In F. G. B. D'Arcais (Ed.), *Studies in perception*. Milano: Aldo Martelli-Giunti, 1975.
Kardos, L., & Barkóci, I. The role of "equiterminal" parts of locomotor behavior in animal learning. (In Hungarian). Az M. T. A. *Biológiai Osztályának Közleményei*, 1953, 97–114.
Kardos, L., & Radics, L. Locomotor learning and spatial orientation IV: The use of detour and the so-called mnemonic field. (In Hungarian). *Magyar Pszichológiai Szemle*, 1972, *XXIX*, 350–372.

Leeper, R. The role of motivation in learning: A study of the phenomena of differential motivation control of the utilization of habits. *Journal of Genetic Psychology,* 1935, *46,* 3–40.

Mackintosh, N. J. *The psychology of animal learning.* New York: Academic Press, 1974.

Postman, L. A pragmatic view of organization theory. In E. Tulving & W. Donaldson (Eds.), *Organization of memory.* New York: Academic Press, 1972.

Rescorla, R. A., & Durlach, P. J. Within-events learning and Pavlovian conditioning. In N. E. Spear & R. R. Miller (Eds.), *Information processing in animals: Memory mechanisms.* Hillsdale, New Jersey: Lawrence Erlbaum Associates, 1981.

Ruggiero, F. T., & Flagg, S. F. Do animals have memory? In D. L. Medin, W. A. Roberts, R. Davis (Eds.), *Processes of animal memory.* Hillsdale, New Jersey: Lawrence Erlbaum Associates, 1976.

Russel, I. S. Animal learning and memory. In D. Richter (Ed.), *Aspects of learning and memory.* New York: Basic Books, 1966.

Spear, N. E. *The processing of memories: Forgetting and retention.* Hillsdale, New Jersey: Lawrence Erlbaum Associates, 1978.

Spear, N. E. & Miller, R. R. (Eds.) *Information processing in animals: Memory mechanisms.* Hillsdale, New Jersey: Lawrence Erlbaum Associates, 1981.

Thomson, D. A., & Tulving, E. Associative encoding and retrieval: Week and strong cues. *Journal of Experimental Psychology,* 1970, *86,* 255–262.

Tolman, E. C. *Purposive behavior in animals and men.* New York: Appleton, 1932.

Warden, C. J. The historical development of comparative psychology. *Psychological Review,* 1927, *34,* 57–85.

7 The Future Study of Learning and Memory from a Psychobiological Perspective

Norman E. Spear
State University of New York, Binghamton, USA

I address the general area that may be termed the *psychobiology of learning and memory*. It remains an important part of experimental psychology, although the future may see aspects of this work conducted increasingly under the heading *neuroscience*. Thirty or 40 years ago much of this area fell under the heading of *learning theory*, then later *animal learning*, and more recently *animal memory;* throughout, segments of this area have been labeled with the prefix, *physiological basis of.*

Generally speaking, the past 20 years of this work has seen a shift from concentration on motivational determinants of learned performance to more direct investigation of learning and memory itself. Concurrently, there has been a perhaps related increase in the use of humans as experimental subjects in psychobiological studies. It has become increasingly important to integrate what is known about human learning and memory with the related knowledge we have acquired from psychobiological experiments with animals. This is so even for issues of special neurophysiological significance, such as the effects of brain damage, drugs, and neurophysiological maturation on learning and memory. I suggest that both of these trends will accelerate during the next 20 years.

From what sources can we seek empirical support for such assertions and predictions? For the first assertion, my approach is to present a survey, admittedly arbitrary and cursory, of what has been published about the role of motivation in learning and memory. For the second, I illustrate how information gathered from psychobiological studies with human subjects can combine with that from research programs requiring the use of animals as subjects to address a classical issue often raised in the psychological literature on learning and memory.

TRENDS IN THE STUDY OF MOTIVATIONAL
INFLUENCES ON
LEARNING AND MEMORY: A BRIEF NOTE

The past 20 years have seen a shift in this area, from focus on experiments and general theories of learning that emphasize the role of motivational factors in learning to focus on the more direct study of learning and memory and their environmental and physiological determinants. This is seen in the trends of publications during this period. I refer to the relevant journals of the American Psychological Association for illustration. Twenty years ago was 1961; reports written at that time may be assumed to have been published in the 1962 editions of the journals.

In the major theoretical journal, *The Psychological Review*, 19% (8) of the 43 papers published in 1962 dealt with the relationship between learning and motivation based largely on experiments with animals as subjects. In contrast, last year's edition (1980) of *The Psychological Review* had no articles on this topic among its 28 entries, although 21% (6) dealt in some fashion with the psychobiology of learning and memory (these figures and those mentioned below are summarized in Table 7.1).

In the *Journal of Experimental Psychology* in 1962 (Vol. 63 only), a similar percentage of its 103 articles, 18% (19), covered the topic of animal learning and motivation. What was the *Journal of Experimental Psychology* 20 years ago is today divided into three separate volumes, one entitled *Learning, Memory and Cognition,* another entitled *Human Perception and Performance,* and the third, *Animal Behavior Processes.* Combining these journals for 1980, there were 147 articles. The percentage of separate publications on learning or motivation with

TABLE 7.1
Percentage Published Reports of Learning Experiments Concerned
with Motivation versus Psychobiology of Memory

Journal	Interaction between Learning and Motivation	Psychobiology of Learning and Memory
Psychological Review		
1962	19%	5%
1980	0	21%
Journal of Experimental Psychology		
1962 (Vol. 63)	16%	2%
1980	3%	14%
Journal of Comparative and Physiological Psychology		
1962	22%	23%
1980	5%	27%

animal subjects was about the same as 20 years ago, 17% (25). Yet, the relative emphasis on motivation in these articles declined sharply from 20 years ago. Whereas about 90% of the pertinent articles 20 years ago (Vol. 63) were primarily concerned with the effects of motivation or conditions of reinforcement on learned performance, only about 10% reported studies of animal learning and memory in and of itself. In contrast, 80% of the pertinent articles in 1980 dealt directly with the topic of learning and memory rather than its interaction with motivation. I suggest later that throughout the next 20 years the issue of motivation may reemerge in relation to certain neurochemical factors that seem important for learning and memory.

In some sense, the present area of the psychobiology of learning and memory was better anticipated 20 years ago by the *Journal of Comparative and Physiological Psychology* than by the *Journal of Experimental Psychology*. In the 1962 issue of the former, 101 articles studied the psychobiology of learning and motivation with animal subjects. More than 50% of these dealt relatively directly with learning and memory, its environmental and neurophysiological determinants—a good deal more than the 10% on this topic published that year by the *Journal of Experimental Psychology*. In view of the increasing use of human subjects in this area, it is notable that seven papers in the 1962 *Journal of Comparative and Physiological Psychology* dealt with learning and memory among children or among human adults with abnormal brain function.

Today the topics covered by the *Journal of Comparative and Physiological Psychology* of 20 years ago are represented in scores of journals. These articles now appear not only in relatively hard-core neuroscience journals such as *Neuropsychologia* or *Brain Research* but also in journals traditionally associated with human cognition at the behavioral level only. For instance, the *Journal of Verbal Learning and Verbal Behavior* and *Journal of Experimental Psychology: Learning, Memory and Cognition* have begun to publish articles on learning and memory among humans suffering brain damage or the influence of drugs. These are trends I expect will continue through the year 2000. It is therefore appropriate that the issue I discuss next addresses equally the psychobiological study of learning and memory with either animals or humans as subjects.

CATEGORIES OF LEARNING AND MEMORY

The major issue I wish to consider is whether it is useful to think of a unitary learning or memory mechanism that is fundamental to the acquisition and expression of knowledge. This is an old issue and in some ways a very simpleminded one. But the fact is that such a conception of learning and remembering seems to underlie a good deal of work on the psychobiological basis of memory. The notion that there is a single unitary "memory" that may be enhanced or impaired is surprisingly prevalent in this area. Although psychologists and neuroscientists have become more careful about it, it is still not uncommon to see references to drugs, lesions, or environmental conditions that are assumed simply to enhance or disrupt "memory." Are there in fact discrete occasions in which the memory process as a whole is poor and others in which it is good? Are there some people with uniformly "good memories" and others with poor? Do some animals possess a more effective system for learning and memory than others? In comparison to adults, do infants and children have an intrinsically inferior mechanism, at the neurophysiological level, for learning and remembering?

I have found that my own response to these questions is very unsatisfying, something like, "No, there is no unitary memory capacity that can be enhanced or impaired . . . but maybe there is." In pondering the sorts of evidence that could resolve this issue, I have also found the substance a good bit more interesting than my nonanswer. I expect that this issue will become increasingly more interesting by the year 2000, as will the classes of evidence that I discuss next.

Ontogenetic Changes in Learning and Forgetting

One of the example questions I mentioned before was whether a unitary learning or memory capacity improves ontogenetically. A good deal of the work in my laboratory is directed toward understanding *infantile amnesia*—I have a long-standing interest in why adult humans remember little or nothing of their activities before the age of 3 years. Experimental analysis of infantile amnesia requires an animal model. Our model is the rat, and for now I shall focus more on the developing rat's learning than on its forgetting.

To review briefly, the rat is an altricial animal. Its central nervous system and corresponding behaviors are strikingly "immature" at birth, in a manner similar to that of the human (Campbell & Coulter, 1976; Campbell & Spear, 1972). Only a few years ago it was thought that infant animals of any altricial species were unlikely to show much learning or remembering of anything. For the rat, little significant learning of any kind seemed evident until after the first week of life, and instrumental learning seemed unlikely until about 11 days of age. It was as if learning is unimportant to the infant rat.

Two developments led to a change in this view. One was theoretical, influenced by the views of Peter Anohkin (1964). For Anohkin and his followers, the major unit for psychobiological analysis is the "functional system" by which is meant a: "functional combination of different organizations and processes on the basis of the achievement of the final effect [p. 56]." Examples of such functional systems are those for alternative types of feeding or for sexual behavior, systems that most obviously emerge in mature fashion at quite different ages. An important point is that when a functional system becomes effective will depend on its adaptive value at that particular age. Anohkin's position is that a functional system is: "indissolubly connected with the final effect of adaptation [p. 56]."

From this orientation, developmental psychobiologists have taken the view that seemingly ineffective behaviors by infants do not primarily indicate that the animal is an incomplete, incompetent adult. What might appear to be deficient learning from the perspective of the adult's adaptational needs is considered instead to be an indication of the immature animal's contrary solution to the particular problems of physiological regulation met at that particular age. We are beginning to learn how different the ecological challenges at different stages of development really are and that if its genes are to survive, the organism must be capable of meeting the challenges of infancy as well as those of adulthood.

The second development corrected the misleading practice of assessing developmental differences in learning and memory by testing the associative capacity of infants in the same ways as were customary for adults. As a consequence of Anohkin's influence, supplemented by some careful observational and experimental studies of the developing animal, psychologists began to solve this problem of experimental design in another way—by carefully accommodating the organism's age, specific ecological niche, and age-related stimulus and response dispositions, when testing infantile associative capacities and characteristics. Recent methods for analyzing the associative processes of the physiologically immature rat have therefore taken into account that during the first 2 weeks of life, the rat is dominated by tastes, odors, temperature differences, and ultrasounds, yet with suckling and crawling its only notable instrumental behaviors; that thereafter, visual stimuli and noises of different frequencies than before appear to gain in importance, increased mobility requires new mechanisms for the pup's return to the nest, and items of a familiar taste but somewhat new texture begin to be consumed.

By taking this approach, the laboratories of Alberts (Martin & Alberts, 1979), Amsel (1979), Blass (Blass, Kenny, Stoloff, Bruno, Teicher, & Hall, 1979), Campbell (Campbell & Stehouwer, 1979; Haroutunian & Campbell, 1979), Hall (Johanson & Hall, 1979), Leon (1979), Nagy (1979), Rosenblatt (1979), Rudy (Rudy & Cheatle, 1979), and many others (Spear, 1979, 1983) have suggested that perhaps especially during the infancy of rats, different sets of event contingencies are not learned and remembered with uniform effectiveness. Certain tasks readily acquired by adults lead to less learning or none at all in infants, whereas with other tasks, learning seems equally effective for infants and older animals. To what extent this is a matter of task complexity or of differences in the number or type of elements that require processing for successful task performance is a problem that has not yet been sorted out completely. But, along with identification of these limitations has come the realization that we have severely underestimated the associative capacity of developing animals, and humans too, from birth to adolescence.

Within the past few years it has been shown in the previously mentioned laboratories that rats 3 or 4 days of age can acquire an aversion to an odor paired with either an illness or a cold temperature and can show significant retention several days later, either in terms of odor preferences or change in the animal's heart rate response when exposed to the aversive odor. It has been found that rats only a week old can learn a spatial discrimination about as rapidly as older rats, as long as the reward is a reunion with mother. Rats several days younger than 1 week can show higher-order conditioning, and rats only slightly older can learn and remember an active avoidance response. And as a final example, it has been shown that when rats are only 36 hours old, they can learn to discriminate between two miniature switches in order to receive milk and learn also to move the correct switch but not the incorrect one. Further evidence suggests that the newborn rat uses its capacity for classical and instrumental learning for such challenges as finding a nipple for its first postnatal meal a few minutes after birth.

Aside from establishing that previous experiments used the wrong techniques, why is it interesting that rats have been found to have good capacity for learning and memory during the first few days of life? It is interesting because this capacity seems not to be evident for all kinds of events at a particular age. The capacity to learn and remember depends on what is to be learned and remembered, and in a manner that does not seem to depend on simple sensory or perceptual deficiencies. For instance, there is no doubt that infant rats can detect a footshock during the first week of life. They are in fact somewhat more sensitive to it than older animals. Yet during this period, such infants are on certain occasions unable to acquire an aversion to an odor paired with a footshock, even though under the same circumstances an aversion to that odor is readily conditioned if paired instead with an illness or an electrical shock to the stomach. Also, a preference to that odor can be acquired if it is paired with an injection of milk. As another example, 7-day-old rats that cannot learn a position discrimination in order to escape a footshock can do so if reward is access to an anesthetized mother rat.

We have found other evidence to indicate how misleading was the view that infants are simply deficient in terms of a unitary memory capacity. (1) Infants trained and tested in the context of odors from their home nest seem more mature than otherwise, for some learning tasks. In this sort of "home" environment, for example, infants behave as if they were several days older in their learning of an aversion to a particular location or in learning to withhold a punished response. I might note that analogous effects have begun to appear for human infants tested in the home rather than the laboratory. There are, however, some things that the infant rat learns more slowly in the home, such as a conditioned aversion to a taste or odor that is paired with an illness. (2) In further contrast to the expectations of a generally deficient memory, we have found that the infant rat sometimes learns more than the adult about redundant aspects of a particular task. (3) We have been surprised to find that even when processing multiple elements of compound stimuli, infants often can be as effective in learning as adults and show similar potentiation or overshadowing effects from one component to another. When an interval is interpolated between the conditioned stimulus and the unconditioned stimulus, however, the limitations of the infant become evident in this situation. For instance, when an hour elapses between the tasting of two flavors of different kinds and amounts and an illness, infants tend to acquire an aversion to only one flavor or the other, whereas adults tend to learn about both flavors (Steinert, 1980).

What about long-term retention? Does not the phenomenon of infantile amnesia suggest some fundamental deficiency in the infant's capacity, relative the adult's, for holding acquired associations in memory over long periods? The pertinent facts on this matter are not yet in. The data indicate, for instance, that when forgetting of both infants and adults is alleviated by prior cueing treatments that precede a retention test, there is still a greater net forgetting by the younger animals. Yet we know that on certain occasions when infantile amnesia appears complete in terms of a particular measure of instrumental learning, it is clearly incomplete in terms of some classically conditioned elements in the situation. We also know that infants can be more susceptible than adults to retroactive and proactive interference in retention. It seems that rather than a basic deficiency in some fundamental, physiologically based capacity for processing memories, these cases of infantile amnesia are at least as likely due to differences in stimulus selection or other psychological factors (for reviews of such work, see Spear, 1978, 1979; Spear & Parsons, 1976).

To summarize so far, recent progress in ontogenetic research on learning and memory has required a rejection of the view that the infant rat learns and remembers less well than the adult because it has a fundamentally deficient memory capacity. I can amplify this briefly with an example from the results of studies with human infants that have begun to parallel our experience with the infant rat. During the early portion of the twentieth century, some psychologists stated that the human infant has little or no capacity for learning and memory before the age of about 6 months. Even within the past 5 years, theories in this area have been built on the assumption that the human's capacity for remembering is limited to a few minutes or hours until the age of 6 to 8 months. It is now quite clear, however, that the newborn infant can show substantial learning of either a classical or instrumental nature and, moreover, can show a reliable capacity for quite long-term retention by 2–3 months of age. The innovative research project by Professor Carolyn Rovee–Collier of Rutgers University provides an especially notable example. For this project, an ingeniously simple instrumental learning task has been developed. A ribbon is attached from an overhead mobile to the infant's ankle, and the infant learns to move the mobile by kicking. In very systematic fashion, Professor Rovee–Collier has shown that this task yields many of the fundamental characteristics of instrumental learning. Of more pertinence here, she has also found in studies modeled after work on the alleviation of forgetting in infant rats that although instrumental learning in these human infants is forgotten rather rapidly, over a period of a week or so, quite substantial remembering can be shown as long as a month after learning, if a reactivation treatment to promote memory retrieval precedes the retention test (Rovee–Collier, Sullivan, Enright, Lucas, & Fagan, 1980).

In summary, recent progress in ontogenetic research has depended on rejection of the view that it is a fundamentally deficient memory capacity of the infant that leads to its relatively poor learning and rapid forgetting.

Dissociation in the Expression of Human Knowledge

Just as the infant rat may fail to exhibit learning under some circumstances while readily manifesting it under others, a similar selectivity of memory—an apparent dissociation between what is expressed and what could be remembered—is found among humans. Broad consideration of such dissociation may be found elsewhere (Isaacson & Spear, 1982; for humans in particular, see chapters in this volume by Fagan & Rovee–Collier, Isaacson & Spear, Schacter & Tulving, and Spear & Isaacson). The following are some illustrations:

1. Persons classified as *global amnesics* have been characterized clinically as having complete absence of permanent memory for new information. A variety of careful experiments have shown, however, that these amnesics do in fact show significant retention for some aspects of an episode while denying verbally that they remember anything about it. I refer here to individuals with relatively discrete lesions in the temporal regions of the brain or with Korsakoff's syndrome, such that the memory dysfunction is accompanied by no substantial perceptual difficulties nor decrease in general IQ. The dissociation phenomenon is illustrated in the following examples: (a) Weiskrantz and Warrington (1979) found that an eyeblink response could be classically conditioned in such amnesics and retention shown after a minute or even 24 hours later; when questioned afterward, however, these subjects not only denied that any learning had occurred but also gave no indication of remembering anything about the rather obtuse apparatus used to deliver an air puff to their eye and to measure their responding. (b) Among the amnesics tested over the years have been two musicians who were quite capable of performing adequately and even learning a new tune with practice. Afterward, however, these patients would give no verbal indication of being aware that they had learned a new tune nor that they had performed at all (Luria, 1966; Starr & Phillips, 1970). (c) Finally, the well-studied amnesic, H. M., who had bilateral temporal lesions surgically induced years ago to control epileptic seizures, has frequently displayed this sort of dissociative memory for episodes. Although able to learn and remember visual form discriminations over several minutes, a reverse-mirror drawing over periods of 24 hours, a tactile maze over a period of 2 years, and a particular perceptual learning task over a period of 13 years, he has in each case stated that

he could not remember having participated in such a task before (Corkin, 1982, personal communication; Milner, 1962; Milner, Corkin, & Teuber, 1968; Sidman, Stoddard, & Mohr, 1968).

2. Squire and his colleagues have studied this kind of dissociation in memory with patients suffering anterograde amnesia from one of three sources, a discrete lesion in the diencephalon, Korsakoff disease, or a recent series of bilateral electroconvulsive shocks (Cohen & Squire, 1980). They used a task that seems to reflect a sort of dissociated memory in normal humans. For this task, subjects must learn to read words presented backward, as mirror images. Kolers (1976) had found that long after participating in this task, normals remembered the general skill of reading words presented in this way, even though they forgot the specific materials they had read earlier. Cohen and Squire found a similar, though exaggerated, effect with the amnesics: very rapid forgetting of the specific items, much more rapid than for normal control subjects, and yet good retention of the general skill over a period of 3 months. In discussing this dissociation in memory, these authors distinguish between "procedural" or rule-based information and "declarative" or data-based information. Analogous distinctions have been made often in cognitive psychology and applied in the study of artificial intelligence with computers.

3. Persons susceptible to hypnosis are known to exhibit a type of memory dissociation termed *source amnesia*. For this effect, hypnotically susceptible individuals are given new information when under hypnosis, then questioned about it when released from the series of hypnotic suggestions. Several careful experiments have established that these individuals may readily exhibit this new knowledge and yet indicate complete ignorance as to where they had learned it, even though the learning had occurred only a few minutes earlier (for reviews, see Hilgard, 1977; Schacter & Tulving, 1982).

4. For experimental psychologists, it is hardly news that what the experimenter chooses to measure might not be the most sensitive index of learning. And it is similarly no surprise that normal persons dissociate verbal and nonverbal behaviors, "say one thing and do another." We know that humans can learn a general rule for solving anagrams without being able to verbalize the rule, can have their verbal behavior conditioned by subtle feedback remarks such as "good" and yet be unable to state why their verbal behavior changed, and can employ verbal mediators as mnemonic aids in learning associations and yet be unable to verbalize the particular mediator (Ericsson & Simon, 1980, Nisbett & Wilson, 1977). But, the extreme cases of dissociation seem more than merely a matter of sensitivity of measurement or a distinction between verbal and nonverbal learning. The phenomenon is more general than that. For instance, unilateral, circumscribed damage to the occipital region of the brain can be associated with a similar affliction in spite of no real memory lead. I refer to the phenomenon termed "blindsight" by Weiskrantz and his colleagues (Weiskrantz, 1980).

Patients with these lesions state quite explicitly that they cannot see a particular object in space; yet they can identify the location of the object quite accurately when asked to do so "as if there were in fact something there."

5. We have known for some time that normal humans can have striking dissociation in what is remembered. One example is the "selector mechanism." Identified and analyzed by Underwood, Postman, and their colleagues, the selector mechanism refers to the human's precision in remembering which items were *not* among a learned list of verbal units, even when they remember rather poorly what actually was on the list. For instance, Underwood (1964) described an experiment with paired associate learning in which, among 1424 errors, only one was a word that did not appear somewhere in the list (someone said "yellow" when the correct response was "canary").

6. Dissociation in memory among normal humans is evident in the several variables that determine how well a set of words is recalled and yet have no influence on how accurately each word is identified as to its frequency in the set. Reference here is to a distinction sometimes made between "controlled" and "automatic" processing (Hasher & Zacks, 1979; Schneider & Shiffrin, 1977). Experiments from the laboratory of Professor Lynn Hasher and her colleagues provide good examples (Hasher, 1981). In these experiments, subjects were presented a list of words that differed in their repetition within the list; some words were presented only once, some twice, some three times, and so forth. The subjects then were either asked to recall the words or they were shown all words from the list and asked to judge how frequently each had appeared. The effects of a variety of variables on free recall in these experiments are of some interest, although not particularly surprising: (a) Over an age range of 5 to 80, from preschool children to the elderly, free recall first increased from childhood to adulthood and then began declining after about age 60; (b) learning-disabled children were impaired in recall relative to normals; (c) college students or working-class adults scored as extremely depressed in mood had poorer recall than normals; (d) subjects either uninformed or misinformed about the subsequent recall test had poorer recall than those given explicit instructions to expect the test; (e) college students with relatively low scores on the Scholastic Aptitude Test recalled less well than those with high scores; and (f) with successive practice opportunities on a particular list, free recall improved from trial to trial. The real interest here is in the contrasting effect of these variables on frequency estimation or, I should say, the absence of any effect of these variables on frequency estimations. Accuracy of frequency estimation was not affected by any of these variables—not by age of the subject, nor by a specified "learning disability," nor by extreme mood state, nor by intention to learn, nor by differences in the subjects' SAT scores, nor by practice. Again, this invariance in memory for frequency of occurence occured in spite of quite substantial differences, for each variable, in recall memory.

7. One final bit of evidence from normal adults illustrates still another case of dissociation in memory for one aspect of an episode from that of another. There seems no doubt that what is remembered about a relatively neutral story can be biased in striking fashion by the particular title or theme assigned to the story prior to its presentation. For instance, a story about a man walking through the woods would be remembered quite differently if the title were "The Hunter" rather than "The Escaped Convict." A similar biasing can be introduced by suggesting a new theme or implicit modification of the facts of a previously learned passage when it is recalled; from that point on the subject will remember the original passage as biased. Yet, in view of 100 years worth of evidence for quite precise and faithful—unbiased—memory for specific stimuli, are lexical aspects of the original passage dissociated and preserved independently of a titular or thematic bias? The answer is, yes. Precise memory for the lexical content can be established, dissociated from the biased memory, if the subject can be convinced at the time of testing that the previously assigned theme was a mistake and that, instead, the story dealt with the alternative theme. For instance, the subject is told at the test something like, "I am terribly sorry that this passage was not to have been assigned the theme of 'The Hunter,' but instead its title was supposed to be 'The Escaped Convict'." When this occurs, the subject's recall of the exact words of the passage actually improves, independent of either biasing, as if the subject has returned to a "reproductive" mode of remembering and abandoned a "reconstructive" mode (Hasher, Attig, & Alba, 1981; Hasher & Griffin, 1978).

Summary to This Point

What I have been trying to illustrate are instances in which the expression of one aspect of a stored memory seems dissociated from that of another aspect. The expression of knowledge about a particular episode is not "all or none." Extreme cases of memory dysfunction are in fact characterized by a sparing of certain kinds of knowledge in spite of the apparently complete obliteration of others. This pattern suggests that truly global impairment of a general memory capacity is unlikely.

That such a concept is misleading as well is shown by tests of the ontogeny of memory and learning in infant animals and humans. The discovery of unexpected associative capacities in very young animals was practically a monthly occurrence during the last few years of the 1970s, indicating the error in assuming a relatively deficient capacity for learning or memory among infants. What seems to have been mistaken for such age-specific associative capacities is more likely an age-specific stimulus selection process that may depend on the maturation of separable functional systems.

Finally, a wide variety of individual differences and environmental circumstances that affect recall of a set of words do not affect accuracy in judging how frequently each word was presented. Categorizing these different kinds of processing, or different consequences of processing different materials, has occurred frequently and with some success, both heuristic and analytic. We have, for example, *declarative knowledge* as a term to represent "knowing that," and *procedural knowledge* for "knowing how"; and we have *automatic processing* for information such as frequency of occurrence, in contrast to *controlled processing* for recall of verbal items. Like the evidence concerning ontogenetic and dissociative characteristics of memory, these functional categorizations imply that an assumption of a general capacity for learning or memory is inappropriate.

Some quite different attempts to categorize human learning took place at a symposium organized by Arthur Melton almost exactly 20 years ago (Melton, 1964). Comparison would be instructive although there is not the space for it here. About 10 years ago another widespread categorization procedure was in terms of a stage analysis that included variants of "short-term memory" and "long-term memory." This, too, has largely been replaced. Still of value, although not really comparable to these other categorizations, is the distinction between "memory storage" and "memory retrieval". I think we can expect to see continued attempts at categorization of this kind in the year 2000. At that time we probably will have found that the distinction between storage and retrieval is no longer particularly useful. It has become increasingly apparent that these two steps in remembering have perhaps more in common, in terms of function as well as process, than is useful for purposes of categorization (Spear, 1981; Spear & Mueller, 1983).

What will be the basis of our distinctions in the year 2000? I would hazard the guess that as areas of neuroscience become more fully integrated with experimental psychology, we shall see increasing use of something akin to Anohkin's notion of functional systems. Such a notion has the advantage of incorporating biological as well as psychological considerations.

Some (Apparently) Contrary Evidence: Alcohol and Memory

I have tried to argue that the implicit treatment of learning and memory as global capacities within an individual is a misleading one that psychologists and other neuroscientists should avoid. I now contradict myself by citing some of our recent evidence to suggest impairments in learning and memory that seem, at least today, quite global in their character. I refer to the effects of alcohol on learning and memory in humans. At least in our hands—Steve Lisman, Christian Mueller, and myself—alcohol has seemed to disrupt all aspects of learning and with surprising, almost boring, uniformity. With blood alcohol levels at about .08%–.10% in our experiments, learning seems always to be impaired, whatever the response measure and whatever the nature of the processing required by the subject. I briefly list some examples from our experiments:

1. When persons are given a list of words to remember, it is well known that the more the semantic processing in the encoding of each item, the better it will be remembered. Subjects asked to use a word in a sentence remember it better than if asked instead if it rhymes with another word or if it is presented in capital or lowercase letters. It has been suspected that semantic processing in particular is unlikely or deficient when subjects are intoxicated with alcohol. One might think, therefore, that if intoxicated subjects could be induced to encode words at the semantic level, they might learn and remember as well as sober subjects or at least show less of a deficit. We have conducted two extensive studies to test this idea and have found uniformly, among a wide variety of conditions, that the alcohol deficit is stable regardless of the type of encoding engaged in by the subject. At least two other studies in other laboratories have found the same.

2. From the same rationale, one might think that persons intoxicated with alcohol are simply deficient in rehearsing in a conducive, semantic fashion. We have conducted four substantial experiments to determine whether the alcohol deficit could be reduced when intoxicated subjects are made to rehearse in an explicitly semantic manner. Although these experiments have yielded interesting results in other respects, the memory deficit among subjects given alcohol has been remarkably constant regardless of type of rehearsal.

3. Three cases of invariance in the alcohol deficit can be mentioned without explaining the hypotheses for these studies: (a) When subjects are given part of a set of words to cue their recall of the remainder—"part-list cueing"—net recall is impaired by alcohol intoxication to the same degree as if no cueing had occurred; (b) subjects tested for recall show an increment in subsequent recall; such "learning on test trials" is impaired among intoxicated subjects to the same degree as occurs for learning on study trials; (c) in spite of the indications of invariance in memory for frequency judgments, we have found that the alcohol deficit occurs in terms of recognition memory with a magnitude roughly comparable to that when recall is measured.

4. Finally, although studied less thoroughly than the previous factors, our data suggest that neither amount of retroactive interference, proactive interference, nor forgetting that occurs during a retention interval have any special relationship with alcohol intoxication; the alcohol-induced deficit in memory occurs to about the same extent regardless of retroactive interference, proactive interference, or retention interval.

Collectively, what these sets of experiments seem to be telling us is that this drug, alcohol, has the sort of pervasive influence on memory conceivable as a basic deficit in a global capacity for memory. It may be no coincidence that alcohol also has rather ubiquitous effects throughout the brain, but functionally speaking, this is in any case exactly opposed to the lesson intrinsic to the earlier evidence I discussed.

Recently, another set of drug treatments also has seemed to affect a general capacity for memory (or perhaps for attention), although in this case the drugs seem to have an enhancing rather than impairing effect. I refer to the research on neuropeptides that has been conducted primarily by Professors DeWeid, Bohus, Gispen, and their colleagues in the Netherlands. With either animals or humans as subjects, they have found that performance on several memory tasks may be facilitated by certain pituitary hormones, such as ACTH and vasopressin. For humans, this facilitation has been most marked among individuals otherwise impaired in learning and memory, such as the very elderly or the mentally retarded. This work has been summarized in a number of papers (e.g., Bohus, 1982). It seems too early to judge whether the source of these effects is a change in a global memory capacity. Some variations of these neuropeptides seem to alter attentional or motivational factors, whereas others may act directly on some learning and memory mechanisms. In another sense, however, these effects are of special interest in relating past and future work on the psychobiology of learning and memory. I mentioned earlier that one trend during the past 20 years has been a decrease in studies of the effects of motivation on learning and memory. The primary endogenous origin of the neuropeptides that may exert important control over learning and memory is the pituitary, which is in turn controlled by the hypothalamus. These structures have also been recognized for many years as modulators of a variety of motivational effects. We may therefore see in the future, the conjoint manipulation of motivational and learning variables in a manner analogous to that of the past but with an important difference: Focus will be on how learning is altered biochemically by the neurotransmitters and neuromodulators released by motivational variables rather than on the consequences of an intervening variable termed *motivation*.

SUMMARY

I have tried to focus on two alternative ways of conceptualizing variation in the effectiveness of learning and memory. One is in terms of a global memory capacity that determines in rather uniform fashion all cases of learning and memory; the other is in terms of something like "functional systems", involving different classes or kinds of memory processing for different effects of special relevance to contemporary adaptation. Although the classifications of different kinds of learning or memory by humans seem of a different sort than are presently used when discussing experiments with animal subjects, some convergence of these concepts has begun (Hulse, Fowler, & Honig, 1978; Spear & Miller, 1981) and may be accomplished more fully by the year 2000. I have suggested also that the study of the psychobiology of learning and memory will see an increasing use of humans as subjects. Finally, as a secondary point, I noted that the decreasing interest in motivational factors over the past 20 years may be reversed by the year 2000, although the research and theories touching on this topic may be rephrased in terms of neurotransmitter activity rather than the intervening variable, "motivation."

REFERENCES

Amsel, A. The ontogeny of appetitive learning and persistence in the rat. In N. E. Spear & B. A. Campbell (Eds.), *Ontogeny of learning and memory.* Hillsdale, N.J.: Lawrence Erlbaum Associates, 1979.

Anohkin, P. K. Systemogenesis as a general regulator of brain development. In W. A. Himwich & H. E. Himwich (Eds.), *The developing brain, progress in brain research.* Amsterdam: Elsevier, 1964.

Blass, E. M., Kenny, J. T., Stoloff, M., Bruno, J. P., Teicher, M. H., & Hall, W. G. Motivation, learning, and memory in the ontogeny of suckling in albino rats. In N. E. Spear & B. A. Campbell (Eds.), *Ontogeny of learning and memory.* Hillsdale, N.J.: Lawrence Erlbaum Associates, 1979.

Bohus, B. Neuropeptides and memory. In R. L. Isaacson & N. E. Spear (Eds.), *The expression of knowledge.* New York: Plenum Press, 1982.

Campbell, B. A., & Coulter, X. Ontogeny of learning and memory. In M. R. Rosenzweig & E. L. Bennett (Eds.), *Neural mechanisms of learning and memory.* Cambridge: MIT Press, 1976.

Campbell, B. A., & Stehouwer, D. J. Ontogeny of habituation and sensitization in the rat. In N. E. Spear & B. A. Campbell (Eds.), *Ontogeny of learning and memory,* Hillsdale, N.J.: Lawrence Erlbaum Associates, 1979.

Campbell, B. A., & Spear, N. E. Ontogeny of memory. *Psychological Review,* 1972, *79,* 215–236.

Cohen, N. J., & Squire, L. R. Preserved learning and retention of pattern-analyzing skill in amnesia: Dissociation of knowing how and knowing that. *Science,* 1980, *210,* 207–210.

Ericsson, K. A., & Simon, A. J. Verbal reports as data. *Psychological Review,* 1980, *87,* 215–251.

Fagen, J. W., & Rovee–Collier, C. K. A conditioning analysis of infant memory: How do we know that they know what we know they knew? In R. L. Isaacson & N. E. Spear (Eds.), *The expression of knowledge.* New York: Plenum Press, 1982.

Haroutunian, V., & Campbell, B. A. Emergence of interoceptive and exteroceptive control of behavior in rats. *Science,* 1979, *205,* 927–929.

Hasher, L. The automatic encoding of information into memory. Invited address at meetings of the Eastern Psychological Association, New York, 1981.

Hasher, L., & Griffin, M. Reconstructive and reproductive processes in memory. *Journal of Experimental Psychology: Human Learning and Memory,* 1978, *4,* 318–330.

Hasher, L., Attig, M. S., & Alba, J. W. I knew it all along: Or, did I? *Journal of Verbal Learning and Verbal Behavior,* 1981, *20,* 86–96.

Hasher, L., & Zacks, R. T. Automatic and effortful processes in memory. *Journal of Experimental Psychology: General,* 1979, *108,* 356–388.

Hilgard, E. R. *Divided consciousness: Multiple controls in human thought and action.* New York: Wiley, 1977.

Hulse, S. H., Fowler, H., & Honig, W. K. *Cognitive Processes in Animal Behavior.* Hillsdale, N.J.: Lawrence Erlbaum Associates, 1978.

Isaacson, R. L., & Spear, N. E. (Eds.). *The expression of knowledge.* New York: Plenum Press, 1982.

Johanson, I. B., & Hall, W. G. Appetitive learning in 1-day old rat pups. *Science*, 1979, *205*, 419–421.

Kolers, P. A. Reading a year later. *Journal of Experimental Psychology: Human Learning and Memory*, 1976, *2*, 554–565.

Leon, M. Mother–young reunions. In J. M. Sprague & A. N. Epstein (Eds.), *Progress in psychobiology and physiological psychology*, (Vol. 8). New York: Academic Press, 1979.

Luria, A. R. *Human brain and psychological processes*. New York: Harper & Row, 1966.

Martin, L. T., & Alberts, J. R. Taste aversions to mother's milk: The age-related role of nursing in acquisition and expression of learned association. *Journal of Comparative and Physiological Psychology*, 1979, *93*, 430–445.

Milner, B. Les troubles de la memoire accompagnant des lesions hippocampiques bilaterales. In *Physiologie de Phippocampe*. Paris: C.N.R.S., 257–272, 1962. (English translation in P. M. Milner & S. Glickman (Eds.), *Cognitive processes and the brain*. Princeton, N.J.: Van Nostrand, 97–111, 1965).

Milner, B., Corkin, S., & Teuber, H. L. Further analysis of the hippocampal-amnesic syndrome: Fourteen-year follow-up study of H. M. *Neuropsychologia*, 1968, *6*, 215–234.

Melton, A. W. (Ed.) *Categories of human learning*. New York: Academic Press, 1964.

Nagy, Z. M. Development of learning and memory processes in infant mice. In N. E. Spear & B. A. Campbell (Eds.), *Ontogeny of learning and memory*, Hillsdale, N.J.: Lawrence Erlbaum Associates, 1979.

Nisbett, R. E., & Wilson, T. D. Telling more than we can know: Verbal reports on mental processes. *Psychological Review*, 1977, *84*, 231–259.

Rosenblatt, J. S. The sensorimotor and motivational bases of early behavioral development of selected altricial mammals. In N. E. Spear & B. A. Campbell (Eds.), *Ontogeny of learning and memory*. Hillsdale, N.J.: Lawrence Erlbaum Associates, 1979.

Rovee–Collier, C. K., Sullivan, M. W., Enright, M., Lucas, D., & Fagen, J. W. Reactivation of infant memory. *Science*, 1980, *208*, 1159–1161.

Rudy, J. W., & Cheatle, M. D. Ontogeny of associative learning: Acquisition of odor aversions by neonatal rats. In N. E. Spear & B. A. Campbell (Eds.), *Ontogeny of learning and memory*. Hillsdale, N.J.: Lawrence Erlbaum Associates, 1979.

Schacter, D. L., & Tulving, E. Memory, amnesia and the episodic/semantic distinction. In R. L. Isaacson & N. E. Spear (Eds.), *The Expression of Knowledge*. New York: Plenum Press, 1982.

Sidman, M., Stoddard, L. T., & Mohr, J. P. Some additional quantitative observations of immediate memory in a patient with bilateral hippocampal lesions. *Neuropsychologia*, 1968, *6*, 245–254.

Spear, N. E. *Processing of memories: Forgetting and retention*. Hillsdale, N.J.: Lawrence Erlbaum Associates, 1978.

Spear, N. E. Memory storage factors leading to infantile amnesia. In G. Bower (Ed.), *The psychology of learning and motivation* (Vol. 13). New York: Academic Press, 1979.

Spear, N. E. Extending the domain of memory retrieval. In N. E. Spear & R. R. Miller (Eds.), *Information processing in animals: Memory mechanisms*. Hillsdale, N.J.: Lawrence Erlbaum Associates, 1981.

Spear, N. E. Ecologically determined dispositions control the ontogeny of learning and memory. In R. V. Kail & N. E. Spear (Eds.), *Comparative perspectives on the development of memory*. Hillsdale, New Jersey: Lawrence Erlbaum Associates, 1983.

Spear, N. E., & R. R. Miller (Eds.). *Information processing in animals: Memory mechanisms*. Hillsdale, N.J.: Lawrence Erlbaum Associates, 1981.

Spear, N. E., & Mueller, C. W. Consolidation as a function of retrieval. In H. Weingartner & E. S. Parker (Eds.), *Memory consolidation: Towards a psychobiology of cognition*. Hillsdale, N.J.: Lawrence Erlbaum Associates, 1983.

Spear, N. E., & Parsons, P. Alleviation of forgetting by reactivation treatment: A preliminary analysis of the ontogeny of memory processing. In D. Medin, W. Roberts, & R. Davis (Eds.), *Processes in animal memory*. Hillsdale, N.J.: Lawrence Erlbaum Associates, 1976.

Steinert, P. A. Stimulus selection among preweanling and adult rats as a function of CS amount and quality using a taste aversion paradigm. Unpublished doctoral dissertation, State University of New York at Binghamton, 1980.

Underwood, B. J. The representativeness of rote verbal learning. In A. W. Melton (Ed.), *Categories of human learning*. New York: Academic Press, 1964.

Weiskrantz, L. Varieties of residual experience. *Quarterly Journal of Experimental Psychology*, 1980, *32*, 365–386.

Weiskrantz, L., & Warrington, E. K. Conditioning in amnesic patients. *Neuropsychologia*, 1979. *17*, 187–194.

III
PERCEPTUAL AND
COGNITIVE PSYCHOLOGY

Several of the chapters in this part are very much in the mainstream of contemporary cognitive psychology. George Mandler's exhuberant analysis of consciousness in terms of schema and processing limitations exemplifies the new freedom from the proscriptive constraints of behaviorism. Mandler speculates about the functions of consciousness, its organization and phenomenal characteristics, as freely as William James did 30 years before J. B. Watson proclaimed psychology's emancipation from such concepts.

James would have been very much at home with Mandler's thinking. What seems new, besides the breaking of the bonds of behaviorism, is the appeal to empirical and often experimental research. Mandler and his associates typically measure reaction times (another 19th-century custom!) for recall of previously presented lists that are organized into categories and clusters of various sizes; similar methods are used to study the organization of long-term memory. The results emphasize the importance of "chunking" and a strict limitation on the number of items that can be remembered in any chunk.

The concept of "schema" is Mandler's key theoretical tool for analyzing the structure of consciousness. It is interesting to consider how his use of this constructivist concept relates to that of Piaget and others. It is also interesting to consider the explanatory power of the concept and whether it can be evaluated by the experimental techniques of cognitive psychology.

Also in the mainstream of contemporary cognitive psychology is the chapter by Walter and Eileen Kintsch. Here we get their theory of reading comprehension. Like Mandler, they express themselves with a sense of freedom from the constraints of behaviorism. Extremely modest in comparison with the general theories of learning that dominated psychology 30 years ago, the Kintsch's are content to theorize about the specific mental representations and processes of reading. Furthermore, they envision that the psychology of the Year 2000 will be more content with specific models for understanding the mental operations required by different tasks. But they also want their theorizing to stimulate the construction of tests measuring individuals with respect to different levels of their model. There is an obvious concern with practical applications. As with so much of psychological theorizing, one can ask whether the supporting research is not also consistent with other ways of thinking about the same problem, and in this case with commonsense notions about reading comprehension.

At a conceptually simpler level, but still very much in the information-processing mainstream of cognitive psychology, is the chapter by Paul Fraisse. Reviewing his experiments on the perceptual processing of words and drawings, conducted over the past quarter-century, Fraisse shows us how reaction times can be used to analyze into component parts the processing of information. His flow diagram breaks down "encoding storage" into separate bins for phonetic and semantic storage, with the addition of stimulus uncertainty and discriminability as two interrelated factors. Ingenious experiments pinpoint the differences between the processes involved in naming and in reading, with naming necessarily having a semantic component. Fraisse defends his concentration on simple materials and on simple but basic processes as propaedeutic to the study of more complex processes.

Allen Parducci's chapter on the relativity of judgment presents another example of the new freedom of experimental psychologists to write about the mind. In this case, the concern is with value experiences, a concern that has been largely neglected by contemporary cognitive psychology. Parducci believes that understanding of the relational character of such experiences comes from simple psychophysical experiments, but he regards such research more as a source of hypotheses than as a test of his grander theory of happiness. In general, he is skeptical about the possibility of rigorous tests of any theory that is genuinely psychological, and also about attempts to apply psychological theories to practical problems.

The systems approach of the "Slovak Experimental School of Psychology" is presented in the chapter by Damian Kováč. Rejecting simpler paradigms for what they leave out, Kováč's basic conceptual formulation reads:

$$B = f[\Psi(O, S)],$$

that is, behavior is a function *mental* states and processes under different organismic conditions and in different environmental situations. "Data obtained through scientific procedures may grow into psychological scientific facts only when they give testimony to the entire reflexive-regulatory process between '*S*' and '*B*' mediated by mental functions." Kováč presents teasing glimpses of several interfunctional research projects conducted by the Slovak school. The emphasis is upon perception and memory. The reader can sense a movement away from psychology's past. Kováč's vision of the future of experimental research seems to have much in common with that of cognitive psychologists in the West.

8 The Construction and Limitation of Consciousness

George Mandler
University of California, San Diego, La Jolla, USA

I have chosen to discuss some aspects of the problem of consciousness. The investigation of the role of consciousness has once again become central to theoretical and empirical work on human thought and action. Because the future of experimental psychology is one of the themes of this volume, discussing a currently active topic seems to be one way of looking into that future. Another way of approaching that theme might be to let one's imagination wander in order to predict what experimental psychologists will be doing 20 or 50 years from now. Such fantasies are typically unconstrained by reality; they are more likely to reveal the wishes and hopes (or fears and forebodings) of the predictor. I prefer to look briefly at our past and at important problems facing us today.

I do have one concern about our enterprise here. As I surveyed the array of eminent contributors to this volume, I realized that the experimental psychology of the year 2000 will not be marked by the activities of my colleagues here. Experimental psychology in the year 2000 will be the psychology of women and men who are currently active in their own laboratories, who are mainly less than 40 years old, and who are not here.

Experimental psychology of the past 60 years was marked, particularly in the United States, by the behaviorist interlude. Behaviorism was a particular symptom of American society—its pragmatism and its avoidance of the fanciful. As a result we learned much about experimental method and little about fruitful, imaginative theory. One of the consequences of the behaviorist period was the commitment to data and the careful gathering thereof. Data collection in well-controlled experiments became an end in itself, and that attitude can still be found today—particularly in some of the more remote corners of American psychology.

The last 20 years have seen important changes in experimental psychology. One of the signs that is symptomatic of an increasing maturity is the closer tie between experimentation and theory. The functional approach to experimental psychology—determining the relationship among empirical variables—is still with us (and has its role to play), but it has been replaced by the traditional scientific role of experimentation—providing evidence for theoretical models and ideas. Such a shift needed, of course, the lifting of the behaviorist veil and the opening of vistas of the theoretical possibilities of the human mind. At the same time, experimental method has become more sophisticated, as the classic model of the experimental and control group design and appropriate large number statistics has given way to well-controlled studies of few individuals and to new statistical techniques. Finally, the pursuit of laboratory-bound traditional (and often imaginary) problems has been replaced by investigations of theoretically and experientially relevant questions.

Consciousness was proscribed as an area of study during the behaviorist period in the United States, but it is now beginning to enjoy the fruits of new theoretical endeavors. The study of consciousness is also a good example of research that cannot be engaged without constant interplay of theory and data. I shall therefore discuss some new theoretical developments in the study of consciousness and then put some results from my laboratory within that perspective.

THE FUNCTIONS OF CONSCIOUSNESS

Consciousness—at the extremes—has been viewed either as the central and only problem of psychology or as an epiphenomenal curiosity of no theoretical importance. One of the most encouraging signs of recent years has been the approach to consciousness in terms of its functions, the processes that determine its occurrence or construction, and its utility in the course of information processing (Marcel, 1983b; Natsoulas, 1977; Norman & Shallice, 1980; Shallice, 1972). I first briefly review some of my previous discussions of these functions (Mandler, 1975a, 1979b, 1982a).

When are conscious processes most obvious? First of all in the process of construction and integration of mental and action structures. Essentially this refers to the use of consciousness in the learning process. Thoughts and actions are typically conscious before they become well-integrated and subsequently automatic. Thus, for example, learning to drive a car is a conscious process, whereas the skilled driver acts automatically and unconsciously.

Second, conscious processes are active during the exercise of choices and judgments, particularly with respect to any action requirements. These choices, often novel ones, require the consideration of possible outcomes and consequences and frequently involve what the behaviorist literature calls "covert trial and error."

Third, conscious processes exercise an important function during "troubleshooting." Thus, many automatic structures become conscious when they somehow fail in their functions, when a particular habitual way of acting fails or when a thought process cannot be brought to an appropriate conclusion. The experienced driver becomes "aware" of where she or he is and what she or he is doing when something new and different happens; when a near miss or a police car or an unexpected traffic light are suddenly registered. The troubleshooting function of consciousness permits repair of current troublesome or injudicious processing, and subsequent choice from among other alternatives. These arguments stress the role of consciousness in action, in contrast to a contemplative, reflective view of conscious states. A similar approach to the role of consciousness in the execution and voluntary initiation of actions has been explored by Norman and Shallice (1980).

Having listed some of the conditions that give rise to conscious states, I now move to a more detailed consideration of the structures and processes that contribute the contents of consciousness. Central to these are knowledge representations embodied in the concept of schemas.

THE SCHEMA AS A BUILDING BLOCK OF CONSCIOUSNESS

I use the term *schema* to conform with current usage but also to evoke similarities with Bartlett's and Piaget's usage. My own preference in recent years has been to refer to cognitive structures, which I now include under the term *schema*. The concept of schema also overlaps with some aspects of Miller, Galanter, and Pribram's (1960) use of "plan" and "image."

Schemas are built up in the course of interaction with the environment. They are available at increasing levels of generality and abstraction. Thus, schemas may represent organized experience ranging from discrete features to general categories. For example, one schema may represent a horse's head, and another one facilitates the perception of a particular animal as a horse because of the concatenation of certain features (variables of a schema) such as a head, a tail, a mane, a certain size, or a range of colors. That same horse is categorized as an animal because of the occurrence of certain defining characteristics of that class of events.

I use schema here as a category of mental structures that organize past experience, and that includes Piaget's invention of the schema as structuring our experience and being structured by it. A more recent exploration by Rumelhart and Ortony (1978) provides some of the specifications of schemas developed below.

The schema that is developed as a result of prior experiences with a particular kind of event is not a carbon copy of that event; schemas are abstract representations of environmental regularities (Franks & Bransford, 1971). Schemas vary from the most concrete to the most abstract; they are available for the perceptual elements of an event as well as for the abstract representation of its "meaning" or gist.[1] We comprehend events in terms of the schemas they activate, though we have different ways of talking about different kinds of comprehension. Perception is "comprehension of sensory input" (Rumelhart & Ortony, 1978); one sense of understanding involves comprehension of semantic relations; and some value judgments are based on the comprehension of structural relations. Finally, it should be noted that generic schemas have modal (or even canonic) values of variables. This property responds to the notion of schematic prototypes (Rosch, 1978; Rosch & Mervis, 1975), which affect the likely congruity of specific instances of objects and events.

Schemas operate interactively, i.e., input from the environment is coded selectively in keeping with the schemas currently operating while that input also selects relevant schemas (Marcel, 1982b; McClelland, 1981; McClelland & Rumelhart, 1980). Whenever some event in the environment produces "data" for the schematic analysis, the activation process proceeds automatically (and interactively) to the highest (most abstract) relevant schema. At the same time, I assume that the activation of a schema also involves the inhibition of other competing schemas. Evidence from the environment activates potential schemas, and active schemas produce an increased readiness for certain evidence and decreased readiness (inhibition) for other evidence. The particular interaction between the contextual environmental evidence and the organism's available schemas constricts perception and conception to specific hypotheses, constructions, and schemas.

Most, if not all, of the activation processes occur automatically and without awareness on the part of the perceiver/comprehender. When and under what cirumstances do we become aware of any part of the processing stream? We must find at least a tentative answer to that question, because clearly most aspects of processing are never conscious.

THE CONSTRUCTION OF CONSCIOUS EXPERIENCE

Marcel (1983b) has addressed the problem of consciousness for the general perceptual process. His view of mental structures is consistent with the one presented here—he is concerned with structures and the conditions under which they reach the conscious state (Mandler, 1975a, Chapter 3). However, in contrast to the view that structures *become* conscious so that consciousness is simply

---

[1]I am using *concrete* and *abstract* here as essentially equivalent to *specific* and *general*. Though the distinction between these two sets of terms is potentially important, it does not interact significantly with my theme.

a different state of a structure, Marcel sees consciousness as a constructive process in which the phenomenal experience is a novel construction to which two or more activated schemata have contributed. Treisman and Gelade (1980) recently proposed a constructive view of focal attention that is very similar to Marcel's proposition.

A precursor of these views is the theoretical account of automatic activation and conscious processing contributed by Posner and his associates (Posner & Boies, 1971; Posner & Snyder, 1975). Their position also distinguishes between automatic pathway activation and conscious processing. The conscious processing discussed by Posner and Snyder (1975) is: "a mechanism of limited capacity which may be directed toward different types of activity [p. 64]." In that sense, they hold to the more traditional position that consciousness is "directed toward" an unconscious structure or process that then becomes "conscious."

The constructive approach to consciousness is also relevant to speculations about the nature of introspective (verbal) reports. Ericsson and Simon (1980) have provided an excellent theoretical account of the generation of such reports. However, their account is primarily concerned with the relationship between information available in short-term memory (STM) on the one hand and verbalized information on the other. STM seems to operate as a (more respectable?) substitute for consciousness. Ericsson and Simon note that they use "attended to," "heeded," and "stored in STM" as synonymous expressions; they assert that recently attended information is kept in STM and is "directly accessible" for producing verbal reports; and that the products of automatic processing are not available to STM. The question of what it is that is available in STM (consciousness) is never specifically addressed, but it is implied that that information somehow directly represents cognitive processes. In contrast, I would argue that these "available" contents of STM are themselves the product of constructive processes. A theory of introspection needs to specify how "heeding" and "attending" operate and also how such processes determine (construct) specific conscious contents.[2]

Marcel (1983b) notes that: "that of which we are conscious are structural descriptions." We can be conscious only of experiences that are constructed out of activated schemas. We are not conscious of the process of activation or the

---

[2]There is a need to clear up currently shifting distinctions among such concepts as short-term memory, primary memory, working memory, and consciousness. Short-term memory and primary memory have been used interchangeably, though William James introduced the concept of primary memory as essentially equivalent with momentary consciousness. Similarly, working memory is frequently used to refer to a blackboard conception, very similar to the limited-capacity notion of consciousness. On the other hand, some writers (such as Ericsson and Simon) seem to use short-term memory as equivalent with momentary, limited-capacity consciousness. I would prefer to use consciousness to refer to material that is phenomenally immediately available and needs no retrieval, whereas short-term memory should be reserved to the limited amount of information that is quickly retrieved, often without the expenditure of processing resources.

constituents of the activated schemas.[3] A constructed conscious experience depends on the activated schemas of one or more of the constituent processes and features. The schemas that are available for constructive consciousness must be adequately activated (i.e., have produced a record in Marcel's sense) and must not be inhibited. The advantage of postulating that several such activated schemas construct consciousness is that we thereby can achieve the phenomenal unity of conscious experience. Consciousness constructed from more than one activated schema takes advantage of alternate ways of viewing the world and also integrates some optimal amount of the available information. Marcel (1983b) advances his hypothesis in order to argue that phenomenal experience is: "an attempt to make sense of as much data as possible at the highest or most functionally useful level possible." When a categorical or a value judgment is sought—by an actor's intentions or by an experimenter's instructions—the "most functionally useful" level of abstraction is a general schema or the relational aspect of a schema. And even then what is constructed as a conscious, phenomenal accompaniment is not the awareness of congruity but the direct apprehension of category membership or valuation.

A similar interpretation of consciousness was advanced by John (Thatcher & John, 1977). He noted that in consciousness: "information about multiple individual modalities of sensation and perception is combined into a unified multidimensional representation," that is, that "consciousness itself is a representational system."

Finally, Marcel (1983b) argues that as we learn to interpret the significance of a set of cues: "*we are aware of that significance instead of and before we are aware of the cues.*" Although Marcel's argument was specifically intended for the phenomenon of category access without access to instantiation, it applies pari passu to a number of judgments, such as evaluation, feeling tone, and general familiarity. Marcel and others (Fowler, Wolford, Slade, & Tassinary, 1981; Intraub, 1981; Marcel, 1983a) have shown that, under some conditions of minimal attention to or exposure of instances of verbal or visual categories, there is evidence that people "know" (consciously) to which category a specific event belongs (e.g., furniture, landscape) without being able to identify which particular item (piece of furniture or specific scenes) they had witnessed. Parker (1977) has shown that semantic incongruity in a visual display is recognized (peripherally) even before the direct fixation of the incongruous object. It is of course obvious that we are customarily conscious of events and objects in our environ in a constructed fashion; we are aware of the important aspects of the event but hardly ever are aware of all our potential knowledge of the event (Köhler, 1947). Similarly, I would argue it is possible that one can know the

---

[3]The contrast is introduced by Marcel as a distinction between the results of activation processes and their records. Whereas the former are generally unconscious processes, it is the latter—the records of these processes—that may become available to consciousness.

value of an event before one is aware of the details of the event that is being judged. A similar disjunction between the awareness of structural and event-specific information has been reported for some clinical observations.[4] This general approach to the problem of consciousness of abstract and concrete aspects of an event is also consistent with those arguments that claim immediate access to complex meanings of events (Lazarus, 1981).

We are apparently never conscious of all the available evidence that surrounds us but only of a small subset. What is the nature of that limitation?

THE LIMITATION OF CONSCIOUS EXPERIENCE

In recent intellectual history, one of the earliest references to the limitation of human attention was made by Charles Bonnet (1720–1793). Antoine Louis Claude Destutt de Tracy (1754–1836) elaborated on the notion that only six "objects" can be apprehended by the mind at any one time. Hamilton (1859) introduced the notion into the modern era and noted that it applied to both single objects and groupings of objects. By 1890 William James had firmly established the limited capacity concept as a cornerstone of our knowledge about consciousness/attention, and G. A. Miller (1956) made it a central thesis of modern approaches to human information processing.

The limited capacity of attention should be an excellent candidate as a pervasive characteristic of human beings. Our colleagues who are often overly eager to ascribe evolutionary and genetic origins to a variety of human characteristics and differences might well focus on limited conscious capacity, which is found across groups, societies, races, and even ages. As Dempster (1981) noted in an extensive review of the available data: "there is little or no evidence of either individual or developmental differences in capacity [p. 87]." He defines capacity as "attentional capacity" or as the limited amount of attention that is available "for activating internal units stored in long-term memory [p. 87]."

Such a general characteristic of human functioning as limited attentional capacity should have a rather important role to play in thought and action. I assume in the first place that the limited-capacity characteristic of consciousness serves to reduce further the "blooming confusion" that the physical world potentially presents to the organism. Just as sensory end organs and central transducers radically reduce and categorize the world of physical stimuli to the functional stimuli that are in fact registered, so does the conscious process further reduce the available information to a small and manageable subset. Similarly,

---

[4]Warrington (1975) reports on patients who could identify the category name of an object, but not the object name. Similarly Sheinkopf (1970, cited in Osgood, May, & Miron, 1975) has shown that anomic aphasics, who have difficulty in naming and word finding, perform like normals in a visual–verbal synesthesia task (Osgood, 1960).

Marcel (1983b) has proposed that conscious states are constructed so that they are functionally useful and make optimal sense of all the available data. I assume, somewhat circularly, that the limitation of conscious capacity defines what is in fact cognitively manageable. Whereas we do not know why the reduction is of the magnitude that we observe, it is reasonable to assume that some reduction is necessary. Just consider a need for pairwise comparisons (in a choice situation) among n chunks in consciousness; clearly the number n must be limited if the organism is to make a choice within some reasonable time span.

Posner and Snyder (1975) note that the: "limited-capacity mechanism may serve an important inhibitory function . . . [by] giving priority to a particular pathway [p. 65]." Shallice (1972) and Norman and Shallice (1980) have elaborated the function of attention in the execution of action; attention is restricted to the central aspects of action selection and execution. The limitation of capacity prevents other structures and schemas from competing overtly with the selected mechanism.

There are occasions and stimuli that demand conscious capacity and construction almost automatically. Among these are intense stimuli and internal physiological events such as autonomic nervous system activity. Whenever such events claim and preoccupy some part of the limited-capacity system, other cognitive functions will suffer, i.e., they will be displaced from conscious processing and problem-solving activities will be impaired (see Mandler, 1979b, for a review). Particularly in the case of the interruption or failure of ongoing conscious (and particularly unconscious) intercourse with the world, signals from both the external and the internal world will require conscious representation.

The question arises whether we are really "conscious" of five or six discrete events. The arguments for a constructive view of consciousness seem to counsel against such a view. If we consider consciousness as an integrated construction of the available evidence—a construction that seems to be phenomenally "whole"—then it is probably more likely that the limitation to a certain number of items or objects or events or chunks refers to the limitation of these elements *within* the constructed holistic conscious experience. I would argue therefore that whatever schema guides the conscious experience is necessarily restricted to a certain number of features or relations. Cognitive "chunks"—organized clusters of knowledge—can operate as units of such constructed experience, just as the experience itself acts as a constructed holistic chunk. For example, as I look out my window I am aware of the presence of trees and roads and people—individual organized schemas. I may switch my attention—reconstruct my conscious experience—to focus on one of these events and note that some of the people are on bicycles, others walk, some are male, some female. Switching attention again I see a friend and note that he is limping, carrying a briefcase, and talking with a person walking next to him. In each case a new experiential whole enters the conscious state and consists itself of new and different organized chunks.

In arguing that the limited capacity of consciousness is represented by the number of events that can be organized within a single constructed conscious experience, I respond to the intuitively appealing notion that we are both aware of some unitary "scene" and have available within it a limited number of constituent chunks. I have discussed elsewhere (Mandler, 1975a) the manner in which these momentary conscious states construct the phenomenal continuity and flow of consciousness.

The construction of individual chunks is consistent with the cognitive mechanisms embodied in the distinction between integrative and elaborative processing (Mandler, 1979a, 1982b). Integration refers to the process whereby the elements of a structure become more strongly related to each other, the structure itself develops its own unique constituents, and relations among the elements of a cognitive structure (a schema) become stable. This process produces organized chunks of knowledge that act as single units, are stored and retrieved as units, and may themselves become elements or features of a larger cognitive structure. Elaboration on the other hand refers to the establishment of relationships among structures, the kind of network that is basic to the notion of structural meaning. The relations of a unit of knowledge to other such units determines its meaning and its function in memorial storage and retrieval (Craik & Tulving, 1975; Mandler, 1967). Integration and elaboration have a dialectic relationship (Mandler, 1982b). The integration of a particular set of elements may be viewed as the elaboration of one of its constituent members, and conversely elaboration of a particular event involves the integration of the events that are related to the target event.

Experimental evidence

In this final section I confine myself to experimental work from our laboratory on the construction and limitation of consciousness. Limitations of time and space prevent me from reviewing the experimental literature, and the following discussion should therefore be seen primarily as illustrative and certainly not exhaustive. In particular, I do not refer to the extensive literature on divided attention that has provided another avenue of approach to the problem of limited capacity.

My interest in the limited-capacity notion started with an extensive project on the organization of memory (Mandler, 1967, 1968). Given a large number of unrelated words, people tend to sort them into no more than about seven categories and then retrieve the material in clusters organized by category and by suborganizations within each category. I concluded, following and adapting Miller (1956), that the "basic limit of the organizing system" was set at $5 +/- 2$ items.

In 1975 I summarized a number of studies from our laboratory that demonstrated the effect of organizational limitations on different aspects of memorial storage and retrieval (Mandler, 1975b). In one study we showed that the organizational model could be accommodated by a processing model that assumed that retrieval times were determined by the organization of the memorial material into chunks. Patterson, Meltzer, and Mandler (1971) demonstrated that the retrieval of categorized material produced relatively short inter response times (IRTs) within organized clusters and longer IRTs between clusters. Figure 8.1 shows this finding, with IRTs within categorically related clusters staying relatively flat, but subjects taking increasingly longer to retrieve successive categories. This study confirmed the sensitivity of reaction times to the retrieval of organized material.

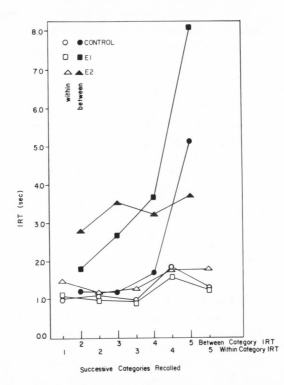

Successive Categories Recalled

FIG. 8.1.   Mean IRTs (interresponse times) for successive access to items within categorical clusters and access between clusters in the recall of lists consisting of five items from each of five categories (from Patterson, Meltzer, & Mandler, 1971). The upper row of numbers on the abscissa represents the four between category transitions, and the lower row represents the positions for the within-category IRTs. Group E1 was not given the category names during recall, and the "between" function shows the increasing time needed for successive category access. Group E2 was given the category names and therefore does not show such increasing IRTs. The Control group was not told about the categorical character of the list either at input or output; their overall recall was also lower than that of the two experimental groups.

As far as retrieval processes were concerned, Patterson (1972) showed that not only the kind of cues used for retrieval but also the size of the category that is retrieved are important determiners of retrieval efficiency. If category size becomes large (i.e., as it increases in size beyond four items), only some subset of its members are retrieved and that subset changes from one retrieval attempt to the next. Similarly, Meltzer (1971) demonstrated that subjects' estimates of the size of a category were strong determinants of recall. People tend to overestimate the size of categories that are smaller than five and underestimate the size if it is larger. These estimates, in turn, determine how much time a subject will spend on attempts to retrieve from a category.

A study by Mandler and Graesser (1976) addressed the notion that the clusters of items that appear in the recall of lists of unrelated words must have some organizing principles—they are not just random collections of about five items. We demonstrated by an analysis of multiple repeated recalls that subjects construct focal dimensions that serve as the organizing points for the list. These focal dimensions determine the content of the chunks and each dimension organizes about five items. Dimensional foci are established in order to accommodate the words in the list—the items that need to be organized. One of the results of this process is that it determines the unified organized nature of chunk. Another consequence is the way in which such a process handles the problem of list length. As more items need to be organized, they are recruited around the relevant dimensions that are—if necessary—subdivided. The number of stable focal items changes little with list length, but the items that are organized by these foci increase as list length increases, thus making greater recall from longer lists possible.

All the studies reported above used the rather artificial procedure of presenting people with lists of (categorized or unrelated) words and asking them to retrieve them at some later time. If the kind of process we have speculated about truly characterizes the human processing system, then the same kind of effects should be observable in the direct retrieval from semantic memory. Following earlier work, we started in 1971 to examine the characteristics of direct output from long-term semantic storage. Typically subjects are asked to name all the members of a natural semantic category that come to mind. These categories could be animals, occupations, kitchen utensils, etc. Dean (1971) examined such protocols for both temporal and semantic clustering. He found that fast sequences of emissions (with short IRTs) characterized clusters with five or fewer members. When subjects were later asked to sort the words they had given into groups that "belonged together," the modal size of these categories was six. When the emission protocols were compared with the sorting categories, the emissions protocols showed clusters of related items (i.e., items that were sorted together) that were mostly less than five in size, with a mean of 3.7.

In a more extended study by Graesser and Mandler (1978), we confirmed first of all the importance of focal items that organize the structure of the emitted

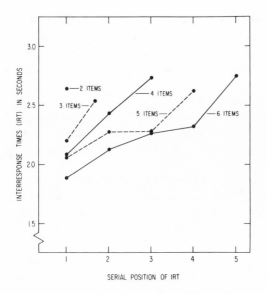

FIG. 8.2. Interresponse times as function of cluster size and output position within clusters (from Graesser & Mandler, 1978).

items. As in the learning of lists, the semantic organization of natural categories also depends on certain focal dimensions. Inspections of the temporal functions for each of the subjects in the experiment again confirmed the presence of fast intracluster and slower intercluster response times. Once an organized chunk is accessed, up to approximately five items from the cluster are quickly produced. However, the search for new chunks produces increasingly longer IRTs between the fast clusters. We also noted that the IRTs within clusters indicated that the chunk was first retrieved as a whole and then produced. Figure 8.2 shows that regardless of the number of items within a temporally defined cluster, the *last* item was given at the same general speed. In other words, after entry into an organized cluster there is no search process, but rather what determines the IRTs is the number of items that still were to be produced. The clusters are retrived as units; when many items are in the cluster, initial response times are fast, but the final item is no more difficult to retrieve if it is the second or the sixth.

If organized units containing about five items are the basic building blocks of this kind of semantic storage, then the number of items that can be produced for any of the natural categories should depend on the number of clusters or chunks that can be produced. That result is shown in Fig. 8.3, which plots the total number of items emitted against the size of the fast clusters (chunks) and against the number of these clusters that were produced. Clearly the number of items that are stored for these natural categories depends not on the number that are stored within chunks but on the number of different such chunks that are available. These data also confirm the notion that, regardless of the kind of category that is accessed, the number of items that can be stored within an organized unit is strictly limited.

I indicated earlier that consciousness is apparently necessary for the adequate encoding into and retrieval from long-term storage. The evidence summarized here does not speak directly to this issue, but it does indicate that some limitation of capacity is operating in the encoding and retrieval of memorial material, both experimentally generated and naturally established. What these data do indicate is that organized groups with no more than about five members are retrieved from larger conceptual categories. In retrieving our knowledge of natural categories we seem to retrieve a small organized chunk that is identified by some theme or concept (e.g., farm animals from animals, kitchen furniture from furniture, and metals from physical substances). The retrieved cluster contains only few of the items that could be classed under that particular theme or concept, but the capacity limitation prevents access to more than about five at any one time. The phenomenal experience that accompanies these retrievals also seems to specify some conceptual group and its momentarily limited number of instances. Our research has shown that, whereas extensive material may be potentially available, any one retrieval attempt will produce only a limited subset of that material. In particular the retrieval of natural categories showed that, whereas subjects produce about the same number of items on successive attempts at emitting the

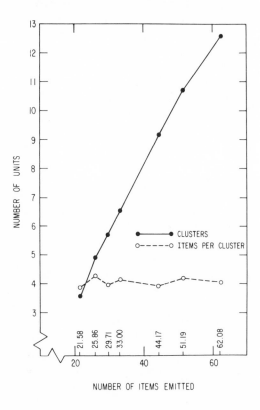

FIG. 8.3. Mean number of clusters and mean number of items per cluster as a function of the total number of items emitted (from Graesser & Mandler, 1978).

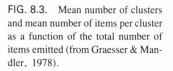

whole category, there is considerable variation in which items will actually be emitted during any specific attempt.

We also have some direct evidence that the limitation of capacity occurs within some organized unit. In Graesser and Mandler (1978) we requested subjects to find some common meaning for sets of randomly selected, unrelated words. The size of these sets varied from 1 to 12. The mean time to find a common-meaning dimension for these sets of words increased to set size 6 and then flattened out, and the mean number of words reported to fit a particular meaning dimensions was 6.5. In other words, subjects were able to find a single meaning dimension for about five or six words, but seemed unable to fit more items to that dimension. In this particular case, the dimension is semantic; in other cases the organizing principle may be spatial or serial or some other organizational process. In general, the limitation of consciousness is a function of the number of objects/events that can be accommodated by some unitary organizing principle, whether the objects are words, series of digits, or complex chunks. I now turn to an example of very simple spatial organization.

The phenomenon of subitizing, baptized and explored by Kaufman, Lord, Reese, and Volkmann (1949), has long been a mainstay in the definition of the limited-capacity phenomenon. Kaufman et al. used the term *subitizing* to refer to the rapid, confident, and accurate report of the numerosity of arrays of elements presented for very brief exposures. The phenomenon is restricted to arrays of six or fewer elements (usually simple dots). It is an extension of the limitation known at least since the eighteenth century (i.e., that the immediate apprehension of the numerosity of a random array of objects or events is limited to arrays of six or fewer objects). Our experiments (discussed in detail in Mandler & Shebo, 1982) showed that subjects give very fast responses to canonical patterns of one to three elements, engage in mental counting for arrays consisting of four to six elements, and estimate the numerosity of the array if there are more than six or seven elements. Of particular interest to the present discussion is the phenomenon of mental counting. It appears that after exposures of the arrays as short as 200 msec subjects are able to hold the array in consciousness and to count the elements in it. Of particular interest is the temporal slope, the function relating reaction times to the size of arrays. The temporal slope for mental counting—in the absence of physical evidence—is identical with the counting slope for physically present arrays that are presented for unlimited exposures. However, people apparently cannot hold more than six elements in their mind's eye; arrays larger than seven that are presented for brief periods cannot be subsequently counted. This finding suggests that a perceptual field, such as an array of elements, can be organized for conscious construction but that the number of elements that can be consciously constructed is limited. This is very similar to my initial argument that the limited capacity of consciousness may well be the number of chunks or constituents that can be accommodated in a single organized construction.

One of the difficulties of the experimental investigation of human consciousness is the fact that the very act of inspection interacts with the contents of the conscious construction. I have discussed this peculiar psychological indeterminacy principle elsewhere (Mandler, 1975a). It is obvious that a report about some conscious state will require conscious capacity that will in turn reduce the capacity available to the inspected event and thereby change it. In our subitizing study, we were able to take one step toward circumventing this problem. In one of our experiments, we required subjects not to give the number of elements they saw displayed, but rather to indicate whether they thought they *could* give such a number judgment if required. In other words, the subject does not count or estimate the mental arrays but rather reports on its cognitive clarity. In contrast to the numerosity judgments that show significant positive temporal slopes as the array size increases, these judgments of the apprehensibility of the arrays produce essentially flat slopes for the range of array size that produces accurate responses. The conscious construction of these arrays makes them "look countable," and the judgment provides a more direct access to the phenomenal appearance of the array when it is not distorted by the requirement of mental counting. The speed of the response is essentially unaffected by the number of elements. On the other hand, whether or not a clear percept of the countable array *can* be constructed is constrained by a limitation of the number of elements (or chunks) that can be organized.

FUTURE DIRECTIONS

Although we appear to have clarified the nature and function of human consciousness, the experimental work has only begun to mine the richness of the theoretical possibilities. We need to know more about the constructive process and the attentional mechanisms that guide the system toward one out of several possible constructions. We need to explore innovative methods for determining the time course of the constructive process and to determine more exactly the relationship between automatic activation of potential schemas and their availability for conscious construction.

I have suggested one approach toward the interaction of integrative and elaborative processes in the construction of the units of thought and action (Mandler, 1979a). If a particular task is not well integrated, it will require maximal conscious capacity for its performance. Once it is compacted into chunks that require little conscious capacity, other new knowledge can be obtained. Knapp (1979) showed that the acquisition of new syntactic structures by very young children depends on the automatization of their precursors and of other currently-being-integrated syntactic structures. The relation among integration, elaboration, and conscious capacity in the acquisition of new information is a useful guide for teaching purposes (see the iso-capacity curves in Mandler, 1979a).

We need continuing explorations of the mechanisms that produce coherent schemas that act as unitary chunks. The latter adventure is particularly exciting because it is a promising approach to a problem that has bedevilled psychology for decades if not centuries—the specification of the basic psychological unit. That approach will combine the insights of Gestalt psychology, which specified some of the phenomenal units, with the methods of modern cognitive theory.

ACKNOWLEDGMENTS

Preparation of this chapter was supported in part by Grant BNS 79–15336 from the National Science Foundation. Parts of this chapter have been adapted from sections in "Thought processes, consciousness, and stress," in V. Hamilton and D. M. Warburton (Eds.), *Human stress and cognition: An information processing approach.* London: Wiley, 1979; and from "The structure of value: Accounting for taste," presented at *The 1981 Carnegie Symposium on Cognition and Affect* (Technical Report No. 101), Center for Human Information Processing, University of California, San Diego.

REFERENCES

Craik, F. I. M., & Tulving, E. Depth of processing and the retention of words in episodic memory. *Journal of Experimental Psychology: General,* 1975, *104,* 268–294.

Dean, P. *Organizational structure and retrieval processes in long-term memory.* Unpublished Ph.D. thesis. University of California, San Diego, 1971.

Dempster, F. N. Memory span: Sources of individual and developmental differences. *Psychological Bulletin,* 1981, *89,* 63–100.

Ericsson, K. A., & Simon, H. Verbal reports as data. *Psychological Review,* 1980, *87,* 215–251.

Fowler, C. A., Wolford, G., Slade, R., & Tassinary, L. Lexical access with and without awareness. *Journal of Experimental Psychology: General,* 1981, *110,* 341–362.

Franks, J. J., & Bransford, J. D. Abstraction of visual patterns. *Journal of Experimental Psychology,* 1971, *90,* 65–74.

Graesser, A. C. II, & Mandler, G. Limited processing capacity constrains the storage of unrelated sets of words and retrieval from natural categories. *Journal of Experimental Psychology: Human Learning and Memory,* 1978, *4,* 86–100.

Hamilton, W. *Lectures on metaphysics and logic* (Vol. 1). Edinburgh: Blackwood, 1859.

Intraub, H. Identification and processing of briefly glimpsed visual scenes. In D. F. Fisher, R. A. Monty, & J. W. Senders (Eds.), *Eye movements: Cognition and visual perception.* Hillsdale, N.J.: Lawrence Erlbaum Associates, 1981.

Kaufman, E. L., Lord, M. W., Reese, T. W., & Volkmann, J. The discrimination of visual number. *American Journal of Psychology,* 1949, *62,* 498–525.

Knapp, D. *Automatization in child language acquisition.* Unpublished Doctoral dissertation, University of California, San Diego, 1979.

Köhler, W. *Gestalt psychology.* New York: Liveright, 1947.

Lazarus, R. S. A cognitivist's reply to Zajonc on emotion and cognition. *American Psychologist,* 1981, *36,* 222–223.

Mandler, G. Organization and memory. In K. W. Spence & J. T. Spence (Eds.), *The psychology of learning and motivation: Advances in research and theory,* (Vol. I). New York: Academic Press, 1967.

Mandler, G. Organized recall: Individual functions. *Psychonomic Science,* 1968, *13,* 235–236.

Mandler, G. *Mind and emotion.* New York: Wiley, 1975. (a)

Mandler, G. Memory storage and retrieval: Some limits on the reach of attention and consciousness. In P. M. A. Rabbit & S. Dornic (Eds.), *Attention and performance*(V). London: Academic Press, 1975. (b)

Mandler, G. Organization and repetition: Organizational principles with special reference to rote learning. In L. G. Nilsson (Ed.), *Perspectives on memory research.* Hillsdale, N.J.: Lawrence Erlbaum Associates, 1979. (a)

Mandler, G. Thought processes, consciousness, and stress. In V. Hamilton & D. M. Warburton (Eds.), *Human stress and cognition: An information processing approach.* London: Wiley, 1979. (b)

Mandler, G. The structure of value: Accounting for taste. In M. S. Clark & S. T. Fiske (Eds.), *Affect and cognition: The 17th Annual Carnegie Symposium on Cognition.* Hillsdale, N.J.: Lawrence Erlbaum Associates, 1982. (a)

Mandler, G. The integration and elaboration of memory structures. In F. Klix, J. Hoffmann, & E. van der Meer (Eds.), *Cognitive research in psychology* Amsterdam: North Holland, 1982. (b)

Mandler, G., & Graesser, A. C. II. Analyse dimensionelle et le ''locus'' de l'organisation. In S. Ehrlich & E. Tulving (Eds.), *La memoire sémantique.* Paris: Bulletin de Psychologie, 1976. English version: Dimensional analysis and the locus of organization. Technical Report No. 48, Center for Human Information Processing, UCSD, January 1975.

Mandler, G., & Shebo, B. J. Subitizing: An analysis of its component processes. *Journal of Experimental Psychology: General,* 1982, *111,* 1–22.

Marcel, A. J. Conscious and unconscious perception: I. Experiments on visual masking and word perception. *Cognitive Psychology,* 1983, in press. (a)

Marcel, A. J. Conscious and unconscious perception: II. An approach to consciousness. *Cognitive Psychology,* 1983, in press. (b)

McClelland, J. L. *Networks of interacting processors as models of perception and memory.* Unpublished manuscript, 1981.

McClelland, J. L., & Rumelhart, D. E. *An interactive activation model of context effects in perception,* Part I. (CHIP Report # 91), Center for Human Information Processing, University of California, San Diego. La Jolla, Calif., 1980.

Meltzer, R. H. *Retrieval limitations: Output effects.* Unpublished Doctoral thesis, University of California, San Diego, 1971.

Miller, G. A. The magical number seven, plus or minus two: Some limits on our capacity for processing information. *Psychological Review,* 1956, *63,* 81–97.

Miller, G. A., Galanter, E. H., & Pribram, K. *Plans and the structure of behavior.* New York: Holt, 1960.

Natsoulas, T. Consciousness: Consideration of an inferential hypothesis. *Journal for the Theory of Social Behavior,* 1977, *7,* 29–39.

Norman, D. A., & Shallice, T. Attention to action: Willed and automatic control of behavior. (CHIP Technical Report No. 99), Center for Human Information Processing, University of California, San Diego. December, 1980.

Osgood, C. E. The cross-cultural generality of visual–verbal synesthetic tendencies. *Behavioral Science,* 1960, *5,* 146–169.

Osgood, C. E., May, W. H., & Miron, M. S. *Cross-cultural universals of affective meaning.* Urbana: University of Illinois Press, 1975.

Parker, R. E. *The encoding of information in complex pictures.* Unpublished Doctoral dissertation. University of California, San Diego, 1977.

Patterson, K. E. Some characteristics of retrieval limitation in long-term memory. *Journal of Verbal Learning and Verbal Behavior,* 1972, *11,* 685–691.

Patterson, K. E., Meltzer, R. H., & Mandler, G. Inter-response times in categorized free recall. *Journal of Verbal Learning and Verbal Behavior,* 1971, *10,* 417–426.

Posner, M. I., & Boies, S. W. Components of attention. *Psychological Review*, 1971, *78*, 391–408.

Posner, M. I., & Snyder, C. R. R. Attention and cognitive control. In R. L. Solso (Ed.), *Information processing and cognition: The Loyola symposium*. Hillsdale, N.J.: Lawrence Erlbaum Associates, 1975.

Rosch, E. Principles of categorization. In E. Rosch & B. B. Lloyd (Eds.), *Cognition and categorization*. Hillsdale, N.J.: Lawrence Erlbaum Associates, 1978.

Rosch, E., & Mervis, C. Family resemblances: Studies in the internal structure of categories. *Cognitive Psychology*. 1975, *7*, 573–605.

Rumelhart, D. E., & Ortony, A. The representation of knowledge in memory. In R. C. Anderson, R. J. Spiro, & W. E. Montague (Eds.), *Schooling and the acquisition of knowledge*. Hillsdale, N.J.: Lawrence Erlbaum Associates, 1978.

Shallice, T. Dual functions of consciousness. *Psychological Review*, 1972, *79*, 383–393.

Sheinkopf, S. *A comparative study of the affective judgments made by anomic aphasics and normals on a nonverbal task*. Unpublished Doctoral dissertation, Boston University, 1970.

Thatcher, R. W., & John, E. R. *Foundations of cognitive processes*. Hillsdale, N.J.: Lawrence Erlbaum Associates, 1977.

Treisman, A. M., & Gelade, G. A feature-integration theory of attention. *Cognitive Psychology*, 1980, *12*, 97–136.

Warrington, E. K. The selective impairment of semantic memory. *Quarterly Journal of Experimental Psychology*, 1975, *27*, 635–657.

9 Perceptual and Mnemonic Functions: A Psychological Paradigm

Damián Kováč
Institute of Experimental Psychology, Slovak Academy of Sciences

The Slovak school of experimental psychology is characterized with respect to its psycho-regulatory conception, its methodological-integrative approach, and its principle of interfunctionality. The psycho-regulatory paradigm is presented in an historical overview of leading paradigms of experimental psychology. Psychologists study how mental functions regulate behavior under controlled states of the organism in various situations. Experimental projects on visual-spatial discrimination and on word discrimination illustrate our methods of research. Perceptual and mnemonic processes are inferred from the results of some 200 experimental projects carried out at our institute. We expect our future research on these problems to proceed at both microanalytic and macroanalytic levels of analysis.

It may seem old fashioned to be concentrating today upon traditional sensory and perceptual problems when there are exciting new fields, such as artificial intelligence. Yet, we found no more satisfactory alternative when as the first postwar Slovak generation we began to develop a new experimental program for psychology in Czechoslovakia. Naturally, in those years of Pavlovian psychology, perceptual experiments could not be designed in the classical way of Gestalt psychology. Later when we shifted the focus of our research to memory, we felt that we were already within the mainstream of events in cognitive psychology. However, we would have objected had anyone assigned us to the mainstream, for our methods differed from those typically employed by cognitive psychologists.

What then are the special characteristics of our approach? I beg to be excused for commencing my answer with an enumeration of our most general theses:

1. Psychological phenomena need no longer be regarded merely as premises or deductions: they are a plausible part of reality, open to study by the methods generally employed in scientific research.

2. Experience and behavior should not be studied in isolation, as phenomena separate from each other. Nevertheless, psychologists are called to uncover the laws of mental representation and its impact on behavior—primarily in man.

3. Psychology is now at the heart of scientific research on the as yet weakly established science of man.

These three theses lead to the methods we use in our research. They characterize what has been called (e.g., by Lienert, 1974) "The Slovak Experimental School of Psychology."

PSYCHIC REGULATION AND METHODOLOGICAL INTEGRATION

Although it cannot be claimed that general psychological systems have grown out of a dialectical process of history, yet there is a certain continuity in the development of research methods in psychology. This can be appreciated from a consideration of the leading historical paradigms: (1) experience is a function of the stimulus, the original paradigm for mentalism; (2) response is a function of stimulation, the paradigm for the behavioristic revolution; and (3) behavior is a function of both stimulation and organismic factors, the paradigm for various neo-behaviorisms. All of this reflects a faith in Laplacean determinism, with classical mechanics as the model of a scientific theory. The original single-factor paradigms permitted the development of psychological laws, such as the Weber-Fechner function relating stimulus to experience and Ebbinghaus' laws in which memory for stimuli is manifested in overt responses. However, it is now clear that such oversimplified formulations ignore important aspects of the psychological processes. The same stimulus elicits different responses, depending on the state of the organism. Living systems have laws of their own, a freedom to partially overcome the basic determinism.

A classic example of the application of a two-factor paradigm to sensory perception can be found in the review chapter on reaction time by Woodworth and Schlosberg (1954), with its three subchapters entitled "Stimulus Dependence," "Organismic Dependence," and "Correlations and Uses." However, the ecological validity of even this sophisticated research must be questioned in the light of what we now know about how "perceptual promptness" combines with various personality traits (such as aggressiveness) to determine performance, as in driving by visual guidance. Furthermore, as long as organismic factors are conceived strictly in neurophysiological terms, prospects are dim for genuine psychological laws. Recent investigations have shown the usefulness of including among organismic factors the psychic image of future behavior (Shvyrkov, 1978). We must not substitute for an inadequate physicalistic paradigm a simplistic biological paradigm that excludes the psychic.

We must cease treating psychology as the science of behavior and instead start treating it as a science of man (cf., Ananiev, 1969). Among other things, man is a perceiving and remembering personality, a multiplane reality, a bio-psycho-social entity. Some of this can be seen in the well-known approaches of Lewin (1978) and Fraisse (1978).

At our institute, we have been concerned about such questions and how different answers might affect our experimental research and also our theoretical interpretations. Our answers are best revealed by a very general description of some of our recent research.

RECENT RESEARCH

Consider first a laboratory experiment on subjective uncertainty and memory. Our hypotheses concerned how the effects of different degrees of mental uncertainty, assumed to result from different experimental manipulations, would affect recall and recognition. We attempted to manipulate uncertainty by having the experimenter comment either positively, negatively, or not at all, upon the performance of our subjects (see Fig. 9.1). Thus, our interpretation of the effect of these comments was in terms of states of subjective uncertainty. Our interest here is not in the results (memory was affected by our experimental manipulations) but rather in how we interpreted them.

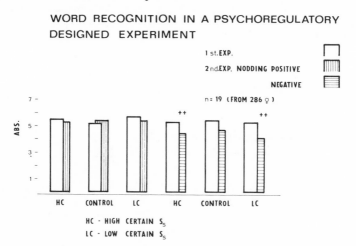

FIG. 9.1.   Recognition of words by subjects with: (HC) high subjective uncertainty, (LC) low subjective uncertainty, and (CO) control group. (For details, see Kovac, 1980b.)

In contrast to the simpler paradigms that have dominated the history of experimental psychology, our interpretation assumes that behavior is a function of the stimulus, the biological organism, and certain mental states. What are these mental states? We conceive them to be (cf., Lomov, 1981) the subject's active reflections as they regulate his behavior, adapting his organism to the environment, actively changing the environment, and in perfecting himself as a personality living in an environment (Kováč, 1980a). Whatever criticisms this paradigm might evoke, it is unique insofar as it is genuinely psychological in its concerns.

With this paradigm, the choice of experimental methods is restricted to: (1) direct access to mental representations, as they are actually experienced or stored, and (2) recording behavior regulated by these representations. Thus, we have a group of self-reporting methods and a group of recording methods. Our paradigm requires us to integrate them to discover the laws of psychology, as we conceive them. I can illustrate how we do this and how it is related to our psychoregulatory conception by describing a concrete research project.

This research investigated how conclusions about visual-spatial discrimination are affected by whether the research takes account of the subject's *experience*. In one experiment, subjects sorted cards into piles in accordance with whether an intermediate point on the card was closer to a point to its left, to its right, or exactly in the middle. In a second experiment, the card-sorting was the same but subjects also had to rate on a five-point scale their degree of uncertainty (see Fig. 9.2). Had we been following a traditional paradigm, we would have done just one experiment or just the other. By doing both experiments, we believe that we are including the subjective state of the subject in our analysis of the effects of stimulus relationships upon behavior. We believe that subjective states are directly accessible to the subjects for rating. We also believe, however, that this can yield laws that are genuinely psychological only by integrating these subjective states with the effects of stimuli on discriminatory behavior. Only by such integration can the entire reflexive-regulatory process between stimulus and behavior be understood.

PERCEPTION AND MEMORY IN AN
INTERFUNCTIONAL CONTEXT

Using this integration of research methods as the basis for our psycho-regulatory approach, we have completed some 200 research projects at the Institute of Experimental Psychology, Slovak Academy of Sciences. Naturally, our earlier work did not follow this paradigm completely. Moreover, a new principle which we call *interfunctionality* has come to guide the major part of our research on perception and memory. We deduce interfunctionality from the dialectical category of world unity (Lomov, 1982). The basic idea is that mental phenomena

VISUO SPATIAL DISCRIMINATION

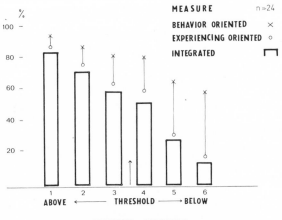

FIG. 9.2.   Visual-spatial discrimination expressed as a measure of performance (card sorting—asterisks), self-report (subjective uncertainty—circles), and as an integrated measure (columns) derived from weighting both measures according to the psychoregulatory principle. (For details see Kovac, 1980b.)

originate in man at various levels of reality. In contrast to multifactorial research, interfunctional research presumes three stages: (1) an experimental search for intrapsychic relations that both precede and follow the phenomena being studied; (2) an experimental search for the origin of these phenomena; and (3) an experimental search for the various levels of the regulatory system as it affects behavior—i.e., the psychological structure under investigation. Fig. 9.3 illustrates this notion of interfunctionality. Thus, in interfunctional studies of perception and memory, we investigate how these fit into a framework of other cognitive processes, how they relate intrapsychically to each other. Our aim is to uncover dependencies between various aspects of the stimulus situation and various organismic variables as they cooperate in the "birth of psychic images." The ultimate goal is to reveal laws describing how the regulatory action of mental representation determines behavior.

In the study of perception, our experiments have led to improved interfunctional interpretations (Kováč, 1970, 1980b). Changes in the physical stimulus provide only potential information for perception; with the higher animals, and especially with man, one must consider both the probabilistic character of the stimulus and its meaning, including its social context. Organismic factors enter into all principles of perception. The sensory information in the stimulus is but the raw material out of which the subject forms percepts in accordance with his individual experience and social conventions. Memory also enters into percep-

DIFFERENTIATED SCHEME OF PSYCHOLOGICAL METACATEGORIES

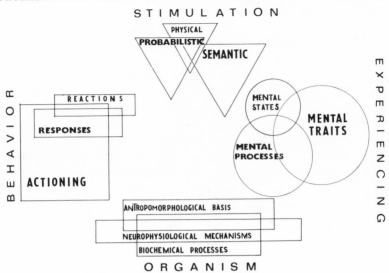

FIG. 9.3.   Scheme of four meta-categories differentiated by variables commonly used by experimental psychologists.

tion. Learning produces perceptual schemas and sets. In sum, perception is never simply a base for cognitive activity but is itself one of the higher cognitive processes.

As with perception, we have attempted to conceptualize the results of our research on memory within the interfunctional framework (Halmiova, 1981; Ruisel, 1980; Sipos 1978). We doubt that in the case of man memory can be explained solely in terms of underlying biochemical and neurophysiological principles. The initial functioning of memory as a mirror gives way to semantic memory which in turn makes possible categorical-systemic memory. Memory constitutes that subsystem in man's cognitive functions that connects his phylogenetic attributes to the new and diverse ontogenetic attributes of human personality.

Memory is manifestly more dependent upon organismic factors than it is on perception. Certain components of memory are already fully developed during the preschool age, whereas others are still changing in response to sociocultural conditions during middle adulthood. There is a kind of neurodynamic compensatory effect: Persons with greater strength of excitation tend to perform better on memory tasks, but persons with a weakness of excitation tend to perform more reliably.

Memory can improve through partial recall, intentional forgetting, and other laboratory techniques; however, it can also improve through selective processing of stimuli, organizing information in storage and in recall, and through social contact. A crucial problem for memory research is the transfer from short-term to long-term storage. Although numerous models are available for describing this process, there are unfortunately few valid facts.

We regard memory processes as subsystems of intellectual functions of the type measured by intelligence tests. However, we find that the relationships between memory and intelligence are not straightforward: the role of intellectual abilities in memory grows with the difficulty of the tasks and is more striking with recall than with recognition.

We also find that memory is in a complex intrapsychic relationship with personality. Recall is clearly selective, sensitive to the hierarchy of human needs, to the subject's interests, and to the particular nature of the recall task. The well-known generalizations about the effect of anxiety upon memory performance require modification in view of our experiments showing that although anxiety does tend to lower the score, anxious subjects perform above the norm on free recall and recognize more details in tests of recognition. We also find that although pathology affects recall more than recognition, the magnitude of this difference depends on the level and overall intactness of the subject's intellectual abilities.

In summary, our research supports the view that perception acts as a mental regulator of the response components of behavior by which man maintains the indispensable contact between outside environment and inner conditions. The function of memory is to serve man as a permanent mental regulator, affecting all components of behavior, making possible the continuity of man as a human being and thereby the possibility of his own improvement.

WHERE DO WE GO FROM HERE?

The Institute of Experimental Psychology, Slovak Academy of Sciences, along with the related psychological teams in Czechoslovakia whose work the Academy coordinates, will continue to investigate the cognitive functions of personality—conceived as regulators of various activities. Our work will not be artificially restricted to laboratory problems but will be concerned with behaviors that occur in everyday life.

I assume that basic cognitive processes will, even in the Year 2000, still be the central concern of psychological research.

I also assume that, following known trends in other domains of science, research on perception and memory will proceed along two extreme approaches: microanalysis at one extreme, macroanalysis or synthesis at the other. Microanalysis is attractive in that it evolves constantly more sophisticated techniques for research and growing cooperation of psychologists with designers, linguists, neuropsychologists, biochemists, and others. Macroanalysis represents the natural consequence of psychology's coming of age after a century of development. Macroanalysis also reflects the demands of practice. Psychology seems to be aiming at a greater unification of theory. It also aims at practical applications. The nomothetic character of experimental psychology has been joined, sometimes in apparent competition, by an idiographic concern with applications—with particular success in the clinical domain.

And it is this extension of experimental methods that may ultimately play the decisive role, not as a deadlock but as a *via regia* in the historical process toward the unification of psychology.

REFERENCES

Ananiev, B. G. *Chelovek kak predmet poznanya*. Leningrad: Izd. LGU, 1969.

Fraisse, P. Psychologie: Science de l'homme ou science du comportement? *XXI Congres International de Psychologie, Actes*. Paris: Presses universitaires, 1978.

Halmiová, O. *Pamäťová hľadacia činnosť*. Bratislava: Veda, Vyd. SAV, 1981.

Kováč, D. Problema psikhicheskoy regulyatsiyi: Metodologiya, teoriya, eksperiment. *Psikhologichesky Zhurnal*, 1980, *1*, 47–57. (a)

Kováč, D. Psychická regulácia a poznávacie procesy. In *Psychologické výskumy v ČSSR: 1976–1980*. Praha: ČSPS, 1980. (b)

Lewin, K. *Principles of topological psychology*. New York: McGraw-Hill, 1936.

Lienert, G. A. *Closing speech at the third Meeting of psychologists from Danubian countries*. Smolenice, 1974.

Lomov, B. F. Laws in psychology. *Studia Psychol.*, *23*, 303–315, 1981.

Ruisel, I. *Interfunkčné vzťahy osobnosti a percepčno-mnemických procesov*. Záverečná správa VIII-5-2. Bratislava: Vyd. SAV, 1980.

Shvyrkov, V. B. *Neyrofiziologicheskoe izucheniye sistemnykh mekhanizmov povedeniya*. Moskva: Izd. Nauka, 1978.

Šípoš, I. *Pamät' a znovupoznanie*. Bratislava: Veda, Vyd. SAV, 1978.

Woodworth, R., & Schlosberg, H. *Experimental psychology*. 2nd edit., Methuen, London 1954.

10 Perceptual and Judgmental Relativity

Allen Parducci
University of California, Los Angeles, USA

Like so many students of psychology, I came to the field looking for answers to questions that probably cannot be answered. In my case, the primary question· was concerned with the relational character of value experiences. If the pleasantness or painfulness of any particular event is determined by how that event compares with other events we have experienced, does it not follow that there must always be an even balance between pleasure and pain? The logic of this despairing inquiry goes something like this: Life is a succession of events, some of which can be characterized with respect to experienced value (pleasantness, goodness, etc.). A succession of highly valued experiences raises our standards so that what was once satisfying becomes dissatisfying. The psychological process of comparison guarantees an even balance between positive and negative experiences.

Before studying psychology, I thought that this rather debilitating philosophy possessed an a priori status. It just had to be true, by definition. A proper understanding of what constitutes a value experience seemed to entail that the degree of value—positive or negative—depends on comparison with the average level of prior events.

Adaptation-Level Theory

In psychology, I found a formal representation of this notion of an even balance in the theory of adaptation level developed by the late Harry Helson (1947, 1964). The essence of adaptation-level theory is that for any contextual domain of experience there is a neutral point, a stimulus devoid of experienced value, which is located at the mean of all stimuli constituting that contextual domain:

$$AL = \Sigma \frac{s}{N},\qquad(1)$$

in which AL is the adaptation level (viz., the particular stimulus value that would be judged "neutral"), and $\Sigma\ s/N$ is the mean of the stimulus values (psychologically scaled—e.g., log transformations of the physical values of the stimuli). The judged value of any particular stimulus is either positive or negative, depending on whether it is above or below adaptation level; its degree of positivity or negativity is directly proportional to its difference from adaptation-level:

$$J_i = s_i - AL. \tag{2}$$

The most distressing implication of this theory (one that Helson apparently never drew himself) is that just as deviations of scores from their mean sum algebraically to zero, so the judged values must also, according to adaptation-level theory, sum to zero:

$$\Sigma\ J = \Sigma\ s - N(\Sigma \frac{s}{N}) = 0. \tag{3}$$

Although there might be runs of positive or negative value experiences (judgments), these must eventually balance out when life stops its unbroken climb or descent. In the long run, the overall balance would level out to equal amounts of pleasure and pain.[1]

For me, the most novel feature of adaptation-level theory was its empirical testability (falsifiability). Helson showed how crucial experimental tests could be performed using simple psychophysical stimuli: One had only to obtain category ratings for a series of such stimuli and then determine whether these ratings were consistent with the quantitative predictions of adaptation-level theory. Strong tests were possible because the context of psychophysical stimuli affecting the judgment of any particular stimulus appears to be largely restricted to the set of stimuli presented in the experimental session.

I do not propose to review the whole history of this research. What is most important for my present purposes is that the notions I had entertained about a necessary balance of positive and negative value experiences could perhaps be disproven by experimental research. Rationalistic philosophy seemed to have given way to empirical science!

Note that I was not bothered by the fact that Helson was primarily concerned with perceptual rather than value experiences, how heavy a particular weight felt rather than how pleasant a day seemed. The a priori argument for the relativity of judgment applied equally to perceptions, to experienced values, or to any other type of dimensional categorizations. Helson's tests with lifted weights were therefore just as interesting to me as Beebe–Center's earlier tests with the pleasantness of odors or colors. Indeed, adaptation-level theory can be considered a later, more quantitative, and more general version of Beebe–Center's (1929) law

---

[1]This argument is developed further in Brickman and Campbell (1971) and in Parducci (1968, 1973).

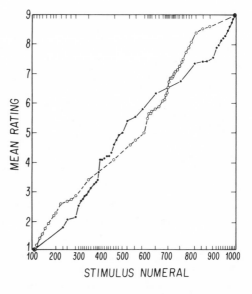

FIG. 10.1   Mean ratings of two sets of numerals (spacing for open-point set shown on upper abscissa, for solid-point set on lower abscissa). Rating functions steeper where numerals are more closely spaced. Intertwining functions inconsistent with adaptation-level theory (adapted from Birnbaum, 1974).

of affective equilibrium: "The affective value of the experiential correlate of a stimulus varies conversely with the sum of the affective values of those experiences preceding this correlate which constitute with it a unitary temporal group."

What became most important for me was that the experimental test be conducted under circumstances that restrict comparisons to those stimuli under the control of the experimenter. Psychophysical experiments using the method of single stimuli seem to meet this requirement. For example, subjects in such experiments are discomfitted by having to rate the very first stimulus in the series selected for presentation: With what are they supposed to compare it? As a consequence, the initial rating is largely independent of the particular physical value presented. Subjects do compare the second stimulus with the first; and after just a few presentations they have already established a complete scale of judgment—one that is obviously dependent on the particular set of stimuli already presented.

Even better than psychophysics, by this criterion of experimental control of context, is the judgment of numerical magnitude. I found that if I presented different sets of numerals (with the members of each set listed on a single page), the rating of the magnitude of any particular numeral seemed completely determined by its relationship to the other numerals on the same page. With such complete and easy experimental control, adaptation-level theory has proven easy to falsify.

Perhaps the clearest type of negative instance is illustrated by the rating scales plotted in Fig. 10.1. Note that the abscissa represents simply the numerals printed on a page, with 100 as one endpoint of the range, 1000 as the other endpoint, and 550 exactly in the middle. It was common practice in adaptation-level research to represent the stimuli by log transformations of their physical values. A log or any other monotonic transformation might thus be applied to the abscissa of Fig. 10.1 without doing violence to adaptation-level theory; but there is no single transformation that could make both these functions linear (as entailed by Equation 2, earlier), not even if one also transformed the ordinate (i.e., assigned different numerals to represent the categories). These double cross-overs appear irretrievably inconsistent with the basic principles of adaptation-level theory.[2]

Parametric manipulation of the frequency distribution of numerals (Parducci, Calfee, Marshall, & Davidson, 1960) showed that rating scales for numerical magnitude are not determined by the simple averaging process posited by adaptation-level theory. Manipulation of the stimulus mean had little effect when the median and midpoint were held constant. However, independent manipulation of these other stimulus parameters had large systematic effects on the rating scale.

Range-Frequency Theory

The key to a more adequate account of judgmental relativity is illustrated by Fig. 10.2, which plots the ranks of the stimuli in each of the two sets whose empirical ratings were plotted in Fig. 10.1. These ranks are a priori in the sense that they do not depend on empirical data. Nevertheless they show, in exaggerated form, the same intertwining relationship found for the empirical ratings. This similarity of form cannot be accidental.

What it suggests is that subjects tend to follow the principle of assigning the same number of contextual stimuli to each category. It is as though there had to be just as many small numerals as large ones (and, let us generalize freely, just as many unpleasant experiences as pleasant ones). Have I rejected Helson's theory only to adopt another principle of equal balance?

Some 30 different sets were used in the experiment on judgments of numerical magnitude (Parducci et al., 1960). Although the data were generally consistent with the principle that equal numbers of numerals tended to be placed in each rating category, the nonlinearity of the rating scales was never as exaggerated as the plots of the ranks of the stimuli in the respective sets. Just as in the comparison of Fig. 10.1 and 10.2, the actual rating functions were always closer to linearity. This suggested that another principle of judgment was linearizing the empirical rating scale.

That other principle asserts that subjects use their rating categories to divide the stimulus range into equal subranges, with each category corresponding to one of the subranges. For example, if the numerals in a set ranged from 100 to 1000, those between 100 and 200 would be rated "1—very very small" on a nine-category scale, those between 200 and 300 would be rated "2—very small," and

---

[2]An algebraic demonstration of this point may be found in Birnbaum (1974).

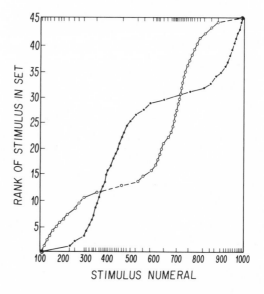

FIG. 10.2. Ranks of numerals in respective sets for which ratings were plotted in Fig. 10.1. Ranks exaggerate intertwining of rating functions, showing tendency toward equal-frequency scales.

so on up to numerals in the subrange of 900 to 1000 which would be rated "9—very very large." In conditions with only six categories, each category would be applied to a subrange of 150, that is, (1000-100)/6.

This second principle leaves room for optimism and also for pessimism about the balance of pleasure and pain, depending on one's view of life. The optimist can imagine a life in which events are concentrated near the top of the range. Insofar as subjective evaluations divide the range into equal subranges, most events would be experienced as pleasant. On the other hand, any piling up of events near the bottom of the range would tip the scale to the unpleasant side. Life would be an even balance only insofar as events were symmetrically distributed around the midpoint of the range.

Although no subject conforms strictly to the equal-frequency principle nor to the equal-subrange principle, the actual rating scales can always be represented as a compromise between these two principles. Subsequent work with psychophysical dimensions, such as lifted weight, loudness, pitch, numerousness of dots, and visual size, led to a simple algebraic model for describing a compromise between these two principles:

$$J_i = wR_i + (1 - w)F_i, \tag{4}$$

in which J_i is the judgment of Stimulus i, R_i is what the judgment of that stimulus would be if subjects were dividing the range into equal subranges, F_i is what it would be if the same number of stimuli were assigned to each successive category, and w is a weighting factor between 0 and 1, representing the relative influence of the range and frequency principles.

The range principle can represented as follows:

$$R_i = (s_i - s_{min})/(s_{max} - s_{min}), \tag{5}$$

which identifies the range value for Stimulus i as the ratio of the difference between its stimulus value, s_i, and the value of lower endpoint of the contextual set, s_{min}, divided by the range of the stimulus set (that is, by the difference between the upper endpoint, s_{max}, and the lower endpoint).

The frequency principle can be operationalized by a parallel equation:

$$F_i = r_i - 1/N - 1, \tag{6}$$

in which the frequency value of the ith stimulus, F_i, is equal to the difference between its rank in the contextual set, r_i, and the rank of the lowest stimulus, 1, divided by the difference between the rank of the highest stimulus (N when there are N contextual stimuli) and 1.

In combination, Equations 4, 5, and 6 permit an interesting algebraic deduction about the overall balance of judgment:

$$\bar{J} = w[\bar{s} - (s_{max} - s_{min})/2]/s_{max} - s_{min}, \tag{7}$$

which says that the mean of all the judgments is proportional to the difference between the mean of all the contextual values minus their midpoint, divided by their range.[3] Statisticians may not recognize this as an orthodox measure of skewness, but it correlates almost perfectly (though negatively) with more conventional measures. Because its constant of proportionality (w) is the weighting of the range principle, Equation 7 asserts that the overall mean of the judgments is limited in how far positive (or negative) it can go by the degree to which judgments are reflecting the equal-frequency principle.

When one leaves the domain of simple numerals on a page and turns to more orthodox psychophysical dimensions, it is not so clear how the stimulus values should be measured to determine the range values. However, one can infer range values from empirical judgments by substituting the latter along with the a priori frequency values into Equation 4. This can be done for one set of stimuli, and the resulting range values can then be used to predict the ratings for other sets of stimuli with the same endpoints. This was the procedure followed for the four sets of squares whose ratings are shown in Fig. 10.3 (in this case, the range values were obtained from ratings of a rectangular set, with w assumed to be

---

[3]In presenting these equations in terms of judgments, I have omitted the transformation from subjective (internal) judgment to overt category rating. This is assumed to be linear, with an additive constant equal to the numeral assigned to represent the bottom category (or middle category in the case of Equation 4) and a multiplicative constant equal to the range of these assigned numerals (usually the category ranks).

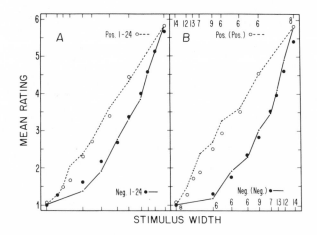

FIG. 10.3.   Predicted functions and empirical ratings (points) for sets of nine squares varying with respect to spacing of sizes (Panel A) or with respect to both spacing of sizes and relative frequency of presentation (Panel B). Functions predicted from range-frequency model (Equation 4), with range values inferred from a rectangular (i.e., equally spaced) set and with equal weighting of range and frequency values ($w = 0.5$). Ratings reflect direction and degree of skewing in accordance with range-frequency theory (from Parducci & Perrett, 1971).

0.5). Although the ratings of particular sizes are predictably lower for the negatively skewed sets, the mean of all ratings is higher (because the higher ratings are made so much more frequently). In fact, the mean of all ratings is more than half a category-step higher for the Negatively Skewed set in the left panel and almost a full category-step higher for the Neg–Neg set in the right panel (where the effects of frequency are added to those of spacing).

All the ratings were used to obtain the best-fit weighting ($w = 0.4$) and range values for the concentrations of sweetness portrayed in Fig. 10.4. Again, the

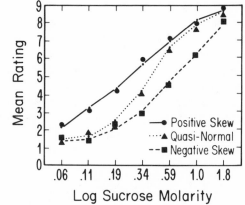

FIG. 10.4.   Ratings of sweetness for seven concentrations of sucrose presented in three different distributions, with relative frequencies as follows:
    Positive Skew (7– 4-3-3-2-1-1),
    Quasi-Normal (1-2-4-7-4-2-1),
    Negative Skew (1-1-2-3-3-4-7).
Data fitted by range-frequency model, Equation 4, with $w = 0.4$ (From Riskey, Parducci, & Beauchamp, 1979.)

power of the range-frequency model is illustrated by the accuracy with which differences between scales are captured using the single empirical constant, w. And again, the overall mean of the ratings is higher for the Negatively Skewed set, lower for the Positively Skewed set. The perfect balance that I had assumed to be a necessary feature of judgmental relativity is found only for symmetrical distributions. The way to get a high overall mean of judgments is to stack the stimuli near the top of the range, whatever the absolute values of the endpoints defining the range.

Implications of Range-Frequency Theory

Faced with these findings, I reluctantly abandoned my earlier commitment to the perfect balance between pleasure and pain. The a priori assumptions that I had made were completely undermined by the empirical results of experiments in which the entire stimulus context seemed under experimental control. Philosophy had to be revised in the light of science.

But still faithful to my original concerns, I have not wanted to end with the rejection of philosophy. In terms of the Utilitarian definition of happiness as the overall balance of pleasure over pain (Bentham, 1789), Equation 7 provides a new rule: Happiness is a negatively-skewed distribution! This assumes that everyday value experiences reflect the same relativistic principles as do category ratings in laboratory experiments.

Can such a rule have clear implications for everyday life? To preview the remainder of this section, my answer is "no"—at least not in a strict sense. More generally, I want to argue that none of our experimentally derived principles have clear implications for the psychology of everyday life. And yet, well-controlled research in the laboratory constitutes an attractive source of hypotheses.

Consider how the rule of skewing might be applied to experiences outside the laboratory. If we are unhappy with respect to any particular domain of our lives (for example, with our material circumstances), if our experiences in this or any other domain seem to balance out on the negative side, the rule of skewing tells us that the set of events constituting our context for judgment is positively skewed. But it does not tell us what these events are or how we can change their skewing. It may be difficult to identify the context when it is not the particular stimuli selected by an experimenter. What is the range of incomes against which we compare our own incomes? Most of us poor scholars do not compare ourselves with the very rich; we do not feel impoverished when we learn that some corporation president has a salary of a million dollars a year. However, our sense of affluence is affected by invidious comparisons with others much closer to ourselves, others who are getting what we might well have gotten.

The basic difficulty in applying laboratory principles is one of establishing rules of correspondence or bridge principles (Hemple, 1966). In the present example, how can one relate "context," a theoretical concept, to the particular events affecting our experiences in everyday life? Perhaps the endpoints of a real-life context might be identified by noting which events elicit our most extreme judgments, such as those that are most satisfying and those that are most dissatisfying.

The rule of skewing suggests that those who are unhappy should either increase the frequency of events near the top of their range (but that is likely to be precisely what they have been trying unsuccessfully to do) or else drop the top of the range from their context for judgment (i.e., lower their standards). Note that these two possibilities are in apparent opposition. We all assume that we can achieve more if we set higher standards, keeping some upper endpoint or goal in mind so that we are discontent with what we have already achieved. However, achieving more is then likely to be the cue for still higher aspirations which in turn create dissatisfaction with our actual achievements.

Suppose that unhappy people were to opt for the second route, lowering their standards. In laboratory experiments, the physical range of contextual stimuli can be narrowed by dropping out the higher values; but even with psychophysical stimuli, subjects may continue to maintain the same scale of judgment—as though the missing values were continuing to function as part of the context (Parducci, 1956). Even if we could spell out the particular conditions that produce restriction of the contextual range in the laboratory, it does not seem that we would be able to predict when such restriction would occur in everyday life. The problem is that although we may understand in a general way some basic principles of judgment, we cannot know how to apply them to complicated situations. And the contexts for everyday value judgments are extraordinarily complicated. Not only can they include the publicly observable events that other people might interpret as affecting our judgments but also the imaginary experiences, such as pleasureable (or fearful) anticipations of events that we may never have actually encountered. It would seem particularly difficult to allow for imaginary events in our attempts to understand everyday value experiences.

This is not an argument against using experimental research as a springboard for speculation about judgments outside the laboratory. My argument is not that we should avoid such speculation, but rather that we should not think that practical applications follow logically from our experimentally derived principles. The record is replete with examples of how such speculation can go awry.

Consider a familiar example from the conditioning laboratory: the principle of reinforcement. Although learning theorists do not agree on what reinforcers have in common (other than that they reinforce), the success of experimental psychologists in reinforcing the behavior of laboratory rats and pigeons has encouraged educators and social philsophers to apply the same principle to the classroom. In America, teachers were instructed to find positive reinforcers that they could give immediately after their students had responded appropriately. Praise was identified as a reinforcer analogous to food, the "creative" productions of the child as the responses analogous to bar-presses and key-pecks. Punishment, which did not seem to have desirable effects in the laboratory, was to be avoided.

The results have been impressive. No longer are children beaten by teachers in America. Instead, it is the teachers who are beaten by their students. In my own city, Los Angeles, teachers receive extra remuneration, called "combat pay," for serving in the less-disciplined schools (like serving in a war zone). Meanwhile, the level of academic achievement shifts progressively downward in America. This decline is substantiated not merely by the testimonials of nostalgic professors but also by 18 years of successive drops in scores on the best of our standardized tests. The drop in the United States is across the entire distribution, even the higher scorers achieving less now than the higher scorers of two decades ago.

It would be unfair to credit all of this decline to improper application of the principle of reinforcement. The notion that children are happier when you set lower standards for them (as suggested by the relativistic approach to judgment) also deserves some credit, as does the Freudian notion that children are less anxious when they can express their repressed feelings. Unfortunately, I can find no hard evidence that happiness is replacing achievement. Indeed, one of my university students gave me a psychological interpretation of why the new freedom may not even encourage the sense of freedom. Hearing her complain about parental restrictions, I pointed out how much more freedom her generation has in comparison with earlier generations. "Apply your own principles," she retorted, "it is precisely because we are now so free that even the least restriction has become insupportable!"

Future Research on Judgmental Relativity

Because this relativism seems so basic to the judgment process but also so alien to the absolutist way people ordinarily think about their value experiences, I hope that it will come to occupy a bigger place in the experimental psychology of the future. Everyone gives lip service to judgmental relativity but no one does anything about it. Psychologists could make an interesting contribution just by dramatizing the extent to which life is ruled by this kind of relativism. However, our contribution might be more interesting if we could come to a deeper understanding of how it works in those laboratory situations where we do appear to have considerable experimental control.

Theoretical developments of the not too distant future should make present notions about judgmental relativity seem quaintly superficial. For example, I was completely surprised to find that the relative weighting of the range tendency (w in Equation 4) varies directly with the number of categories (Parducci, 1981). Although the absence of the number-of-categories effect with simultaneous presentation suggests that this effect somehow depends on memory, its proper interpretation remains a mystery. As one consequence, I have been pushing research on "open" scales in which subjects are free to choose their own categories and to use as many or few as they wish. I used to fear that such freedom would lead only to anarchy, but it turns out that open scales are not much harder to derive than conventional scales (i.e., when subjects have been restricted to a specified set of categories). Preliminary research suggests that open scales show at least as much sensitivity to skewness as do conventional five-category scales—which is how many categories the typical subject generates when using open scales.

When thinking about practical applications, the concern with what gets included in the context or domain of comparison looms large. This is the problem of *anchoring,* studied most thoroughly by my co-editor, Viktor Sarris. In his parametric research, Sarris has studied the effects of interpolating unjudged stimuli into the regular series presented for judgment. What his research demonstrates is that although the anchoring effects of these interpolated stimuli increase with increasing distance from the regular series, beyond a certain optimal distance they exert progressively less influence on the scale of judgment (Sarris, 1967, 1976). It seems useful to think of these anchors as combining with the extreme values of the regular series (perhaps as a weighted average in which the anchors are weighted less with increasing distance) to establish the endpoints of the subjective range. The same account may apply to the decreased anchoring effects of whole sets of unjudged stimuli when these are too distant from the regular series. Recent research (Sarris & Parducci, 1978) is consistent with this interpretation, and I hope the problem can be pursued further.[4] We need greater understanding of what constitutes a contextual domain of judgment such that the component events are evaluated independently of events in other domains.

The possibility of natural anchoring at the center of the scale, for example the break-even point in gambling (Marsh & Parducci, 1978), raises interesting problems for any contextual theory of judgment. Is this simply a matter of transfer of a well-established context from the past, or is it a striking exception to the general claim for judgmental relativity? There has been too little work on transfer of the effects of past contexts. Again, I hope that this problem will be pursued experimentally.

Other recent research suggests that there may sometimes be an interaction between range and frequency effects (Parducci, Knobel, & Thomas, 1976). With highly skewed distributions, the effective endpoint of the range may be extended out beyond those extreme stimuli that are presented most frequently. It is as though their high frequency suggests that stimuli still more extreme might eventually be presented. More generally, I would like to see further research on the relationship between the range of physical values and the psychological range that we infer from subjects' category ratings.

---

[4]This and other problems of anchoring are discussed in a forthcoming chapter (Parducci, in press).

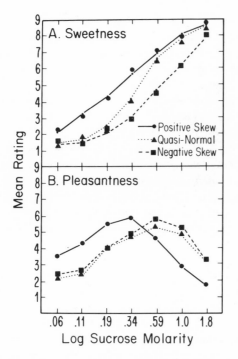

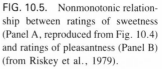

FIG. 10.5. Nonmonotonic relationship between ratings of sweetness (Panel A, reproduced from Fig. 10.4) and ratings of pleasantness (Panel B) (from Riskey et al., 1979).

There is one property of hedonic scales that creates particular difficulties for the range-frequency theory of judgment. This is apparent when there is a *nonmonotonic* relationship between the hedonic ratings and the physical dimension on which the stimuli vary. For example in the research on sweetness by Riskey et al. (1979), ratings of pleasantness were found to be highest at intermediate levels of sacharine concentration (Panel B of Fig. 10.5). Although the point of greatest pleasantness shifted as expected with the skewness of the contextual set, it is not clear how the particular ratings of pleasantness could be derived from a range-frequency analysis. Given my philosophical concern with value judgments, it should be clear that I am urging continued research on this problem.

My own interests have been increasingly devoted to translating range-frequency principles into a theory of happiness. Certainly, it is quite a jump from psychophysical experiments to speculation about the conditions for a positive balance of pleasure over pain. The crucial assumption is that everyday value experiences can be understood as internal judgments, even in the absence of overt ratings.

If experienced values do follow the relativistic principles of category ratings, the happy life is one in which the contextual distributions of values are skewed negatively. The practical problem is to establish the conditions for this skewing. It was experimental research that convinced me of the critical role of skewing. But I do agree with Gergen (Chapter 3) that in trying to understand how this might work in the real world, the primary value of the research may be to *vivify* particular theoretical conceptions. Though Gergen encourages modesty about the experimental research, he is liberating in his suggestion that *all* such research amounts to the promotion of values. The values that I want to promote are those summed up by the word ''happiness.''

The Future of Experimental Psychology

In trying to imagine the more general character of the experimental psychology of the twenty-first century, my first concern is that it should remain firmly rooted in skepticism. The experimental approach must not yield to the wave of antiintellectual faith—whether in creationism (anti-Darwinism), astrology, diet, or exercise—that currently threatens even our universities. We must continue to ask for evidence. Professor Eysenck, years ago, showed us the importance of experimental design for evaluating the effects of psychotherapy. This kind of enlightened skepticism may be the chief benefit of training in experimental psychology. I hope that such training will be strengthened, even for those students who will never perform laboratory experiments themselves. But we should also apply the experimental approach to the evaluation of this kind of training—in particular, we should be more concerned with how well it transfers to practical situations outside the particular courses in which such training is offered.

I am not courageous enough to predict the directions experimental psychology will have taken 20 years hence, and none of the other contributors to this book seems anxious to make the attempt either. Our interest seems to be more in what psychologists *should* be doing rather than in trying to predict what they actually will be doing. But I would like to discuss some of the hopes for the experimental psychology of the future expressed by other participants in this volume.

Although my own interests are often practical or applied (what could be more pragmatic than the concern with happiness?), I am uneasy about the appeals for ''representative design.'' How can principles generated from even the most representative of experiments escape the hazards intrinsic to any attempt to apply laboratory-generated principles to everyday life? Furthermore, there is an added problem of confounding. The purpose of experimental design is to unconfound conditions that are ordinarily confounded. Insofar as we select experimental conditions that are ''representative,'' we are more likely to be deceived by this confounding. For example, earlier research supporting the mean as the predictor of adaptation level employed representative frequency distributions of stimuli in which the mean, median, and midpoint of the stimuli were hopelessly confounded. It required independent manipulation of these parameters (i.e., the study of some most *unrepresentative* distributions) to establish the range-frequency account of contextual effects. An historical model for unrepresentative experimental design was provided by the brothers Weber, who generated their laws of wave motion not by observing the confused and hopelessly complicated waves out in open sea but rather by unrepresentative manipulations of waves in their own little tub of brandy. The one brother, Ernst, then applied this approach to the problem of discrimination, generating what is perhaps the first experimentally derived, quantitative law of psychology—one that has outlasted so many of the "laws" that came later.

I am pleased by the surprisingly philosophical tone of some of these chapters. Experimental psychology has already had its flirtation with "dustbowl empiricism." Its prospects for an inspiring relationship seem more promising with contemporary versions of the older discipline from which it sprang. Philosophy has two virtues that compliment corresponding vices in psychology: (1) attention to those psychological problems that have concerned thinking people since antiquity; and (2) a realistic modesty about what can be accomplished. In his chapter, Professor Gergen emphasises the limits of knowledge. Psychology, even experimental psychology, has purported to go so far beyond these limits that it loses credibility. A modest consideration of the possibility that our most important role may be as generators of interesting hypotheses would make it easier for us to concentrate upon matters of enduring concern.

Experimental psychologists should feel free to speculate about the complicated world outside their laboratories, just like everyone else. Insofar as our theories have weathered tests within the laboratory, our proposals for applying these theories to everyday affairs may even have some claim to special attention. However, it seems to me that we should try to remain clear about the hazards of this kind of adventure.

REFERENCES

Beebe–Center, J. G. The law of affective equilibrium. *American Journal of Psychology*, 1929, *41*, 54–69.

Bentham, J. *The Principles of morals and legislation*, 1789.

Birnbaum, M. H. Using contextual effects to derive psychophysical scales. *Perception & Psychophysics*, 1974, *15*, 89–96.

Brickman, P., & Campbell, D. T. Hedonic relativism and planning the good society. In M. H. Appley (Ed.), *Adaptation-level theory: A symposium*. New York: Academic Press, 1971.

Helson, H. Adaptation-level as frame of reference for prediction of psychophysical data. *American Journal of Psychology*, 1947, *60*, 1–29.

Helson, H. *Adaptation-level theory*. New York: Harper & Row, 1964.

Hemple, C. G. *Philosophy of natural science*. Englewood Cliffs, N.J.: Prentice-Hall, 1966.

Marsh, H. W., & Parducci, A. Natural anchoring at the neutral point of category rating scales. *Journal of Experimental Social Psychology*, 1978, *14*, 193–204.

Parducci, A. Direction of shift in the judgment of single stimuli. *Journal of Experimental Psychology*, 1956, *51*, 169–178.

Parducci, A. The relativism of absolute judgment. *Scientific American*, 1968, *219*, 84–90.

Parducci, A. A range-frequency approach to sequential effects in category ratings. In S. Kornblum (Eds.), *Attention and performance IV*. New York: Academic Press, 1973.

Parducci, A. Category ratings: Still more contextual effects! In B. Wegener (Ed.), *Social attitudes and psychophysical measurement.* Hillsdale, N.J.: Lawrence Erlbaum Association, 1981, (in press).

Parducci, A. Category ratings and the relational character of judgment. In H.-G. Geissler & V. Sarris (Eds.), *Modern trends in perception.* Berlin: VEB Deutscher Verlag der Wissenschaften, in press.

Parducci, A., Calfee, R. C., Marshall, L. M., & Davidson, L. P. Context effects in judgment: Adaptation level as a function of the mean, midpoint, and median of the stimuli. *Journal of Experimental Psychology,* 1960, *60,* 65–77.

Parducci, A., Knobel, S., & Thomas, C. Independent contexts for category ratings: A range-frequency analysis. *Perception & Psychophysics,* 1976, *20,* 360–366.

Parducci, A., & Perrett, L. P. Rating scales: Effects of relative spacing and frequency of stimulus values. *Journal of Experimental Psychology Monograph,* 1971, *89,* 427–452.

Riskey, D. R., Parducci, A., & Beauchamp, G. K. Effects of context in judgments of sweetness and pleasantness. *Perception & Psychophysics,* 1979, *26,* 171–176.

Sarris, V. Adaptation-level theory: Two critical experiments on Helson's weighted-average model. *American Journal of Psychology,* 1967, *80,* 331–334.

Sarris, V. Effects of stimulus range and anchor value on psychophysical judgment. In H.-G. Geissler & Y. M. Zabrodin (Eds.), *Advances in psychophysics.* Berlin: VEB Deutscher Verlag der Wissenschaften, 1976.

Sarris, V., & Parducci, A. Multiple anchoring of category rating scales. *Perception & Psychophysics,* 1978, *24,* 35–39.

11 Perceptual Processings of Words and Drawings

Paul Fraisse
University René Descartes, Paris, France

For many years, I have studied by means of a number of experiments, one simple process: that which consists in naming what we see. I am interested in studying information processing in such a simple situation because I think that we should achieve a more precise understanding of the basic processes in order to explain better the complex processes. And perception is the source of all information. I speak of perception, but it would also be possible to speak of immediate memory, because, in some experiments, the subjects were asked to name not just a single but several stimuli.

Let me make a preliminary observation. Although my experiments are very close to those of many researchers who are working in the same field, but I believe they do have an original character. In my experiments, subjects were asked to name what they saw, with a variety of possible responses. On the other hand, most workers in this area generally use a binary system of response: yes or no, A or B, presence or absence of a stimulus, and subjects are required to choose among two possible responses.

I attempt to present a synthesis of my findings, but unfortunately I do not have time to compare them with other results in the same area. My purpose is to analyze the different processes involved in the naming response or, in other words, to find out the intermediate variables that may be postulated to explain the results (Fraisse, 1969).

First of all, naming occurs in response to two different types of stimulation. In one case, the subject is asked to name an object or the pictorial representation of an object. In this case, I speak of denomination, or naming. In the other case, the subject has to name a written word; this is a reading response. My purpose is to use these two kinds of material to investigate the differences in the processes involved in naming and reading.

I begin with a rough model (diagramed in Fig. 11.1) that is common to all workers in this field.

Given a stimulus to be perceived visually, the first stage is iconic storage. This iconic storage is a stage in itself. You may have iconic storage without being capable of naming the stimulus afterward; for example, if you don't know Chinese and if you look at a Chinese sign, you will have only iconic storage. My first purpose is to identify the variables involved in this process and to show their influence on the duration of the naming process.

The second stage is encoding storage. It consists of the recognition of the icon that was perceived in the first stage. At this point, it is necessary to make a distinction. If the stimulus is a word written in Roman orthography, a European subject is capable of naming the stimulus, in other words, of reading the word, without necessarily understanding its meaning. For reading a word, it is only necessary to have phonetic coding, the subject using the phonetic rules of his or her own language. But when the stimulus is an object, for coding the icon the object has to be recognized, before it can be given a name. Naming is impossible if the subject is presented with an unknown object.

In the case in which I am interested, in order to give a verbal response, semantic coding has to occur prior to naming. The encoding storage involves two aspects: a phonetic one and a semantic one. One of my aims is to study the relationships between these two types of encoding.

I assume that prior to the occurrence of a verbal response there exists a stage generating the response in which there is also articulatory coding. The role of this stage will appear clearly when subjects are asked to give several successive verbal responses.

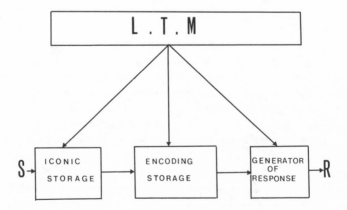

FIG. 11.1.   A simplified model of information processing leading to a verbal response. LTM = long-term memory.

Let me now consider different stages and present the results that permitted me to find the variables involved at every stage, as well as the relations or correlations between these stages.

Iconic Storage

To study this form of storage, I used two methods. One is classical: It consists of measuring the recognition threshold for stimuli presented tachistoscopically. I also used a second method, but not systematically. It consisted of using various presentation durations and observing the repercussions of these variations on the duration of the subsequent stages. In this case, what is measured is the reaction time between the stimulus and the response, which is, in some way, the sum of the duration of all processes; but I tried to delimit the respective contribution of each process to the global duration.

When using the threshold method, I found, like many authors, that recognition threshold is very low, which means that subjects are capable of recognizing a simple stimulus such as a word or a drawing after less than 20 msec in normal lighting conditions. This duration is very short in comparison with the total duration of the naming process, which is at least 300 msec and often more.

I thoroughly investigated the role of two variables on the recognition threshold, namely uncertainty and discriminability (or graphic complexity). These variables are of particular interest for all my other studies.

The role of uncertainty is evident when a subject has to recognize a stimulus belonging to a set of stimuli that he or she learned before. The recognition threshold increases as the logarithm of the number of possible stimuli, according to the general laws of information theory. This is true for meaningless syllables (Fraisse & Blancheteau, 1962), as well as for words (Fraisse, 1967a). For example, the recognition threshold is 12 msec when there are two possible stimuli and 18 msec when there are 16 possible stimuli. The same holds with geometric figures (Fraisse, 1967a). From a survey of the literature, it appears that in French as well as in English recognition threshold of words depends on use frequency (Fraisse, 1964a), and frequency is one aspect of uncertainty. This is confirmed by the fact that, if a subject is presented in advance with the different possible words, the effect of use frequency is no longer observed (Fraisse, Kassou, & Krawsky, 1963).

The role of graphic complexity is also well known and trivial, in some sense. As early as 1952, McGinnies, Comer, and Lacey showed that word recognition threshold was increasing with word length. I have been particularly interested in the comparison of recognition thresholds for words and drawings when the naming response is the same. For instance, I compared the recognition threshold for the written word "square" with the recognition threshold for the pictorial representation of a square. Recognition threshold was 8.9. msec in the case of the drawing and 14.2 msec in the case of the written word. The same is true with more complex drawings and words. For instance, for an octagon, recognition threshold was 11.2 msec in the case of the drawing and 17 msec in the case of the written word. In this experiment, uncertainty was kept constant and identical for drawings and words (Fraisse, 1960). I found the same result when I used children aged 7 to 11 years as subjects (Fraisse & McMurray, 1960).

I found an interaction between uncertainty and discriminability in the case of geometric figures but not in the case of words (Fraisse, 1967a). But I have some doubts concerning this result, because the material used could have been better. It suffices to say that the quantitative effect of uncertainty and graphic complexity was less strong in the case of words than in the case of geometric figures.

Graphic complexity may be considered not only in terms of simple features but also in terms of the nature of the stimuli. I compared the recognition threshold for eight objects (such as a key, an arm-chair, a plane) in four conditions, the stimuli having always the same size: I used the object (a toy), a drawing of this object with shadows, a photograph, and a line drawing. With subjects ranging from 7 years to adulthood, I obtained the same results. The lowest threshold was found for drawings with shadows, a type of drawing that emphasizes the form of the object, and the highest for line drawings, a type of drawing that is simpler but does not give enough information on the form and nature of the stimulus (Fraisse & Elkin, 1963).

To conclude this point, I shall note that if, in general, the recognition threshold for objects and drawings is lower than the recognition threshold for words, it is however possible to find drawings that will be as difficult to recognize as words are; it is a question of graphic presentation.

Encoding Storage

In order to study the processes intervening at this stage, I measured verbal reaction times (VRT). The problem with this index is that it consists of the sum of different processes. To analyze this duration, I had to compute the differences between the means obtained in different situations or the correlations between visual recognition threshold and verbal reaction time.

I later show that uncertainty and discriminability have an effect on verbal reaction time. But first I have to present the major finding concerning encoding storage. There is a difference of at least 100 msec between the coding (reading) of words and the coding (naming) of objects, colors, geometric figures, or drawings. I have done a number of experiments on this. Let me give a simple example: The material consisted of 15 words designating very familiar concrete objects (animals, plants, objects) and the 15 corresponding pictorial representations. I attempted to minimize the effect of iconic storage by using long enough presentation durations and also by a direct control. I now say a few words on this control because it is very important for my purpose. The 30 stimuli (15 words and 15 drawings) were presented tachistoscopically, and subjects were asked to press a key as soon as they recognized a stimulus. The mean reaction time was 249 msec for drawings and 259 msec for words. Let me recall here that the recognition threshold is about 10 to 20 msec. This illustrates that the process of reaction is rather long, even when the response is very simple: Switch off by pressing a key. There was a small difference between the means for words and drawings (10 msec, $p < .10$); this result confirmed my first finding concerning the fact that in general words have a greater graphic complexity than drawings. With the same material, but in a different session, the subjects were asked to give a naming response to each stimulus. In this case, mean reaction time was 473 msec for words and 563 msec for drawings. The difference is now 90 msec ($p < .005$) (Fraisse, 1968). This result is not new. It was found by J. Mck Cattell in 1885. But it has to be explained in the framework of the information processing model that I have presented.

As soon as a subject can translate the graphic code into a phonetic one or, to put it differently, as soon as he can read, there is a close and univocal correspondence or compatibility between S and R. We can give a verbal response even if we do not understand the meaning of a word. I should add that the difference in verbal reaction time between naming and reading is also found in children as soon as they have a mastery of reading (Ligon, 1932).

With drawings, the process is more complex. First, the subject has to recognize the object and after to give it a name. We can recognize an object (a kind of stone, for example) without being capable of finding its name. In the coding of a concrete object, there is first a semantic coding and later a phonetic coding. One needs a minimum of 90 sec. to perform this translation. This leads me to assume that the encoding storage of words differs from the encoding storage of objects and that for objects there is a double coding: first a semantic, and then a phonetic one.

Let me give another example (Fraisse, 1967b). If you take the same form (O) and present it together with 3 letters (OBKF) in one condition, and with three geometric figures (square, triangle, cross) in another condition, in each condition you have the same graphic stimulus and the same uncertainty, but the verbal response is different. In one case, the response is "O," and in the other case it is "circle." I also used a control condition with a simple verbal reaction time to O and to the word circle to investigate the role of the nature of verbal responses. The results were as follows:

Reading O	Naming a circle
453 msec	619 msec
Reaction time to O	Reaction time to circle
304 msec	333 msec

It is clear that the large difference between reading and naming is explained neither by the situation (the same stimulus) nor by the nature of the response.

Another way to give evidence of this double process is to use Posner's paradigm. I asked the subjects to compare two words (identical or different), two drawings (identical or different), or two stimuli: a word and a drawing. In 50% of the cases, the drawing corresponded to the word; in 50% of the cases, there was no relation between the word and the drawing. Subjects had only to decide whether the two stimuli presented simultaneously were identical or different by saying "yes" or "no." The presentation duration was not limited (Fraisse, 1970).

The results were in total agreement with the previous ones.

Identical

word–word	561 msec
drawing–drawing	521 msec
word–drawing	687 msec

These results permitted me to study the relations between the iconic and the encoding storage. Even though the range of measurements is very different, I found in many experiments (Fraisse, 1964a) a correlation of .50 to .80 between recognition threshold and verbal reaction time. However, this correlation was found only when the material belonged to the same category (words or drawings). When the material consisted of both drawings and words, the correlations were more or less negative. The positive correlation between recognition threshold and verbal reaction time implies the existence of a common factor. The simplest hypothesis is to consider that a specific difficulty of retrieval from long-term storage plays a role in iconic recognition and in the encoding stage.

If we want to have a better understanding of these facts, we must first of all study the effect of uncertainty and discriminability at the encoding stage.

Concerning discriminability, its effect on word encoding is small. For example, the verbal reaction time to "square" is 601 msec and to "octagon" 637 msec (Fraisse, 1964b). This an example of the effect of word length. Let me remind you that subjects were shown the stimuli before the experiment. This small difference must be compared with the effect of the discriminability of the corresponding geometric figures (VRT was 701 msec for square and 963 msec for octagon, Fraisse, 1964b).

Another way of varying the discriminability is to modify presentation duration (Fraisse, 1968, 1980). When presentation duration is twice the threshold value (11.5 msec for words and 8.6. msec for geometric figures), VRTs are equal. The difficulty of perceiving the words that have a more complex graphic presentation compensates the difficulty of encoding geometrical figures. When presentation duration is three times the threshold value, the effect of the double coding of geometric figures appears; with longer durations, there are no more marked effects of the duration of the stimulation.

In other experiments, I attempted to minimize this effect of the difficulty of iconic coding on verbal reaction time by using long durations. The effect of uncertainty then appeared. But this effect is totally different in the case of words from that with drawings or geometric figures. It is well known that in the case of words there is no effect of uncertainty (Pierce & Karlin, 1957). But this is true only when there is a long practice with a few words. Personally, I found that with 4 possible words verbal reaction time was 475 msec and with 16 possible words it was 526 msec, the subjects having been presented with the words before the experiment (Fraisse, 1968).

Assuming that the frequency of words is related to a kind of uncertainty, when we have to read a word, verbal reaction time is also not related to word frequency. Neither is it, as I found, related to a more subjective index that I termed *word familiarity*. This index was calculated by using a rating method with the same population of subjects.

The results concerning the effects of uncertainty are quite different with drawings. For instance, the difference between naming a square and reading the word square is 100 msec when there are 4 possible stimuli and 205 msec when there are 12 possible stimuli. With an octagon as a stimulus, the difference increases from 326 msec. to 584 msec. with the same variation of uncertainty. There is an interaction of uncertainty and discriminability in the case of objects or drawings. The more difficult the coding of the stimulus at the iconic stage, the more time consuming the semantic coding (Fraisse, 1967a). If the effect of word frequency in language is considered as an aspect of the uncertainty of naming, a correlation between verbal reaction time to drawings and frequency is found, whereas there was no effect or only a very small one on reading.

These different examples have shown that the naming process differs from the reading process. When naming, we are obliged to find the relation between the signifier and the signified; we have to refer to meaning.

Let me give another kind of example of the specificity of semantic coding. French students with a good knowledge of English were asked to read French words or the corresponding English words in one condition and to translate English words into French or French words into English. Translation was always longer than reading. Translation from a foreign language to the native language is always faster than the contrary, but what I want to emphasize is that in the reading condition, with English and French words, there was no effect of the number of stimuli (from 2 to 16). Reading foreign words took just a little more time (535 msec opposed to 491 msec, a 44-msec difference). In the translation condition, verbal reaction time was longer and also increased with the number of possible stimuli, that is to say with uncertainty (when passing from 2 to 16 possible stimuli, the increase was 131 msec when translating from English to French and 122 msec from French to English). The increase was linear when

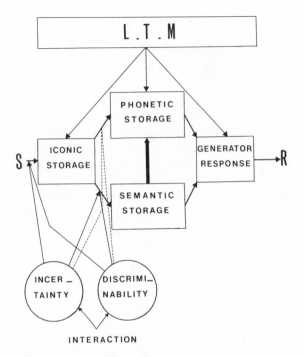

FIG. 11.2. A model representing the information processes discussed in this work. It shows in particular differences between processes at the level of encoding storage and sequential order of treatment in the case of denomination (naming) of concrete stimuli.

taking the logarithm of the number of possible stimuli. Translating requires a semantic coding, whereas semantic coding is not necessary when reading words of foreign languages, as long as they are written in Roman characters in our countries (Fraisse, 1966).

The Organization of Response (s)

The time taken for iconic recognition is a part of verbal reaction time; it is very short. We know the complexity of the encoding stage and we know that discriminability and uncertainty may be responsible for an increase of VRT.

In several experiments I measured the verbal reaction time to a single stimulus easy to discriminate, using long presentation durations. I already said that the verbal reaction time to the sign O was 304 msec when the response was a letter and 333 msec when it was a circle (Fraisse, 1967b). In another experiment subjects were asked to name a color or to read the name of a color. Verbal reaction time was 236 msec for the reading response and 261 for the naming response (Fraisse, 1964b).

In these two experiments, the specific difficulty of the naming response was found again; furthermore, it was found that verbal reaction time to a single stimulus was more than half the total verbal reaction time when there is uncertainty. In normal conditions, there is always a sort of uncertainty when we have to read or to name something.

To have a good understanding of the total process it is necessary to take into account the specific time necessary for the elaboration and the emission of the response.

Because it was difficult to analyze this process with only one response, I devised a new experimental procedure. The subject received simultaneously or successively many stimuli and was asked to give a verbal response as quickly as possible. In the reading condition, stimuli consisted of letters or words; in the naming condition, they consisted of geometric figures.

When the number of responses is equal to the number of stimuli presented simultaneously, that is to say when the number of stimuli was within the limits of the span of apprehension, the latency of the first response increased linearly with the number of responses. For a maximum six stimuli–responses, the regression equation was:

$740 + 54n$ for words

$1032 + 62n$ for geometric figures.

It should be emphasized that the number of correct responses decreases with the increase in the number of stimuli. There were 50% correct responses for 3–4 words and for 4–5 geometric figures (Fraisse, 1977).

How can this increase in latency with the number of stimuli be explained? Is it due to the duration of the encoding process when there are many stimuli? My answer is negative. It is based on another experiment where the material consisted only of letters with two different presentation conditions (Fraisse & Smirnov, 1976). In one condition, letters were presented simultaneously for a relatively short duration (80 msec); in the other condition, letters were presented successively on a screen. Each letter was presented for 600 msec, with an interval of 300 msec. Latencies were about the same in the two conditions: 672 msec $+ 72n$ for the simultaneous presentation and 704 msec $+ 50n$ for the successive presentation. In the latter case, the subject had as much time as he or she needed for coding each successive letter. But the results were about the same as when the letters were presented simultaneously for brief durations. On the basis of these results, we must conclude that the increase in latency with the increase in the number of correct responses is not due to a problem of encoding, but that it is a later process attributed to the activity of a generator of responses.

My experiment of 1977 provides me with a further argument. In this study, not only the first response latency had been recorded but also the temporal intervals between each response. Two results were found: (1) The first result is that temporal intervals between responses were almost equal, if the number of responses and the location of the interval in the series were taken into consideration. It has to be noted that the last interval was always a little longer. (2) The second result is that the mean of temporal intervals between the beginning of two verbal responses is 513 msec in the reading condition and 655 msec in the naming condition. The same phenomenon, with the same amplitude, as when working with only one stimulus, was found in the two conditions. It can be hypothesized that words are stored in the phonetic stage and geometric figures in the semantic stage. The subject has to retrieve each stimulus from these stores and to elaborate each of the responses as a unique one.

But why is there a 50 to 70 msec lengthening of the first response with every additional response?

My results do not allow any assumption. But by reasoning analogically, it seems that this particular increase in latency corresponds to the verification of each response before the beginning of the oral response. You all know that Sternberg (1966, 1975) found that in memory search there is an increase of about 40 msec in the "yes–no" response latency when there is a one letter increase in the store. In visual search, when the subject has to say if a stimulus that was shown to him or her before is present or not on a screen, the lengthening in the latency is about the same in visual search as in memory search (Gilford & Juola, 1976).

It seems that before giving an answer, the subject controls each possible response and it takes about the same time as a memory search or a visual search of one element.

We should now go further in the comprehension of response elaboration. When the number of responses is equal to the number of stimuli, there is a lengthening of the first response latency with the increase in the number of responses. As I already said, I explain this lengthening by a preliminary verification of what is stored at the level of the semantic or phonetic storage.

But the latency is also lengthened for a definite number of responses when the number of stimuli is higher than the number of possible responses, in other words, when the number of stimuli is larger than the memory span. This result has been observed many times with letters, digits, words, and geometric figures (Fraisse, 1977, 1978, 1979).

Let me take only the example of my last research (1979) on this question. Six letters were presented for 150 msec. In one condition, the subject was asked to name all the stimuli he could recognize. Six letters is beyond the memory span; the memory span is between three and four letters in this type of condition. Sometimes the subject gives fewer responses, sometimes more.

I plotted response latencies against the number of responses. Let me remind you that the number of stimuli was always six. You see that in this case latencies become longer and longer as the number of responses decreases. My assumption is that the subject, who can perceive in the best case about six letters, is after the

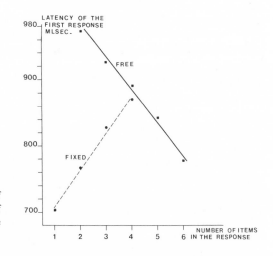

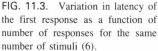
FIG. 11.3. Variation in latency of the first response as a function of number of responses for the same number of stimuli (6).

stage of verification, searching for the missing responses. This search takes approximately 47 msec.

It has been possible to verify this assumption. With the same material, the subjects were asked to give a definite number of responses (from 1 to 4). Here again, the first result was found: Response latency increased with the increase in the number of responses. This increment was 56 msec.

At this stage of response elaboration, I have determined the existence of two specific processes: the verification or the control of responses before the beginning of verbal responses. But when the subject is aware that the number of his or her responses is less than the number of stimuli, there is a search for the missing responses. The verification of and search for an element take about the same time.

Let me mention that in my experiments this duration is 50 msec, whereas American authors found 40 msec; this difference is due to the fact that I did not use as many trials as they. This time must be taken into account for explaining the total verbal reaction time. The minimum time necessary for the encoding and for the response elaboration is about 200 msec in reading conditions and 300 msec in naming conditions. Uncertainty, complexity, and number of responses increase latency, according to the laws I established.

I think that my results are original in two ways. First, they reveal the necessary successive coding from semantic to the phonetic storage. In the case of words, phonetic coding suffices, but, in general, there are two parallel processes through phonetic and semantic storage. It is appropriate to speak of storage because, as it has been shown, when there are many responses, there is storage at this stage.

The second result throws a new light on the elaboration of responses: a scanning of the available responses and a search for the missing ones. At this stage the duration for giving the response is important, and it is measured with a single reaction time to a name or to a drawing (about 250 msec).

This research on information processing provides an initial set of results. They are particularly concerned with fundamental processes that are common to all adults and also to children as soon as they can read. As a first step for future research it would be important to know in what measure the relative difficulties of phonetic coding and semantic storage are affected by genetic, cultural, and pedagogic differences. Another problem is that of long-term memory retention of different forms of coding in extending the problem to the processing of information transmitted via the auditory channel.

Research to come should demonstrate the role of these processes in more complex tasks, comparing for example information presented in a written text or by a drawing in the case where a comparison has a meaning.

In neuropsychology it would be interesting to know whether or not phonetic coding and semantic coding involve the same cerebral structures. One could test this with respect to the two hemispheres of the normal subject by peripheral presentations of stimuli and in the case of subjects with neurological problems by systematically exploring the difference between reading and denomination (naming).

Finally, I believe that the relative difficulty of verbal coding of concrete stimuli should be especially taken into account in pedagogical research. Learning from concrete data is perhaps more enriching, but it must be recognized that it entails considerable difficulties in denomination.

REFERENCES

Fraisse, P. Recognition time measured by verbal reaction to figures and words. *Perceptual and Motor Skills*, 1960, *11*, 204.

Fraisse, P. Relations entre le seuil de reconnaissance perceptive et le temps de réaction verbale, *Psychologie Française*, 1964, *9*, 77–85. (a)

Fraisse, P. Le temps de réaction verbale: Dénomination et lecture. *L'Année Psychologique*, 1964, *64*, 21–46. (b)

Fraisse, P. La durée de la traduction—thème et version—de mots isolés. *Bulletin de Psychologie*, 1966, *XIX*, 593–602.

Fraisse, P. Le rôle de l'incertitude et de la discriminabilité dans la reconnaissance perceptive. *L'Année Psychologique*, 1967, *67*, 61–72. (a)

Fraisse, P. Latency of different verbal responses to the same stimulus. *Quarterly Journal of Experimental Psychology*, 1967, *19*, 353–355. (b)

Fraisse, P. Motor and verbal reactions to words and drawings. *Psychonomic Science*, 1968, *12*, 235–236. (a)

Fraisse, P. Durée de présentation de mots isolés et rapidité de lecture. *Psychologie Française*, 1968, *13*, 31–57. (b)

Fraisse, P. Why is naming longer than reading. *Acta Psychologica*, 1969, *30*, 96–103.

Fraisse, P. Reconnaissance de l'identité physique et sémantique de dessins et de noms. *Revue Suisse de Psychologie pure et appliquée*, 1970, *29*, 76–84.

Fraisse, P. Latence des réponses en mémoire immédiate. Noms et figures géométriques. *L'Année Psychologique*, 1977, *77*, 325–342.

Fraisse, P. La latence des réponses complètes et incomplètes en mémoire immédiate. *L'Année Psychologique*, 1978, *78*, 39–60.

Fraisse, P. Responce latency in immediate memory: Free number of responses versus fixed number of responses. *Bulletin of the Psychonomic Society*, 1979, *13*, 127–129.

Fraisse, P. Des modes de relation entre la durée de l'identification perceptive et le temps de réaction verbale. *L'Année Psychologique*, 1980, *80*, 433–447.

Fraisse, P., & Blancheteau, M. The influence of the number of alternatives on the perceptual recognition threshold. *Quarterly Journal of Experimental Psychology*, 1962, *14*, 52–55.

Fraisse, P., & Elkin, E. H. Etude génétique de l'influence des modes de présentation sur le seuil de reconnaissance d'objets familiers. *L'Année Psychologique*, 1963, *63*, 1–12.

Fraisse, P., Kassou, A., & Krawsky, G. Rôle de la fréquence des mots et de la connaissance préalable de l'échantillon sur la durée des seuils de reconnaissance. *Bulletin de Psychologie*, 1963, *XVII*, 409–411.

Fraisse, P., & Mc Murray, G. Etude génétique du seuil visuel pour quatre catégories de stimuli. *L'Année Psychologique*, 1960, *60*, 1–9.

Fraisse, P., & Smirnov, S. Response latency and the content of immediate memory. *Bulletin of the Psychonomic Society*, 1976, *8*, 345–348.

Gilford, R. M., & Juola, J. F. Familiarity effects on memory search and visual search. *Bulletin of the Psychonomic Society*, 1976, *7*, 142–147.

Ligon, E. M. A genetic etudy of color naming and word naming. *American Journal of Psychology*, 1932, *44*, 103–110.

Mc Ginnies, E., Comer, P. A., & Lacey, O. L. Visual recognition thresholds as a function of words longth and word frequency. *Journal of Experimental Psychology*, 1952, *44*, 65–69.

Pierce, J. R., & Karlin, J. E. Reading rates and the information rate of a human channel. *Bell Systems and Technics Journal*, 1957, *36*, 497–516.

Sternberg, S. High speed scanning in human memory. *Science*, 1966, *153*, 652–657.

Sternberg, S. Memory scanning: New findings and current controversies. *Quarterly Journal of Experimental Psychology*, 1975, *27*, 1–32.

12 Studies in Text Comprehension: Toward a Model for Learning from Reading

Walter Kintsch
Eileen Kintsch
University of Colorado, Boulder, USA

Interest in "learning" has fluctuated more widely in the past decades than women's fashions. If my memory serves me right, I did not hear a single lecture or discussion on learning as a graduate student in Vienna in the 1950s. When I came to America, however, learning was almost the sole topic where I went to graduate school, and I quickly succumbed to the fascination of habit strength and drive–reward interactions. However, I had hardly graduated when all that became passé, and learning, together with my beloved Markov models, disappeared into history's storage closet. The students at Colorado during the past 10 years have heard about as much about "learning" as I had years ago at Vienna. What has happened? Has America caught up with Europe? Or have we relapsed into the dark ages?

Neither, we think. American learning psychology had overreached itself and was forced to retrench and repair its bases. Thorndike, Hull, Skinner, and Tolman, in spite of many good ideas and early successes, could not deliver what they had promised. Weaknesses became apparent in their approach, and a cognitive viewpoint became dominant in experimental psychology both in Europe and America. "Learning" became a nonissue, not so much because it was tainted by the collapse of the great theories of the 1930s and 1940s but because psychologists realized that they did not have the conceptual and experimental tools to tackle it. The incredibly ambitious global theories of Hull and Skinner were replaced first by miniature models of learning and eventually by a shift away from questions of learning per se to the psychological processes underlying learning—perception, attention, memory, and knowledge use. A cognitive theory today is typically small in scope and concerned with mental representations and processes operating on these representations. Well-known examples are the buffer model of short-term memory (Atkinson & Shiffrin, 1968), the scanning model of memory retrieval (Sternberg, 1969), semantic memory models for verification times (Smith, Rips, & Shoben, 1974), or problem-solving models for river-crossing puzzles (Newell & Simon, 1972). There is no general cognitive theory of human information processing, but an ever growing body of data and theories for limited domains adds up to a rich structure and a slowly evolving consensus view. These developments are described in some detail in Kintsch (1977).

An essential change brought about by the information-processing reorientation of experimental psychology consists in the demotion of some very influential commonsense terms that psychology has inherited from everyday language use. Not only learning, but intelligence, comprehension, and problem solving are among them. These global concepts turn out to be not very useful because they subsume too many distinct and disparate subcomponents under one label, thereby suggesting that there is some unitary psychological process or trait indicated by that label. Learning in one situation may be a completely different process than learning in another situation, having in common not more than the superficial fact that in both situations some eventual improvement in performance occurs. There can be no such thing as a general learning theory because learning processes in different tasks are all quite different and obey their own laws. Instead, what we are going to have are process models for particular behaviors (e.g., typing, reading comprehension, solving physics problems) that will eventually be expanded to include learning processes: the change from some particular initial state of performance to a final desired state.

We believe learning in this new form will once again become an important topic in psychology, and although at this point we are quite unable to sketch the contours of the future psychology of learning, we can do something much more modest. In line with our prediction that the future will bring detailed process models of specific behaviors, we would like to outline a model of text comprehension (Kintsch & van Dijk, 1978; van Dijk & Kintsch, 1983) that may serve as a starting point to understanding certain kinds of learning processes.

Framework for a Model of Text Comprehension

When we say *learning from written text,* we mean the ability to remember and use the information the text contains. Comprehension, we assume, forms the backbone of this process: People simply do not remember what they do not understand. If our goal is to specify the mechanism responsible for text memory, we must first understand the comprehension processes that underlie it.

This also proves to be a formidable undertaking, for again we are dealing with a complex, catch-all term. How do we deal with the fact that one can sometimes understand each phrase and sentence in a text without grasping the overall meaning, whereas on another occasion one can gain a pretty fair idea of the gist of a text without ever ploughing through the details? Depending on the purpose for which the reading is done, either method might get you in trouble. If you want to assemble a bicycle or repair an electronic instrument, knowing the gist of the instructions won't take you very far. On the other hand, phrase-by-phrase comprehension does not provide much enjoyment from a mystery story or illumination when trying to understand a scientific argument. A comprehension model must deal with the fact that there are different levels of comprehension: Local-level processes parse the individual words or short phrases into propositions, the underlying meaning of the text. The propositions themselves have to be interrelated and organized to form a coherent structure, called the *text base*, that represents the meaning a particular reader has derived from a given text. But these are still local-level processes. The process by which a reader derives the gist of the text must also be modeled. In the model described in the following, this process is represented by the construction of macropropositions, which subsume the detailed information and their organization as a macrostructure. In a long text macrostructures must be hierarchical, being subsumed under ever more general categories. Thus, in a model of comprehension we have to deal with meaning units corresponding to phrases and short sentences, on the one hand, and paragraphs and whole chapters on the other.

Rather than attempting to model such a complex system in its totality, it is possible to decompose it into simpler subsystems, as proposed by Simon (1969). Although independent subsystems are too simple to be informative, and totally interactive systems too clumsy to deal with, a partially interactive system that allows interactions only among the outputs of the various subsystems can give a model the flexibility it needs while keeping it manageable.

Decomposition has the further advantage of permitting some components of the system to be fully modeled, whereas others are neglected. Thus, the model developed by Kintsch and van Dijk (1978) has concentrated mainly on three components of the comprehension process.

First, it attempts to specify the processes by which a coherent text base is constructed from the individual meaning units. However, it does not concern itself with the underlying parsing level that converts the linguistic representation into semantic units. Instead, the basic meaning units are simply provided as a starting point for the model.

Second, the model focuses on the use of knowledge in this process, how people employ their knowledge to construct a text base, and how the knowledge they bring to a text in turn becomes modified by the new material (i.e., how the new knowledge becomes integrated in the memory system). Again, the important problem of how knowledge is retrieved from long-term storage is bypassed, with the relevant knowledge simply being supplied to the system.

Finally, higher-level processes are also dealt with in this model—the level of macrostructure formation, how people develop a notion about the gist of a text. Briefly, we assume that people use certain well-learned strategies, often cued by the text, that allow them to infer the macrostructure unconsciously as they read.

Before describing how the model works, two other basic assumptions must be discussed, namely that we are concerned with building a psychological model, one that deals with how real people comprehend in real time, and that the model must be testable.

As psychologists we have to be concerned with the psychological reality and plausibility of our model. It is not enough to show how a coherent text base can be constructed; we must also show how it can be constructed in real time, subject to the memory and processing constraints of the human system. One consequence of our psychological orientation is that processing in our model is based on strategies rather than rules. Giving rules to a system, assuming they are correct, will guarantee the correct outcome: As long as you keep applying them, the text will eventually be parsed, a macrostructure will be formed and assimilated into the reader's knowledge structure. However, these computations may be long and tedious, making heavy demands on the reader's resources. Strategies, on the other hand, are heuristics—quick and easy to apply and usually correct, though one can't count on it. There is some evidence that people operate via strategies rather than grinding through a set of rules (Bever, 1970; Clark & Clark, 1977). In reading through a text, they may notice certain cues that will trigger a set of preprogrammed operations, allowing them to quickly infer the intended meaning of the text. This may occur at many different levels in the comprehension process, from word identification on up. One important goal of recent work on the model has been to specify these strategies and to show both how people use them and how a computer program equipped with appropriate strategies can likewise understand text.

The second consequence of our psychological orientation is a continued emphasis on *testability*, which distinguishes our approach from various AI projects. Whereas we in no way want to minimize the role that self-observation (introspection) plays in constructing a model of comprehension, we also find useful the traditional methods of the experimental psychologist. On the one hand, they serve as avenues of exploration when self-observation becomes uninformative; on the other, they serve as valuable, objective checks on introspective results, as well as on model predictions.

How the Model Works

So far we have been discussing in very general terms the framework for a model of text comprehension. In the following section we briefly summarize how such a model works; however, the reader is referred to other publications for more detailed presentations. The basic model is described in Kintsch and van Dijk (1978) and more currently in Miller and Kintsch (1980). Its further elaboration and expression as a computer program will be available in van Dijk and Kintsch (1983) and Miller (forthcoming), respectively.

We assume that comprehension occurs as a parallel process at several levels. Each processing level produces a special representation as its output. Although processing at each level is independent of other levels, their outcomes interact and may influence processing at other levels. Each level, then, is subject to correction and control from other levels in the system.

The basic components of the model are depicted in Fig. 12.1. The verbal representation of the text—strings of words organized into phrases, sentences, and paragraphs—serve as input to the system. A sequence of semantic units, called atomic propositions, are derived by a parsing process. This operation is, however, not specified in the model that focuses instead on the higher processing levels: the organization of the semantic units into text propositions and the formation of a macrostructure.

The process by which the atomic propositions are organized into text propositions involves several operations. First, a decision is made to focus on a particular semantic unit, for example, a predicate, around which the incoming text material may be organized. A corresponding knowledge structure, or frame, is retrieved from long-term memory, whose slots may be filled by related semantic units, or they may be appended to it as modifiers. A frame, then, is like an expectation of what a small portion of the text is about. When incoming semantic units no longer fit the slots of an activated frame, it is replaced in working memory by a new one. The old, filled-in frame is stored in episodic text memory. Thus, reading a text results in the storage of a sequence of interrelated chunks of text information, called *text propositions*. Their form is determined both by a reader's knowledge and interests, as well as the meaning units themselves and how they were expressed in the text.

At the same time the text is being organized via the text propositions, the reader is forming a notion about the gist of the text, what we call *macrostructure formation*. The text propositions are subsumed into even higher superordinate propositions, by processes of selection and generalization, to form a hierarchical representation of the text at a global level. For what the reader ends up with after reading a long text is not a mass of interrelated details but (ideally) just the important points. The reader uses a variety of strategies, signaled by the text, that enable him or her swiftly and unconsciously to identify macrorelevant text prop-

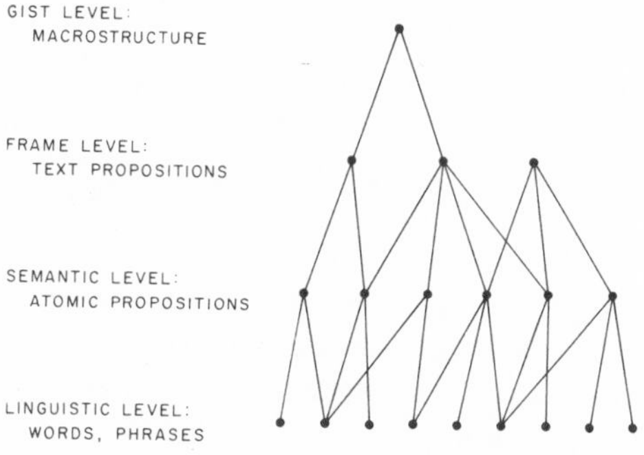

GIST LEVEL:
MACROSTRUCTURE

FRAME LEVEL:
TEXT PROPOSITIONS

SEMANTIC LEVEL:
ATOMIC PROPOSITIONS

LINGUISTIC LEVEL:
WORDS, PHRASES

FIG. 12.1.   Levels of processing in the model of discourse comprehension.

ositions. These may in turn influence processing at lower levels. Usually, for example, the most superordinate proposition is chosen, the one that contains many other propositions. Furthermore, an author uses various importance tags to signal the macrorelevance of parts of the text (e.g., these may be rather obvious semantic cues such as "finally," "the basic assumption here," "thus"; or syntactic cues like passivization, that signals the object as sentence topic). Readers will also focus on particularly surprising or interesting pieces of information. Finally, rhetorical schemata set up certain expectations and hence serve as organizing principles for the macropropositions (e.g., a definition is usually of the form class + special characteristics; the Methods section of a psychological report has slots for materials, subjects, etc.).

At this point it may help to work through a concrete example, such as the sentence in Fig. 12.2, which is to be taken as part of a longer text. The parsing process derives the underlying semantic units (atomic propositions) from the sequence of words. A syntactic strategy is used to choose the predicate READ as the basis for organizing the propositions. The corresponding frame is summoned from long-term memory and its slots filled with appropriate text material. Because READ requires a human agent, "John" is specified as agent; the object must be some kind of written text—"paper" in this case, to which "excellent" is appended as modifier; an instrument slot, though possible, has no candidates (e.g., "glasses," "magnifying glass") and thus is not activated; however, the location slot is specified. A macroproposition, "John's trip to Frankfurt," has been generated on the basis of this proposition and others like it in the text that are not shown. This macroproposition may in turn be subordinate to other propositions further up in the hierarchy (e.g., "the congress on experimental psychology in the year 2000"). Note that macropropositions may be inferred without ever being directly stated in the text.

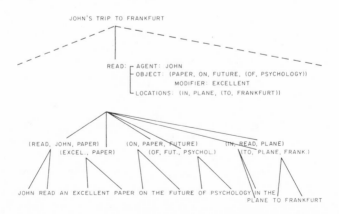

FIG. 12.2.   A sample text analysis provided by the model of comprehension.

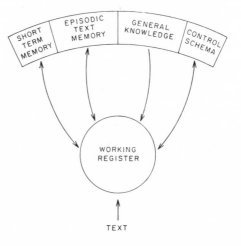

FIG. 12.3. The components of the
memory system according to the
model of comprehension.

To account for how these operations are carried out in real time, the model assumes that processing a text occurs in cycles. Due to the limited capacity of human short-term memory, a sequence of words only about the length of a single sentence (Miller & Kintsch, 1980) is processed at each pass. The components of the memory system are schematically depicted in Fig. 12.3. As each segment of text enters working memory, it undergoes the multilevel analyses described previously. These processes are dominated by a control schema representing the reader's goals, interest, his or her knowledge of the type of text he or she is reading (e.g., whether it is a scientific report, newspaper article, or mystery story), and other high-level information. The short-term buffer is readily accessible to the working register and contains the currently dominant macroproposition but only a single text proposition, to which various semantic units are added as processing continues. When a new text proposition is generated, the old one is stored in episodic text memory, along with the macropropositions that are also formed from time to time. Thus, episodic memory contains both the set of interrelated text propositions and their developing superstructure as well, and this is what constitutes the long-term memory representation of the text. Retrieval depends on the extent to which this representation is well structured and interconnected.

The probability that a proposition will be stored depends on both the amount and the type of processing it has received. Propositions that are structurally central (i.e., that have many connections to other, subordinate propositions) participate in more processing cycles and hence are more likely to be retained and available for recall. However, there are also qualitative differences in processing at every level that influence their retrieval probability. Thus, propositions that were used to infer a macroproposition are more strongly related to it than irrelevant ones; macropropositions that fill slots in a schematic structure (such as a definition schema) and semantic units that fill slots in a frame are more likely to be recalled than less centrally involved propositions.

Competence of the Model

What evidence do we have that the formal approximation of text comprehension provided by this model is a valid one? We can test our model in two ways: First, we can compare model predictions with experimental data from actual readers engaged in various comprehension-based tasks. In Miller and Kintsch (1980), for example, results from recall and summarizing tasks are reported that support the basic model. Secondly, by trying to express the model as a computer program we can test the general principles that were inferred from linguistic analysis and psychological experimentation. For example, can we simulate the strategies used to form coherent text bases and the role of knowledge use in that process or, on a different level, the strategies used to generate macrostructures? Currently our work in this area is concerned with further refining the model to handle the necessary computational burden and to adapt it to a greater variety of materials and tasks. Ultimately, given the necessary annotations and the appropriate knowledge base, our program should be able to "understand" any arbitrary text (i.e., build a representation of the meaning of that text). Such a representation can then be used as the basis for exploring other cognitive tasks.

Before talking about possible future applications of the model, at this point we would like to go into more detail on the role of experimental data in cognitive research. Testing and theorizing, we claim, go hand in hand. A theory, however elegant and parsimonious, that cannot be subjected to experimental tests will tell us little about how real people comprehend a passage of text. On the other hand, running into the field with a barrage of random experiments and no theory to relate them to is like sowing wheat in the wind: Some may sprout and bear the grain, but we are unlikely to find out where or why. What conclusions, for example, have we been able to draw from years of research on adjunct questions? Why can't readability formulas tell us what makes a given textbook difficult to read, so that rewriting need not be such a painful process of trial and error?

The experiment now described (Kintsch & Yarbrough, 1982) may shed some light on this issue. This experiment was designed to explore two basic assumptions of the text comprehension model, namely, the notion that there are different levels of comprehension, ranging from local-level microprocesses to global-level macroprocesses, and that people use strategies to organize the meaning as they read. One group of strategies, familiar to experienced writers and readers, involves rhetorical forms such as argument, definition, procedural description, comparison, and contrast. An author may signal the reader directly, or in some less-obvious ways, that a given paragraph is a definition ("X is defined as . . ."). To the extent that this is succesful, the appropriate schema (class + primary, secondary characteristics) is summoned to the reader's mind and used to organize the material in that paragraph. According to the Kintsch and van Dijk model, texts that are clearly organized according to familiar rhetorical schemata should be easier to comprehend than otherwise comparable texts that lack such organization. Meyer's (Meyer, Brand, & Bluth, 1980) finding that clear-cut rhetorical structures are easier to recall than loose, listlike structures, agrees with this prediction. The reason for this, according to the model, is that schematically well-organized texts make it easier for the reader to form the macrostructures. However, this would only be reflected in a test that is sensitive to macrolevel processes and not in a test that taps processing at the microlevel.

To test this hypothesis, subjects were given 10 essays to read that were either in a good or a bad rhetorical form. The well-formed essays followed closely familiar rhetorical schemata (such as definition, procedural description, comparison and contrast, classification, illustration) and were provided with explicit cues to alert readers to their structure. These cues were deleted in the bad form, and the actual order of the paragraphs deviated from the ideal rhetorical form; however, care was taken not to destroy normal coherence at a local level (e.g., pronoun reference). The content and length (from 205 to 240 words) remained the same for the two types of text.

Two kinds of tests were prepared to evaluate comprehension at both the micro- and macroprocessing levels. A simple cloze test in which every fifth word was deleted from the text, the blanks to be filled in by the subject, was used for the former, because it reflects, for the most part, how well each sentence or phrase is understood in its local context and has little to do with the overall organization of the text. To evaluate gist comprehension, direct questions about the macrostructure were used; for example, "What is this text about?" and "What are the two major points in the article?". The same questions were asked for the good and bad versions of the text.

Table 12.1 shows the main results of the experiment. The subjects' ability to answer questions relevant to macrostructure was greatly facilitated by texts with good rhetorical form. Their answers were 58% correct for such texts, compared to only 29% correct for the texts whose structure had been destroyed. This is in sharp contrast to results on the cloze test, where performance was the same for both text types: Correct words were supplied 41% of the time on the good versions and 42% on the poor versions. Hence the theoretical prediction of different levels of comprehension is upheld by these results. Performance on the

TABLE 12.1
Percentage Correct on Question Answering and Cloze Tests as a
Function of Rhetorical Structure

		Topic Question	Main Idea Question	Cloze Test
Rhetorical form:	Good	58	47	41
	Bad	29	29	42

cloze test is determined by local processes that are fairly independent of global organizational processes. These higher-level processes, however, appear to be strategy-based processes that are sensitive to structural organization. Texts that have a familiar rhetorical structure are easier to comprehend and answer questions about because they contain explicit cues to the appropriate rhetorical schema. Our subjects were able to use these schemata to organize the meaning of the texts as they read. With the bad versions of the texts, however, subjects were less likely to activate the right schemata because such explicit cues were lacking. Furthermore, even if the right ones were found, which is quite possible, although it demands more effort, they would be more difficult to use because the order of the text units did not conform to the subjects' schema-based expectations.

Future Applications

The notion of different levels of comprehension that are differentially sensitive to various types of tests has exciting implications for educational testing. It is clearly false to assume that comprehension is an ability that can be measured by a single, general *comprehension test*. Instead we must evaluate separately the bundle of psychological processes captured by this conglomerate term we have inherited from everyday language. Only a collection of different tests, each tuned to some specific aspect of the total process, will provide adequate results. The testing question is clearly preliminary to research on learning, for only if we know how to evaluate comprehension can we ask what has been learned from reading.

This becomes a feasible undertaking within the framework of an explicit comprehension theory that tells us what the individual processing levels are, how they interact (e.g., how failure to understand at one level can be compensated for at another level), and what the memory representation is for a given reader. Our work is merely a first step in this direction. The present model will by no means be the best nor the last word on the subject, but even as a rough approximation it provides the tools for getting at the issues that interest us.

First of all, we can use the model to analyze the products of the comprehension process, such as recall protocols and summaries, as done in Miller and Kintsch (1980). Such analyses could easily be extended to other tasks like question answering. Indeed, this is a particularly useful kind of comprehension task, because the questions can be directed at different levels of the comprehension process; that is, we can design questions that specifically tap a reader's knowledge of local-level details, on the one hand, or his gist retention on the other, or we can use them to gauge his prior knowledge of the subject matter. Applying this principle of theoretically motivated tests to educational materials would make it much easier for a teacher to pinpoint an individual student's problem with a given text.

Secondly, the model can also be used to study the ongoing comprehension process, and in fact much of our work has been concerned with readability problems. We have been able to show that certain factors isolated by the model do indeed affect comprehension during reading (Kintsch & Vipond, 1979). These include: (1) the connectedness of the text base (i.e., the number and kinds of inferences required to form the connections between semantic units and text propositions); (2) the short-term memory demands on the reader—it is more difficult to connect related elements that are widely spaced in the text because the appropriate proposition may no longer be available in the short-term memory buffer, and to reinstate it requires more time and effort; and (3) the background knowledge for a given text that a reader must have in order to quickly and effortlessly summon the appropriate frame or schema. These factors, singled out by the model, have been experimentally manipulated using various texts and reader characteristics, but it remains a major problem to be able to predict the difficulty of any arbitrary text for a given reader. First of all, we need to apply the model to a much greater quantity and variety of text materials, but just as important we need to account for many different kinds of readers. For when we talk of readability, we do not simply mean a list of factors embedded in a text; instead, we mean the product of a given reader's interaction with a given text. Hence an easy text for one reader can be quite difficult for another, depending on how much each one already knows of the subject, what processing strategies he or she uses, the capacity of his or her individual short-term memory. This, of course, calls into question the search for a quick and easy readability test. Much to the despair of our textbook publishers, there probably never will be some magical formula that they can use to advertise their products. However, it may be well within our grasp at this point to develop a battery of comprehension tests that will tell us where in a given text and for a given sample of target readers a breakdown in comprehension is likely to occur. Then we shall at least be able to rewrite the text accordingly.

To go from theory to applications is by no means a trivial step. To work out such a battery of comprehension tests for a given text is a huge job in itself. In addition, much more experimental work is needed, both on readability and on the retention and use of the material read. For although it is certainly true that learning depends on comprehension, there are undoubtedly other factors that influence our ability to learn from a text.

The pursuit of a new, general theory of learning, however, is probably just as illusionary a goal now as it was 50 years ago. Just as there can be no general, overall theory of comprehension, no magical readability formula, we are unlikely to be able to specify a general learning process. However, what we may look forward to, perhaps even before the year 2000, is an understanding of the specific demands and operations involved in a particular cognitive task.

REFERENCES

Atkinson, R. C., & Shiffrin, R. M. Human memory: A proposed system and its control processes. In K. W. Spence & J. T. Spence (Eds.), *The psychology of learning and motivation: Advances in research and theory* (Vol. 2). New York: Academic Press, 1968.

Bever, T. G. The cognitive basis for linguistic structures. In J. K. Hayes (Ed.), *Cognition and the development of language*. New York: Wiley, 1970.

Clark, H. H., & Clark, E. V. *Psychology and language*. New York: Harcourt, Brace, Jovanovich, 1977.

Kintsch, W. *Memory and cognition*. New York: Wiley, 1977.

Kintsch, W., & van Dijk, T. A. Toward a model of text comprehension and production. *Psychological Review*, 1978, *85*, 363–394.

Kintsch, W., & Vipond, D. Reading comprehension and readability in educational practice and psychological theory. In L. G. Nilsson (Ed.), *Perspectives on memory research*. Hillsdale, N.J.: Lawrence Erlbaum Associates, 1979.

Kintsch, W., & Yarbrough, J. C. The role of rhetorical structure in text comprehension. *Journal of Educational Psychology*, 1982, *74*, 828–834.

Meyer, B. J. F., Brand, D. M., & Bluth, G. L. Use of top level structure in text: Key for reading comprehension of ninth-grade students. *Reading Research Quarterly*, 1980, *16*, 72–103.

Miller, J. R., & Kintsch, W. Readability and recall of short prose passages: A theoretical analysis. *Journal of Experimental Psychology: Human Learning and Memory*, 1980, *6*, 335–354.

Newell, A., & Simon, H. A. *Human problem solving*. Englewood Cliffs, N.J.: Prentice-Hall, 1972.

Simon, H. A. *The artificial sciences*. Cambridge, Mass.: MIT Press, 1969.

Smith, E. E., Rips, L. J., & Shoben, E. J. Structure and process in semantic decisions. *Psychological Review*, 1974, *81*, 214–241.

Sternberg, S. The discovery of processing stages: Extension of Donder's method. *Acts Psychologica*, 1969, *30*, 276–315.

van Dijk, T. A., & Kintsch, W. *Strategies of comprehension*. New York: Academic Press, 1983.

IV DIFFERENTIAL, SOCIAL, AND DEVELOPMENTAL PSYCHOLOGY

The bringing together into Part IV of three important areas of psychology, *differential* (Chapters 13–15), *social* (16 and 17), and *developmental* (18), reflects a faith in the future unification of such diverse fields of study. The basis for this faith is explored and illustrated by concrete examples. Thus, Hans Eysenck's present contribution deals explicitly with "biosocial man" and the "unification of psychology," supported by his experiments bridging differential, physiological, and clinical psychology. Jan Strelau's very different orientation from Warsaw nevertheless seems to support this same integration. David Magnusson's data from Sweden relate differential, social, and developmental psychology. And Philip Zimbardo, with his imperialistically social orientation, seems to encompass all of traditional psychology. In addition to the integrative push of these particular chapters, Part IV is characterized by methodological approaches that incorporate features of both experimental and correlational analyses.

Eysenck's data are striking in their strong support for genetic factors, with heritability coefficients as high as 70 or 80%. Particularly impressive are the correlations above .80 that he finds between a physical component of the EEG and a standard measure of intelligence, the Wechsler IQ. Insofar as these findings are replicated and digested, one may look forward to revolutionary changes in theorizing about the biology of intelligence. Strelau's neo-Pavlovian approach places much more emphasis upon the social environment, though this is interpreted with respect to a regulative theory of temperment that is moulded on nonspecific psychophysiological functioning. Magnusson's data lead him to his interactive position: The individual personal equation (e.g., amount of intellectual ability, level of anxiety, etc.) manifests itself differently in different specific situations. It will be interesting to see how these three positions fare as we approach the year 2000. Will there be theoretical reorientations that integrate their different kinds of data?

From an experimental paradigm for the "dynamics of action," Julius Kuhl and John W. Atkinson deduce systematic variability under the influence of various inner and outer conditions, even over a period for which an individual's cognitive structure would normally be assumed to be constant. Their research program combines a concern with individual differences and more general cognitive processes.

Zimbardo's chapter, besides presenting a provocative review of dominant theoretical influences in the field of social psychology, reflects the widespread contemporary importance of cognitive psychology. His own research includes daring demonstrations of social phenomena of great practical significance. In his prognostications for the future, Zimbardo emphasizes the methodological possibilities of technological advances, particularly as we enter the age of personal computers.

The chapter by John Nesselroade and Paul Baltes concludes Part IV with a sober look into the possibilities of extracting causal information from correlational data. They illustrate their argument for path analysis and causal modeling with examples from recent research, including an analysis of interindividual differences in intraindividual stages of development.

Part IV covers a great deal of psychology, substantive, methodological, and theoretical. Perhaps what these chapters have most in common is that none of them are content to restrict their attention to the traditional methods of experimental psychology. In their different ways, they each broaden the possibilities of the experimental approach. Whether this broadening will lead to a multitude of disparate disciplines, or whether it will lead back to a more fully integrated psychology remains a question to be answered by future developments.

13 The Biology of Individual Differences

Hans Jürgen Eysenck
University of London, England

The study of individual differences has always formed an important part of experimental psychology, ever since the early days of Sir Francis Galton; even Wundt, who is often represented as being inimical to the study of individual differences, made an important contribution to the description of personality by suggesting the transformation of the traditional Greek typology of the four temperaments into a two-dimensional system closely resembling that later on advocated by this author. In spite of this early inclusion of personality variable into Wundt's system of physiological psychology, the paths of experimental psychology (in the narrow sense) and of the study of individual differences have tended to diverge. Cronbach (1957), in his Presidential Address to the American Psychological Society, pointed out that there were two disciplines of scientific psychology and that psychology would be unlikely to prosper unless they could be brought together into one integrated whole. This hope, strongly supported in my writings (Eysenck, 1967), has only been fulfilled very partially; in spite of much lip service, experimentalists and psychometrics have tended to go their own way, and integration is still in the future.

There are, of course, some signs that integration is proceeding, although not at a very fast rate. The work of Teplov, Nebylitsyn, and Strelau, on the development of the Pavlovian concepts of typology, and the work of Gray, Claridge, and this author in the English-speaking countries has made some attempts to bring these two disciplines more closely together, and there is a growing amount of interest in this approach (Eysenck, 1981a, 1981e; Mangan, 1981).

The plea for a unification of these two disciplines of scientific psychology is based primarily on two facts. The first of these relates to the obvious difficulties encountered by experimental psychology (and also by its various applied branches, such as industrial, educational, clinical, and social psychology), namely that the accepted method of functional analysis, $a = f(b)$, has run into unexpected difficulties. The major one of these is simply that in the majority of experiments main effects are relatively weak, and the error term in the analysis of variance very strong. In other words, there is a great deal of noise in the system, and the signal-to-noise ratio will not become acceptable unless this noise is reduced. Evidence is accumulating that the major part of the noise is contributed by individual differences; extraverts and introverts, to take but one example, react quite differently to identical stimuli, and unless these differences are taken into account the greater part of the total variance would be relegated to the error term. This is not an acceptable situation, and it clearly can be resolved only by the recognition of the importance of individual differences. Physicists and chemists recognize the fundamental importance of careful analysis and description of elements, alloys, etc. entering into their experiments and do not use random samples of matter; psychologists must follow this example and describe in detail the relevant personality characteristics of the people entering into their experiments. Recognition of this fact is growing slowly but surely, and it is to be hoped that the rate of recognition will accelerate in the near future and that by the year 2000 both experimentalists and applied psychologists will have learned this lesson.

The second important recognition seems to be that just as experimental psychology needs the work of the student of individual differences, so work on personality and intelligence needs the concepts of experimental psychology in order to formulate causal theories to go beyond the purely descriptive types of work carried out by factor analysts and others. Correlational methods and factor analysis are necessary but not sufficient tools in the construction of a proper theory of personality, and no model of personality is conceivable that does not incorporate the concepts of experimental psychology (Eysenck, 1981a). Recognition of this fact by students of personality and intelligence is only beginning to dawn, and many are still hostile to the implied integration. However, if psychology is to prosper, then the study of individual differences will have to follow this path of integration and accept the need for causal theories based on the findings of experimental psychology.

Any such integration can only be fruitful if it takes into account the fact that no model of man is acceptable that does not recognize the importance both of biological and of social factors in the individual's development. The biosocial nature of man (Eysenck 1980a, 1980b, 1980c) has not always been recognized by psychologists, who either tend to overemphasize the social factors to the exclusion of the biological ones (as is typical of traditional behaviorists, cognitive psychologists, psychoanalysts, and others) or who stress biological factors without paying due regard to social factors (e.g., the early "instinct" psychologists, or some modern geneticists and sociobiologists). Psychologists must recognize the tri–une nature of the brain (McLean, 1969) (i.e., the fact that both morphologically and functionally the brain shows evidence of three major evolutionary phases—the brainstem and hindbrain [the so-called reptile brain], the paleocortex [limbic system], and the neocortex). We cannot doubt the importance of social factors and the second signaling system, as Pavlov called it, both of which are linked to the neocortex, but equally or even more important in many ways is the limbic system, and hence the importance of genetic and biological factors in neurosis, criminality, and other types of human behavior (Eysenck, 1976, 1977a,b). My own theories, accounting for the phenomena of neurosis and criminality in terms of Pavlovian conditioning and suggesting methods of treatment based on the same paradigm, may of course be in error, but the general principle that biological factors play an important part in social phenomena (in addition of course to social and environmental factors) can hardly be gainsaid in the light of the available evidence.

The stress on genetic factors, both in the genesis of differences in intelligence (Eysenck, 1979) and personality (Fulker, 1981) would appear to contradict the major beliefs of psychologists during the last 50 years, but the evidence is becoming more and more conclusive that genetic factors do play a large part in the causation of individual differences in both personality and intelligence and that to deny these biological factors is to fly in the face of a great deal of experimental work, fortified in recent years by developments of statistical technique in the biometrical analysis of genetical factors. These studies are not concerned so much with the simple quantification of heritability but rather with the elucidation of the genetic architecture involved. Thus, whereas it is important to know that at the present time, and in our type of society, genetic factors account for something like 80% of the total variance as far as individual differences in IQ are concerned, it is at least equally important to know that a sizable proportion of this genetic variance is nonadditive, involving strong directional dominance effects and strong assortative mating effects. It is equally important to know that between-family environmental influences are twice as strong as within-family environmental influences and that interaction effects of any kind are rather weak (Eysenck, 1979). It is important to know that as far as personality dimensions like neuroticism, extraversion, and psychoticism are concerned, additive genetic causes are equally as important as in the causation of intellectual differences but that here nonadditive causes like dominance and assortative mating play no part and that within-family environmental differences are much more important than are between-family environmental differences. A great deal has been learned about the genetic architecture of personality and intelligence in recent years, and the tempo of discovery is accelerating; we may be sure that during the next 20 years we shall see a great advance in our understanding of these obscure and difficult topics.

We thus conceive of a man (or woman) as being born with certain predispositions that, in interaction with environmental forces, will lead him to develop behavior patterns characteristic of extraversion–introversion, neuroticism–stability, or psychoticism–superego control. Through these personality differences he will be more or less likely to develop criminal tendencies, neurotic or psychotic disorders, successful or unsuccessful adaptation to educational and professional experiences, patterns of sexual behavior, and quite generally a lifestyle characteristic of him and setting him off from all other people. The particular functions determined by heredity are of course biological; what is genetically determined is the general level of cortical arousal, mediated by the reticular formation, and in turn influencing the degree of extraverted or intro-verted behavior of the person concerned, and the functioning of the autonomic system, coordinated by the limbic system or visceral brain, and in turn giving rise to overemotional or underemotional reactions to various types of stimuli. We now possess some understanding of the pysiological underpinning of personality (Stelmack, 1981), and there is a rich literature linking these personality and physiological factors with laboratory investigations and work in social areas (Eysenck, 1976). Even the field of social attitudes and ideology can find partial explanations of human behavior in these terms (Eysenck & Wilson, 1978). It is not an unreasonable prediction to say that advance in these areas will increase our understanding and make possible a more complete system of explanation and prediction in the course of the next 20 years.

This type of work may illustrate the importance of using concepts derived from experimental psychology, like cortical arousal, to give a causal explanation of the descriptive theories of extraversion, neuroticism, and psychoticism. Such causal theories enable us to break out from the circular arguments of correlational and factorial analysis and to make predictions that can be tested along the ordinary lines of experimental psychology. We extend the functional paradigm mentioned before so as to include personality as a relevant variable, and in its simplest form the new paradigm reads: $a = f(b, P)$ (i.e., a *[the dependent variable] is a function of b* [the independent variable] interacting with personality in a predictable manner determined by the general theory in question). A few examples may illustrate the way the principle works in general experimental psychology and in various applied areas.

To begin with, let us take an experiment by Howarth and Eysenck (1968) from the area of the experimental study of memory. The whole area has been surveyed in M. W. Eysenck (1977), with particular reference to individual differences. In the experiment to be quoted, groups of introverts and extraverts were taught paired associates to a given level, and recall was tested immediately after learning and after intervals of 1 minute, 5 minutes, 30 minutes, and 24 hours. Different groups were of course used for each of these recall intervals, and the following prediction was made. Introverts, having a higher level of arousal, would consolidate the memory trace better than extraverts, who have a low level of arousal (Eysenck, 1981b). However, following Walker's theorem, it was also taken into account that while consolidation was proceeding, the neural traces were not available readily for recall. Thus extraverts, having poor consolidation,

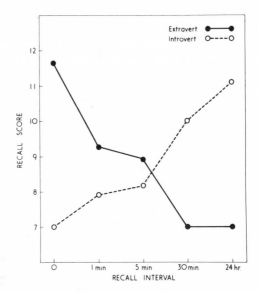

FIG. 13.1.   Recall as a function of recall interval, for introverts and extraverts (from Howarth & Eysenck, 1968).

would have the memory traces readily available soon after learning, but because of the poor consolidation they would forget readily over time; thus the course of their recall should be indicative of forgetting (i.e., show a decline). Introverts, on the other hand, should show poor recall immediately after learning, because consolidation interfered with recall; they should then show improved memory over time (i.e., show reminiscence, (Eysenck & Frith, 1977). Figure 13.1 shows the actual results obtained, which bear out this prediction in detail. Note that a simple averaging over all groups (i.e., a failure to take personality into account) would have resulted in a flat record wrongly indicating that recall interval had no influence on recall. Thus the old-fashioned paradigm: $a = f(b)$ would tell us that the dependent variable (recall) was not affected by the independent variable (recall interval), throwing all the variance into the error term. The extended paradigm: $a = f(b, P)$, by introducing personality into the equation, shows us that much of the variance can be rescued from the error term and becomes part of the interaction. This is typical of many experiments in this and other fields, as is made clear by M. W. Eysenck (1977), who also goes in great detail into the ways in which causal explanations can be linked with experimental work in this field.

In another example, consider Fig. 13.2, which shows the operant conditioning of extraverts and introverts when noise and light are reinforcement. Both groups have the same operant level of pushing a button, but when the reinforcement is introduced, it will be seen that extraverts increase the frequency in order to obtain loud jazz music from a jukebox and bright light, whereas introverts reduce the frequency of pushing the button in order to remain in quiet and dark conditions, very much as predicted by the hypothesis that extraverts are sensation seeking because of their low level of arousal. Had the two groups been thrown

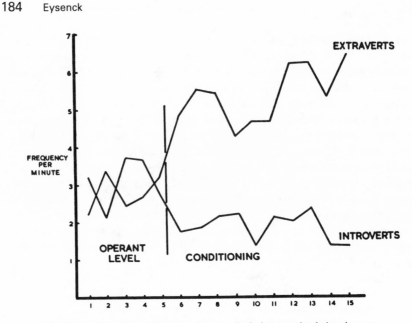

FIG. 13.2.   Frequency of button pushing to obtain intense stimulation, by extraverts and introverts (from Weisen, 1965).

together, the results would again have been to show that reinforcement had
neither a positive nor negative effect, with the major portion of the variance
going into the error term.

As the third and last example, consider the work of Shigehisa and Symons
(1973a, 1973b). This relates to effect of intensity of visual stimuli on auditory
sensitivity, in relation to personality. There have been many tests of the hypothesis that increasing the intensity of stimulation in one sensory field would, by
increasing arousal, decrease the threshold in another, but the outcome has been
contradictory and indecisive. Shigehisa and Symons argued that this result might
be due to differential interaction of the effect with personality and demonstrated
convincingly that indeed introverts and extraverts show quite different effects,
with introverts showing what Pavlov called "transmarginal" inhibition even
with relatively weak sensory input, thus reversing the predicted trend, whereas
extraverts showing no such reversal. Shigehisa and Symons went on to replicate
the experiment and to reverse it (i.e., to show that auditory stimulation produces
similar effects on measures of visual thresholds, again modulated by personality
variables). Here again we see clearly that the old-fashioned paradigm, leaving
out personality, is quite incapable of dealing with what is a very straightforward
prediction; only the integration of personality variables into the experiment can
make results replicable and meaningful.

Let us next consider a simple experiment in educational psychology (Eysenck, 1978). Here it has often been shown that experimental comparisons between different methods of treatment tend to give support only to the null hypothesis; in other words, both methods work equally well (or poorly!). The introduction of personality into the picture often serves to demonstrate quite clearly that two methods apparently equal in effectiveness differ sharply, one being much better for introverts, the other for extraverts. Figure 13.3 shows the effect of such an experiment (Leith, 1974), comparing the reactions of introverts and extraverts to discovery learning and reception learning types of teaching, respectively. It will be seen that on both the posttest and the delayed test introverts do much better with the traditional method of reception learning (i.e., ordinary teaching of principles), whereas extraverts do much better with discovery learning (i.e., the new method in which they are asked to find out for themselves principles and results). Without this division into two different personality groups, the two methods would have appeared to give identical or similar results.

In a recent experiment, McCord and Wakefield (1981) reported the outcome of an experiment testing the effects of praise and blame, respectively, on extraverted and introverted pupils. Overall there was little difference between the two groups, but, as predicted, extraverts responded much more strongly to praise, introverts to blame. The prediction follows from Gray's principle that introverts are more responsive to pain stimuli, extraverts to stimuli activating the pleasure centers. Here again then it is only the invocation of personality factors that rescue the major portion of the variance from the error term and gives us information that may be useful in dealing in a practical manner with classroom situations.

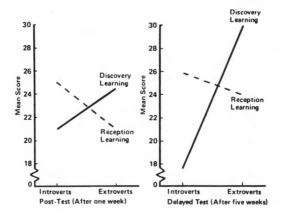

FIG. 13.3.   Effects of discovery and reception learning in introverts and extraverts (from Leith, 1974).

Extraversion/introversion, of course, is not the only personality variable that may be relevant to the evaluation of educational treatment. In an experiment by Leith and Trown (1975), almost 500 boys and girls took part in an experiment that contrasted the effects of "supportive" and "explorative" strategies in mathematics teaching in four junior schools, the mean age of the children being 10 years and 6 months.

In the case of the supportive strategy, the sequence employed, over each of the 12 sections of learning material, was that of teacher-provided statement of organizing principle, followed by related pupil activity with mathematical models and subsequent restatement of principle by the teacher. Such statements were both spoken and written on the blackboard. The same activities with models were used in the exploratory strategy, but this time at the beginning of each section of the learning sequence. Each statement of principle by the teacher was delayed until pupils had been given the opportunity to perceive the relationship themselves and had been encouraged to attempt an appropriate generalization.

Results are shown in Table 13.1. "Anxiety level distinguished between those who were able to profit greatly from the learner-centered exploratory approach and those whom it clearly handicapped. . . . The teacher-centered supportive strategy, on the other hand, was almost equally effective at each level of anxiety" (Leith & Trown, 1975, p. 18). Overall differences (i.e., neglecting the personality interaction dimension) would have led to the quite erroneous conclusion that strategies were identical in their effects. It may be noted that in this experiment there was an ability effect (in the expected direction) but no ability-treatment interaction. The results of the experiment, as the authors emphasize, are very germane to an evaluation of the Nuffield mathematics scheme, suggesting that this may improve the performance of some (nonanxious) children and make worse the performance of other (anxious) children. Such a conclusion cannot of course be based on the results of a single experiment and cannot be extrapolated to other subjects, but it does suggest the importance of proper experimental investigation of interaction effects.

Let us next turn to the field of social psychology. Of interest here is a study by Leith (1974), dealing with the personality interaction in a paired learning situa-

TABLE 13.1
Strategy-Anxiety Interaction (by Sex). Mean Scores for Retained
Learning [from Leith & Trown, 1975 (N per cell $= 40$)].

	Boys		Girls		All Pupils	
	Low Anx.	High Anx.	Low Anx.	High Anx.	Low Anx.	High Anx.
Supportive strategy	15.98	15.26	16.63	17.73	16.30	16.49
Exploratory strategy	20.30	12.35	18.30	14.25	19.30	13.29

TABLE 13.2
Comparisons of Achievement and Behavior of Same and Different
Anxiety Level Pairs (from Leith, 1974 (Heterogeneous Ability Pairs in
Brackets, Homogeneous Ability Pairs Without Brackets).

Opposite anxiety pairs	Achieved	74% (32%)	More on the posttest than same anxiety pairs
Opposite anxiety pairs	Achieved	98% (113%)	More on the transfer-test than same anxiety pairs
Opposite anxiety pairs	Spent	59% (36%)	More time in showing solidarity, raising other's status, giving help, and rewarding than same anxiety pairs
Opposite anxiety pairs	Spent	121% (132%)	More time asking for orientation, information, confirmation than same anxiety pairs
Opposite anxiety pairs	Spent	11% (20%)	Less time in disagreeing, passively rejecting, withholding help than same anxiety pairs
Opposite anxiety pairs	Spent	49% (25%)	Less time in showing antagonism, deflating other, asserting self than same anxiety pairs

tion (i.e., learning in a situation where two learners are paired with each other).
In this experiment, pairing was on the basis of anxiety/neuroticism, pairs being
either similar in score on this variable, or opposite (i.e., one anxious, the other
stable). Table 13.2 shows the main results; it can be seen that quite extraordinary
improvements over the ''same'' pairings are shown in ''unlike'' pairings. Opposite anxiety pairs showed something like a 100% superiority over the same
anxiety pairs on the transfer test! (The pairs were subdivided according to heterogeneity to homogeneity in ability; the figures in brackets refer to the heterogeneous pairs.) Table 13.3 shows the results of a similar experiment using
extraversion/introversion instead of anxiety/neuroticism. It can be seen that

TABLE 13.3
Achievements of Students Learning in Homogeneous or
Heterogeneous Personality Pairs or as Individuals (from Leith, 1974)

		Methods		
Personality		*Homogeneous Pairs*	*Heterogeneous Pairs*	*Individuals*
Introverts		32.2	27.3	30.0
Extraverts		30.6	27.7	25.4
	Significance of differences (one-tailed)	N.S.	N.S.	$p < .01$
	Homogeneous vs. heterogeneous pairs: $p < .01$			
	Homogeneous pairs vs. individuals $p < .025$			

GENERAL ANXIETY

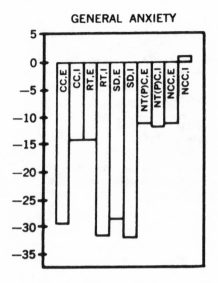

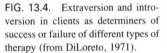

FIG. 13.4. Extraversion and introversion in clients as determiners of success or failure of different types of therapy (from DiLoreto, 1971).

when working individually introverts were significantly superior; this superiority vanished when the students worked in pairs. Homogeneous pairs here worked better than heterogenous pairs, regardless of whether the pair was made up of two extraverts or two introverts. These results open up fascinating vistas for both research and educational practice.

In the field of clinical psychology, the work of DiLoreto (1971) may serve as an indication that different methods of therapy may be differentially effective with different types of personality. DiLoreto compared the effects of Roger's client-centered therapy, Ellis's rational–emotional type of therapy, and Wolpe's desensitization technique with a nontreatment control. The effectiveness of the treatment was judged on a number of different scales; all tended to give similar results. What is shown in Fig. 13.4 is the reduction on follow-up of neurotic and anxiety-induced behaviors. It can be seen that the client-centered therapy was very effective for extraverts but completely ineffective for introverts; conversely, rational–emotional therapy was very effective for introverts but quite ineffective for extraverts. Desensitization treatment was equally effective for both, and the nontreatment equally ineffective for both groups. Thus personality interacts very strongly with client-centered and rational–emotional type therapy, an interaction that would not have been discovered had personality not formed an integral part of the design of the experiment.

In yet another area, namely psychopharmacology (Eysenck, 1981d), the effect of smoking a cigarette was assessed on the CNV (contingent negative variation) as a measure of cortical arousal. The prediction was made in terms of a theory relating nicotine administration through cigarette smoking to cortical arousal, but in a curvilinear fashion to incorporate "transmarginal" inhibition effects. As Fig. 13.5 indicates, extraverts under sham smoking conditions (S.S.) (i.e., handling an unlit cigarette) are in a lower state of arousal than when they are in a condition of real smoking (R.S.), and consequently smoking increases their CNV. Introverts, on the other hand, are in a higher state of arousal under conditions of sham smoking, and smoking a cigarette decreases their CNV. This prediction was shown to be verified by experiment (O'Connor, 1980), and again it is clear that omitting the personality variable would have shown no effect as far as the independent variable (smoking a cigarette) is concerned, thus relegating all the important informations available from the experiment to the error term.

It would be possible to continue almost ad infinitum an account of experiments in the various psychological fields mentioned to indicate the generality of this conclusion, but time does not allow, and adequate accounts will be found in Eysenck (1967, 1976, 1981a). To put the position in a general form, and to point up the similarity with research in physics, consider Fig. 13.6 (Eysenck, 1964). The upper part shows the effect of imposing a load on a wire, and the consequent elongation (dependent variable) of that wire. For two different materials or alloys, A and B, the effect of the same load can be seen to be quite different, giving rise to elongations of alpha or beta, respectively, depending on the nature of the substance involved. The law in question is Hooke's Law of Elasticity: stress $= k \times$ strain, where k is a constant (the modulus of elasticity) that depends on the nature of the material and the type of stress used to produce the strain. This constant k (i.e., the ratio stress/strain) is called Young's modulus and corresponds to individual differences in personality in psychology.

The lower part of Fig. 13.6 illustrates this principle in two groups of subjects, differing in neuroticism: an unemotional group (A) and an emotional group (B). Identical stresses produce different strains; to produce an identical strain, different stresses have to be imposed on the two groups. This illustrates very clearly that in the field of emotion and stress, too, individual differences must be taken into account to avoid errors of design and interpretation.

So far we have dealt with personality factors; much the same may be said with regard to intelligence. Here too individual differences are of the utmost importance, and here too physiological theories are now coming to the fore. This work

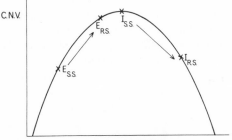

FIG. 13.5.   Effects of sham smoking and real smoking on CNV in extraverts and introverts (from O'Connor, 1980).

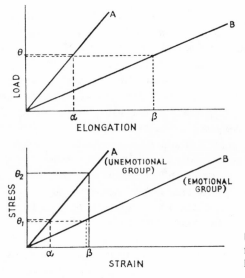

FIG. 13.6.   Effect of individual differences in physical (top) and psychological experiments (bottom).

has been largely concerned with the applications of the EEG. Resting levels here have not on the whole proved very successful in attempts to relate the EEG to intelligence (Cattell, 1971; Lindsley, 1961; Vogel & Broverman, 1966), and evoked potentials have been more widely used.

Ertl (1968) was the first to look at these responses with a view to relating them to IQ and showed that latencies were longer for subjects with low IQs than for subjects with high IQs. This early work was followed by many replications, some successful, others not (Barry & Ertl, 1965; Chalke & Ertl, 1965; Ertl, 1971; Ertl & Schafer, 1969; Osborne, 1969; Plum, 1972; Rhodes, Dustman, & Beck, 1969; Shucard & Horn, 1972); these leave little doubt that correlations between .2 and .4 can be obtained in this way, and somewhat higher correlations can be found by also using amplitude. Evoked potentials tend to correlate equally with the different aspects of intelligence (i.e., verbal and spatial), and this suggests the idea of dealing with a true correlate of general mental ability.

This early work, although interesting and important in some ways, was subject to criticism. In the first place, the correlations, although interesting, were too low to be of practical importance or theoretical import. In the second place, the findings were not a product of a theory and hence were difficult to interpret. This position was changed recently, due to work done in my department by Alan and Elaine Hendrickson. Alan Hendrickson (1972) originally worked out a theory to explain many memory functions, in terms of cortical information processing, and this theory has led to a new measure of evoked potentials that has a proper theoretical background and leads to much higher correlations between evoked potentials and intelligence (Hendrickson & Hendrickson, 1980). The theory goes into great detail of synapse functioning at the biochemical level and also of neurotransmission on the physiological level; clearly it would be inappropriate here even to try to summarize the theory. I instead simply state its main features, which are two. In the first place, the observed averaged evoked potential trace recapitulates and makes visible in some degree the message that is passed through the neurons and synapses of the cortex. In the second place, during this processing of information errors occur, and different people are differently prone to making errors of this kind. Persons making few errors will tend to have high intelligence, and persons making many errors will tend to have low intelligence, due to the failure of information processing to give accurate information. Recognition of error frequency is possible because the evoked potential, as is well known, is usually recorded as the average of a number of different (in our case, 90) time-locked evocations of the response. Errors will therefore give different traces to be averaged and will thus simplify the complexity of the final waveform. We can thus measure the amount of error by looking at the complexity of the waveform, and also the variability of each point on the wave over the 90 trials averaged. These scores have a sound theoretical basis, they are reliable, and they give a sound physiological underpinning to our attempts to measure intelligence.

Figures 13.7 and 13.8 show typical averaged evoked potentials for high-IQ and low-IQ subjects, respectively, using in the one case auditory and in the other visual stimuli. The auditory stimuli have proved the more successful, giving higher correlations with IQ, and will therefore be the ones to be referred to in the next paragraph. Note in both figures the much more complex waveform characteristic of the brighter children, and the much simpler and less-complex waveform characteristic of the duller children. These differences are so obvious that they can be seen with the naked eye and without any detailed measurement.

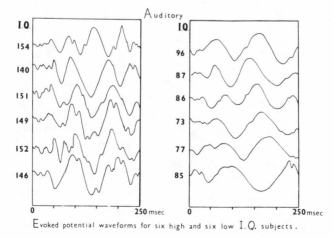

FIG. 13.7.   Averaged evoked potentials in bright and dull children (from Eysenck, 1981c).

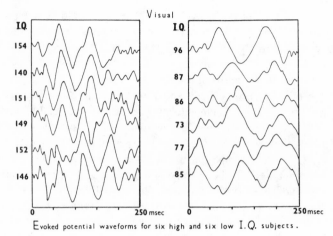

Evoked potential waveforms for six high and six low I.Q. subjects.

FIG. 13.8.   Averaged evoked potentials in bright and dull children (from Eysenck, 1981c).

Repeat reliabilities of these measures are very high and so are intraclass correlation of MZ twins.

Several experiments have shown the high degree of validity achieved using this measure of intelligence (Eysenck, 1981a). These studies used various medium-sized groups of adults and also a sample of some 220 schoolchildren. The criterion was the Matrices (for the adults) and the Wechsler (for the children). Taking only the children sample, as being more representative and larger than the others, a correlation of .83 was found between the full-scale Wechsler and the evoked potential measure; this is higher than the correlation between the Wechsler and the Binet or some other accepted measures of IQ. The factor analysis of 11 subtests of the Wechsler plus the evoked potential measure resulted in one very strong general factor, on which the evoked potential measure had a loading of .91; this was much higher than the next highest loading of .80 of the vocabulary test. Thus the evoked potential measures whatever the Wechsler measures with greater reliability and validity than any of the tests included in that IQ measure. There are the added advantages that the evoked potential does not depend to any degree on education, is not affected by cultural factors, and is not dependent on motivational or relational factors as the subject is not asked to do anything but listen passively.

Again, our outlook for the future is clearly simply a projection of the past and the present. As in the case of personality, so here too it is confidently anticipated that a clarification will take place on the physiological basis of intelligence, that many problems in the intellectual field will be solved by reliance on these new methods, and that the new methods will be accepted as a much purer measure of the genotypic intelligence that was hitherto measured only with difficulty by phenotypic IQ tests adulterated to a considerable degree by cultural and educational factors. Among the topics that can now be investigated experimentally are the growth of intelligence in very young children (EEGs can be taken almost from birth), the decline of intelligence with age (where hitherto great difficulties have arisen because of the contamination of IQ tests with cultural factors), and the relationship between verbal and nonverbal ability and the two hemispheres of the brain (where presumably evoked potentials can be recorded separately from the two hemispheres and the differences compared with the differential performance on tests). It thus seems likely that in the next 20 years a considerable advance will be made in our knowledge of intellectual differences, their causation, and their consequences.

On the whole, therefore, I am optimistic about the future progress in the study of individual differences. I predict that it will become much more experimental than hitherto, that theories regarding causal factors will be advanced with much greater confidence, that the links among behavior and physiology and biochemistry will be elaborated to a considerable extent, that genetic factors will be investigated in a much more determined manner than hitherto, and that intellectual abilities too will be subjected to the same type of investigation and explanation. Over 2000 years ago the Greek philosopher Theophratus wrote a book on personality in his 99th year, in which he stated the perennial problem of this branch of psychology: "Why is it that while all Greece lies under the same sky and all the Greeks are educated alike, it has befallen us to have characters variously constituted?" This question has haunted mankind for a long time; it now looks as if we are beginning to find an answer to it, and by the turn of the century we may have advanced sufficiently to give an answer with some degree of confidence.

REFERENCES

Barry, W. M., & Ertl, J. P. Brain waves and human intelligence. In F. B. Davis (Ed.), *Modern educational developments: Another Look*. New York: Educational Records Bureau, 1965.

Cattell, R. B. *Abilities: their structure, growth and action*. Boston: Houghton Mifflin, 1971.

Chalke, F. C. R., & Ertl, J. P. Evoked potentials and intelligence. *Life Sciences*, 1965, *4*, 1319–1322.

Cronbach, L. J. The two disciplines of scientific psychology. *American Psychologist*, 1957, *12*, 671–684.

DiLoreto, A. O. *Comparative psychotherapy: An experimental analysis*. New York: Aldine–Atherton, 1971.

Ertl, J. P. Evoked potentials, neural efficiency and I.Q.. *Paper presented at the International Symposium for Biocybernetics,* Washington, D.C., 1968.

Ertl. J. P. Fourier analysis of evoked potentials and human intelligence. *Nature*, 1971, *230*, 525–526.

Ertl, J. P., & Schafer, E. W. P. Brain response correlates of psychometric intelligence. *Nature*, 1969, *223*, 421–422.

Eysenck, H. J. (Ed.). *Experiments in motivation.* London: Pergamon, 1964.

Eysenck, H. J. *The biological basis of personality.* Springfield, Ill.: Thomas, 1967.

Eysenck, H. J. *The measurement of personality.* Lancaster, Pa.: Medical and Technical Publishers, 1976. (a)

Eysenck, H. J. *Sex and personality.* London: Open Books, 1976. (b)

Eysenck, H. J. *You and neurosis.* London: Temple Smith, 1977. (a)

Eysenck, H. J. *Crime and personality* (3rd ed.). London: Routledge & Kegan Paul, 1977. (b)

Eysenck, H. J. The development of personality and its relation to learning. In S. Murray–Smith (Ed.), *Melbourne studies in education.* Melbourne: University Press, 1978.

Eysenck, H. J. *The structure and measurement of intelligence.* New York: Springer, 1979.

Eysenck, H. J. The biosocial model of man and the unification of psychology. In A. J. Chapman & D. M. Jones (Eds.), *Models of man.* Leicester: British Psychological Society, 1980. (a)

Eysenck, H. J. The biosocial nature of man. *Journal of Social and Biological Structures, 1980, 3,* 125–134. (b)

Eysenck, H. J. Man as a biosocial animal. *Political Psychology, 1980, 2,* 43–51. (c)

Eysenck, H. J. *A model for personality.* New York: Springer, 1981. (a)

Eysenck, H. J. Arousal, intrinsic motivation, and personality. In H. I. Day (Ed.), *Advances in intrinsic motivation and aesthetics.* New York: Plenum, 1981. (b)

Eysenck, H. J. The psychophysiology of intelligence. In C. D. Spielberger & J. N. Butcher (Eds.), *Advances in personality assessment.* Hillsdale, N.J.: Lawrence Erlbaum Associates, 1981. (c)

Eysenck, H. J. Psychopharmacology and personality. In W. Janke (Ed.), *Symposium on personality and response variability to psychotropic drugs* (Provisional Title). London: Pergamon Press, 1981. (d)

Eysenck, H. J. Pavlovian concepts and personality dimensions: The nature of modern typology. In G. Mangan (Ed.), *Essays in honour of V. D. Nebylitsyn.* London: Pergamon Press, 1981. (e)

Eysenck, H. J., & Frith, C. *Reminiscence, motivation and personality.* New York: Plenum, 1977.

Eysenck, H. J., & O'Connor, K. Smoking, arousal and personality. In A. Remond & C. Izard (Eds.), *Electro-pysiological effects of nicotine.* Amsterdam: Elsevier/North Holland, 1979.

Eysenck, H. J., & Wilson, G. D. *The psychological basis of ideology.* Lancaster: Medical and Technical Publishers, 1978.

Eysenck, M. W. *Human memory: Theory, research and individual differences. London: Pergamon Press, 1977.*

Fulker, D. W. *The genetic and environmental architecture of psychoticism, extraversion and neuroticism. In H. J. Eysenck (Ed.), A model for personality.* New York: Springer, 1981.

Hendrickson, A. E. An integrated molar/molecular model for the brain. *Psychological Reports, 1972, 30,* 343–368.

Hendrickson, D. E., & Hendrickson, A. E. The biological basis of individual differences in intelligence. *Personality & Individual Differences, 1980, 1,* 3–33.

Howarth, E., & Eysenck, H. J. Extraversion, arousal, and paired-associate recall. *Journal of Experimental Research in Personality, 1968, 3,* 114–116.

Leith, G. O. Individual differences in learning: Interactions of personality and teaching methods. In *Personality and Academic Progress Proceedings,* 14–25. London: Association of Educational Psychologists, 1974.

Leith, G. O., & Trown, E. A. The influence of personality and task conditions on learning and transfer. *Programmed Learning, 1975, 7,* 181–188.

Lindsley, D. B. The reticular motivating system and perceptual integration. In D. E. Sheer (Ed.), *Electrical stimulation of the brain.* Austin: University of Texas Press, 1961

Mangan, G. L. *Temperament and personality: The psychophysiology of individual differences.* London: Pergamon Press, 1981.

McCord, R. R., & Wakefield, J. A. Arithmetic achievement as a function of introversion–extraversion and teacher-presented reward and punishment. *Personality and individual differences,* 1981, in press.

McLean, P. D. *A triune concept of the brain and behavior.* Toronto: University of Toronto Hincks Memorial Lecture, 1969.

O'Connor, K. The contingent negative variation and individual differences in smoking behavior. *Personality & Individual Differences,* 1980, *1,* 57–72.

Osborne, R. T. Psychometric correlates of the visual evoked potential. *Acta Psychologica,* 1969, *29,* 303–308.

Plum, A. *Visual evoked responses: Their relationship to intelligence.* Miami: Unpublished Doctoral dissertation, University of Florida, 1968 (quoted by Shucard & Horn, 1972).

Rhodes, I. E., Dustman, R. E., & Beck, E. C. The visual evoked response: A comparison of bright and dull children. *Electroencephalography and Clinical Neurophysiology,* 1969, *27,* 364–372.

Shigehisa, T., & Symons, J. R. Effect of intensity of visual stimulation on auditory sensitivity in relation to personality. *British Journal of Psychology,* 1973, *64,* 205–213. (a)

Shigehisa, T., & Symons, J. R. Reliability of auditory responses under increasing intensity of visual stimulation in relation to personality. *British Journal of Psychology,* 1973, *64,* 375–381. (b)

Shucard, D. W., & Horn, J. L. Evoked cortical potentials and measurement of human abilities. *Journal of Comparative and Physiological Psychology,* 1972, *78,* 59–68.

Stelmack, R. M. The psychophysiology of extraversion and neuroticism. In H. J. Eysenck (Ed.), *A model of personality.* New York: Springer, 1981.

Vogel, W., & Broverman, D. M. Relationship between EEG and test intelligence: A commentary. *Psychological Bulletin,* 1966, *65,* 99–109.

Weisen, A. *Differential reinforcing effects of onset and offset of stimulation on the operant behavior of normals, neurotics and psychopaths.* University of Florida: Unpublished Doctoral thesis, 1965.

14 Biological Determination of Personality Dimensions

Jan Strelau
University of Warsaw, Poland

For many hundreds of years the differentiation between endogenous and exogenous determinants of personality has existed. The major contribution made by Kant and especially by Wundt consists in assuming that biologically (i.e., internally) determined traits of personality (temperament) compose the formal aspect of behavior.

The constitutional concept of personality, also strongly developed in Germany (Kretschmer, Conrad), extracted the content and direction of behavior directly from the human organism, ignoring the fundamental role of the social environment.

Pavlov's view of types of nervous system, generating from experimental research in CRs in animals, was a new approach in seeking biological bases in personality. The neo-Pavlovian approach in human nervous system properties investigation, developed by Teplov, Nebylitsyn, Merlin et al., is an example of experimental research in the biological foundations of personality.

The interactive approach in personality, which stresses that humans are biosocial beings, pays more attention, depending on the taken position, to the biological or social determinants of personality.

Our own concept of biologically determined reactivity and activity of behavior is an example of the regulative theory of temperament. It is assumed that the biological basis of personality (temperament) is a product of biological evolution, whereas personality (the content and direction of behavior) is a product of social environment, moulded on the bases of psychophysiological mechanisms.

It is our belief that future research will support the hypothesis that the psychophysiological mechanisms, being a nonspecific factor in molding personality, do not determine the development of personality, which is primarily a product of sociohistorical conditions.

BIOLOGICAL DETERMINATION OF PERSONALITY DIMENSIONS

Some of the First Ideas of Biological Determinations of Personality

The interest in elucidating individual differences in human behavior dates back as far as the beginning of the history of science. The search for the answer to the question of what the main determinants of personality are went from the start in two quite different directions. In one case the external world was stressed as the main factor in molding personality, in the other one the "forces" inside the individual were assumed to be the most important determinants of people's individuality. Hippocrates–Galen's conception of temperaments serve as an example of internally determined personality, whereas the concept of character given by Theofrastus may serve as an illustration of externally determined personality.

Simplifying matters somewhat, one might say that in many cases the endogenous concepts of personality that stress the importance of biological mechanisms in its moulding are treated within the category of temperament, whereas the concepts of exogenous-determined personality, which stress in first place the importance of the social environment in personality molding, are treated as personality theories in their narrow sense, where the phenomenon of personality is limited to the human only (Hjelle & Ziegler, 1981; Leontev, 1975).

In line with our interests, the first direction of research in personality is discussed; however, one must bear in mind that to limit personality molding to the biological or social determinants only means reductionism that leads always in such cases to wrong and even harmful conclusions.

In German philosophy, and during the first period of experimental psychology, attempts were made to link the biologically determined traits of personality (temperament) with the formal characteristics of behavior. This may be assumed to mark the beginning of a proper understanding of the role of the biological mechanisms in determining personality traits.

Thus, for example, Kant, taking into account vital energy (Lebenskraft) that may be characterized by a dimension with excitability at one pole and drowsiness on the other, and the relations between emotions and activity, introduced in his "Antropologie," a model of four simple temperaments in analogy to his four syllogistic figures. As a matter of fact, it must be mentioned that the concept of Lebenskraft reminds one of the modern concept of the intensity of behavior dimension introduced by Duffy and is very close to the theory of activation–arousal elaborated by the McGill School.

Wundt (1911), for whom the phenomenon of individual differences was rather a source of error in psychological measurements, could not ignore the fact that people differ in the intensity and speed of changing emotions, and these two dimensions of emotion (strong–weak, slow–rapid), which are purely formal characteristics of human reactions, constituted the bases of his typology that he limited to the four classical temperaments.

What was revolutionary in Wundt's understanding of temperament was the idea that temperamental traits could change from situation to situation. This concept—not accepted by the majority of investigators of biological determinants of personality, who stress the stability of these mechanisms—has been developed within the contemporary transactional model by one of my students, Eliasz (1981), who gives some empirical evidence supporting the idea of transituational changes in temperamental traits.

There is also another important idea in Wundt's theory of temperament, namely, the claim that there are neither good nor bad temperaments. Any temperament has its advantages and disadvantages depending on the individual's situation. This modern "interactionistic" kind of thinking expressed in Wundt's concept of temperament passed unnoticed even by Teplov (1961) and Nebylitsyn (1972), who devoted a considerable place in their publications to the evaluation aspect of temperament, more particularly, of nervous system properties, taking a position similar to that of Wundt.

Apart from this direction in grasping the biologically determined dimensions of personality, where the energy aspect of behavior or the intensity and speed of reactions were highlighted without direct connections with content of behavior, in Germany there developed another line of research that is known as *constitutional psychology,* the main representatives of which are Kretschmer (1944) and one of his students, Conrad (1963). The extreme constitutional position of Conrad is less known in the psychological literature but illustrates better than any other the essence of the constitutional thinking. According to Conrad, the variety of body structures and the relation between body structure and temperament in humans can only be explained by referring to specific dominant genes determining the type of body structure and related temperamental traits. Conrad, describing one of his types, the so-called hypoplastic body type (Kretschmer's astenic one) that corresponds with the "spiritualistic" temperament, characterizes the type among others as one disposed to cosmopolitanism, internationalism, and intellectualism (p. 172).

According to this position, like all other constitutional typologies, including Sheldon's well-known temperament typology, the content and direction of behavior is determined by biological mechanisms (genes, endocrine system) or by the individual's body structure. This kind of thinking, being independent of the investigators intention, the "scientific" justification of racist or fascist ideology, was inacceptable to psychologists, especially by those who were involved in personality research. One of the reactions was to remove almost completely the term *temperament* discredited by constitutional psychologists from psychological textbooks and personality monographs.

The Pavlovian Approach in Physiological Bases of Personality

In the same period when constitutional typology was gaining popularity in Germany, Pavlov, researching CR activity in dogs, developed the idea of nervous system types, which constitute, according to him, the physiological bases of personality that he called "temperament." Following his "nervism" paradigm, by which any behavior is governed by the nervous system, he assumed that observed individual differences in CR activity, such as efficiency and speed of CR formation, CR magnitude, and durability, are determined by certain properties of the central nervous system (CNS, i.e., strength of excitation and inhibition, balance, and mobility of nervous processes). Combinations of these properties constitute the type of nervous system. There is no need to describe here his NS typology, which has become popular in the Western countries, especially over the past 2 decades (Gray, 1964; Mangan, 1982; Nebylitsyn, 1972; Strelau, 1975).

Let me emphasize only some facts that are especially important for better understanding of the new ideas in Pavlov's treatment of the biological determination of personality dimensions.

First, Pavlov revealed that the physiological basis of personality lies in some features of excitation and inhibition of the CNS. This idea, elaborated later by his Russian students, has been strongly developed in the West by Eysenck (1970) in his discussion of the physiological bases of extraversion–introversion.

Second, Pavlov was the first to link biologically determined individual differences in conditioning with some aspects of personality, especially with temperament. This line of research has been further developed by some of his students (Ivanov–Smolensky, 1953; Krasnogorsky, 1958). However Spence's anxiety theory (1960) and Eysenck's concept of extraversion–introversion (1970) are the most popular theories in elaborating the link between certain personality dimensions and individual differences in conditioning.

Third, in treating NS type as the physiological basis of temperament, Pavlov paid attention primarily to the functional significance of the basic properties of the NS, stressing their role in regulating the relations between the organism and the requirements of the environment. Therefore it is not accidental that he used the notions "type of nervous system" and "type of higher nervous activity" interchangeably. This approach is represented in the Teplov–Nebylitsyn school (Nebylitsyn, 1972; Teplov, 1961) and constitutes the main direction of research conducted by the Ural group headed originally by Merlin (1973). It is also an idea strongly developed in our laboratory (Strelau, 1974, 1981).

Pavlov, who was influenced by the Hippocrates–Galen theory of temperament, did not avoid influences of the constitutional typologists thinking. He assumed the type of the NS to be a genotype, rather resistant to changes under environmental influences. Evaluating his four types of NS, he classified the weak type (weak, excitatory, and inhibitory processes) as a limited one, with a narrowed vital range. Individuals representing this type may be recognized as valuable only under special conditions, having been reared in hothouse atmospheres (Pavlov, 1951–1952). Giving this kind of NS types description he limited to a high degree the content and direction of the individual's behavior to his or her genotype.

The fixation on types rather than on properties, combinations of which constitute different configurations, was one of the reasons why Pavlov was not greatly interested in explaining the physiological nature of separate properties of the NS, limiting them almost to some general features of the upper segments of the CNS, mainly to the cortex.

A new approach to the biological foundations of personality has been developed by the Neo-Pavlovians, mainly by the Teplov–Nebylitsyn school (the so-called Moscow group) and by Merlin and his students (the Ural group), both centers doing research on people.

Separate nervous system properties, rather than types of NS, became central in the interests of Teplov's laboratory. He and most of his students assumed that such properties should be treated not only as physiological mechanisms of temperament but also as physiological tokens of abilities (Golubeva, 1980; Russalov, 1979).

One of the main contributions of the Teplov school lies in their research showing links between strength of excitation and the biologically determined phenomenon of sensory sensitivity (Teplov, 1961; Nebylitsyn, 1972). This led, among other things, to finding common elements between the Pavlovian nervous system properties and such concepts as extraversion–introversion (Eysenck, 1981; Eysenck & Levey, 1972) or arousal theory (Gray, 1964).

Most of the research conducted during the past 15 years has been concentrated on EEG methods for diagnosing NS properties. Using numerous indicators related to the amplitude, frequency, and energetic characteristics of bioelectrical activity, including basal records, photodriving reactions, and EP, Nebylitsyn and his students attempted to interpret the individual differences in EEG characteristics within the concept of nervous system properties, introducing some new features like dynamism of nervous processes (Nebylitsyn, 1972) and "activatability" (Golubeva, 1980), the latter resembling the concept of arousability introduced by Gray (1964). Without going into details available in the original studies (Golubeva, 1980; Russalov, 1979), one may say that the research shows that most of the NS properties are not so mutually independent as has been thought earlier. If one were to use the accepted EEG indices of activation level, it should be stated that at least such NS properties, like strength of excitation, dynamism of excitation, balance in dynamism, share a part of their variance together with the physiological mechanisms of activation. It may be that the EEG method will become the area within which investigators searching for physiological bases of personality will find a common language, regardless of whether they are looking for the physiological mechanisms of extraversion–introversion, strength or dynamism of the nervous system, sensation seeking, stimulus intensity modulation, or any other biologically determined personality dimension.

Whereas Teplov and Nebylitsyn were specially interested in studying the essential nature of physiological mechanism of nervous system properties, Merlin and his students concentrated mainly on the psychological aspects of these properties. They gathered evidence in support of the hypothesis that the same configurations of nervous system properties may constitute the physiological bases of different temperamental traits, among which they include: extraversion–introversion, rigidity, anxiety, impulsivity, emotional stability, emotional excitability, and the reverse (i.e., the same temperamental traits may be determined by several combinations of nervous system properties, Belous, 1976). This statement seems of considerable importance in understanding the physiological determination of personality dimensions, because it emphasizes the lack of their univocal subordination to physiological mechanisms.

One of the regulatory mechanisms that guarantees efficient functioning in individuals with different nervous system properties has been called style of action (work), codetermined, according to Merlin (1973), by the type of NS. Following their particular interest in preparatory and executive actions, the Merlin group showed that in weak and slow NS types preparatory dominates over executive activity, which ensures individual's proper functioning in strongly stimulating or rapidly changing situations. An opposite regularity may be observed in strong or mobile individuals in whom there is either a balance between both kinds of activity or predominance of executive over preparatory actions. Assuming that individuals have the possibility to develop a proper style of action (i.e., one that is adequate to their NS type), the significance of NS properties in determining the efficiency of functioning plays a secondary role, in view of the fact that the weakness or inertia of the individual's NS properties, can be compensated by the given style of action. Among other things, this means that there is no direct relation between an individual's NS properties and given activity results.

In general one may say that, according to the Russian investigators of Pavlov's typology, the type of NS or particular properties of nervous processes that are mainly treated as the physiological bases of temperament do not directly influence the content or direction of behavior. Neither is there a direct relation between temperament and personality. Relating these two phenomena, Leontev (1975) stressed that temperamental traits, which are the outcome of biological evolution, do not determine the direction of personality development that is primarily set by the social environment. In other words, personality should be treated as a resultant of social–historical evolution.

Man as the Biosocial Being: Different Understanding of the Contribution of the Biological Factor into the Interaction with Environment

In speaking about the biological bases of personality dimensions, I have limited myself mainly to the investigations involved with the Pavlovian tradition in this area. However it would be unfair if one were to neglect such concepts as Eysenck's well-known theory of personality and the interesting modification given by Gray, Zuckerman's concept of sensation seeking, Petrie's idea of stimulus intensity modulation with the physiological interpretations made by Buchsbaum, Buss and Plomin's three-dimensional theory of temperament, or the interactional concept of temperament proposed by Thomas and Chess that is growing in popularity, and several others I shall not mention here.

In all of them, major attention is paid to the biological determination of personality or of some dimensions considered as belonging to personality. However, answers to the question of what comprises the physiological bases of given personality dimensions differ, as well as the dimensions themselves. For instance, Eysenck (1981), in discussing the biological nature of extraversion–introversion, stresses the importance of the cortex-reticular formation loop in determining these dimensions; Zuckerman, 1979, stresses the importance of some neurotransmitters, norepinephrine and dopamine, in molding the sensation-seeking dimension; Thomas and Chess, 1977, who have underlined the importance of biological determination of temperament, do not give any answer at all about what really is the physiological mechanism of temperament; nor do Buss and Polomin, 1975, whose temperament theory is a descriptive one.

All the preceeding authors generally accept the idea that a human is a biosocial being, by which is meant that human development is a resultant of the interaction of biological and social factors. However, they differ in the extent of attention paid to the significance of the biological factor in this interaction. For example, according to Eysenck, extraverts, with a decreased level of cortico-reticular activity (i.e., with low arousability), are poor in conditioning and poor in socialization, both of these facts having strong influences on the development of a number of personality traits and attitudes. If we accept Eysenck's hypothesis and he shows convincing evidence for it, we are compelled at the same time to support the presupposition that the content and direction of human behavior is to a great extent inherited, which evokes much doubt and can hardly be accepted even by biologically oriented psychologists.

Let me give an example illustrating a different view of the importance of the biological factor in molding personality, within the framework of the aforementioned theories. Thomas and Chess, who developed the idea of nine biologically determined temperament dimensions, show that depending on the environment, especially on family-rearing conditions, individuals may develop quite different personality patterns, and temperamental dimensions comprise only one of the many factors that codetermine to some degree the molding of personality. Their significance, however, takes on special importance in those cases where the parents or educators ignore the child's biologically determined personality traits (i.e., his temperament).

Temperament as Biologically Determined Personality Dimensions

Taking as a starting point the Pavlovian typology, in particular the research trend developed by Teplov in which I have been involved since the mid-1950s, my students and I have developed a theory of temperament that might be understood as biologically determined personality dimensions. In view of the essential feature of this concept we have proposed to call it the *regulative theory of temperament.*

By temperament I understand a set of formal, relatively stable behavioral traits expressed in the energy level of behavior and in the temporal characteristic of reactions. Temperament, a product of biological evolution, is in large part genetically determined, but it may change under durable environmental conditions (e.g., temperature, nutrition, noise). We emphasize the fact that temperament as such does not rule out the possibility of indirect influences. As one of the regulative mechanisms of behavior, temperament is manifested in all kinds of activity, regardless of direction and content. We have concentrated primarily on the energy level of behavior, by which we cover all those traits that are determined by relatively stable individual differences in the physiological mechanism responsible for the accumulation and release of energy in the organism.

Our studies led us to single out two basic properties of behavior: reactivity and activity. By reactivity I understand a property that determines the intensity (magnitude) of reaction that is characteristic for a given individual and is relatively stable. Reactivity constitutes a dimension that runs from (sensory or emotional) sensitivity at one pole to extreme endurance under strong stimulation at the other. Thus conceived, reactivity resembles nervous system strength.

We decided to abandon the notion of nervous system strength for a number of reasons (Strelau, 1974). One of the most important was that nervous system strength is essentially an explanatory concept of rather limited scope, saddled with given tradition. Pavlov and his students used to ascribe this property to cortical processes almost entirely. More recently, notably at Nebylitsyn's laboratory, some attention has also been paid to subcortical processes. Our view is that the physiological mechanism of reactivity is even more complex than that, forming a bloc of several systems: the endocrine system, the autonomous nervous system, certain neural centers in the brainstem, and some features of the cortex— a bloc of relatively stable structures within the given individual.

Another reason for abandoning the notion of nervous system strength has been our desire to underline the behavioral aspect of our interest in temperament. Finally, the notion of nervous system strength is burdened—as are all the other properties of the nervous system—with certain typological tradition. One drawback of this tradition is the emphasis on innateness or even immutability of the properties (Pavlov, 1951–1952; Teplov, 1961), a claim that appears doubtful in the light of recent evidence, including that produced in our laboratory (Eliasz, 1981).

Coming back to reactivity, we assume that it might be, among others, experimentally measured by taking into account the ratio of the magnitude of reaction to the intensity of acting stimuli. Reactivity is the higher, the less intensive the stimulus evoking a just noticeable reaction (the lower the sensitivity threshold) and, also, the weaker the stimulus needed to disrupt efficient responding (the lower the person's endurance), and vice versa: A person with low reactivity displays low sensitivity and high endurance.

Without going into the details of the physiological mechanism of reactivity, we simply suggest that in highly reactive individuals this mechanism tends to reinforce stimulation. Both external and internal stimuli evoke in these persons stronger reactions than in low-reactive individuals. A high-reactive individual has therefore a high Stimulation Processing Coefficient (SPC). Low-reactive individuals possess a physiological mechanism that tends to depress stimulation: A stimulus of a given intensity evokes in them a weaker response than in high-reactive persons. Hence the former have a low SPC (Matysiak, 1980).

In addition to reactivity we have isolated another property that bears testimony to the energy level of a person's behavior, namely, activity, conceived as a property on which individuals vary in the intensity or frequency with which they undertake actions or engage in tasks. Irrespective of its specific character or direction (which depend on the person's tasks or goals), activity functions also as a regulator of the amount of stimulation, the demand for which is determined by the person's reactivity level. High-reactive persons (with high SPC) can do with weaker stimulation to reach what for them is an optimal level of activation (Hebb, 1955). Hence their demand for stimulation, and naturally their activity in search for such stimulation also, is lower than in low-reactive persons. The latter are in need of strong stimulation, being driven by the desire to function at an optimal activation level. Thus, low-reactive individuals (with low SPC) have strong demand for stimulation and also for activity as a regulator of that demand.

Activity may serve either as a direct or an indirect source of stimulation. It is a direct source in the sense that the person's motor activity results in activation of the receptors, and the latter pass on this activation to higher nervous centers (Fiske & Maddi, 1961). This type of stimulation arises on the basis of the well-known mechanism of feedback afferentation. Moreover, a behavior that arouses certain emotions for the performed action possesses a particular stimulation capacity itself in that the excitation-inducing factor is the emotional process accompanying the given action. Activities may thus be a source of stimulation chiefly because they generate certain emotions, which in turn elicit a particular state of activation.

Activity is also an indirect source of stimulation, chiefly in that it serves the person in the choice of those situations, settings, and tasks that supply the desired amount of stimulation. Evidence obtained in our laboratory from studies on rats (Matysiak, 1980) suggests that the aforementioned relationship between activity and reactivity applies only to activities that generate stimulation in a direct fashion (through feedback afferentation or by generating emotions). High-reactive individuals may manifest a great deal of activity in their behavior, provided that the goal of their activity is to reduce or avoid stimulation. In one case we have to do with positively oriented activity (stimulation seeking), in the other case negatively oriented activity (stimulation avoidance), as shown by Matysiak (1980).

Working with a concept of temperament that focuses on reactivity as the principal dimension, we have carried out a series of studies on the regulative functions of temperament in human activities. Among other things, it has been shown that reactivity is decisive for the formation of the person's style of action, that reactivity codetermines tolerance to stress, that it influences preferences for actions that supply necessary amounts of stimulation, and that it shows a definite relationship to the individual's personality as one of the factors in the formation of this personality, without however directly causing its development.

There is no place to present the results of research; however, let me illustrate some of the main regularities that have been discovered during the last 10 years in our laboratory. For example, taking into account the style of action understood

TABLE 14.1
Preference of Different Action Styles in High-
and Low-Reactive Individuals

Style of Action	Reactivity	
	High	Low
Predominance of actions leading directly to the goal (primary actions)	<	
Preparatory actions	>	
Corrective actions during task performance	>	
Corrective activity after task is performed	=	
Control actions	>	
Continous actions	<	
Intermittend actions	>	
Homogenous actions during continuous activity	<	
Heterogenous actions during continuous activity	>	

TABLE 14.2
Efficiency and Preference of Behavior in Situations Differing in
Stimulation Load in Individuals with High and Low Reactivity

	Reactivity	
Situations and Activities	*High*	*Low*
Risk-taking behavior in decision games	<	
Decision making in time-limited situations: easy tasks	=	
Decision making in time-limited situations: difficult tasks	<	
Preference of professions and activities of low stimulation value (librarians, avoiding athletic activity)	>	
Preference of professions and activities with high stimulation value (lawyers, mountaineers, parachutists)	<	
Sporting activities in highly competitive situations	<	
Sporting activities during training	=	

as the mode of performing an act peculiar to the individual, it has been stated that the number and time spent on realizing the separate styles depends on the individuals reactivity level. Some of our data are comprised in Table 14.1, which gives information if a separate style of action dominates in the high- or in the low-reactive individuals. It has to be mentioned, however, that if the high- and low-reactive individuals have the possibility to realize their own style of activity and are not limited in its performing by natural or laboratory conditions, there is no difference between them in the efficiency of performance. Similar facts have been confirmed in the Pavlovian typology research (see p. 201).

Taking as another example the preferences of actions or situations differing in stimulation load, we have data that show that highly reactive individuals show a low need for stimulation, whereas low-reactive ones may be characterized by a high need for stimulation. Table 14.2 illustrates some of the general trends established in our experiments where the differences between high- and low-reactive individuals in their level of performance or the preference to perform given activity in situations differing in stimulation load have been taken into account. If the high-reactive individuals have the possibility to lower the stimulation value of the situation in which activity is performed, for example, by realizing their own style of action (i.e., by performing a given amount of preparatory, control, or corrective activities) that may highten the chance of performing primary actions, the differences between high- and low-reactive individuals may disappear.

Most of the research we are conducting at present and that is planned for the next few years focuses on the empirical verification—in laboratory experiments as well as in field studies—of our hypotheses concerned with the regulative functions of the basic temperamental traits.

Summarizing our considerations and at the same time looking to the future of research on the biologically determined dimensions of personality that I prefer to call temperament, it is my belief that we shall be able to gather more and more data convincing us that the physiological bases of personality neither determine nor directly influence the development of personality. They are rather of a nonspecific character and only in interaction with the environment, especially the social, they may codetermine the development of personality in a given direction. From the physiological mechanisms of personality alone, it is not possible to predict the direction of an individual's development. The higher on the developmental ladder (onto- and phylogenetically) the individual is, the lower the specific influence of this mechanism. This rather pessimistic picture from the viewpoint of the biologically oriented personality researcher is in fact a very optimistic one for the human individual, because what his or her personality will be is not predestined by nature. The knowledge of physiological mechanisms underlying given personality dimensions helps, however, to understand their nature and provides information on one of the important codeterminants of personality development, one that cannot be ignored, like other factors influencing the molding of the individual's personality.

REFERENCES

Belous, V. V. Mathematical models of temperament from the point of view of systems theory. In V. S. Merlin (Ed.), *Temperament*. Perm: Ministerstvo Prosveshcheniya RSFSR, Permski Gosudarstvenny Pedagogicheski Institut, 1976, 16–44 (in Russian).

Buss, A. H., & Polomin, R. *A temperament theory of personality development*. New York: Wiley, 1975.

Conrad, K. *Der Konstitutionstypus. Theoretische Grundlegung und praktische Bestimmung* (2nd ed.). Berlin: Springer Verlag, 1963.

Eliasz, A. *Temperament a system regulacji stymulacji*. Warszawa: Państwowe Wydawnictwo Naukowe, 1981.

Eysenck, H. J. *The structure of human personality*. London: Methuen, 1970.

Eysenck, H. J. (Ed.). *A model for personality*. Berlin–New York: Springer Verlag, 1981.

Eysenck, H. J., & Levey, A. Conditioning, introversion–extraversion and the strength of the nervous system. In V. D. Nebylitsyn & J. A. Gray (Eds.), *Biological bases of individual behavior*. New York and London: Academic Press, 1972.

Fiske, D. W., & Maddi, S. R. A conceptual framework. In D. W. Fiske & S. R. Maddi (Eds.), *Functions of varied experience*. Homewood: Dorsey, 1961.

Golubeva, E. A. *Individual properties of human memory (psychophysiological investigation)*. Moskva: Pedagogika, 1980 (in Russian).

Gray, J. A. *Pavlov's typology*. Oxford–Frankfurt: Pergamon Press, 1964.

Hebb, D. O. Drives and the CNS (conceptual nervous system). *Psychological Review*, 1955, *62*, 243–254.

Hjelle, L. A., & Ziegler, D. J. *Personality theories*. New York: McGraw-Hill, 1981.

Ivanov–Smolensky, A. G. On the investigation of types of higher nervous activity in animals and man. *Zhurnal Vysshei Nervnoi Deyatelnosti*, 1953, *3*, 1, 36–54 (in Russian).

Krasnogorsky, N. P. *Higher nervous activity in children*. Leningrad: Medgiz, 1958 (in Russian).

Kretschmer, E. *Körperbau und Charakter* (17-18th ed.). Berlin: Springer Verlag, 1944.

Leontev, A. N. *Activity, consciousness, personality.* Moskva: Izdatelstvo politicheskoy literatury, 1975 (in Russian).

Mangan, G. L. *The biology of human conduct. East–West models of temperament and personality.* London: Pergamon Press, 1982.

Matysiak, J. *Różnice indiwidualne w zachowaniu zwierzat w świetle koncepcji zapotrzebowania na stymulacje.* Wrocław–Warszawa: Ossolineum, 1980.

Merlin, V. S. (Ed.). *Outline of the theory of temperament* (2nd ed.). Perm: Permskoye knizhnoye izdatelstvo, 1973.

Nebylitsyn, V. D. *Fundamental properties of the human nervous system.* New York–London: Plenum Press, 1972.

Pavlov, I. P. *Complete works* (2nd ed.). Moskva–Leningrad: Akademia Nauk SSSR, 1951–1952 (in Russian).

Russalov, V. D. *Biological bases of individual-psychological differences.* Moskva: Nauka, 1979 (in Russian).

Spence, K. W. *Behavior theory and learning. Selected papers.* Englewood Cliffs, N.J.: Prentice-Hall, 1960.

Strelau, J. Temperament as an expression of energy level and temporal features of behavior. *Polish Psychological Bulletin,* 1974, *5,* 119–127.

Strelau, J. Pavlovs typology and current investigations in this area. *Netherlands Tijdschrift voor Psychologie,* 1975, *30,* 177–200.

Strelau, J. (Ed.). *Regulacyjne funkcje temperamentu.* Wrocław–Warszawa: Ossolineum, 1981.

Teplov, B. M. *Problems of individual differences.* Moskva: Izdatelstvo APN RSFSR, 1961 (in Russian).

Thomas, A., & Chess, S. *Temperament and development.* New York: Brunner/Mazel Publishers, 1977.

Wundt, W. *Grundzüge der physiologischen Psychologie* (6th ed.) Vol. III. Leipzig: Verlag von W. Engelmann, 1911.

Zuckerman, M. *Sensation seeking: Beyond the optimal level of arousal.* Hillsdale, N.J.: Lawrence Erlbaum Associates, 1979.

15

The Situation in an Interactional Paradigm of Personality Research

David Magnusson
University of Stockholm, Sweden

That behavior cannot be understood and explained per se but only in relation to the situational conditions under which it occurs and can be observed has been a general theme since the 1920s among psychologists interested in molar, social behavior. It has been explicitly stated from various perspectives by behaviorists, field theorists, personologists, trait psychologists, psychodynamists, and those arguing for an interactional approach to the study of human behavior (Allport, 1966; Barker, 1965; Cattell, 1963; Kantor, 1924, 1926; Lewin, 1951; Murphy, 1947; Murray, 1938; Sells, 1963; Stagner, 1976; Tolman, 1951; Wachtel, 1977). Sometimes it has been stated that trait theorists have neglected or at least underestimated the role of situational conditions for understanding and explaining behavior. Then it is particularly interesting to recognize the strong statement about the importance of considering the situational context by one of the most devoted trait theorists, namely Raymond B. Cattell (1963) when he wrote: "Lack of allowance for the situation is one of the main causes of misjudging personality [p. 27]." His attitude to this problem was also manifested in his formulation of the "specification" or "behavioral equation."

IMPORTANCE OF THE SITUATIONAL CONTEXT IN BEHAVIOR

The consideration of situational factors for understanding behavior has not been restricted to researchers in psychology. For ethologists it has always been natural to refer to situational context, for example, in terms of perceived territories, in explanatory models of *animal* behavior. From their various perspectives, anthropologists and sociologists have also made important contributions—too often overlooked in the theoretical debate in psychology—to the theoretical discussion about the role of situational conditions for human behavior.

Thus situations and situational conditions have not been a neglected issue in the *theoretical* debate in psychology or in neighboring disciplines, and there is not much new in proposing that we should consider the situational context in models of personality. Those who argue that situations play an important role in the processes underlying human behavior have certainly won the battle of words in this respect.

If we take the theoretical formulations seriously, they have important and, in some respects, far-reaching consequences for research strategies, for models of measurement, for which type of data are appropriate, and for methods for data collection and analysis. This is true in many fields of research: Not only for research on molar, social behavior but also for research on perception, cognition, and information processing in general; stress and anxiety; emotions; and psychophysiological processes. And the consequences are important both for research on contemporaneous behavior and for research on development (Magnusson, 1981).

Given the background of almost total agreement among theorists over a long period of time about the importance of including the situational context in models of personality and the serious consequences of these theoretical formulations, it is surprising and also embarrassing to recognize how little impact on empirical research these formulations have had. It is only recently, and slowly at that, that the formulations have led to research in the two obvious directions: (1) systematic analyses of the lawfulness of person by situation interactions; and (2) systematical analyses of the situations in which behavior is observed, as a basis for research on lawful interactions. One indication of this paucity of available research is the fact that we are almost totally lacking in adequate conceptualizations, distinctions, and an appropriate language for situations and for person–situation interactions.

It is the purpose of this chapter to draw attention to the importance of considering in a systematic and informed way the situational context in which behavior occurs in the planning, carrying-through, and interpreting empirical research on personality. I do not suggest that we should devote all our resources to this kind of research or that it is the most important task in psychology. But I do believe that taking seriously the consequences of the theoretical formulations about the role of the situational context for human functioning is *one* of the directions that we must follow in order to reach the ultimate goal for theorizing and empirical research in psychology, namely to understand why individuals think, feel, react, and act as they do in real-life situations.

In analyses and discussions about lawfulness of individual functioning, a distinction must be made between lawfulness in terms of manifest behavior and lawfulness in terms of perceptions, thoughts, and feelings. There is not a one-to-one relation between these two levels of functioning. For example, one and the same intention may be manifested in different ways in different situations for the same person and in different ways for different persons in the same situation. The same behavior may reflect different intentions at different occasions for the same person and different intentions at the same occasion for different persons (Hammond, 1955, and his discussion of *equifinality* and *equipotentiality*). One important task for theorizing and research is to investigate the way these two systems interact in a continuous, bidirectional process.

Consideration of the situational context is essential in analysis at both levels of individual functioning (manifest behavior and perception–cognition). It would lead too far afield to go into all these problems; therefore, I restrict myself to a discussion of situational conditions and their influence on *manifest behavior*. I fulfill my purpose by discussing basic distinctions with respect to situational effects, with respect to behavior models, with respect to types of data, and by presentation of three empirical studies. The theoretical distinctions and the empirical studies are used as the background for some suggestions about directions for future research.

Needless to say, my concentration on the level of manifest behavior does not imply that the issue of situational effects on perceptual–cognitive processes is less important. For example, I believe that we would arrive at more functional and thereby more effective models for perceptual and cognitive processes, for information processing, and for decision making if we started more explicitly than hitherto from two reasonable hypotheses implying differential situational effects: (1) that one and the same kind of situational information may evoke different kinds of cognitive processes and cognitive strategies in different individuals; and (2) that different situational information may evoke different kinds of cognitive processes and cognitive strategies in the same individual.

THEORETICAL MODELS AND THEIR IMPLICATIONS

Two Types of Situational Effects[1]

During the 1970s the role of situations has been especially stressed by those advocating an interactional paradigm of research, in which behavior is regarded as an aspect of the continuous reciprocal interaction process between person and situational factors (Magnusson & Endler, 1977). In that process two kinds of

---

[1]The term *situation* is used here to denote situation-bound contextual sources of influence on behavior in a wide sense. (For a more systematic discussion about definitions and distinctions, the reader is referred to Magnusson, 1978, 1981, and Pervin, 1978, among others.)

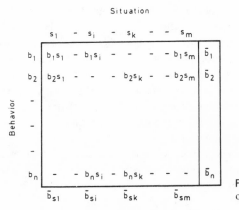

FIG. 15.1. Matrix of raw data for one individual.

situational effects on behavior can be distinguished: general and differential effects.[2]

When situational effects are *general,* the rank order of individuals for a certain behavior is the same across situations, independent of their nature. It is only the intensity of the specific behavior under consideration that changes with variation in situational conditions, and it does so monotonically across individuals. General situational effects are expressed in the means of reactions for situations and reflected in the main variance due to situations in a reaction by situation matrix of data (Fig. 15.1) for a certain individual.

The implication of *differential* situational effects is that rank orders of individuals for a certain kind of behavior will vary across situations. The existence of differential situational effects is revealed in the interaction variance in a person by situation matrix of data.

Models of Behavior

The quality of conclusions drawn from empirical research is dependent on the properties and quality of the data obtained. No sophisticated method for data treatment can save poor or inappropriate data. But the appropriateness of data for illuminating a psychological problem is determined, among other things, by the assumed model of behavior. Too often methods for data collection are used and methods for data treatment applied without making explicit the important connection with an underlying behavioral model.

Most personality theories have concentrated mainly on the lawfulness of mediating cognitive processes, using different intervening variables and hypo-

---

[2]In the discussion about person × situation interactions, it has been emphasized that the person–situation interaction is a bidirectional, reciprocal *process,* in which the traditional distinction between independent and dependent variables is not always obvious. However, the relation between situational factors and behavior is discussed in such terms here, for simplicity.

thetical constructs to explain behavior. Less theoretical interest has been devoted to the lawfulness of actual behavior; this has been taken for granted and used for testing hypotheses derived from theories and models for mediating processes. However, the need for coherent and explicit models of the lawfulness of behavior is just as obvious as it is for models of lawfulness of mediating processes. This is, of course, the case when behavior per se is the object of research, but it also applies when interest is focused on models for cognitive processes and behavioral criteria are used to test the validity of such models (Magnusson, 1980).

A crucial aspect of any model of behavior is the assumption made about consistency of behavior (i.e., the type of lawfulness of behavior that is assumed). With respect to situational effects, two different models can be distinguished (Fig. 15.2).

A Trait Measurement Behavior Model.   The predominant behavioral model, in empirical research, can be derived from a trait measurement model (Magnusson, 1976). (The trait measurement model should be clearly distinguished from the trait personality *theory.*) The theoretical base for that model is two assumptions: (1) Each individual has a certain position, his "true score," on each of a number of latent dimensions of basic personality factors, say, independence, anxiety etc.; and (2) there is a monotonic relation between individuals' positions on such dimensions and their positions for relevant manifest behaviors. These assumptions are reflected in the well-known formula in classical test theory ($t_j = T_j + e$), in which an obtained test score is regarded as the sum of a true component (T) and an error component (e). Taken together, the two assumptions lead to the conclusion that the rank order of individuals for a certain type of behavior will be stable across situations. Lawfulness of behavior is sought in stable rank orders of behavior (i.e., in relative consistency).

The assumption about stable rank orders of individuals across situations implies that possible differential situational effects are *not* taken into account or reflected in data for actual behavior. Across situations, individuals differ for a

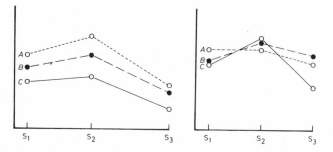

FIG. 15.2.   Cross-situational profiles for a certain type of behavior for three individuals (A, B, C) according to (a) trait-measurement (b) an interactional model of behavior.

certain behavior only with respect to the general level of intensity (expressed in means or sums of data across situations), which make up the variance due to persons in a person × situation matrix of data.

Most empirical research in personality during the last 4 decades has used the relative consistency hypothesis, implicitly or explicitly. However, its generality and validity were questioned early by Hartshorne and May (1928) and have been the object of much research since then (see Bowers, 1973; Ekehammar, 1974; Endler, 1982; Endler & Magnusson, 1976; Epstein, 1979; Magnusson & Endler, 1977; Mischel, 1968, for summaries). This has been one of the central issues in research connected with the debate on person by situation interaction during the 1970s. Empirical studies of cross-situational consistency have been concerned with different kinds of data (test data, inventory data, ratings, etc.), for different samples of individuals and of situations. For the present discussion the following conclusions that can be drawn from these studies are of special interest:

1. The degree of relative consistency of behavior, expressed in stability of rank orders of individuals, varies systematically with the similarity among situations across which behavior is observed. This was well illustrated in a study by Magnusson, Gerzén, and Nyman (1968). Using ratings of behavior as raw data, they obtained coefficients for relative consistency of about .70 when there was no variation in situational conditions between the observations, whereas the stability coefficients gave a distribution around 0 when the situations were varied with respect to both group composition and task.

2. The degree of consistency varies with type of behavior as well as with type of data. Thus, the degree of validity of the relative consistency hypothesis about stable rank order cannot be settled once and for all. It is an important task for empirical research to investigate when and to what extent it is valid. However, across variables, types of data, and situations, the main variance due to persons is substantial. The general level of behavioral responses, reflected in means across situations, is an important characteristic of individuals and is needed for adequate description and classification.

An Interactional Model of Behavior.   The basic assumption in an interactional model of behavior is that lawfulness is to be sought in individuals' partly unique *patterns* of stable and changing behaviors across situations that differ in character (i.e., lawfulness in behavior lies in coherent cross-situational patterns rather than in stable rank orders). In terms of data, individuals are then best described by cross-situational profiles having two characteristics: (1) a general intensity level; and (2) an individually unique part. (In terms of underlying mediating processes, interindividual differences in patterns of behavior are interpreted in terms of interindividual differences in the perception and interpretation of the situations across which the individuals are observed.) This implies an important difference in relation to the trait measurement model of behavior:

Variations across situations in rank-order positions for a certain type of behavior are assumed to reflect valid and important information about the individuals and will be treated as true variance (Magnusson, 1976). Thus the classical formula for an obtained test score for individual j should be extended to include a situation-bound component T_s and be written $t_j = T_j + T_{j_s} + e$. For an adequate and effective description we must add another parameter to the general trait level considered in the trait measurement model, namely, the individually unique part of the cross-situational profiles (i.e., the part of the profiles that remains when the variance reflected in the mean profiles for individuals is partialled out). To summarize, an interactional model of behavior assumes two person parameters: (1) the general trait level, reflected in the main variance due to persons; and (2) the unique cross-situational profile, reflected in the interaction variance in a person × situation matrix of data for each type of behavior.

The relative importance of the two sources of person variance depends on the specific character of the situations across which behavior is observed, the sample of individuals studied, and the person variables investigated (Endler, 1975; Magnusson, 1976; Mischel, 1973; Sarason, Smith, & Diener, 1975). That the idiographic part of the cross-situational profiles is significantly stable across time was demonstrated in a recent empirical study by Magnusson and Stattin (1981), who studied the stability of inventory data over a period of 6 months.

Two Types of Data

In empirical personality research two kinds of data, reflecting different situational effects on behavior, are used as a basis for description and classification of individuals. They can be designated *trait-bound* and *situation-bound* data, respectively (Goldfried & D'Zurilla, 1969; Goldfried & Kent, 1972).

Trait-Bound Data.   A trait-bound datum represents an individual's general trait level (his or her "true score") for a certain type of behavior. It is obtained as a mean or as a sum of responses across situations (the last column in Fig. 15.1). Thus, trait-bound data are not representative of, nor do they reflect, an individual's responses in a specific situation or a specific type of situation. It is in itself an aggregation of observations cross-situationally and over time, often in an unspecified and uncontrolled way.

The situations to be considered are generally not defined, at least not very clearly. The domain of situations may be defined, say as working life, family, etc., but generally no attempts are made to group the situations on the basis of their similarity in evoking or promoting a certain type of behavior or on the basis of perceived similarity. These kinds of data reflect the basic assumption that each individual can best be described by a true score for each basic dimension and that the purpose of using such data is to estimate this true score. Variations across situations in rank orders of individuals are regarded as *error variance*.

Trait-bound data are obtained in two main ways:

1. By allowing the individual himself to generalize across a defined sample or an unlimited, undefined population of situations ("Do you often show . . .?," "Do you generally feel . . .?"). This is the type of raw data usually obtained by answers to single items in traditional types of *inventories*. Obviously, this type of data has some drawbacks, due to the fact that the situational conditions to which the self-generated ratings refer are unknown.

2. By allowing raters to give a judgment based on observations of the individual across situations of different character, either *directly* (as in teachers' *ratings* of their pupils) or *indirectly* (as in an interview). The variance in ratings as raw data depends on the conditions for the observations that form the basis of the judgment of the rater, the range of situational conditions, the number of situations, the length of the observation period, etc.

Trait-bound data obtained by inventories and by ratings predominate in empirical personality research, and their characteristics are fundamental for evaluating their effectiveness as a basis for description and classification of individuals. One implication is that person factors based on trait-bound data are defined in terms of and are homogeneous only with respect to behaviors, and the situational factors are not controlled. Data from such instruments do reflect individual differences in mean levels of behavior but do not account for cross-situationally unique differences in patterns of behavior. Thus, differential situational effects on data are not taken into account.

Situation-Bound Data. The characteristic of situation-bound data is that each datum refers to behavior in a situation of known properties or to situations that are similar in some relevant aspect(s). In Fig. 15.1 each cell represents a situation-bound datum. A special, but very illustrative case in which situation-bound data are common and have proved their efficiency for personality description and classification is intelligence research.

A test item can be regarded as a well-defined situation that presents each individual with a specific task. For a random sample of items from a population covering different areas of intelligence, the correlations vary from very high for similar items to very low for dissimilar items. By factor analysis, data for specific items (situations) are grouped into factors on the basis of the degree of cross-item (cross-situational) similarity.

An intelligence factor can be described and discussed in terms of the tasks (situations) that define it (e.g., logical problems) as well as in terms of the appropriate behavior (logical ability). Then, what is called an *intelligence factor* is homogeneous with respect to both the kind of behavior and the kind of situations. A factor score is obtained by aggregation of data across the same kinds of situations for a certain type of behavior. Thus, the important situation factors are under control.

Individual profiles of factor scores for a number of homogeneous factors based on situation-bound data can, according to this view, be regarded as cross-situational profiles of behavior. Each profile reflects the individual's general level of intelligence as well as the specific, unique part of his intelligence profile. In this tradition, intelligence research is in accordance with a mechanistic interactional model of behavior.

Comments. The characteristics of situation-bound data and trait-bound data must be considered when using data and interpreting results in empirical research, both when raw data are used without aggregation and when they are aggregated (e.g., by factor analysis). When raw data are used, the consequences are rather obvious, the most obvious being that raw trait-bound data are aggregated data in themselves. When data are used for factor analyses, the differences in character of the data that are actually used for conclusions (i.e., factor scores) are concealed to such an extent that it is rather difficult to see them.

Factor analysis was originally developed in the area of intelligence, using situation-bound data. The items are grouped into homogeneous factors on the basis of cross-situational similarity for a relevant sample of individuals. Thus, the total variance in the person by response by situation data matrix is used for finding the relevant set of factors, and, consequently, the resulting set of factors explains the reliable common variance in the total person × situation × response matrix of data. A factor score for a certain individual reflects the individual's performance in a certain type of situation defined by a certain type of tasks, requiring that kind of performance. Among other things, this implies that such a factor score will have high predictability with respect to that kind of performance in relevant types of situations.

Later the use of factor analysis was extended to other areas of personality research, where trait-bound data were frequently used. Of course, using such data for factor analysis was technically correct. However, the researchers did not always (or not even often) recognize the fact that using trait-bound data will yield factors of somewhat different character from using situation-bound data in the analyses. A factor analysis on trait-bound data will use only the common variance in the person by response matrix, and consequently the factors will reflect only the common variance in the person by response matrix of data with neglect of the variance due to situations, A factor is defined by items that rank-order individuals in the same way without reference to situational conditions. This implies that factor scores based on trait-bound data should have lower predictability with respect to a certain kind of behavior in a certain type of situation than scores for factors that are based on situation-bound data.

The difference in characteristics between situation-bound data and trait-bound data makes it necessary to consider which type of data is used in empirical research. Results obtained with the two types of data are not comparable without reservations and cannot be used interchangably in research on, for example, cross-situational and longitudinal stability.

It has been suggested that some kinds of person variables (e.g., intelligence) are more stable person characteristics than others (e.g., temperament variable) (Mischel, 1973). With reference to the preceding discussion, it should be observed that research in these two areas has been dominated by different types of data. Most of the research on stability of intelligence has used situation-bound data, whereas most research on the stability of temperament variables has used the traditional type of inventory data. This circumstance may have contributed at least partially to the reported differences in the stability data between these two types of person variables (intelligence versus temperament).

EMPIRICAL ILLUSTRATIONS OF THE ROLE OF SITUATIONS

The systematic and lawful nature of the relation between situational conditions and individuals' perceptions of and reactions to situations is illustrated here by three empirical studies performed in my research group. They are selected from a series of studies in which the role of situational conditions has been investigated in the domain of anxiety-provoking situations. The studies are not presented in order to show decisive results. The purpose is illustrative rather than substantial, and the comments are therefore restricted to implications of the results for methodology and research strategy that are the focus of interest here. (For further discussion of the results, the reader is referred to the original reports.)

AGE DIFFERENCES IN SITUATION PERCEPTION

The starting point for this study was the question of age, sex, and cultural differences in the perception and interpretation of anxiety-provoking situations. The problem has been investigated using data for the age levels 12, 15, and 18, for youngsters from Hungary, Japan, Sweden, and Yemen. Data from Hungary is used here to illustrate a way for analyzing situations and investigating interindividual responses to anxiety-provoking situations (Magnusson & Oláh, 1981).

Principally, the problems focused upon imply two main steps in the procedure. First, we need an empirical definition of the population of anxiety-provoking situation, and, second, we must investigate the structure among the situations in terms of categories or dimensions. To reach that goal, the following procedure was used.

Across sex and age levels (12, 15, and 18 years) a sample of about 130 subjects was drawn. The basic data for age and sex comparisons were free descriptions of anxiety-provoking situations given by each individual. The instructions asked each subject to describe as carefully and concretely as possible the most anxiety-provoking situations he or she had experienced or could imagine. Then the subjects were asked to describe which specific element in that situation was associated with his or her experience of anxiety and *why* this specific element was anxiety provoking. The instruction was repeated three times, which allowed each individual to produce three anxiety-provoking situations.

According to modern social learning theories, behavior develops in a process in which two types of expectations are formed: *Situation-outcome contingencies* (which means that certain situational conditions imply certain outcomes) and *behavior-outcome contingencies* (which means that certain behaviors by the individual will lead to certain consequences). With reference to such theories two schemes for the classification of situations have been developed (Magnusson & Stattin, 1981). The categories in each of the schemes are shown in Table 15.1.

Using the subscheme "Situational Characteristic," situations are classified on the basis of the descriptions of *what* element in the situations is associated with experiences of anxiety. Using the subscheme "Expected Consequences," the situations are classified on the basis of the descriptions of *why* these situational elements are anxiety–provoking. The psychometric properties of data obtained by the subschemes have been investigated to estimate the reliability of data obtained by them. The analyses have shown that the procedure is reliable to a satisfactory extent.

TABLE 15.1
Categorizing Schemes for (a) Situation Characteristics and (b)
Expected Characteristics

(a) Situation Characteristics	*(b) Expected Consequence*
Person	*Physical–Bodily*
1. Self	1. Physical pain
2. Parents	2. Physical injury
3. Other closely akin adults	3. Uneasiness
4. Siblings	4. Unrealistic
5. Authorities outside the family	*Personal–interpersonal*
6. Equals	5. Personal inadequacy
7. "Dangerous" people	6. Loss of self-control
8. People in general	7. Death
Situation	8. Punishment
9. Demand of achievement	9. Guilt
10. Medical situations	10. Shame
11. Accidents	11. Rejection
12. Common phobia	12. Separation
13. Animals	*Global*
14. Archaic situations	13. Societal
15. Supernatural horror	
16. Macro-social	

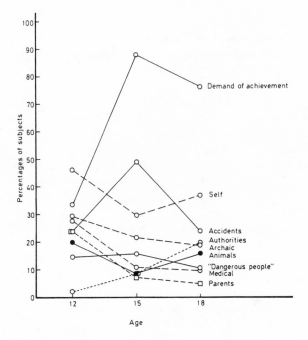

FIG. 15.3.   Age curves for the percentage of boys reporting different categories of Situational Characteristics.

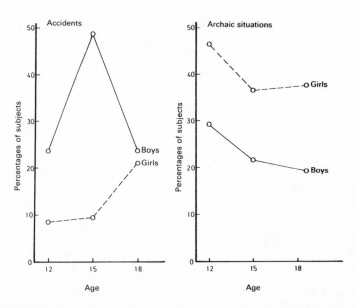

FIG. 15.4.   Sex differences in age trends for reports of Accidents and Archaic Situations as Situational Characteristics.

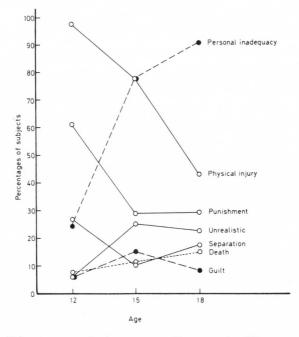

FIG. 15.5.   Age curves for the percentage of boys reporting different categories of Expected Consequences.

Figure 15.3 presents the age trends for the most frequent Situational Characteristics reported by boys. For each age level the percentages of boys who reported the specific category are reported. Figure 15.4 shows sex differences in age trends for the categories Accidents and Archaic situations. In Fig. 15.5 the age trends for Expected Consequences for boys are shown in terms of the percentage of boys who reported the different types of situations. Figure 15.6 shows sex differences in age trends for the two Expected Consequence categories of Personal Inadequacy and Separation.

The most fruitful way of using the subschemes is to use them in conjunction with each other. The two sets of categories are then matched in a contingency table with *m* rows (the number of categories for Activating Conditions) and *n* columns (the number of categories for Expected Consequences).

Comments.   Statistical analysis showed strongly significant sex and age differences for specific categories and strong sex by age by category interactions both for Situational characteristics and Expected consequences. This demonstrates the necessity of taking into account the situational conditions under which observations are made in research on age and sex differences. This finding implies, among other things, that we need to have an adequate sampling of situations for well-defined samples of individuals.

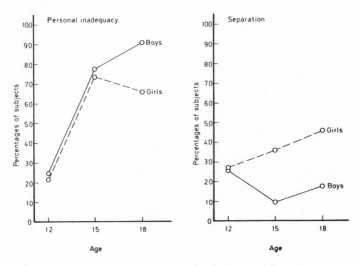

FIG. 15.6.   Sex differences in age trends for the Expected Consequences. Personal inadequacy (a) and Separation (b).

INTERINDIVIDUAL DIFFERENCES IN BEHAVIOR

The importance of considering both general and differential situational effect on individual reactions as they are reflected in partly unique cross-situational profiles can be illustrated by results from a study reported by Magnusson and Ekehammar (1975).

Teenage boys and girls answered an S–R inventory, employing 17 situations and 18 modes of response. For each situation each subject reported the degree of experienced intensity of each mode of response. The situations represented three main types of situations designated Threat of Punishment, Anticipation Fear, and Inanimate Threat. The models of response represented two types of anxiety reactions, somatic and psychic anxiety.

Two main types of analyses were made. First, individuals were classified (for each sex separately) into homogeneous groups on the basis of cross-situational profile similarity by Latent Profile Analysis (LPA). Three distinct groups of individuals were obtained for both girls and boys. Second, a five-way analysis of variance with partially nested sets, comprising the following factors, was performed: Sex Profiles (LPA) nested within Sex, Individuals nested within Profiles and Sex, Responses, and Situations. In Fig. 15.7 the results of the analysis of data from the girls are shown, and in Table 15.2 results concerning cross-situational profile characteristics are presented. For girls, profile I (comprising 59% of the girls) was characterized by: (1) low anxiety level; (2) high transsituational consistency; and (3) high response consistency. (Low response consistency means that the difference between psychic and somatic reactions was large.)

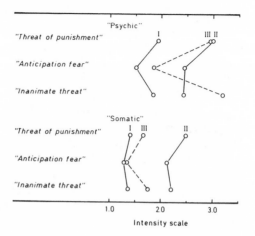

FIG. 15.7. Mean cross-situational anxiety profiles for three homogeneous groups of girls, obtained by Latent Profile Analysis.

Profile II (17%) was characterized by: (1) high anxiety level; (2) comparatively high transsituational consistency; and (3) high response consistency. Profile III (24%) was characterized by: (1) moderate anxiety level; (2) low transituational consistency; and (3) low response consistency.

For boys, profile I (53%) was characterized by: (1) low anxiety level; (2) high transituational consistency; and (3) high response consistency. Profile II (36%) was characterized by: (1) moderate anxiety level; (2) comparatively high transsituational consistency; and (3) low response consistency. Profile III (11%) was characterized by: (1) high anxiety level; (2) low transituational consistency; and (3) moderate response consistency.

Comment.   This study is an illustration of the appropriateness of an interactional model of behavior in which individuals differ with respect to general level of intensity *and* with respect to partly unique cross-situational profiles for the

TABLE 15.2
Profile Characteristics of LPA Groups
(from Magnusson & Ekehammar, 1975)

Profile Characteristic	Girls			Boys		
	Profile I	*Profile II*	*Profile III*	*Profile I*	*Profile II*	*Profile III*
Transsituational inconsistency (MS_S)	.05	.10	.44	.03	.05	.39
Response inconsistency (MS_R)	.27	.32	1.76	.13	.58	.33
Mean overall anxiety	1.56	2.50	2.12	1.29	1.68	2.01

behavior under consideration. The study shows the possibility of using the information about cross-situational profiles classifying individuals into homogeneous groups as a basis for generalizations.

Cross-Cultural Differences in Behavior

In a cross-cultural study of reactions to anxiety-provoking situations, youngsters in Hungary, Japan, and Sweden rated their own reactions to a number of hypothetical situations (Magnusson & Stattin, 1978). Figure 15.8 shows reaction profiles across three situations from youngsters in the three countries.

Figure 15.8 clearly reveals that youngsters in the three countries differ not only on the mean level of anxiety reactions across situations; they also differ (and this is of no less interest) on their characteristic profiles of reactions across situations.

Comments.   In support of a trait model of personality it has been argued that the same type of personality factors have been found in different cultures using data from the traditional type of personality inventories. In an analysis of data for state anxiety collected among youngsters in Hungary, Japan, and Sweden, the same factors (psychic and somatic anxiety reactions) were defined in the same way in the three cultures. Such findings do not contradict the result presented previously nor the conclusion that it is important to consider the situational context in the interpretation of empirical results in cross-cultural research. The results only demonstrate that individuals from different cultures express anxiety by the same kind of reaction. However, what evokes, promotes, and prohibits various types of behaviors differs to some extent among cultures.

Conclusions

The distinctions discussed with respect to situational effects on behavior, behavior models, and types of data and the empirical illustration presented show that interindividual differences, age differences, sex differences, and differences

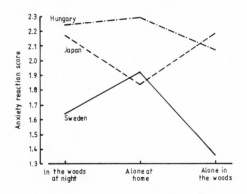

FIG. 15.8.   Cross-situational anxiety reaction profiles for youngsters in Hungary, Japan, and Sweden.

among cultural and subcultural groups cannot be meaningfully and effectively investigated and understood without reference to the specific characteristics of the situations in which behavior is observed. This implies, for empirical research, a need to consider the situational conditions under which behavioral data are obtained in a systematic way in planning, carrying through, and interpretation of empirical studies. The distinctions and conceptualizations discussed in this chapter and the results of the empirical studies presented can form the background to a few suggestions for further research in the proposed direction.

CONSEQUENCES OF AN INTERACTIONAL PARADIGM

As stated earlier, an interactional model of behavior assumes that a person is best characterized by his partly unique *pattern* of stable and changing behaviors across situations. Several obvious consequences follow from this model.

Situation-Bound Data

First, this view implies a need for more situation-bound data (i.e., data that stand for and reflect individual functioning in specific situations having known qualities). The characteristics of these data and the reasons for the advantages of using them are discussed on page 218. Among other things, situation-bound data are a necessary prerequisite for aggregation of data in a meaningful and useful way. In many connections, aggregating of data is needed in order to enable us to use reliable measures. However, for the actual properties of aggregated data to be known and for the data to be used effectively, they must be based on situation-bound data of known qualities.

The need for situation-bound data is a challenge for further development of methods for data collection, using the methodological prototypes that traditional factor intelligence tests offer. In the area of anxiety such instruments have been introduced by Endler, Hunt, and Rosenstein (1962) in their S–R format and by Spielberger (1972) by his STAI for studying trait and state anxiety (see also Magnusson, Dunér, & Zetterblom, 1975, who presented a method for studying norms by situation-bound data).

Idiographic Approach

Second, an interactional view favors the use of an idiographic approach to personality research. The renewed interest in the idiographic approach to personality research has been expressed by several researchers during recent years. An extensive analysis and discussion of the idiographic approach is given by Pervin (in press).

One common argument offered against an idiographic approach in personality research is that it is suitable for case studies but does not permit the same degree of generalization as is possible for its nomothetic counterpart. It should be stressed that the idiographic approach is not restricted to case studies and does permit generalization, in principle and in practice, of no less quality than is possible for nomothetic research. Individuals can be grouped into homogeneous categories on the basis of pattern similarity, and this can be used for comparison and generalization (see the second of the studies reported here). The advantage of this approach is, among other things, that generalizations refer to persons rather than to variables. Methods for analyzing data by clustering of individuals in this way are rapidly being developed (Krauth & Lienert, 1973; Lienert, 1978; Mårdberg, 1973).

Sampling of Situations

Other implications of an interactional approach can be cited. The results presented earlier demonstrate the importance of Brunswik's proposition that in empirical research we should be as careful in sampling situations that are representative, in the sense of being relevant for the problem under consideration, as we are in sampling individuals (Magnusson & Heffler, 1969). Though this proposition was made very strongly and in spite of its importance for empirical research, it has had strikingly little influence. On the whole, with few exceptions (e.g., Barker's, 1965, and his coworkers' studies on behavioral settings) empirical research has been unaffected by the proposition. Let me take one example of this neglect and its consequences.

In the rapidly growing field of stress and anxiety, most researchers are well aware of the role of situations and have included reference to situational conditions in their models. On the other hand, one is struck by the general lack of consideration given to the systematic variation of situational conditions in this area of research. It has been concluded on the basis of much psychophysiological laboratory work that men react more strongly physiologically than women to stressful situations. And it has been an issue for much discussion whether such differences are genetically determined or the result of a learning process. An analysis of the situations in which the empirical results have been obtained, however, reveals that most often a specific type of situation is used, namely, situations that imply a demand for some sort of achievement. There may be a significant sex difference in the interpretation of such situations, so that men interpret them as being more stressful than women. Referring to the results of the first empirical study presented earlier (that females report situations implying expectations of separation much more frequently tham males), it seems natural to ask what would happen if we investigated physiological reactions in situations implying threat of separation.

Systematic Observation and Description

The first empirical study presented earlier demonstrated the usefulness and importance of systematic observation and systematic description of the phenomena that we investigate in empirical psychological research. I believe that we have underestimated the usefulness and importance of systematic observation and description of the basic phenomena, even before we start the experimentation and hypothesis testing and before we apply our arsenals of technically very sophisticated methods for analysis of data (which we do not always really know what they represent). In other fields of research on behavior, for example, biology, anthropology, and ethology, systematic observation and description of the phenomena under consideration is a natural and expected procedure that does not need any justification. Although systematic observation and description can never be a substitute for experimentation, it is a necessary and important complement.

The results of careful observation and description form the essential basis for the development of adequate and effective theories. Much meaningless experimentation could have been avoided if it had been preceded by careful and systematic observation.

Situational Analyses

A necessary prerequisite for considering situational conditions in a systematic way in the planning, carrying through, and evaluating of empirical research is knowledge expressed in relevant terms about the situational characteristics that may influence behavior and that should be controlled. This statement raises the issue that has been discussed sometimes in terms of taxonomy of situations. When discussing this issue, some researchers have raised the question of whether meaningful taxonomies of situations can be arrived at, and several have expressed their doubts (Block & Block, 1981; Pervin, 1981). If the discussion about a taxonomy of situations is limited to mean that there is one static and final solution for the categorization or dimensionalization of situations and situational conditions, I can agree with it. In a broader sense, though, a taxonomy of situations and situational conditions is both possible and meaningful and is very useful for further progress in psychology.

The starting point for this suggestion is the assumption that there is order and regularity in the environment. Stimuli, patterns of stimuli, and events do not appear in anarchic disorder. That order and regularity exist in the environment is a prerequisite for an individual's purposeful and lawful behavior.

As far as there is order and regularity in the environment, stimuli, patterns of stimuli, and events can be ordered along dimensions and can be grouped into homogeneous categories on the basis of common characteristics (as illustrated in the first study, presented earlier). Order and regularity exist at different levels of generalization along the micromacro dimension of the environment. For example, cultures can be systematically categorized with respect to the kind of paths that individuals use for reaching their goals. For example, situations can be ordered with respect to the kind of reward they offer for a certain type of behavior, and objects can be ordered with respect to how fearful they are.

The statement that order and regularity exist in the environment at different levels does not necessarily mean that there is only one hierarchial system of dimensions and categories that can be established once and for all. What kind of order can be observed and meaningfully mapped in the total environmental space depends on the level of generality of the micromacro dimension and on the vantage point from which it is observed (i.e., on the problem under consideration).

Order and regularity exist in the environment itself and can be expressed directly in terms of physical properties, social and cultural norms, rules, roles, etc., that are attached to specific environments, and biological significance. Order and regularity exist also in individuals' perceptions and cognitive representations of the environment, and therefore it can be described and analyzed in terms of individuals' perceptions of or reactions to the environment.

The conclusion is that it is possible to investigate and describe the environment in systematic terms. It is an important task to uncover and map the order of the environment at relevant levels of generalizations for the problems under consideration. This is a goal in itself, but it is an essential prerequisite for the formulation of more effective questions, for the planning and performance of research that yields data that can be accumulated, and for the formulation of more effective theories of personality.

The previous statements imply that one cannot expect one single, definite solution to the problem of categorization and dimensionalization in this area. The essential base for analyses of situations is the set of psychological problems that we want to investigate and elucidate. The appropriate method of data analysis will vary depending on the problem, the situational characteristics being investigated, and the kind of data (quantitative or qualitative) being collected.

For fruitful research on situations we should avoid the fallacies of differential psychology, where research and also theorizing have to a large extent been steered by the *methods* of data collection and analysis. It is essential that research on situations is based on careful systematic observation and description and steered by theoretical analyses and the formulation of psychological problems within a theoretical framework. If we follow such a strategy, systematic research on situations will produce knowledge of basic importance that will contribute to a better understanding of many psychological problems.

CONCLUDING RECOMMENDATIONS

This chapter has focused on the importance of considering the situational context in theorizing and empirical research in personality. To avoid any misunderstanding of my position, I would like to put the view advocated here in a broader perspective. When we describe the process underlying current behavior in terms of person–situation interaction processes and when we discuss individual development in such terms, the problem is not how the person and the situation as two separate parts of equal importance interact. It is, rather, and this is essential, how individuals by their perceptions, thoughts, and feelings function in relation to the environment. Thus, in the process of an individual's dealing with the external world, a fundamental role is played by his or her integrated mediating system of which the main aspects are: (1) his or her cognitions and conceptions of the external world including his or her self-conceptions; (2) his or her way of processing information; (3) his or her emotions; and (4) his or her physiological processes.

The structure and functioning of an individual's mediating system is formed and changes slowly in a process of learning and maturation that takes place in the continuous bidirectional interaction between the individual and his or her environment. It is this system that determines which situations an individual seeks and which he or she avoids (as far as he or she has options), which situational conditions he or she attends to, how he or she interprets single stimuli and patterns of stimuli and events, and how he or she transforms the information about the environment into internal and external actions. A central task for explaining human behavior is to understand the lawfulness of the functioning of the subsystems of perceptions, cognitions, emotions, and physiological processes in interaction with each other and as an integrated total system in current situations, as well as how they develop during the process of maturation and learning.

If we want to arrive at more realistic models for individual functioning, however, the models cannot be restricted to encompass only perceptions, thoughts, feelings, physiological processes, and their interrelations with manifest behavior. As demonstrated earlier, these aspects of individual functioning in current situations are dependent on the character of the situational context. As we proceed toward more integrated models, we must incorporate the situational context in which individuals live and develop in a more systematic and informed way than we have done hitherto. Among other things, such integrated models are needed as a basis for more precise empirical work that is really scientific in the sense that it yields data that can be accumulated and that can be interpreted in a general and common frame of reference. Integrated models incorporating the situational context will help us to reach the dual goal of psychology, namely to explain and understand why individuals feel, think, and act as they do in real life, *and* to contribute to the formation of physical and social environments that are adapted to the needs and potentialities of individuals.

ACKNOWLEDGMENTS

Comments on an earlier version of the manuscript by V. L. Allen, A. Dunér, H. Stattin, and Bertil Törestad are highly appreciated.

REFERENCES

Allport, G. W. Traits revisited. *American Psychologist,* 1966, *21,* 1–10.

Barker, R. G. Explorations in ecological psychology. *American Psychologist,* 1965, *20,* 1–14.

Block, J., & Block, J. H. Studying situational dimensions: A grand perspective and some limited empiricism. In D. Magnusson (Ed.), *Toward a psychology of situations: An interactional perspective.* Hillsdale, N.J.: Lawrence Erlbaum Associates, 1981.

Bowers, K. S. Situationism in psychology: An analysis and a critique. *Psychological Review,* 1973, *80,* 307–336.

Cattell, R. B. Personality, role, mood, and situation perception: A unifying theory of modulators. *Psychological Review,* 1963, *70,* 1–18.

Ekehammar, B. Interactionism in personality from a historical perspective. *Psychological Bulletin,* 1974, *81,* 1026–1048.

Endler, N. S. A person–situation interaction model for anxiety. In C. D. Spielberger & I. G. Sarason (Eds.), *Stress and anxiety* (Vol. 1). Washington, D.C.: Hemisphere (Wiley), 1975.

Endler, N. S. Whence interactional psychology. In A. Furnham & M. Argyle (Eds.), *Social Behavior in Context.* Boston: Allyn & Bacon, in press.

Endler, N. S., Hunt, J. Mc V., & Rosenstein, A. J. An S–R inventory of anxiousness. *Psychological Monographs,* 1962, *76,* 1–33.

Endler, N. S., & Magnusson, D. Toward an interactional psychology of personality. *Psychological Bulletin,* 1976, *83,* 956–974.

Epstein, S. The stability of behavior: I. On predicting most of the people much of the time. *Journal of Personality and Social Psychology,* 1979, *37,* 1097–1126.

Goldfried, M. R., & D'Zurilla, T. J. A behavioral-analytic model for assessing competence. In C. D. Spielberger (Ed.), *Current Topics in Clinical and Community Psychology* (Vol. 1). New York: Academic Press, 1969.

Goldfried, M. R., & Kent, R. N. Traditional versus behavioral personality assessment: A comparison of methodological and theoretical assumptions. *Psychological Bulletin,* 1972, *77,* 409–420.

Hammond, K. R. Probabilistic functioning and the clinical method. *Psychological Review,* 1955, *62,* 255–262.

Hartshorne, H., & May, M. A. *Studies in the nature of character: Studies in deceit* (Vol. 1). New York: Macmillan, 1928.

Kantor, J. R. *Principles of psychology* (Vol. 1). Bloomington: Principia Press, 1924.

Kantor, J. R. *Principles of psychology* (Vol. 2). Bloomington: Principia Press, 1926.

Krauth, J., & Lienert, G. A. *Die Konfigurationsfrequenzanalyse und ihre Anwendung in Psychologie und Medizin.* München: Verlag Karl Alber, 1973.

Lewin, K. *Field theory in social science.* Selected theoretical papers. New York: Harper, 1951.

Lienert, G. A. *Verteilungsfreie Methoden in der Biostatistik: Band II.* Meisenheim am Glan: Verlag Anton Hain, 1978.

Magnusson, D. The person and the situation in an interactional model of behavior. *Scandinavian Journal of Psychology,* 1976, *17,* 253–271.

Magnusson, D. On the psychological situation. Reports from the Department of Psychology, the University of Stockholm, 1978, No. 544.

Magnusson, D. Personality in an interactional paradigm of research. *Zeitschrift für Differentielle und Diagnostische Psychologie,* 1980, *1,* 17–34.

Magnusson, D. Wanted: A psychology of situations. In D. Magnusson (Ed.), *Toward a psychology of situations: An interactional perspective.* Hillsdale, N.J.: Lawrence Erlbaum Associates, 1981.

Magnusson, D. *Persons in situations: Some comments on a current issue.* Invited address at the First European Conference on Personality, Tilburg, May 1982.

Magnusson, D., Dunér, A., & Zetterblom, G. *Adjustment: A longitudinal study.* Stockholm: Almqwist & Wiksell, 1975.

Magnusson, D., & Ekehammar, B. Anxiety profiles based on both situational and response factors. *Multivariate Behavioral Research*, 1975, *10*, 27–44.

Magnusson, D., & Endler, N. S. (Eds.). *Personality at the crossroads: Current issues in interactional psychology*. Hillsdale, N.J.: Lawrence Erlbaum Associates, 1977.

Magnusson, D., Gerzén, M., & Nyman, B. The generality of behavioral data I: Generalization from observations on one occasion. *Multivariate Behavioral Research*, 1968, *3*, 295–320.

Magnusson, D., & Heffler, B. The generality of behavioral data III: Generalization potential as a function of the number of observation instances. *Multivariate Behavioral Research*, 1969, *4*, 29–42.

Magnusson, D., & Oláh, A. *Situation-outcome contingencies: A study of anxiety-provoking situations in a developmental perspective*. Reports from the Department of Psychology, the University of Stockholm, 1981 (No. 574).

Magnusson, D., & Stattin, H. A cross-cultural comparison of anxiety responses in an interactional frame of reference. *International Journal of Psychology*, 1978, *13*, 317–32.

Magnusson, D., & Stattin, H. Stability of cross-situational patterns of behavior. *Journal of Research in Personality*, 1981, *15*, 488–496.

Magnusson, D., & Stattin, H. *Situation-outcome contingencies: A conceptual and empirical analysis of threatening situations*. Reports from the Department of Psychology, the University of Stockholm, 1981 (No. 571).

Mårdberg, B. *A model for selection and classification in industrial psychology*. Reports from the Department of Psychology, the University of Stockholm, 1973 (Suppl. 19).

Mischel, W. *Personality and assessment*. New York: Wiley, 1968.

Mischel, W. Toward a cognitive social learning reconceptualization of personality. *Psychological Review*, 1973, *80*, 252–283.

Murphy, G. *Personality: A biosocial approach to origins and structure*. New York: Harper, 1947.

Murray, H. A. *Explorations in personality*. New York: Oxford Univ Press, 1938.

Murray, H. A. Studies of stressful interpersonal disputations. *American Psychologist*, 1963, *18*, 28–36.

Pervin, L. A. Definitions, measurements, and classifications of stimuli, situations and environments. *Human Ecology*, 1978, *6*, 71–105.

Pervin, L. A. The relations of situations to behavior. In D. Magnusson (Ed.), *Toward a psychology of situations: An interactional perspective*. Hillsdale, N.J.: Lawrence Erlbaum Associates, 1981.

Pervin, L. A. Idiographic approaches to personality. In N. S. Endler & J. Mc V. Hunt (Eds.), *Personality and the behavioral disorders* (2nd ed.). New York: Wiley, in press.

Sarason, I. G., Smith, R. E., & Diener, E. Personality research: Components of variance attributable to the person and the situation. *Journal of Personality and Social Psychology*, 1975, *32*, 199–204.

Sells, S. B. An interactionist looks at the environment. *American Psychologist*, 1963, *18*, 696–702.

Spielberger, C. D. Anxiety as an emotional state. In *anxiety: Current trends in theory and research* (Vol. 1). New York: Academic Press, 1972.

Stagner, R. Traits are relevant: Theoretical analysis and empirical evidence. In N. S. Endler & D. Magnusson (Eds.), *Interactional psychology and personality*. Washington: Hemisphere, 1976.

Tolman, E. C. Psychology versus immediate experience. In *E. C. Tolman: Collected papers in psychology*. Berkeley: University of California Press, 1951.

Wachtel, P. Interaction cycles, unconcious processes and the person–situation issue. In D. Magnusson & N. S. Endler (Eds.), *Personality at the crossroads: Current issues in interactional psychology*, 1977.

16 Perspectives in Human Motivational Psychology: A New Experimental Paradigm

Julius Kuhl
Max–Planck–Institute for Psychological Research, Munich West Germany

John W. Atkinson
The University of Michigan, USA

A persistently ringing telephone can create a very annoying experience. Imagine you are about to leave your office for some reason that seems important enough for you to decide you do not want to pick up the phone if it rings. And sure enough, while you are walking to the door, the phone rings. You continue to walk to the door when you hear the second ring and, while you are opening the door, the third ring makes you return to answer the phone, maybe with that overly friendly tone in your voice that hardly disguises your suppressed anger.

This little example illustrates the difference between the two theoretical positions on human motivation psychology that is dealt with in this chapter. They are: (1) the traditional cognitive-episodic theories of motivation; and (2) a recently proposed cognitive-dynamic theory (Atkinson & Birch, 1970, 1974, 1978). Traditional cognitive-episodic theories are characterized by the various elaborations of Expectancy × Value Theory (Atkinson & Feather, 1966; Edwards, 1954; Heckhausen, 1977). They have been called *episodic* (Atkinson & Birch, 1970), because they miss the temporal continuity of the stream of everyday behavior and of its underlying motivational determinants. Cognitive-episodic theories focus on a given temporal episode (a "situation") and attempt to predict future behavior on the basis of the cognitive construction of that situation in terms of expectancies and incentives. In our illustrative example, a cognitive approach would predict that the actor would leave his office *if* the cognitive evaluation of the two action alternatives in question had yielded a greater expected value associated with leaving than with answering the phone. This account ignores the dynamic changes in motivational tendencies that may occur even if the subjective environment as described by expectancy and value parameters does not change.

Specifically, the behavior of the person in our example may be attributed to the basic dynamic postulate regarding inertial motivation. According to this postulate, the first ring of the phone arouses—on the basis of prior learning experiences—a tendency to approach the phone and to answer it (see Fig. 16.1b). This tendency is assumed to *persist* even in the absence of any motivation stimulus (i.e., during the time between rings). When the second ring occurs, the tendency to answer the phone is further increased until at the third ring it exceeds the initially dominant tendency to leave, which should result in a respective change in behavior.

In dealing with each behavioral episode separately, cognitive theorists neglect the effects of the immediate motivational past of the organism. According to an episodic cognitive approach, each ring may be treated as a separate temporal episode during which the actor has to make a decision between the available action alternatives. If the expected value associated with answering the phone is lower than the one that is associated with leaving, the cognitive approach may be illustrated as in Figure 16.1a. In each episode, the tendency to leave is expected to be stronger than the tendency to answer the phone because the cognitive evaluation of the two alternatives is assumed to be constant throughout the period of observation. Obviously, the cognitive view ignores the persisting quality of motivational tendencies as emphasized in Freud's and Lewin's theory and corroborated by experimental results by Lewin's students (Ovsiankina, 1928; Zeigarnik, 1927). As a result, cognitive theories ignore the cumulative effects of successive arousal of the same action tendency.

The reader might object to the dynamic interpretation of the telephone example that the return to the phone may not be caused by a cumulative effect of successive arousals of the same action tendency but by some cognitive restructuring of the situation elicited by the third ring. At the third ring the actor might think of some reason why that phone call could be an important one. This criticism would miss the point we are trying to make. We do not doubt that a

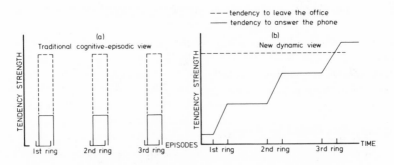

FIG. 16.1.   Traditional cognitive-episodic and new dynamic interpretation of telephone example (see text for details).

change in the cognitive evaluation of action alternatives may produce a respective change in behavior nor do we doubt that such an evaluative change could occur in the described situation. The example merely serves to illustrate the difference between two theoretical positions. Cognitive-episodic theories do not predict a change *if* the cognitive evaluation does not change. The dynamic theory predicts a change even if no cognitive change occurs. The latter theory does not say when this case might occur, it simply states what happens whenever it occurs. In practice, both cumulative dynamic effects and cognitive effects due to evaluative changes may occur simultaneously, which makes it difficult to disentangle the contribution of each of the two factors to behavioral change. The two factors might even be interdependent. The cognitive restructuring mentioned earlier might, for instance, be a *result* of the cumulative increase in the tendency to answer the phone. The person may sense an increased inclination to answer the phone and, as a result, look for a "reason" that justifies this change of intentions. The dynamic theory does not ignore the motivational effect of cognitive mediators. It simply reintroduces a principle of motivation, which has been ignored in traditional cognitive theories of motivation.

Some of the far-reaching consequences of this ignorance are discussed later, especially those related to misconceptions regarding psychological measurement and regarding the theoretical meaning of the commonly observed behavioral inconsistency across situations. The remainder of our chapter has four aims, first, to discuss three developments in past theorizing on human motivation (i.e., the classical cognitive-interactional approach, the more recent elaborated cognitive-episodic approach, and the dynamic approach), and to discuss a recent attempt toward an integration of the cognitive and the dynamic approaches. The second aim is to present two experimental paradigms that are presently used to investigate critical differences between the episodic-cognitive approach and the dynamic approach. The third aim of this chapter is to propose a new experimental paradigm for future research that may promote future unification of motivation theory by providing a common data basis for all three approaches.

THE PAST: THREE THEORETICAL DEVELOPMENTS

If we want to define the tasks for the future, we have to consider what the past has provided us with. Since 1950 there have been three important developments in motivational psychology. The aim for the future is to achieve a conceptual integration of these new developments.

The Classical Cognitive-Interactional Approach

The first development has achieved an integration of what Cronbach (1957) had referred to as the two scientific disciplines of psychology—the study of individual differences and the experimental analysis of the basic process of motivation. An example of a cognitive-interactional model is Atkinson's (1957) model of achievement motivation, which defines a subject's resultant tendency (T_r) to approach a task in terms of the algebraic product of three factors: (1) the difference between the motive to achieve success (M_S) and the motive to avoid failure (M_F); (2) the subjective probability of success (P_s) and (3) the incentive value of success (I_s), which is assumed to be inversely related to P_s (i.e., $I_s = (1 - P_s)$; $T_r = (M_S - M_F) \times P_s \times (1 - P_s)$.

Following Lewin's programmatic conception of the basic problem of motivation that expresses behavior (B) as a function of personal (P) and environmental (E) determinants, $B = f(P, E)$, the interactional approach required simultaneous interest in the behavioral effects of individual differences in P as inferred from diagnostic tests and of systematic manipulations of E as illustrated in research on achievement-related activities (Atkinson, 1958; Heckhausen, 1967). The theory of achievement motivation illustrates this first important conceptual development (Atkinson & Feather, 1966; Kuhl, 1978; Raynor, 1969).

The Elaborated Cognitive-Episodic Approach

The second development in past theorizing focused upon elaborations of cognitive mediators of motivation and action (Heckhausen, 1977; Weiner, 1980). Heckhausen's model is based on several conceptual distinctions regarding expectancy variables that had been neglected earlier. According to his model three conceptually independent expectancies affect the strength of an action tendency, i.e., the expectancy E_{so} that the situation will lead to a certain outcome without personal intervention (situation– outcome expectancy), the expectancy E_{ao} that an action will lead to a certain outcome (action–outcome expectancy), and the expectancy E_{oc} that an outcome is associated with various consequences (outcome–consequence expectancy or instrumentality), which, in turn, may be associated with varying incentive values I_j. The resultant tendency (T_r) to perform a certain action is assumed to be equal to the difference between the action–outcome expectancy and the situation–outcome expectancy, where each is wheighted by the algebraic sum of the products between the incentive values of all n anticipated consequences, each weighted with the expectancy that the action outcome would lead to (or away from) the respective consequence:

$$T_r = (E_{ao} \times \sum_{j=1}^{n} I_j \times E_{ocj}) - (E_{so} \times \sum_{j=1}^{n} I_j \times E_{ocj}).$$

Besides taking account of a variety of expected consequences that may, but need not, be conceived of as steps in a contingent path toward a future goal—as in Raynor's model (1969), Heckhausen's model introduces a motivational principle of *parsimony* according to which a resultant action tendency is dampened to the extent that a person believes that desired consequences can be obtained (or undesired consequences can be avoided) without personal action.

The Dynamics of Action

Atkinson & Birch (1970, 1974, 1978) formulated a mathematical theory of action that describes continuous changes in the strength of competing action tendencies in time, as suggested by Lewin's (1943) programmatic differential equations. Breaking with the traditional view that treats behavioral incidents (e.g., preference) as if they were separate and discrete events in the life of an individual (Fig. 16.1) and merely cognitively mediated reactions to an immediate stimulus situation, the new conception emphasizes the temporal continuity of behavior and of the underlying motivational structure of the individual. The behavior (B) to be explained is seen to be the stream of activity characterized by change from one activity to another even when the environment (E) and characteristics of the person (P) are constant. A change in behavior implies a change in the relative strength of the tendencies that motivate behavior (see Fig. 16.2). What are the determinants of behavioral change?

Instigating Force.   The first determinant of change discussed in the dynamics of action (Atkinson & Birch, 1970) has already been mentioned in connection with our introductory example. Consider the first change from activity X to activity Y in Fig. 16.2. The tendency to engage in activity Y is aroused at a faster rate than the tendencies supporting activity X or Z. The dynamic theory departs from cognitive theories in assuming that any source of motivation, whether it be an external stimulus or an *internal* cognitive activity, determines the *rate of arousal,* which is described in terms of an instigating force (F), rather than the absolute strength of a tendency (see Fig. 16.1). This assumption is based on the already mentioned postulate regarding the persisting nature of motivational ten-

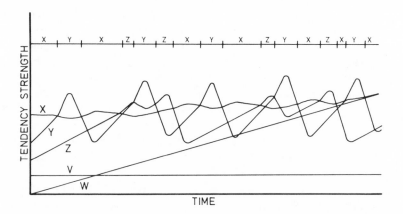

FIG. 16.2.   An example of a stream of activity (X, Y, Z) and the changing motivational state that accounts for it even when the personality and immediate environment are constant.

dencies. Repeated or continous arousal of an action tendency can have a cumulative effect only if the tendency aroused at a given point in time is carried over to a later point in time. It is this cumulative aspect of motivational arousal that explains why also relatively weakly instigated action tendencies—as the tendency to answer the phone in our introductory example—may become dominant and expressed in behavior. According to current cognitive models, an activity that is associated with a lower expected value than another one should never be performed (Heckhausen, 1977). Earlier theories could accomodate this case only by adding a statistical assumption regarding random oscillation to the theory (Cartwright & Festinger, 1943; Hull, 1943). The dynamics of action attributes the occasional performance of a relatively weakly instigated activity to a systematic motivational process rather than to random error. This process may be highly adaptive because it prevents the organism from getting stuck in the performance of the most strongly instigated activity, which would result in a frustration of important though less strongly aroused needs.

Consummatory Force.   Let us return to the stream of behavior illustrated in Fig. 16.2. If action tendencies were affected by instigating forces only, one could not explain why the organism resumes an earlier activity X after having engaged in another one (Y) for a while, unless the environment (represented, for instance, by the cognitive evaluation of the available action alternatives) would change. The dynamics of action assumes an additional factor that reduces an action tendency once it is expressed in behavior. The consummatory force (C) of an activity, when it occurs, is described as a function of two factors: the nature of the activity and the strength of the tendency being expressed in it. The consummatory value (c) of a particular activity describes the degree to which its performance results in a reduction of the underlying tendency. Some activities (e.g., eating fudge cake, succeeding on a task) should have a greater consummatory value than others (e.g., eating peanuts or failing on a task, respectively). The strength of the tendency (T) being expressed in behavior is considered the second determinant of consummatory force (i.e., $C = c \times T$). Although neurobiological research strongly suggests the existence of two separate motivational processes—one that arouses motivation and another that reduces motivation—(Pribram, 1971), cognitive theories of human motivation have been preoccupied with instigating sources of motivation. It is a great challenge for future research to investigate the processes that mediate the consummation of action tendencies in greater detail. A first step in this direction was taken in a paradigmatic experiment by Blankenship (1979), which is discussed later.

The new conception of what brings about changes in the strength of behavioral tendencies may be expressed in a simple differential equation: $dT/dt = F - C$ (Atkinson & Birch, 1970, p. 12). This equation has the following implications. When F, representing the instigating effect resulting from the interaction of person and situation, is greater than C, representing the consummatory effect of the performance of the ongoing activity, the strength of tendency increases. When $C > F$, the strength of tendency decreases. When $F = C$, the strength of tendency stabilizes. And this, given the notion that $C = c \times T$, occurs at a particular level when $T = F/c$. In other words, in a given situation a tendency expressed in an activity will rise or fall in strength, as will the consummatory force of the activity, until finally, if expressed in behavior long enough, the tendency becomes stable at a level equivalent to F/c for that activity. This guarantees variability of behavior even in a constant environment.

The Principle of Time Allocation. A simple generalization deduced from the dynamics of action illustrates this point. The dynamics of action predicts that the amount of time an individual spends in a given activity A is proportional to the ratio between the F_A/c_A-value associated with that activity divided by the sum of F/c-values of all competing activities (Atkinson & Birch, 1970, p. 160; 1978, pp. 145–148);

$$\% \text{ time spent in } A = \frac{F_A/c_A}{F_A/c_A + F_B/c_B + \cdots + F_Z/c_Z}.$$

Note that this principle of time allocation is in contrast to the maximization principle suggested by current cognitive theories. According to these theories, an individual should spend her/his total time performing the activity that has the highest expected value until the cognitive hierarchy of expected values associated with the competing tendencies changes.

While the investigators of Michigan had been working on the *deduction* of the principle of time allocation from the dynamics of action, a research group at Harvard had arrived at a virtually identical principle by way of *induction* from many empirical observations in animal experiments (deVilliers & Herrnstein, 1976). Their empirical "law of relative effect" states in its most simple form that the ratio of the number of responses for each of two alternatives equals the ratio of the frequency of reinforcement for the two alternative responses. Curiously enough, Atkinson & Birch (1970) had coordinated instigating forces that enter the right side of the time allocation equation to the number of earlier reinforcements in the learning history of the organism. An earlier study (Atkinson, 1964, p. 291) had already shown that the time allocation principle also holds in human behavior. Subjects matched the frequencies of pointing to various cards that had different colors to the relative reward frequencies for the different colors. This result shows that also humans do not always maximize the frequency of the action alternative that has the highest expected value. The important implications of this difference between cognitive and dynamic approaches have been pointed out earlier.

The principle of time allocation implies that the traditional way of estimating test reliability on the basis of internal consistency of successive behavioral incidences is inappropriate for a method that taps a behavioral stream. The traditional instrument for assessing individual differences in motive strength (i.e., the TAT), is such a method. The principle of time allocation suggests that change from one activity to another rather than behavioral consistency is expected over an extended period of time. At the same time this principle claims that valid estimates of individual differences in motive strength as reflected in F can be derived from time allocation scores. These two suggestions were, in fact, substantiated by computer simulations based on the dynamics of action that confirmed that valid inferences about motive parameters could be made on the basis of % time-spent-scores even if the temporal consistency of behavior (estimated by Cronbach's alpha) was very low (Atkinson, Bongort, & Price, 1977).

The principle of time allocation also speaks to the recently revived debate regarding the cross-situational consistency of personality attributes (Endler & Magnusson, 1976; Mischel, 1968). It suggests that an individual should engage in a variety of activities even if the latent personality parameters (e.g., motive strength reflected in F) are constant. A recent series of computer simulations (Reuman, Atkinson, & Gallop, 1981) confirmed this expectation. It could be deduced from the dynamics of action that correlations between various behavioral expressions of several motives were low or modest even though the latent motive parameters were held constant. It can be concluded from this simulation result that one cannot infer the lack of stable personality determinants from the observed instability of behavior across situations (Atkinson, 1981). Inferences of this kind result from a neglect of basic motivational principles that leads to a confounding of manifest behavior and its latent determinants.

Facilitators of Behavioral Change.   The dynamics of action contain an additional set of parameters that seem necessary to account for a change from one activity to another. Without those parameters the onset of consummation when an activity is initiated would immediately reduce the underlying tendency, and the offset of consummation of the tendency that has ceased to be performed would increase its strength. As a result the dominance relations would change rapidly between those two tendencies (behavioral chatter) to the extent that neither could be expressed in behavior for a substantial period of time. There are at least three different ways by which a person can increase the likelihood of a successful change from one activity to another: (1) The person may shift the attention quickly from stimuli supporting the performance of the old activity to stimuli supporting the performance of the new one; (2) the onset of full consummation of the tendency supporting the new activity may be delayed; and (3) the offset of consummation of the tendency supporting the old activity may be delayed (Atkinson & Birch, 1970). The process underlying the control of the execution of an intended action (action control), which always requires a change from one activity to another, has received little attention in cognitive theories of motivation. Usually, it is implicitly assumed that there is a one to one relationship between motivation (or intention) and performance.

Recently, a model of action control has been proposed that specifies assumed cognitive (personal and situational) mediators of action control (Kuhl, in press a,b). A questionnaire has been constructed to assess individual differences in action control. The validity of the action control scale could be demonstrated in a study in which the correlations between reported motivation to perform several activities and actual time spent in those activities were considerably higher for high control than for low control subjects. Prolonged exposure to uncontrollable outcomes is considered one of the most potent situational factors that reduce action-control.

So far, experimental results have confirmed the suggested relationship between the assumed determinants of action control and one of the dynamic parameters that facilitate behavioral change, namely selective attention. Specifically, it could be shown that subjects low in action control ("state-oriented" subjects) focused their attention less on stimuli that were relevant for the performance of an ongoing activity than high control ("action-oriented") subjects did (Kuhl, in press b). In another experiment, the verbal reports about the content of thought when working on a task in a repeated failure condition revealed a greater frequency of task-irrelevant thoughts in state-oriented than in action-oriented subjects (Kuhl & Weiß, 1981). Also, state-oriented subjects in a failure condition had a significant performance deficit on a subsequent task that was dissimilar to the task used during failure pretreatment. This effect, which is usually referred to as learned helplessness, was not attributable to a motivational deficit nor to a generalized belief in the uncontrollability of outcomes as assumed by learned helplessness theory (Abramson, Seligman, & Teasdale, 1978). Instead, the experimental results suggest that the generalized performance deficits found in state-oriented subjects following failure pretreatment may be attributed to their inability to focus attention on thoughts that facilitate the execution of an intended action (i.e., solving the task, Kuhl, 1981).

Unresolved Problems. There is no doubt that all three approaches in the preceding sections have made valuable contributions to motivational theory. The interactional approach has led to a more sophisticated conception of interactive processes than earlier attempts (Endler & Magnusson, 1976), the cognitive approach has achieved a more detailed theory of the cognitive processes that may affect motivation (Heckhausen, 1980; Weiner, 1980), and the dynamic approach has led to a more appropriate design and analysis of motivation experiments (Blankenship, 1979; Kuhl & Blankenship, 1979). The great challenge for the future, however, is to overcome the existing separation between and to achieve a unification of the three approaches within one comprehensive theoretical framework. One step toward a conceptual unification of the cognitive and the dynamic approaches has recently been made in a paper that discusses the strengths and weaknesses of the two approaches, proposes coordinating definitions that relate parameters from recent cognitive models to dynamic parameters, and introduces additional cognitive parameters to formu'.ate hypotheses about cognitive anteced-ents of dynamic parameters that describe processes that have been neglected in cognitive research (Kuhl, in preparation).

Specifically, to achieve the integration of the three approaches, experimental research should focus on the following problems:

1. We will have to investigate the behavioral effects of the immediate moti-vational past of the organism in greater detail than we have done until now. How do cognitive mediators of action interact with *inertial* and *cumulative* effects of the frequency and duration of prior exposure to various sources of motivation. Situations, in which cognitive and dynamic processes may have opposing moti-vational effects as in our introductory example, deserve special attention. Future research will hopefully specify situational and personal factors that determine the extent to which dynamic and/or cognitive processes affect behavior.

2. Research should focus on cognitive and dynamic processes that mediate *action control*. Besides selective attention that has been under recent investiga-tion (Kuhl, in press a), a variety of additional processes are conceivable that may mediate the transition from the formulation of an intention to its execution. The parameters that control the delayed onset and offset of consummation in the dynamics of action may be related to cognitive plans that define the sequencing of steps in an action. A person who has learned to start an action sequence—say having dinner—with the more consummating steps (e.g. eating the desert first) may have more problems to actually carry out all steps of the intended action sequence than a person who starts with a subactivity that has a relatively small consummatory value (e.g., having a soup first).

3. Finally, we would like to encourage researchers to concentrate in their work on processes that mediate *consummation*. Past research has almost entirely been preoccupied with cognitive processes that are assumed to arouse motivation (Heckhausen, 1980; Weiner, 1980). We know very little about the processes that make people stop doing whatever they are busy doing.

Before we turn to a discussion of an experimental paradigm for future re-search that may help solve the unresolved problems, we would like to discuss two experimental paradigms that are *presently* used to study the three problems mentioned earlier.

THE PRESENT: TWO EXPERIMENTAL PARADIGMS

The two experiments described in this section may give an illustration of current research concerning the differences between the dynamic principles of inertial motivation and consummation in action on the one hand and the cognitive-episodic conception of motivation on the other hand.

An Illustration of Inertial Motivation

Recently an experiment was designed that illustrates one difference between the traditional cognitive approach and the dynamic theory. According to episodic cognitive theories, subjects should always perform the action alternative having the highest expected value. The dynamic theory does not question motivating effects of the content of thought (Birch, Atkinson, & Bongort, 1974). It covers, however, the case in which effects of the cognitive evaluation of action alternatives may be superseded by the effects of a dynamic process such as inertial motivation. If an activity having a low expected value has been aroused for quite a while, we may make the seemingly paradoxical observation that a person fails to perform an action that has a higher expected value even if the person may freely choose between the two actions.

The Alienation Effect.   In a recent experiment, subjects were first asked to perform a rather boring sequence of routine activities (e.g., sorting cards) for about 45 minutes (Kuhl & Eisenbeiser, 1981). At the end of this period, the experimenter told the subject that there was no need to continue on the task "because you have done all we need" but that the subject should feel free to continue the ongoing activity or switch to another activity (reading a magazine or comic) until the regular time scheduled for the experiment was up. Attractiveness ratings obtained from an independent sample indicated that the reading activity was judged as far more attractive than the sorting task by all but one (of 25) subjects. Nevertheless, about two thirds of the subjects in the experiment did not switch to the more attractive task but continued with the sorting activity. This result suggests that behavior may become temporarily or even chronically alienated from the latent value structure of a person. This "alienation effect" illustrates the behavioral "inconsistency" mentioned earlier that can be deduced from the dynamics of action even if the cognitive determinants of motivation are assumed to be constant.

The Effect of Action Control.   In the just-mentioned experiment, subjects had been subdivided according to their score on the action control scale. As can be seen from Table 16.1, most of the subjects who did switch to the more attractive activity were action oriented (high control), whereas only two state-oriented (low control) subjects switched to the more attractive activity. This result is in accordance with the hypothesis that a disposition toward high action control should facilitate the change from a weakly instigated to a strongly instigated activity or—to put it in phenomenological terms—high action control should help people to actually do what they intend to do on the basis of their own hierarchy of values. Although the occasional performance of a less-preferred activity seems necessary to fulfill all the needs of a person, a strong and chronical alienation of a person's behavior from her/his latent value structure may result in serious disorders such as depression (Kuhl & Eisenbeiser, 1981).

Experimental Investigation of Consummatory Effects

In data on preference or time allocation, the effects of instigating and consummatory sources of motivation are usually confounded. Blankenship (1979) has designed an experiment that has a paradigmatic status as a method to uncouple instigating and consummatory effects. The experiment was designed to study cognitive antecedents of consummatory force (C) that have been widely neglected in motivation research. Specifically, the experiment was conducted to investigate the relationship between task difficulty and consummatory value of success. Special care was taken to ensure that the instigating forces for the tendency to succeed were equal in two subject groups that worked on different difficulty levels of an achievement task. With instigating forces regarding the tendency to achieve success being equal in two groups, differences in time spent on the achievement task (rather than in a nonachievement alternative activity) can be attributed to differences in consummatory forces between the two groups. Earlier and more recent research suggests that the instigating forces for two tasks differing in difficulty should be equal if they are equidistant from the midpoint ($P_s = .50$) of the scale of subjective probability of success (Atkinson & Feather, 1966; Schneider, 1978).

In Blankenship's (1979) experiment (male subjects were given a choice between an achievement task (Target-shooting game) and a joke-rating activity on the screen of a microcomputer. After an initial practice period, in which P_s-levels of .30, .50, and .70, respectively, were established for the three difficulty levels included in the study, the subject was asked to start with joke rating and switch to the easy or to the difficult task (depending on the experimental condition the subject was assigned to) whenever he wanted to. While the experimenter had left the room, the subject could switch back and forth between the jokes and the easy (or difficult) game as often as he wished.

As motivational tendencies are not expected to be subject to consummation until they are expressed in behavior, the latency of the first choice of the achievement task may be considered an unconfounded measure of the instigating force (F) to achieve success. Consequently, the latency measures could be used to check the assumption regarding equality of instigating forces to succeed between

TABLE 16.1
Number of Subjects That Switched to the More Attractive Activity
and Number of Subjects That Stayed with the Less Attractive Activity
(Collapsed Across Experimental Conditions) (from Kuhl and Eisenbeiser, 1981)

Behavior:	More-Attractive Activity	Less-Attractive Activity
State-oriented subjects	2	34
Action-oriented subjects	10	26

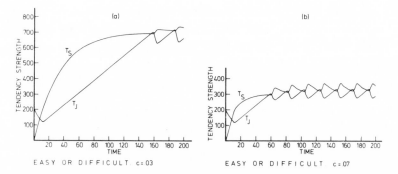

FIG. 16.3.   First durations of an achievement-related activity as a function of low (a) or high (b) consummatory value of success.

the easy and the difficult groups. The mean latencies for initiating the achievement activity were, in fact, almost identical in the two difficulty groups. Figure 16.3 shows the theoretically expected first durations of the achievement activity for tasks differing in consummatory value as simulated on the basis of the dynamics of action (Blankenship, 1979). The empirical results showed a significantly greater first duration of the achievement-related activity for the difficult than for the easy task. The counterintuitive conclusion that may be drawn from this result suggests that consummatory value of success is greater for easy than for difficult tasks. The theoretically innovative aspect of Blankenship's study is that it demonstrates that the observation of high preference for and a high time allocation to a certain activity need not be an indication for a high instigation (F) to perform that activity. Instead, that observation may be indicative of a weak consummatory force for the activity involved. Research on overeating did, in fact, suggest that, in many cases, high preference for food does not seem to be instigated by a strong appetite but seems to be attributable to a low ability to stop eating once it has been initiated in response to tempting cues in the environment (Pribram, 1971; Schachter & Gross, 1968).

THE FUTURE: A NEW EXPERIMENTAL PARADIGM

Past research on human motivation has been based on an experimental paradigm that lags far behind the theoretical developments outlined earlier. Experimental research on human motivation has not made the transition yet that has been achieved in animal research by replacing the maze by the Skinner box. Experiments on human motivation are still based on the episodic stimulus–response paradigm underlying the trial-by-trial maze experiment in animal research. The experimenter confronts the subjects with some stimulus material and observes their response to it. The subjects are usually not allowed to engage in free operant behavior as they are in many situations in everyday life. If we restrict our attention to the subjects' responses to the experimental stimuli, we are unable to investigate the effects of dynamic determinants of motivation (e.g., inertial and cumulative effects of past arousal of the action tendency that is aroused in the experiment, consummatory effects attributable to the performance of an activity, and the matching between the latent motivational structure of the subject and the allocation of time to various activities). Those effects can be studied only if we observe subjects for an extended period of time in an experimental context that encourages subjects to freely alternate between various action alternatives. We need an advanced human analogue of the Skinner box.

Measuring the Stream of Activity.   Our vision of the experimental paradigm for future research in human motivation is outlined in Fig. 16.4. It represents an extension of the experimental paradigm used by Blankenship (1979) to study consummatory effects of working on various difficulty levels of a task. The experiment consists of three parts that correspond to the three developments in motivational psychology discussed earlier. In the first phase of the experiment, personality differences are assessed that may affect the motivational tendencies aroused in the experiment. In the second phase, which should take place on a

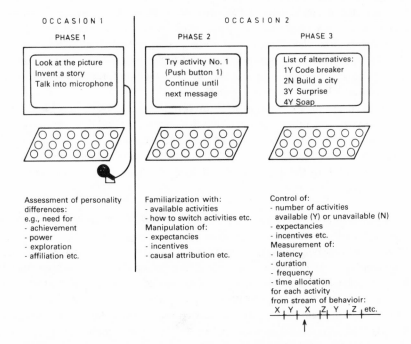

FIG. 16.4.   An illustration of the proposed experimental paradigm for the study of dynamic and cognitive aspects of the stream of behavior.

different occasion, the subject is familiarized with all the action alternatives available. Task-relevant cognitions and the motivational state are assessed or controlled, and selected aspects of the cognitive construction of the situation may be manipulated. In Phase 3 the subject is confronted with the available action alternatives and may alternate freely between them. Expectancies and incentive values of the outcomes associated with the alternative activities may be controlled by an appropriate control of the feedback provided by the computer. Also the number of action alternatives available are controlled. Note that the principle of time allocation derived from the dynamics of action implies that an increase in the number of alternatives will—ceteris paribus—result in a decrease in the proportion of time spent in individual activities. According to cognitive theories the number of alternatives should not affect time allocation provided the most preferred alternative keeps its dominance status. The points in time when behavior changes from one activity to another are recorded during Phase 3. From this protocol, all measurable aspects of the stream of behavior may be derived (i.e., latency, average duration, frequency, and % time spent for all activities).

The last two phases of the experiment should be controlled by an on-line computer. The computer controls the experimental conditions more efficiently and it records the measurable aspects of the stream of behavior more precisely than a human experimenter. Another important advantage of using a computer is the fact that it can control the experiment without the presence of a human experimenter. The motivational effects of the presence of a human experimenter may overshadow the effects of the variables that are under investigation. In the typical experiment on human motivation, the effects of the independent variables are confounded with the effects of the presence of the experimenter. Experiments that include a private control condition suggest that the number of experimental results that are attributable to the motivational effects of the presence of the experimenter rather than to the manipulated variables may be immense (Sacco & Hokanson, 1978). Although the use of a computer may also have some unintended behavioral effects, a computer-controlled experiment provides an important alternative to the experimenter-controlled experiment that has dominated past research.

Separating instigating and Consummatory Effects.   An example for a problem that may be studied on the basis of the proposed paradigm concerns the distinction between instigating and consummatory effects. As illustrated in Blankenship's (1979) experiment, this distinction can be achieved by comparing latency and first duration measures. The separation between instigating and consummatory effects is very important because it enables us to estimate the relative contribution of two separate motivational processes that are confounded in most behavioral measures. Both for a better understanding of motivational processes and for the development of more efficient intervention methods, it is important to find answers in future research to questions like these: Do some people overeat because they have an excessive appetite even in the absence of food, or because it is hard for them stop once they are eating? Do some students achieve less than they could because they have low interest in achievement to begin with, or because they loose their (initially high) interest too quickly once they have started an achievement-related activity? Are some delinquents violent because they have a strong need to behave aggressively toward other people (even if nobody is around), or because they cannot control their aggressive tendencies once these tendencies have been aroused in a given situation? Note that the answers to these questions may be different for different people in the same situation and different for the same person in different situations. To find the answers, we have to make the transition from the type of experiment suggested by the episodic paradigm to the type of experiment suggested by the dynamic paradigm.

Conclusion.   We have made an attempt to describe some theoretical problems left unanswered by past research. We have proposed a change in the experimental paradigm that may help us to find some of the missing answers in future research. The experimental paradigm integrates information about three aspects of motivation that have been studied in the past in separate experimental settings, namely individual differences, cognitive mediators, and dynamic principles. The concrete experimental setup proposed here (Fig. 16.4) may change as a function of future advances in computer technology. Our ultimate dream is a mobile and invisible computer that accompanies our subjects in their natural life settings, which unobtrusively controls selected aspects of their environment, and which unobtrusively records the measurable aspects of the stream of behavior.

REFERENCES

Abramson, L. Y., Seligman, M. E. P., & Teasdale, J. D. Learned helplessness in humans: Critique and reformulation. *Journal of Abnormal Psychology*, 1978, *87*, 49–74.

Atkinson, J. W. Motivational determinants of risk-taking behavior. *Psychological Review*, 1957, *64*, 359–372.

Atkinson, J. W. *Motives in fantasy, action, and society*. Princeton, N.J.: Van Nostrand, 1958.

Atkinson, J. W. *An introduction to motivation*. New York: Van Nostrand, 1964.

Atkinson, J. W. Studying personality in the context of an advanced motivational psychology. *American Psychologist*, 1981, *36*, 117–128.

Atkinson, J. W., & Birch, D. A. *The dynamics of action*. New York: Wiley, 1970.

Atkinson, J. W., & Birch, D. A. The dynamics of achievement-oriented activity. In J. W. Atkinson & J. O. Raynor (Eds.), *Motivation and achievement*. Washington, D.C.: Winston, 1974.

Atkinson, J. W., & Birch, D. A. *Introduction to motivation* (2nd ed.). New York: Van Nostrand, 1978.

Atkinson, J. W., Bongort, K., & Price, L. H. Explorations using computer simulation to comprehend TAT measurement of motivation. *Motivation and Emotion*, 1977, *1*, 1–27.

Atkinson, J. W., & Feather, N. T. (Ed.). *A theory of achievement motivation*. New York: Wiley, 1966.

Birch, D., Atkinson, J. W., & Bongort, K. Cognitive control of action. In B. Weiner (Ed.), *Cognitive views on human motivation*. New York: Academic Press, 1974.

Blankenship, V. *Consummatory value of success, task difficulty, and substitution*. Unpublished doctoral dissertation, University of Michigan, 1979.

Cartwright, D., & Festinger, L. A quantitative theory of decision. *Psychological Review*, 1943, *50*, 595–621.

Cronbach, L. J. The two disciplines of scientific psychology. *American Psychologist*, 1957, *12*, 671–684.

deVilliers, P. A., & Herrnstein, R. J. Toward a law of response strength. *Psychological Bulletin*, 1976, *83*, 1131–1153.

Edwards, W. The theory of decision-making. *Psychological Bulletin*, 1954, *51*, 380–417.

Endler, N. S., & Magnusson, D. *Interactional psychology and personality*. Washington, D.C.: Hemisphere, 1976.

Heckhausen, H. *The anatomy of achievement motivation*. New York: Academic Press, 1967.

Heckhausen, H. Achievement motivation and its constructs. A cognitive model. *Motivation and Emotion*, 1977, *1*, 283–329.

Heckhausen, H. *Motivation and Handeln*. Berlin, Heidelberg: Springer, 1980.

Hull, C. L. *Principles of behavior*. New York: Appleton–Century–Crofts, 1943.

Kuhl, J. Standard setting and risk preference: An elaboration of the theory of achievement motivation and an empirical test. *Psychological Review*, 1978, *85*, 239–248.

Kuhl, J. Motivational and functional helplessness: The moderating effect of state versus action orientation. *Journal of Personality and Social Psychology*, 1981, *40*, 155–170.

Kuhl, J. Action- vs. state-orientation as a mediator between motivation and action. In W. Hacker, W. Volpert, & M. von Cranach (Eds.), *Cognitive and motivational aspects of action*. Amsterdam: North–Holland, in press. (a)

Kuhl, J. Volitional aspects of achievement motivation and learned helplessness: Toward a comprehensive theory of action-control. In B. A. Maher (Ed.), *Progress in experimental personality research* (Vol. 13). New York: Academic Press, in press. (b)

Kuhl, J. *Integrating cognitive and dynamic approaches: A prospectus for a unified motivational psychology*. Prepared for J. W. Atkinson & J. Kuhl (Eds.), *Motivation, thought, and action: Personal and situational determinants* (in preparation).

Kuhl, J., & Blankenship, V. The dynamic theory of achievement motivation: From episodic to dynamic thinking. *Psychological Review*, 1979, *86*, 141–151.

Kuhl, J., & Eisenbeiser, T. *Mediating versus meditating cognitions in human motivation: Action control, inertial motivation and the alienation effect*. Manuscript submitted for publication, Ruhr–University Bochum, 1981.

Kuhl, J., & Weiß, M. *Motivationale und funktionale Hilflosigkeit: Prozeßanalytische Untersuchungen*. Unpublished paper, Ruhr–University Bochum, West Germany, 1981.

Lewin, K. Defining the "field at a given time." *Psychological Review*, 1943, *50*, 292–310.

Mischel, W. *Personality and assessment*. New York: Wiley, 1968.

Ovsiankina, M. Die Wiederaufnahme unterbrochener Handlungen. *Psychologische Forschung*, 1928, *11*, 302–379.

Pribram, H. H. *Languages of the brain: Experimental paradoxes and principles in neuropsychology*. Englewood Cliffs, N.J.: Prentice–Hall, 1971.

Raynor, J. O. Future orientation and motivation of immediate activity: An elaboration of the theory of achievement motivation. *Psychological Review*, 1969, *76*, 606–610.

Reuman, D., Atkinson, J. W., & Gallop, G. *Computer simulation of behavioral expressions of four independent personality traits*. Manuscript in preparation, University of Michigan, 1981.

Sacco, W. P., & Hokanson, J. E. Expectations of success and anagram performance of depressives in a public and private setting. *Journal of Abnormal Psychology*, 1978, *87*, 122–130.

Schachter, S., & Gross, L. P. Manipulated time and eating behavior. *Journal of Personality and Social Psychology*, 1968, *10*, 98–106.

Schneider, K. Atkinson's "risk preference" model. Should it be revised? *Motivation and Emotion,* 1978, *2,* 333–343.

Skinner, B. F. Science and human behavior. New York: Macmillan, 1953.

Weiner, B. Human motivation. New York: Holt, Rinehart, & Winston, 1980.

Zeigarnik, B.- Über das Behalten von erledigten und unerledigten Handlungen. *Psychologische Forschung,* 1927, *9,* 1–85.

17 Social Psychology: What It Is, Where It Came From, and Where It Is Headed

Philip G. Zimbardo
Stanford University, Stanford, California, USA

Social psychology is the conceptual analysis and empirical study of the influences upon an individual's perceptions, thoughts, motives, feelings, bodily processes, and actions exerted by other people—present, imagined, or represented symbolically.

The basic unit of analysis is the individual, although it may also be a collection of individuals in a group. The primary independent variables are people, but they need not be coacting others. The stimulus value of people is also carried in memory, in cognitive schema, in normative expectations, and in partial or indirect forms through their words, visual images, or other mediated sensory qualities. The dependent variables of the social psychologist include virtually all those studied by every other subarea of psychological investigation—from reaction time and heart rate to anxiety, attitudes, and mass movements.

In this broad view of what social psychology is, the field loses some of its uniqueness as a consequence of expanding its territorial boundaries. It is no longer merely the study of the social behavior of people in response to social stimuli. It may involve social behavior such as affiliating or spreading rumors in response to asocial stimuli, such as fear or situational ambiguity. It may also involve social stimuli, such as judgments of other people, but the response may be asocial, such as GSR changes.

The central process in my conception of what social psychology is all about involves the actor's construction of a subjective reality in which he or she exists in patterns of meaningful relationships to other actors and observers over time and across contexts. Using the metaphor of drama, we might say the social psychologist observes the scripts that actors utilize as they face new or old situations, familiar or novel plots, engaged in soliloquies or dialogues. In some cases, the actor is also the playwright who is improvising the script as the moment dictates. At other times, the actor dutifully follows scripts prepared by other more authoritative dramatists.

In this chapter, I outline in a discursive, informal way why I believe social psychology has moved from a rather marginal, peripheral position within the field of general psychology to occupy a position at the very core of what current psychology is all about. Then I suggest future directions I believe we can expect to see social psychological research take in the next decades into the twenty-first century. My analysis is neither encyclopedic in coverage of topics nor comprehensive in referencing the work of my colleagues. It suffers from the egocentric bias of overrepresenting my own research, simply because it is more salient to me and thus most readily retrievable when an argument is searching for support.

In my opinion, the ultimate goal of any inquiry into human nature is to discover the conditions that increase an individual's freedom to optimize his or her potential for personal growth and autonomy. A corollary of this first goal is to use our psychological knowledge to improve the general quality of our social life, be it in dyads, families, work groups, communities, nations, or internationally. To realize these goals, we must study how people define themselves in relation to their physical, social, and spiritual environments.

In attempting to transform reality as given into reality as desired, individuals need to learn how to minimize the unacceptable forms of coercive control that constrain their autonomy. It becomes a task for psychology, and especially social psychology, to specify how the person may be emancipated from freedom-limiting controls (Holzkamp, 1970). Sometimes these controls are imposed by the obvious tyranny of dictators, but there is also the subtle tyranny of rules and roles that force unwitting compliance from us, or the "underground" tyranny of our own guilt, anxiety, and inadequate sense of self-esteem.

The "cognitive revolution" in American psychology has let new light shine into the black box behaviorists imposed on mental processes. Credit for rescuing the minds exiled by the behaviorist manifesto usually goes out to "information processors," psycholinguistics, and computer scientists. However, social psychologists should be acknowledged as having remained loyal to a cognitive psychology even during the darkest reign of radical behaviorism. Indeed, some of the "new look" in cognitive psychology is really just a fresh look backward at what social psychologists have been saying and studying for the past 50 years.

Kurt Lewin (1947) provided the intellectual force that vitalized the field of social psychology. He did so by theory and research that pointed up the significance of a number of interacting processes, among them the role of contextual determinants of perception and judgment, the actor's phenomenological view of the situation, and the force for action arising out of task motivations and interpersonal dynamics.

Although much of Lewinian thought is focused on intraindividual processes, the issues he addressed gave rise to the group dynamics tradition. Despite the importance of group dynamics for our understanding of diverse social phenomena, this approach had the disadvantage of setting social psychology apart from other psychological disciplines, appearing instead to align it more closely with sociology. "Cohesiveness," for example, is a process that exists only *between* people and thus cannot readily be incorporated into other areas of individual psychological thinking.

It remained for Lewin's protege, Leon Festinger, to recognize as central within Lewinian theory, the concept of *discrepancy* and use variants of it to move social psychology away from group process and toward dynamic, individualistic, cognitive processes. For Lewin it was the "discrepancy" between an individual's stand on an issue and his or her perception of the group norm, which energized behavior in compliance-eliciting group settings. This perceived discrepancy between an individual and the group is successively narrowed in Festinger's theories, first as differences on a given dimension wherein a person compares him or herself to other relevant individuals (1954), and then to dissonance generated by two or more ill-fitting cognitions within the head of a single person (1957). The power of Festinger's theory of cognitive dissonance during the 1960s was in part derived from demonstrations of the irrationality of human beings. Man is not a rational animal, but a rationalizing one, asserted Festinger's protege, Elliot Aronson. When faced with possibly contrary evidence from one of their misinformed decisions, people will alter subjective reality, often in rather remarkable ways, in the effort to maintain a favorable self-image.

My research summarized in *The cognitive control of motivation* (Zimbardo, 1969) demonstrated that attempts at dissonance resolution could alter responding not only at subjective and behavioral levels but also at a physiological level. The way experimental subjects *interpreted* the situational constraints on their choices (the magnitude of perceived justifications to take an undesirable action or refrain from a desirable one), along with their perceived freedom to make the decision of their own choosing determined how much dissonance they experienced. Under high dissonance conditions the cognitive apparatus activated was sufficient to diminish or suppress a host of powerful basic motives, such as hunger, thirst, pain, and others.

A second major impetus within social psychology that moved the field to its current cognitive emphasis was the work of the Yale Attitude Change Program and its director, Carl Hovland. Hovland, coming out of a Hullian learning theory approach, proposed a view of the recipient of a persuasive communication as a rational processor of the information it presented. Thus the variables shown to be important in verbal learning were adapted for learning the messages in persuasive communications, among them attention, rehearsal, distraction, comprehension, and incentive.

In contrast to the dynamic models of Lewin and Festinger, Hovland's approach was more structural and "coolly cognitive." The complexity of the persuasion process could be reduced to its separate elements (the communication, the sender, the receiver, the channel of communication, and so forth). But the point of this analytical focus was clearly the mind of the individual audience member who had the task of processing the new input, relating it to what was known already, anticipating the consequences for accepting or rejecting the position it proposed, and then taking an overt action to change one's attitude or not (see Hovland, Janis, & Kelley, 1953).

An often neglected contribution to the development of a cognitively oriented social psychology is that of Gordon Allport and Leo Postman in their classic text, *The psychology of rumor* (1947). They demonstrated what many cognitive psychologists have only recently discovered, namely what a person comprehends and remembers about a given experience is determined to a considerable extent by the knowledge structure the person brings to that experience. The effects of prior values, needs, and prejudices in distorting the transmission of rumors are but instances of the general phenomenon of the biasing effects of what we know on what we perceive. Thus the psychological study of human memory now emphasizes the powerful role of "reconstructive processes" in shaping what is remembered. Old-fashioned "cognitive schema" are helping memory researchers understand how memory for stories, scenes, and people can be biased in ways not possible when such "confounding" was eliminated by "old-look" memory research limited to recall of lists of nonsense syllables.

If Lewin, Festinger, Hovland, Allport, and Postman helped nurture a cognitive social psychology during the years behaviorism was so dominant, then attribution theory is responsible for helping it to mature fully. Harold Kelley (1967) used an analysis of variance paradigm to systematize Fritz Heider's (1958) thinking about how people make inferences from observing others' actions about the dispositions that might have caused those actions. Daryl Bem (1972) contributed the important idea that behavior may *not* be simply the outcome of reflective thought or attitudes or motivational dynamics. Rather, by observing one's own behavior and its contextual determinants, the actor reasons backward to infer what his or her subjective state must have been to give rise to that observable consequence.

Attributional analysis focuses on how we try to explain why certain actors take particular actions in specific situations—but not others. It addresses questions once only the province of the personality psychologist, why different people behave differently in the same situation or why the same person behaves differently in different situations. The scope of an attributional analysis of behavior is limited only to all situations in which organisms attempt to make sense of their own actions or those of others. Even theoretical accounts of the well-established phenomenon of learned helplessness (Seligman, 1975) have benefitted from the cognitive phenomenological perspective provided by a theory of attribution (Abramson, Seligman, & Teasdale, 1978).

Attribution theory offers a rational analysis of the way the average person makes inferences of causality about behavioral events. It assumes a fundamental need to develop an understanding of predictable relationships in order to give stability and meaning to events in our lives. This leads to a *reality orientation* to the world. In addition, the theory assumes that we have a need to be able to predict important events and alter them in desirable directions. This leads to a *control orientation*.

In the process of actively seeking information about "the meaning" of a perceived event, people employ rationally guided search strategies. Nevertheless, *systematic errors* intrude on the process by which people make specific causal attributions and general social inferences. At times, we are blinded by our theories about what ought to be, or we are restricted from considering all available information because of our values or ego defenses. Other times our conclusions are "data-driven," but we are overly impressed with the "hard data" of our own senses and personal experience, thereby distorting the often less vivid, more valid data of population base rates.

The task of reducing complex inferences to simple judgmental operations ("go"/"no go") is often handled by heuristics. Heuristics are cognitive strategies or rules of thumb that facilitate judgment making. In the study of judgmental heuristics and inference strategies, the new social psychology and the new cognitive psychology are joined. The creative work of Amos Tversky and Daniel Kahneman (1980) illustrates how apparently rationally derived judgments may be biased by misuse of two heuristics, those of availability and representativeness. (See also their seminal work on how the framing of decisions can bias our choices, 1981.) Richard Nisbett and Lee Ross (1980) extend this analysis of the use and misuse of higher-order knowledge structures to show how systematic errors in judgment occur when a person's reasoning is distorted by either biased theories or biased data. Nisbett and Ross reveal how the scholar, scientist, and lay person are alike in their vulnerability to such fundamental errors of judgment. In doing so, they underscore a recurring theme in social psychology, namely, that the quest for understanding, prediction, and control, which guides the academic researcher, differs only in sophistication but not in basic quality from that which guides the lives of all "intuitive psychologists"—every thinking man and woman.

In my opinion, the conceptual contributions social psychology has made to our understanding of human nature may be summarized as follows:

1. *Situational control*—emphasizing and experimentally illustrating the subtle yet pervasive extent to which social situations can exert control over the behavior of individuals and groups.

2. *Verbal control*—emphasizing and demonstrating the power of verbal suggestions, instructions, rules, and symbols in influencing behavior.

3. *Cognitive control*—emphasizing and showing that biological, environmental, or physical reality may be less critical determinants of a person's behavior than the cognitive representation that forms his or her subjective reality.

A vivid demonstration of the powerful impact that a social context can exert to alter these dimensions of subjective reality is provided by the simulated prison experiment conducted at Stanford University (Zimbardo 1975). In less than 1 week, a powerful "evil" environment had overwhelmed and transformed the personalities and morality of "good" people. College students preselected (on the basis of clinical interviews and personality tests) as normal and psychologically healthy were randomly assigned to the treatments of either prisoner or guard within a functionally vivid simulation of an American maximum security prison. Living these roles so differentiated the behavior of this group of young men that there were virtually no similarities between them by the end of the experiment. The authoritarian control of the mock guards often became sadistic, "creatively violent," and dehumanizing. The passivity and submission of the mock prisoners, faced with their total loss of control, developed into severe (though transient) emotional and behavioral disorders. The pattern of interaction between these role-playing adversaries is portrayed in the figure.

Current and Projected Directions

One of the major reasons I am a social psychologist is the openness of the discipline to studying any and all ideas and phenomena that relate to people in some social context. There is a tolerance for varied methodological approaches, different levels of analysis, and of basic or applied research. This catholicity encourages a flexibility in selecting what to study, how to study it, and what to do with the results we discover.

Social psychology is the last bastion for generalists in psychology—nothing of man (or woman) is alien to the social psychologist. No wonder then that it is social psychologists who have moved readily into areas where many of their brethren have feared to tread: psychology and law, ecological psychology, psychology of religion, organizational behavior, behavioral medicine, to name only the most prominent new areas of inquiry.

Equally noteworthy is the concern of the social psychologist for applying what is known to help relieve a social problem or to improve the general quality of human life. It should be remembered that the Supreme Court of the United States in its landmark civil rights decision (Brown versus The Board of Education, 1953) that forced racially segregated schools to desegregate relied heavily upon a body of social psychological data. Social psychologists are now working in clinics and mental hospitals teaching basic social skills to mental patients and clients who have difficulty relating effectively to other people. Others are involved in prison litigation to improve the often "cruel and unusual" living conditions that exist in many prisons.

In response to current and projected world-wide energy shortages, social psychologists have begun to investigate sources of psychological resistance to energy conservation and strategies for overcoming them at the individual and

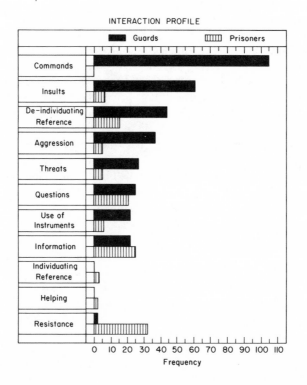

FIG. 17.1.   Interaction profile of guard and prisoner behavior derived from video
tape analyses of 25 occasions over 6 days in the simulated prison environment.

community level. The contributions of diet, exercise, and life-style to making
people prone to coronary attacks is being investigated by teams of social psychologists. Planned community-wide interventions to alter dietary intake of substances that promote risk of heart attack are being shown to be effective (Farquhar, Maccoby, & Wood, 1977). The job stress from working in helping
professions (nursing, police, social work, and others) where there is recurring
emotional overload can lead to "burnout," a phenomenon being remedied by
recommendations of social psychologist Christina Maslach (1982).

My research on shyness studied this pervasive human problem not as a personality trait, but rather as an interpersonal response style. After conducting
thousands of surveys in the United States and eight other countries, I and my

research team made hundreds of in-depth interviews, executed a variety of laboratory and field experiments, and then set up an innovative shyness clinic. In this experimental treatment center, we exchanged our knowledge and service for the opportunity to understand the more profound effects of this social phobia on the lives of the chronically shy. In addition to directly helping the shy clients to minimize or overcome their social inhibitions, I was able to codify the treatment strategies we had learned were useful, conveying this knowledge in popular books for lay audiences (Zimbardo, 1977; Zimbardo & Radl, 1981).

An overview of the cross-cultural dimensions of shyness in college-age students is presented in Table 17.1. It reveals the prevalence and seriousness of this social-emotional problem across many dissimilar cultures.

What might the future hold for social psychological research? The profitable alliances with other disciplines of psychology will continue to flourish. As they do, previously asocial areas of psychology will benefit from incorporating some of the richness inherent in a social psychological perspective of human development and interaction. Social psychology gains by borrowing some more precisely tuned dependent measures, standardized research paradigms, and knowledge of basic processes of mind and behavior.

However, more than an amalgamation may occur in some instances. For example, the study of mental disorders has been the province of psychiatry and clinical psychology. But the methodology they use is largely that of "historical reconstruction," after-the-fact analysis of the possible etiology of a given disorder. What is called for are prospective, longitudinal studies of normal people to follow the course of the transformation of their behavior into dysfunctional response patterns. Moreover, better experimental psychopathology research is needed to test under controlled conditions acute variables assumed to be influential in generating emotional disturbance.

I have been developing a model that attempts to integrate individual forms of psychopathology with social types of pathology (such as mass hysteria, deviant cults, group paranoia). My model borrows the concept of "normality" from social comparison theory (individuals seek to establish the normativeness of their actions by reference to similar others). It is combined with the concept of "rationality" from dissonance theory (individuals seek to establish the causal appropriateness of their acts). Normality and rationality are integrated within an attributional analysis framework (individuals seek to explain perceived discontinuities in their functioning, but their search for an explanation may be biased away from the true explanation and toward false ones). Madness is conceptualized as the outcome of an essentially rational process of trying to account for some perceived significant violation of an expectation regarding personal functioning or status. When biased search processes yield explanations that are not likely to be acceptable to more powerful others, the individual is perceived as irrational. Seeking out others who are similarly agitated or distressed will then at least minimize the person's extent of abnormality. Or, given some persuasive

TABLE 17.1
Cross-cultural Dimensions of Shyness in 18- to 21-year-old Students

	U.S.A.	Israel	Mexico	Germany	Newfoundland	India	Taiwan	Japan
Prevalence of shyness	44%	31	39	43	44	47	55	57
Shyness is a problem	63%	42	79	85	76	83	60	75
Negative consequences (yes)	97%	92	97	100	100	80	93	97
Causes social problems	76%	53	70	84	86	45	64	86
Creates negative emotions	61%	33	55	72	47	40	43	47
Assertion difficulties	68%	30	45	74	90	53	52	90
Others make wrong evaluation	53%	20	22	61	57	33	29	55
Excessive self-consciousness	53%	15	21	61	45	30	32	40
Cognitive and expressive problems	41%	29	50	63	43	27	58	39
Prevents positive evaluations	36%	20	25	56	39	20	38	39

TABLE 17.2
Major Classes of Explanatory Bias with Their Institutionalized and Idiosyncratic
Forms

Focus	Socially Shared (Ideology, Discipline)	Idiosyncratic (Pathology)
1. Body, health, internal functioning	Medicine, Physiology ⎡ Shamanism ⎤ ⎢ Public Health, ⎥ ⎣ Mesmerism ⎦	Hypochondria, hysteria, psychosomatic, anorexia, masochism, impotence, tics
2. Physical environment (actual/symbolic)	Physics, ecology, astrology	Phobias, compulsions, vandalism
3. Social environment (individuals, groups)	Social science	Paranoia, hallucinations, delusions, rationalization, prejudice, violence
	⎡Psychoanalysis⎤	
4. One's past	History Nostalgia	Guilt, denial, amnesia, compartmentalization
5. Nonempirical "reality" spiritual/mystical forces	Religion (sin) Scientology, Parapsychology, Sorcery, Witchcraft	Spirit, possession, compulsion, guilt
6. Structural, ideological	Politics/economic systems	Paranoia, prejudice, fanaticism

skill, the distressed person may arouse the anxieties of others, thereby also appearing more normal in comparison to them. In this model the explanations are the symptoms of madness. Madness is the judgment that the person or the society makes about the unacceptability of the explanations and the social inappropriateness of behaviors generated by those explanations.

As can be seen in Table 17.2, this model proposes that some people are biased, due to their reinforcement, education, or cultural history, toward overuse of certain classes of explanation (biological, social, environmental, temporal, spiritual). The form the pathology assumes is largely determined by the type of biased explanations employed in making sense of perceived discontinuities. For example, paranoia is the pathological outcome only for people who are prone to use socially based explanations to account for discontinuities, whereas phobias should be limited to people who rely most on the physical environment as the modal explanation for a variety of discontinuities.

What is also evident from this analysis is that the same biases when collectively institutionalized result in entire disciplines focused on a "biased" inquiry into the causes of human nature.

In a recent experimental test of part of this approach, normal, healthy college students were put in a laboratory situation paralleling that of many aged mental patients hospitalized for paranoid disorders (Zimbardo, Andersen, & Kabat, 1981). They were partially deaf without awareness that their inability to hear what others were saying was due to a sensory deficit. (The deafness and its lack of awareness were hypnotically induced by a posthypnotic suggestion with amnesia). When a pair of experimenter's confederates talked and laughed in the presence of the subject, he believed them to be whispering, playing a "trick" on him, or plotting against him. His misattribution of what he perceived to be motivated hostility against him resulted in the subject's changing in a significant direction on MMPI scales of paranoia and grandiosity. Other changes in self-ratings, as well as those of judges, corroborate an emerging portrait of this previously normal person as a paranoid-in-the-making. Extensive debriefing and other features of the study ensured that all subjects changed back to their originally healthy status.

The dramatic changes in cognitive functioning in the direction of experimentally induced psychopathology are outlined in Table 17.3.

The value of this approach (which I hope will be used by other researchers in the future) lies in the study of psychopathology within an experimental program that allows us to monitor the cognitive and social processes by which normal, rational people become mad—that is to feel, think, and act in abnormal and irrational ways.

Whereas future research will strive to elucidate more subtle and more molecular processes than past research has, it will also be expanded to the analysis of molar systems, institutional levels of analysis, and broad ecological issues (with their nets of interdependent variables).

Long before the year 2000, our lives are being altered by the advent of microcomputers and macrocomputers. As computers move into our businesses, schools, and homes and become part of our daily experience, more research needs to be done on human–machine interactions, on computer-literacy, -phobia, and -mania.

New studies will be made in vitro, using the storage capacity and convenience of a home computer for collecting daily records of a variety of personal information, habits, preferences, beliefs, worries, decisions contemplated, and so forth.

This electronic communication era makes it possible to have people interact without ever being face-to-face. The "symbolic" dimension of people in a social context will thus assume greater importance as telecommunications involve remote hookups between individuals (as well as teams and nations) whose decisions and interactions are constrained by the programmed features of the computer. New studies are being developed in my laboratory (and those of others) to investigate the effects of various algorithms for turn-taking among members of problem-solving teams whose interactions are directed by computer mediation (Zimbardo, Linsenmeier, Kabat, & Smith, 1981).

TABLE 17.3

Mean Scores on Dependent Measures Distinguishing Experimental from Control Subjects

| Dependent Measures | *Treatment* | | | | |
| | | *Control* | | | |
	Deafness without Awareness (N = 6)	*Deafness with Awareness (N = 6)*	*Posthypnotic Suggestion (N = 6)*	*t(15)*	*P*
Paranoia measures[a]					
MMPI-Paranoia	1.50	.33	−.17	1.838	<.05
MMPI-Grandiosity	1.33	−.83	−1.00	1.922	<.05
Paranoia clinical in- terview form	.30	−.09	−.28	3.667	<.005
TAT					
Affective evaluation	83.35	16.65	33.50	2.858	<.01
Self-assessed creativity	42.83	68.33	73.33	3.436	<.005
Self-rated feelings					
Creative	34.17	55.83	65.83	2.493	<.05
Confused	73.33	39.17	35.00	2.521	<.05
Relaxed	43.33	81.67	78.33	2.855	<.01
Agitated	73.33	14.17	15.33	6.586	<.001
Irritated	70.00	25.00	7.00	6.000	<.001
Friendly	26.67	53.33	56.67	2.195	<.05
Hostile	38.33	13.33	13.33	2.047	<.05
Judges' ratings					
Confused	40.83	27.08	17.67	1.470	<.10
Relaxed	34.17	54.59	65.42	2.839	<.01
Agitated	51.25	24.59	13.75	3.107	<.005
Irritated	45.85	18.92	11.25	3.299	<.005
Friendly	23.34	48.34	65.00	3.385	<.005
Hostile	18.75	5.00	1.67	2.220	<.05

[a]These measures were taken before and after the experimental session; reported means represent difference scores (after minus before).

In the year 2000, social psychologists will have to be even broader general-ists, trained to appreciate the contributions of neuroscientists, systems analysts, and cognitive scientists, as well as those of their colleagues in personality, developmental, and clinical psychology.

But this brave new world will not be to everyone's liking. Many more people will drift into ever greater alienation from the mainstream of their society. Advanced technology and automation will leave a generation or two unemploya-ble—even without projected economic recessions. For many people throughout the world, crime and other acts against society will increase, along with manifestations of personal and social pathology. Youth-oriented cults can be expected to become even more prolific in their recruiting.

The social psychologist must not only apply his or her knowledge in attempting to alleviate such adverse conditions but must discover how to engage the levers of political and economic power to help translate scholarly understanding into pragmatic programs for prevention and solution of these dire social problems. But in this age of uncertainty, there is indeed at least one certainty for the social psychologist: There will be more than enough challenges ahead for both the social researcher and the social change agent. I expect that in the future more academic researchers will adopt the dual-career status of social scientist and advocate for social change (see Maslach, 1975; Zimbardo, 1975).

In conclusion, I turn to the inspired messages for all researchers from these great minds:

The fairest thing we can experience is the mysterious. It is the fundamental emotion which stands at the cradle of the true art and true science.

A. Einstein

Learn your theories as well as you can, but put them aside when you touch the miracle of life.

C. Jung

Social psychological research is stimulated by a quest to understand the mysterious in life, but it should never forget to celebrate the birthday of Everyman and Everywoman.

REFERENCES

Abramson, L. Y., Seligman, M. E. P., & Teasdale, J. D. Learned helplessness in humans: Critique and reformulation. *Journal of Abnormal Psychology, 1978, 87*, 49–74.

Allport, G. W., & Postman, L. J. *The psychology of rumor*. New York: Holt, Rinehart & Winston, 1947.

Bem, D. J. Self-perception theory. In L. Berkowitz (Ed.), *Advances in experimental social psychology* (Vol. 6). New York: Academic Press, 1972.

Farquhar, J., Maccoby, N., & Wood, P. Community education for cardiovascular health. *Lancet, 1977, 1*, 1192–1195.

Festinger, L. A theory of social comparison processes. *Human Relations, 1954, 7*, 117–140.

Festinger, L. *A theory of cognitive dissonance*. Stanford, Calif.: Stanford University Press, 1957.

Heider, F. *The psychology of interpersonal relations*. New York: Wiley, 1958.

Holzkamp, K. Wissenschaftstheoretische Voraussetzungen kritischemanzipatorischer Psychologie (Teil 1 & Teil 1), *Zeitschrift fur Socialpsychologie, 1970, 1*, 5–21, & 109–141.

Hovland, C. I., Janis, I. L., & Kelley, H. H. *Communication and persuasion*. New Haven: Yale University Press, 1953.

Kelley, H. H. Attribution theory in social psychology. In D. Levine (Ed.), *Nebraska symposium on motivation* (Vol. 15). Lincoln: University of Nebraska Press, 1967.

Lewin, K. Group decision and social change. In T. M. Newcomb & E. L. Hartley (Eds.), *Readings in social psychology.* New York: Holt, Rinehart, & Winston, 1947.

Maslach, C. The social psychologist as an agent of change: An identity crisis. In M. Deutsch & H. Hornstein (Eds.), *Applying social psychology: Implications for research, practice, and training.* Hillsdale, N.J.: Lawrence Erlbaum Associates, 1975.

Maslach, C. *Burnout: The cost of caring.* Englewood Cliffs, N.J.: Prentice–Hall, 1982.

Nisbett, R. E., & Ross, L. *Human inference: Strategies and shortcomings in social judgment.* Englewood Cliffs, N.J.: Prentice–Hall, 1980.

Seligman, M. E. P. *Helplessness: On depression, development and death.* San Francisco: W. H. Freeman, 1975.

Tversky, A., & Kahneman, D. The framing of decisions and the psychology of choice. *Science,* 1981, *211,* 453–458.

Tversky, A., & Kahneman, D. Causal schemata in judgments under uncertainty. In M. Fishbein (Ed.), *Progress in social psychology.* Hillsdale, N. J.: Lawrence Erlbaum Associates, 1980.

Zimbardo, P. G. *The cognitive control of motivation.* Glenview, Ill.: Scott, Foresman, 1969.

Zimbardo, P. On transforming experimental research into advocacy for social change. In M. Deutsch & H. Hornstein (Eds.), *Applying social psychology: Implications for research, practice, and training.* Hillsdale, N. J.: Lawrence Erlbaum Associates, 1975.

Zimbardo, P. G. *Shyness: What it is, What to do about it.* Reading, Mass.: Addison–Wesley, 1977.

Zimbardo, P. G., Andersen, S. M., & Kabat, L. G. Induced hearing deficit generates experimental paranoia. *Science,* 26 June 1981, *212,* 1529–1531.

Zimbardo, P. G., Linsenmeier, J., Kabat, L., & Smith, P. Improving team performance and participation via computer-mediated turn-taking and informational prompts. *Office of Naval Research Technical Report* (Z–81–01), 1981.

Zimbardo, P. G., & Radl, S. *The shy child.* New York: McGraw–Hill, 1981.

18 From Traditional Factor Analysis to Structural–Causal Modeling in Developmental Research

John R. Nesselroade*
The Pennsylvania State University, University Park, USA

Paul B. Baltes
Max–Planck–Institute for Human Development and Education, Berlin, West Germany

The construction of explanatory accounts of developmental phenomena rests on both traditional manipulative experimentation and alternative methodological approaches, data sources, and analysis techniques. Because design and analysis needs vary according to the level of theory development and the experimental accessibility of the constructs employed, making the best use of analysis procedures involves some matching of one to the other in relation to a range of exploratory and hypothesis testing objectives. With primary emphasis on multivariate correlational analysis, selected aspects of convergence and divergence of theory and methodology are examined with special attention paid to the development and testing of hypotheses deriving from developmental concerns. Structural modeling techniques offer the promise of a more systematic way for developmentalists to organize and exploit multivariate correlational data in building and testing their theoretical conceptions than has been available heretofore. The techniques are described and some examples illustrating both measurement and causal analysis aspects of structural modeling are presented and discussed in relation to developmental research issues.

INTRODUCTION

The case for conceptualizing and studying developmental phenomena from a multivariate orientation has been presented by a number of writers (Baltes, Cornelius, & Nesselroade, 1979; Baltes & Nesselroade, 1970, 1973; Bentler,

---

The author gratefully acknowledges a year of generous support by the Max-Planck-Institute (1981–82) during which time this chapter was prepared.

1973; Buss, 1973, 1974; Cattell, 1970; Coan, 1966; Dixon & Nesselroade, 1983; Horn & McArdle, 1980; Labouvie, 1974, 1975; Lerner, Skinner, & Sorrell, 1980; Nesselroade, 1970, 1977; Wohlwill, 1973). Perhaps it is some intrinsic similarity between key concepts of developmental theory (e.g., structure) and multivariate perspectives that enhances the combination from the viewpoint of a quest for convergence between theory and methodology. In any event, it seems that many developmental researchers have accepted the principle that, in addition to manipulative experimentation, multivariate–correlational approaches have important features that can and should be exploited in fabricating a better understanding of the phenomena of psychological development.

In this chapter, we examine some elements of the evolution and application of multivariate–correlational methods in relation to the broader context of developmental research and theory building. The discussion focuses on a *descriptive (exploratory analysis)* versus *hypothesis-testing* dichotomy as it applies to both data analysis procedures and theoretical purposes. As with many dichotomies, this one ignores a number of methodological and substantive subtleties, but it is a useful organizational device for our purposes. With respect to procedures, our initial emphasis is on the factor analytic subset of multivariate–correlational methods with a subsequent focus on the use of structural modeling.

SOME FACTOR ANALYSIS HISTORY: ANALYSIS PROCEDURES VERSUS RESEARCH PURPOSES

Multivariate–correlational methods, especially variants of factor analysis, have been used for a variety of purposes. Here we identify and discuss two major past lines of activity, and in subsequent sections we examine current and projected future ones. Table 18.1, a fourfold arrangement, is defined by juxtaposing *data analysis methods* and *research purposes*. Both classifications are identified as being either primarily *exploratory* or *hypothesis testing*. The resulting cells are labeled I, II, III, and IV for convenience in later reference. We wish to empha-

TABLE 18.1
A Heuristic Scheme Classifying Research Purpose and Data Analysis Procedure Combinations

		Research Purpose (Theoretical Orientation)	
		Exploratory	Hypothesis Testing
Analysis procedure (method)	Exploratory	I	II
	Hypothesis testing	III	IV

size that Table 18.1 is only a heuristic device aimed at illustrating the relationship between method and theory.

The research purpose is seen as associated primarily with the theoretical context and status of a given substantive area. Depending on the situation, the research purpose leans in the direction of either being exploratory or hypothesis testing. Data analysis procedures are associated with the actual treatment of data and the dichotomy implies that there are differences in the degree to which the emerging statistical representation is formed by the data versus being imposed on them and tested for goodness of fit. The table illustrates the notion of convergence or divergence between data analytic procedures and research objectives guided by theoretical expectations.

A clear recognition and maintenance of one's research objective is important to putting the various data analysis methods to good use. As noted later, there are some instances where failure to discriminate the name of the procedure from the use made of it leads to an undesirable blurring of purpose. Before discussing these ideas more fully in relation to the four cells of the table, the two dimensions defining it are more fully examined. Subsequently, we consider some applications defined by the two dimensions jointly.

Exploratory Versus Hypothesis-Testing Factor Analysis Procedures

The development and use of procedures for factoring correlation matrices goes back to the turn of the century and runs through the present as exemplified by the work of Burt, Cattell, Eysenck, Guilford, Pearson, Spearman, Thomson, Thurstone, and many others. The concern shown in the literature for ways to utilize the information present in the correlation matrix to guide the analysis (e.g., to determine the number of factors, estimate communalities, and produce good simple structure rotations) underscores an emphasis on the exploratory nature of the procedures being developed.

But even in the "heyday" of the development and application of exploratory factor analytic techniques, hypothesis-testing factor analysis procedures were appearing, too. Mosier (1939), for example, presented a way to determine a simple structure when the factor loadings for certain tests were known. This development, in turn, foreshadowed the presentation of various "Procrustes rotation" procedures (Hurley & Cattell, 1962; Jöreskog, 1966; Schoenemann, 1966) that permitted one to rotate a set of factors to a "best-fitting" approximation of some hypothesized resolution. Eysenck (1950) developed criterion rotation procedures for incorporating a priori informatin into the resolution of factors to test hypotheses about structure differences in groups of people. Guttman (1952) presented multiple group factor analysis for extracting factors in light of hypotheses in such a way that an explicit rotation step was unnecessary. Tucker (1955) proposed an objective definition of the simple structure rotation concept and in so doing used the terms *exploratory* and *confirmatory factorial studies.* Tucker and others proposed ways of transforming factors to test hypotheses about factor invariance across subpopulations. More recently, the confirmatory factor analysis procedure COFAMM (Sörbom & Jöreskog, 1976)—which is a statistically very elegant approach to fitting hypothesized factor models to data and evaluating that fit—has appeared. Acito, Anderson, and Engledow (1980) have provided a comparison of methods of doing hypothesis testing in factor analysis.

In short, 80 years have witnessed a parade of factor analytic innovations that has included both exploratory and hypothesis-testing procedures. Granted, having hypothesis-testing procedures available and putting them to good use in furthering theory development are two different matters. We now turn to a brief examination of the latter in relation to the second dimension of Table 18.1— research purpose.

Exploratory Versus Hypothesis-Testing Purposes

Much early research involving factor analysis was fostered by the belief that descriptive, exploratory analysis was an essential prerequisite to the construction of useful theories about behavior. A major task was to describe and taxonomize behavioral domains by sampling from them and then using factor analysis to create a dimensional structure. But, at the same time, there is a record of factor analytic-based research that was clearly hypothesis testing in purpose. At a fundamental level one might argue that simply using the linear specification equation of factor analysis (Cattell, 1946) and concepts such as simple structure to represent reality is hypothesis testing. But debate about whether or not one is doing hypothesis testing at that level of generality is more like debating the premises of an approach rather than propositions derived from a set of assumptive premises. However, a small shift in conception to Spearman's two-factor model of ability, for example, provides a basis for hypothesis testing factor analytic research for the purpose of theory development. In that instance, one tests within the general framework the adequacy of specific submodels.

There are several examples of hypothesis-testing activity associated with factor analysis that extend clearly beyond the testing of the assumptive specification equation itself. The use of *marker variables* (Cattell, 1966a), for example, to identify or mark previously identified factors in studies designed to extend their relationships to other variable domains has a clear hypothesis-testing aspect to it. Eysenck's investigation of personality dimensions using tools such as *criterion rotation* (Eysenck, 1950) is an hypothesis-testing utilization of the factor model. Guilford's (1967) research on the Structure of Intellect has involved a series of hypothesis-testing factor analyses. These are a few fairly well-known examples to which others could be added, but they suffice to identify a stream of hypothesis-testing factor analytic activity reflecting concern for theory development.

COMBINATIONS OF DATA ANALYSIS PROCEDURES
AND RESEARCH PURPOSES

Obviously, research programs are not based solely on either exploratory or hypothesis-testing objectives. It is more the case that some balance between exploratory and hypothesis-testing work prevails and that the two kinds of activity augment each other as Cattell (1966b) described in discussing the inductive-hypothetico-deductive spiral of research and theory development. Productive increases in hypothesis-testing activity vis-à-vis exploratory analysis clearly rests on an accumulative theoretical base. It also depends, however, on the level of sophistication of available hypothesis-testing procedures, and the presence of the latter does not necessarily coincide historically with the needs of the former, an asymmetry noted by Wittmann (1981). What is perhaps most important is that methodological orientation be informed by theoretical purpose as fully and continuously as possible.

The combinations of procedure and theoretical orientation categories of Table 18.1 fall into two cases of convergence and two of divergence. First, we consider the two cases in which data analysis procedures and research purposes converge on either exploratory (cell I) or hypothesis-testing (cell IV) emphases. The divergent cases (cells II and III) are examined subsequently.

Convergence Between Theoretical Purpose and Data Analysis Procedures

The use of exploratory procedures for exploratory purposes (cell I) is a congruent mapping of technique to purpose and one that characterizes much of the factor analytic work done in the past. Such research has served well, for example, the identification of individual-differences concepts and the construction of measures for their operational expression. In the programs of some researchers, this combination has also been used as a beginning for the identification and structuring of causal relationships (Cattell, 1965).

The second case of convergent crossing of hypothesis-testing data analytic techniques with hypothesis-testing theoretical purposes (cell IV) is central to the latter half of this chapter, and it is considered there in detail. Here we simply point out that aspects of research programs such as those of Cattell, Eysenck, Guilford, Thurstone, and others reflected an awareness of the need for convergence between use of hypothesis-testing data analysis procedures and the testing of hypotheses within the respective personality and ability theoretical frameworks. With a few exceptions, however, the chief one being the general class of "Procrustes rotation" schemes and procedures, powerful analytical tests for hypothesis testing were not available to these investigators. Recent advances in hypothesis-testing procedures, such as those for modeling causal relationships with multivariate–correlational data, represent an increased sophistication in data analysis and statistical manipulation, but they too carry quite clear injunctions about the need for an explicit theory-guided context if the greatest possible value of the procedures is to be realized.

Divergence Between Theoretical Purposes and Data Analysis Procedures

Cases II and III represent a lack of congruence between purpose and data analysis procedures. But as we noted previously, availability of procedures and urgency of theoretical purpose do not necessarily coincide so sometimes adaptations have to occur. One such adaptation of considerable historical significance involved applying exploratory data analysis techniques (e.g., exploratory factor analysis) to the task of testing theory-based hypotheses (cell II). One exemplary area of application, and here our conference honoree made early and important contributions (Lienert & Crott, 1964), is the factor analytic investigation of the age-differentiation hypothesis of human ability development (Burt, 1954; Garrett, 1946; Reinert, 1970). This was done, for example, by factoring ability measures at different age levels to determine the extent to which the number of factors, pattern of loadings, magnitude of communalities, factor intercorrelations, and other indices that the theory indicated were reflective of a differentiation pattern were observable. Although lacking somewhat in statistical rigor and sophistication, a useful and productive phase of research in personality and ability structure development did occur through a combination of basically exploratory procedures with a theoretical framework sufficiently articulated to provide testable hypotheses.

The other divergent case (cell III), in which hypothesis-testing procedures and exploratory theoretical orientation are merged, is important to consider even though it seems somewhat self-contradictory. It includes a class of activity that needs to be explicitly recognized for what it is—an "Achilles heel" of confirmatory analysis. This occurs when there is a shift in purpose from hypothesis testing to exploratory research. For example, in testing hypotheses about a factor-loading pattern by fitting a particular model to data, one may be led to reject the model as a plausible representation of the data. The model may then be modified by, for instance, adding another factor or adding some salient loadings to improve the fit. But these are modifications not given by the theory under which the original hypotheses were formulated. Nor are they independent of the data matrix serving to test the model. Sooner or later the initial model is modified sufficiently to be judged an acceptable fit. Obviously, some modification of models is reasonable when one is elaborating a theoretical framework, but, in successive modification to fit a particular data set, there is surely a point reached where one is no longer doing hypothesis testing but, rather, exploratory analysis. What may have begun as a proper hypothesis-testing study has become essentially an exploratory activity. The final model, then, should be viewed as a new hypothesis and ought to be subjected to a rigorous cross-validation against new data.

The foregoing discussion has emphasized the need for coordination between data analysis procedures and purpose in relation to theory development. In the remainder of this chapter, our intention is to take a closer look at the notion of convergence between analysis procedures and theoretical purpose as it is represented by the case of structural–causal modeling. In so doing, we draw attention to the applicability of this particular realization of methodological and theoretical convergence for a number of developmental research issues having to do with both measurement and explanation.

CAUSAL MODELING AND STRUCTURAL ANALYSIS: TOWARD CONVERGENCE OF PURPOSE AND DATA ANALYSIS IN MULTIVARIATE DEVELOPMENTAL EXPLANATION

The dimension of descriptive versus hypothesis-testing activities is closely identified with strategies for proceeding from the description of a phenomenon to its causal–analytic explication (Baltes, Reese, & Nesselroade, 1977). *Causality*, of course, can be defined in various ways and establishing it is always a matter of successive approximation. There are some rather generally accepted common aspects, however, that help to focus our discussion (Kenny, 1979). Usually, the programmatic empirical study of causal relationships involves in concert four conditions. First, there is the study of *covariation* that may begin with a static conception of a causal pattern derived from observed covariation among variables. Second, further support for a causal interpretation of relationships (covariation) can be obtained by showing a *temporal sequence,* in which putative cause precedes the assumed effect in time. Third, where the nature of the problem permits, demonstration of the causal relationship is enhanced if the causal factor is subjected to *manipulation,* as would be true in the classical experiment. Finally, *replication* completes the classical experimental approach to establishing causal relationships.

Such a sequence is somewhat idealized for the developmentalist, however. For some problems the conditions for establishing causal relationships can be met. For others, one may be limited to trying to assess the usefulness of experimental work on problems bearing only a reasonably close similarity. Still other problems may be defined in a manner that prevents manipulative, experimental attack altogether. For example, maturation refers to a general developmental process but, in the context of manipulative design, it is a troublesome confound (Baltes, Reese, & Nesselroade, 1977). Thus, the developmentalist's conceptions fall over a wide range of the correlational–experimental dimension, and this breadth is mirrored in his or her needs for convergent methodologies. Some methodologies are not experimental, but they can and should be pressed into service to the extent that they help the cumulative growth of theory (Baltes, Reese, & Nesselroade, 1977).

Problems that do not permit experimental manipulation may, however, allow for the observation of covariation among variables and, in some cases, for the introduction of a temporal dimension into the observational sequence. Such correlational data can be used to evaluate hypothesized systems of causal relationships among variables and concepts by means of *structural modeling procedures*—tools designed for that very purpose. Thus, we now turn our attention to cell IV, the case of theory developed to the point of yielding testable hypotheses and convergent (i.e., hypothesis-testing) analysis methods and consider a recent advance that illustrates this level of methodological and theoretical integration.

The important sense in which structural modeling realizes convergence between theory and methodology in relation to hypothesis testing is that to use the procedures one has first to articulate clearly a model of the causal relationships among variables, constructs, etc., with a degree of specificity concerning direction and magnitude that can only come from serious, theory-based consideration of the phenomena one is trying to account for. Provided that a theory-based network of such relationships can be specified, structural analysis procedures offer the means for statistically fitting and evaluating the fit of models to empirical data (Bentler, 1980; Horn & McArdle, 1980; McArdle, 1980; Rogosa, 1979; Sörbom & Jöreskog, 1976).

The early developmental history of structural modeling includes path analysis. Subsequent work, most of it by social scientists (principally economists and sociologists), has led to some rather sophisticated analysis procedures and computer programs. What appears currently to be a very useful general class of procedures for various psychological applications is identified as *causal modeling with latent variables* (Bentler, 1980; Jöreskog, 1973; Wold, 1978). Within that perspective, structural analysis consists of two components. One is called the *measurement model* and the other the *structural model* (Jöreskog, 1973; Jöreskog & Sörbom, 1977, 1982). Wold (1978) uses the terms *inner* and *outer* model for the corresponding components, but, in psychology at least, the terms *measurement* and *structural* models seem to be more prominent, so we shall use them. The characteristics of the measurement model and the structural model, and the relationship between them, is illustrated in Fig. 18.1.

The *measurement model* component is the network of relationships between latent or unobserved variables or constructs and the observed or manifest variables. In the figure, latent variables are symbolized with circles and manifest variables with rectangles. The arrows terminating at the rectangles symbolize the influences acting on the observed variables. Included are both one or more

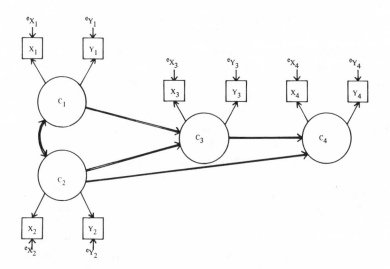

FIG. 18.1. A hypothetical structural analysis consisting of measurement and structural models. The measurement model includes constructs, c, manifest variables, x and y, error sources, e, and their causal linkage signified by single arrows. The structural model includes constructs, c, and their relationships signified by double arrows. One-headed arrows represent causal directionality and two-headed arrows signify covariation without causal attribution.

constructs and also an additional, less-differentiated source composed of errors of measurement and unspecified other influences.

The *structural model* includes the latent variables or constructs and the links, causal and incidental, which theory dictates to exist among them. Both the measurement and structural models are important loci of developmental research questions. Because the measurement model component is so directly related to the general factor analytic model discussed in the first part of this chapter, we consider it in more detail first before examining the structural model more closely.

The Measurement Model: Selected Applications in Developmental Research

The measurement model includes the links between the empirical world and theoretical space. These links can be estimated from empirical data and assigned numerical values indicative of magnitude of association. Specification of the measurement model may include both relationships between manifest and latent variables and characteristics of errors of measurement. To the extent that errors of measurement can be accounted for by the measurement model, one can fit the structural model (the causal system) with "error-free" latent variables. Review and discussion of these and related topics can be found in Bentler (1980), Jöreskog (1973, 1979), and Rogosa (1979).

There is a great deal of congruence between aspects of the measurement model and the common factor model (Bentler, 1980). Common and unique factors are analogous to the latent variables in some measurement models just as the observed variables in common factor analysis correspond to the measurement model's manifest variables. Factor loadings and their derivatives represent the relationships between the two kinds of variables. An essentially confirmatory factor analysis stance is taken in fitting the measurement model. The selection of manifest variables to stand as indicators of the constructs thus represents a set of hypotheses about how to measure the constructs. Obviously such hypotheses will find varying degrees of support depending on the level of pertinent theory development, but the hypothesis-testing orientation underscores the need to choose manifest variables in as theoretically sound manner as possible.

Measurement issues are central to the concerns of developmentalists. The identification and assessment of intraindividual change, interindividual differences in intraindividual change, age-related changes in variability, multidirectionality of change functions, etc., place strong demands on measurement procedures and instruments (Baltes, Reese, & Nesselroade, 1977; Labouvie, 1980; Nesselroade & Harkins, 1980). The measurement model formulation offers a framework for making the problems explicit and for systematically attacking them. We briefly indicate three selected problem areas to clarify the important role that measurement models can play in helping to resolve some of the measurement issues pertinent to developmental research and theory building.

Domain Representativeness

One of the central ideas of a multivariate perspective is that concepts of enough theoretical breadth to make them interesting are probably not adequately indexed by a single observable variable (Cattell, 1946; Cronbach, 1957), the concept of "factor pure" measures notwithstanding. The ability to define a content domain and to specify density and procedures for sampling of variables in order to measure important constructs represents a critical aspect of design in multivariate studies (Cattell, 1952; Humphreys, 1962). If variables are measures of the same concept, they are expected to manifest some common variance but not too much, else they are undesirably redundant. If the concept is a relatively broad one, and a small sample of variables is chosen to represent it, to do so adequately the variables may have to be so diverse that they show a pattern of very low intercorrelations. Thus, external validity concerns (Campbell & Stanley, 1963) apply to construct measurement as well as design. The best guarantee of generalizability is to identify it as a matter of domain specification and representative sampling (tasks, settings, persons, occasions, etc.). Evaluating variables as representative of constructs is one use to which the measurement

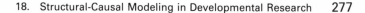

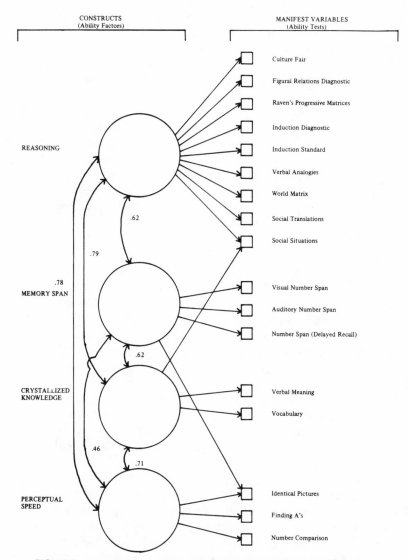

FIG. 18.2. A measurement model representing relationships (salient factor load-ings) between 17 ability tests and four ability factors or constructs. Interrelation-ships among constructs are correlation coefficients and do not imply causal direc-tionality (after Baltes, Cornelius, Spiro, Nesselroade, & Willis, 1980. Copyright (1980) by the American Psychological Association. Adapted by permission).

model component can be put, provided there is a sufficient theoretical base for identifying a content domain. Figure 18.2 illustrates these matters within the context of a larger, developmental investigation (Baltes, Cornelius, Spiro, Nesselroade, & Willis, 1980).

The purpose of the analysis shown in Fig. 18.2 was to develop a stable measurement framework for subsequent assessment of the effects of various cognitive training programs (experimental conditions) for older adult subjects. Horn and Cattell's theory of fluid and crystallized intelligence was used to guide the initial selection of 17 ability tests. The tests were administered to a sample of older adults representing the population from which the training groups would be drawn. Following the rationale of the differentiation hypothesis (Burt, 1954; Garrett, 1946; Lienert & Crott, 1964; Reinert, 1970), alternative "developmental" models of the structure of these measures chosen to represent various levels of the differentiation–integration continuum were then tested against the empirical data for goodness of fit. One of the best-fitting models is presented in Fig. 18.2. Thus, here no causal relationships among constructs (factors) were being tested, but rather the research focus was on using the hypothesis-testing features of the measurement model component to validate a measurement framework.

Measurement Equivalence

Answers to many developmental questions rest on comparisons of one kind or another (e.g., age-based, time-based). The meaningfulness of these comparisons depends, in turn, on the degree that the same concept is measured in the cases involved (Cattell, 1969; Eckensberger, 1973). Thus, the establishment of equivalence criteria and their application is an important aspect of measurement in developmental research. In discussing the concept of measurement equivalence as it pertains to the study of developmental change, Labouvie (1980) identified four highly pertinent questions. He asked: (1) Do instruments measure the same concept in different groups? (2) Are the metrics, or units of measurement, the same? (3) Are differences in observed means reflective of mean differences on the underlying construct? (4) Are the measures equally reliable when used with various groups? Labouvie (1980) indicated that, in general, the study of patterns of divergent and convergent relationships is the empirical avenue to the establishment of important properties of psychological measuring instruments.

The measurement model permits the specification and testing of relationships bearing on measurement equivalence conceptions. Moreover, one may fit models only for the purpose of assessing psychometric properties of measuring instruments as illustrated in Fig. 18.2, or the measurement model can be embedded in a larger context of structural analysis. In either case, questions of measurement equivalence can be translated into some form of hypothesis-testing procedure. For instance, parameters of the measurement model analogous to factor loadings can be examined for strict invariance over age groups or occasions of measurement. Similarly, theory-based predictions regarding constancies or changes in variances, means, etc., of the constructs can be tested.

Development and Use of Change-Sensitive Measures

Researchers who attempt to measure psychological change encounter difficulties on at least two levels. At one level, change scores, even those constructed from observations made with psychometrically sound instruments, have been characterized repeatedly as dubious (Cronbach & Furby, 1970). At another level, in assessing the psychometric properties of measuring instruments due regard has not always been shown for the putative nature of the psychological dimension the instrument was supposed to provide a measure of. For instance, measures of short-term change (e.g., mood and state) involve items that properly show a very low order of test–retest stability, but traditionally a low order of test–retest stability is construed as evidence of unreliability.

It has been proposed that one of the principle reasons for misunderstanding is the failure to discriminate between reliability as a characteristic of the measurement instrument versus stability as a characteristic of the psychological process being observed (Baltes & Nesselroade, 1973; Nesselroade & Bartsch, 1977; Nesselroade, Jacobs, & Pruchno, 1981). Structural modeling has led to more sophisticated techniques for assessing such properties as reliability and stability in empirical data sets (Nesselroade et al. 1981; Wheaton, Muthèn, Alwin, & Summers, 1977). To illustrate concretely, the results of an examination of state anxiety measurement reliability and stability by Nesselroade et al. (1981) are summarized in Fig. 18.3. Self-reports of participants, made with two parallel forms of a state anxiety measure, were repeated four times over a 2-week interval. The analysis was an hypothesis-testing one with indices of reliability (factor loadings in the model shown) specified to be equal both within and between

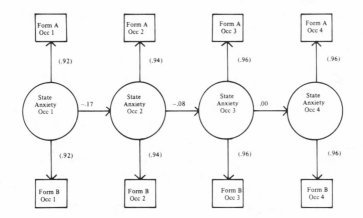

FIG. 18.3. Estimates of test reliability and construct stability based on four repeated measures with two parallel forms of a state anxiety scale. Reliability estimates are in parentheses. Goodness-of-fit index: $\chi^2 = 23.87$; $df = 21$; $p = .30$.

occasions. Stability coefficients were estimated from the data, although it would have been possible to fix them at some value as part of the model specification had one known what values to hypothesize. The fit of the model to the data, as indicated in the figure, was quite good and the results clearly showed the joint occurrence of very *low* anxiety construct stability across occasions and *high* measurement reliabilities within occasions.

Conceptions such as separating stability from reliability estimates need to be incorporated into the construction and evaluation of measuring instruments. For the developmentalist, especially, sensitivity to change ought to be a prized characteristic of the measurement process (see also Nesselroade, Stigler, & Baltes, 1980). Not only do measurement model formulations provide a systematic framework for helping to identify and isolate such parameters, but, in turn, the eventual incorporation of change-sensitive measures into experimental research and structural modeling contexts will enhance their capacity to represent mechanisms and processes of developmental changes.

The Structural Model: Selected Applications in Developmental Research

The structural model, as indicated earlier, includes the latent variables or constructs identified via the measurement model and the causal links or pathways hypothesized to represent their relationships to each other. It is within this component that hypothesized causal links among concepts are estimated and tested. Structural modeling should be seen as part of a scientific process involving successive approximation to explanation and inferences about causality. In principle, outcomes from structural analyses give us evidence about "sufficient" (not necessary) conditions that account for causation in an empirical data set. Structural models can represent static conceptions or they may incorporate an explicit temporal sequence. The closer the design arrangements associated with a data set approach the conditions that permit causal interpretation (e.g., some manipulation, temporal lag), the more likely it is that results from structural modeling indicate causal processes.

If one has a theoretical system developed to the point of permitting hypothesis and specification of a network of causal relationships one can, by using the appropriate analytic procedures (Bentler, 1980; Horn & McArdle, 1980; Jöreskog, 1973, 1979; McArdle, 1980; Rogosa, 1979), estimate the parameters of the model and test its fit to a specific data set. Alternatively, one may test the relative goodness of fit of competing explanatory models. In an important sense, then, structural modeling provides a way to exploit correlational data for the purpose of testing hypothesized causal relationships. In some ways, it is a multivariate–correlational adjunct, if not counterpart, to more traditional manipulative experimentation.

The developmental literature has begun to record the application of modeling procedures to various causal–analytic problems. Applications that involve evaluating the influence of the "Great Depression" experienced by women when they were in their twenties and thirties on their health and well-being during advanced adulthood (Elder & Liker, 1980), testing proposed effects of parental behavior on cognitive development in childhood (Rogosa, 1979), examining the influence that work complexity exerts on intellectual flexibility (Kohn & Schooler, 1978), and testing theory-based deductions regarding the direction of influence in ability changes (Cornelius, 1980) exemplify the range of problems that modeling procedures have already seen. We summarize a couple of examples of applications of modeling to developmental questions to illustrate both the general procedures and to identify some of the variations possible with regard to causal analysis tools such as temporal lag between hypothesized cause and effect.

The Influence of Maternal Behavior on Cognitive Development. The first example of causal–structural modeling involves an examination of the causal influence pattern among maternal behavior, motivation, and cognitive development variables in children (Rogosa, 1979). The causal pattern evaluated was that maternal behaviors (warmth and restrictiveness) exert both a direct effect on child cognitive functioning (Stanford–Binet Intelligence Scale and Peabody Picture Vocabulary Test scores) and an indirect effect mediated by the child's level of motivation (Pupil Behavioral Inventory score and Motivation Rating made during administration of the Stanford–Binet scale). The corresponding measurement and structural models for this set of relationships are presented in Fig. 18.4.

Notable in the example of structural–causal modeling represented by Fig. 18.4 is that although there is an explicit designation of putative cause-and-effect roles, there is no marked time lapse between the observations made of the mother and those made of the child. Yet, the structural–causal analysis can be applied to test the likelihood that the data obtained could have indeed been generated by the explanatory system symbolized in Fig. 18.4. Thus, in line with the distinction between sufficient and necessary conditions, one cannot prove that a given model is the only one that produces a set of data. One can, however, show that a given model probably did not generate them. The emphasis, which is clearly on falsification, reinforces the need to derive the causal model as explicitly and carefully as theory will allow.

In this particular instance, the model-fitting procedures suggested support for the hypothesized mediation of the child's motivation but not for the hypothesized direct effect of maternal behavior on child's cognitive functioning. The analysis of these data can be assimilated into the more general evaluation of the theoretical framework from which the hypothesized causal sequences was derived, and the result also serves as a stimulus for further examination of the potential role of motivation in cognitive development.

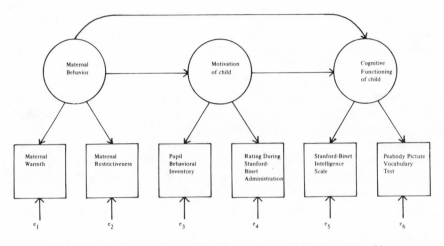

FIG. 18.4. Structural analysis of the effects of maternal behavior on cognitive development of children. Maternal behavior is hypothesized to exert a direct influence on cognitive functioning and an indirect one mediated by the child's level of motivation. Model fitting did not support the hypothesized direct influence (after Rogosa, 1979, courtesy of Academic Press, adapted by permission).

Longitudinally Measured Effects of Performance on Ability.   The second example of structural modeling comes from the field of gerontology. It involved testing a causal representation against data with a 2-year lag between measurements of presumed causes and their effects. The study, which was conducted by Cornelius (1980), focused on causal relationships between speed-related performance and more general fluid and crystalized ability dimensions in elderly subjects. Cornelius fitted the measurement models separately and generated composite scores to represent the constructs in the structural model.

The model is shown in Fig. 18.5. The primary hypotheses being tested were that status on speed-related performance measures at an earlier occasion (the first measurement) would account for status on fluid and crystallized ability dimensions at a later occasion (the second measurement). To a large extent, the outcome was supportive of the hypotheses as shown by the single arrows in the figure. The double arrows represent some cases of significant relationships that were not hypothesized in the structural–causal model but that were added to achieve a satisfactory level of fit. One of these, the path between antecedent crystallized ability level in 1977 and subsequent fluid ability level in 1979, represents a surprising and theoretically very interesting reversal from the descriptions of probable causal mechanisms found in discussions by Horn and Cattell. Horn and Cattell's theory suggests the opposite—a causal developmental link from fluid to crystallized intelligence. Obviously, the relationship discovered by Cornelius would need to be cross-validated to warrant extensive attention.

Cornelius' study illustrates a test of causal implications drawn from the framework provided by fluid and crystallized intelligence theory. Such implications are not subject to direct manipulative experimental investigation, so tests of this sort to extend and clarify aspects of the theory are very important to developmental psychology. Coupled where possible with more traditional manipulative work, causal modeling techniques should help us to fit together more and more pieces of the development puzzle.

The examples given illustrate applications of causal modeling procedures to developmental research. How valuable the procedures will turn out to be as adjuncts to manipulative experimentation is a question that obviously cannot be answered now. Bentler (1980) has argued that, for psychology in general, the need to train students and faculty in understanding and using these modeling procedures is every bit as great as the need to train them in the variety of analyses

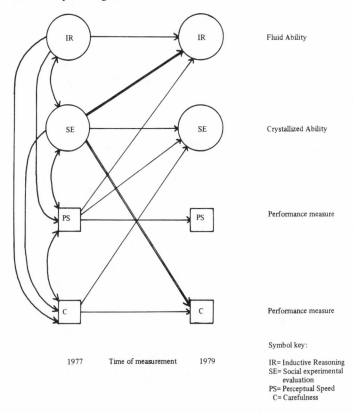

Fluid Ability

Crystallized Ability

Performance measure

Performance measure

Symbol key:

IR= Inductive Reasoning
SE= Social experimental
    evaluation
PS= Perceptual Speed
C= Carefulness

1977   Time of measurement   1979

FIG. 18.5.   Path analytic investigation of ability–performance measure relationships over a 2-year interval. Single arrows represent supported hypotheses concerning direction of causal relationships. Double arrows represent statistically significant relationships not hypothesized in advance (after Cornelius, 1980, adapted by permission of the author).

of variance. This begins to impinge on the topic of what lies ahead—a topic to which we now turn.

WHAT LIES AHEAD?

If the importance of causal modeling does indeed rival that of traditional manipulative experimental work and its alter ego, ANOVA, and if advice concerning what should be done to train properly the next generation of behavioral scientists (Bentler, 1980) is on target, then it appears that structural modeling is in for a long run. Drawing a somewhat facetious analogy from the history of ANOVA in psychology, and if the worst (or best, depending on one's viewpoint) happens, the term *structural analysis* may become synonymous with *design,* and some psychology departments may go so far as to outlaw functionally any other brands of data analysis. There will follow a flurry of methodological innovation and improvements of both general and incredibly specific applicability and perhaps, finally, in an eerie reversal of events, some twenty-first century Cohen (1968) will come along and tell us that structural modeling is just a special case of ANOVA.

On a more serious note, it does seem that, at least over the short run, some likely developments can be foreseen. Causal modeling is making its bid for acceptance as a major tool for the exploitation of multivariate–correlational data. Moreover, the importance of causal modeling lies not only in the data analysis realm. It also encourages (and offers a way of) thinking about and conceptualizing problems that would simply be ignored as intractable from a manipulative, experimental point of view. This possibility is of great interest to developmentalists because a significant portion of current theorizing is most directly translatable into some form of multivariate–correlational data, if at all. Many of the variables and processes at the core of developmental theory are simply not subject to easy manipulation (Baltes, Reese, & Nesselroade, 1977). Rather, their investigation falls within the realm of correlational and quasi-experimental designs. To the extent that structural–causal modeling pans out, then multivariate–correlational methods will further realize their promise for the study of development that we noted at the beginning of this chapter. Whether or not these pursuits will take us into and beyond the year 2000 is another question. Without some truly radical shift in the way developmentalists are doing science, we suspect they will.

REFERENCES

Acito, F., Anderson, R. D., & Engledow, J. L. A simulation study of methods for hypothesis testing in factor analysis. *Journal of Consumer Research,* 1980, *1,* 111–150.

Baltes, P. B., Cornelius, S. W., & Nesselroade, J. R. Cohort effects in developmental psychology. In J. R. Nesselroade & P. B. Baltes (Eds.), *Longitudinal research in the study of behavior and development.* New York: Academic Press, 1979.

Baltes, P. B., Cornelius, S. W., Spiro, A., Nesselroade, J. R., & Willis, S. L. Integration versus differentiation of fluid/crystallized intelligence in old age. *Developmental Psychology*, 1980, *16*, 625–635.

Baltes, P. B., & Nesselroade, J. R. Multivariate longitudinal and cross-sectional sequences for analyzing ontogenetic and generational change: A methodological note. *Developmental Psychology*, 1970, *2*, 163–168.

Baltes, P. B., & Nesselroade, J. R. The developmental analysis of individual differences on multiple measures. In J. R. Nesselroade & H. W. Reese (Eds.), *Life-span developmental psychology: Methodological issues.* New York: Academic Press, 1973.

Baltes, P. B., Reese, H. W., & Nesselroade, J. R. *Life-span developmental psychology: Introduction to research methods.* Monterey, Calif.: Brooks/Cole, 1977.

Bentler, P. M. Assessment of developmental factor change at the individual and group level. In J. R. Nesselroade & H. W. Reese (Eds.), *Life-span developmental psychology: Methodological issues.* New York: Academic Press, 1973.

Bentler, P. M. Multivariate analysis with latent variables: Causal modeling. In M. R. Rosenzweig & L. W. Porter (Eds.), *Annual Review of Psychology.* Palo Alto, Calif.: Annual Reviews Inc., 1980.

Burt, C. L. The differentiation of intellectual abilities. *British Journal of Educational Psychology*, 1954, *24*, 76–90.

Buss, A. R. An extension of developmental models that separate ontogenetic change and cohort differences. *Psychological Bulletin*, 1973, *80*, 466–479.

Buss, A. R. A general developmental model for interindividual differences, intraindividual differences, and intraindividual changes. *Developmental Psychology*, 1974, *10*, 70–78.

Campbell, D. T., & Stanley, J. C. Experimental and quasi-experimental designs for research on teaching. In N. L. Gage (Ed.), *Handbook of research on teaching.* Chicago: Rand McNally, 1963.

Cattell, R. B. *The description and measurement of personality.* New York: Harcourt Brace, 1946.

Cattell, R. B. *Factor analysis.* New York: Harper, 1952.

Cattell, R. B. Higher order factor structures and reticular vs. hierarchical formulae for their interpretation. In C. Banks & P. L. Broadhurst (Eds.), *Studies in psychology in honor of Cyril Burt.* London: University of London Press, 1965.

Cattell, R. B. The meaning and strategic use of factor analysis. In R. B. Cattell (Ed.), *Handbook of multivariate experimental psychology.* Chicago: Rand McNally, 1966. (a)

Cattell, R. B. Psychological theory and scientific method. In R. B. Cattell (Ed.), *Handbook of multivariate experimental psychology.* Chicago: Rand McNally, 1966. (b)

Cattell, R. B. Comparing factor trait and state scores across ages and cultures. *Journal of Gerontology*, 1969, *24*, 348–360.

Cattell, R. B. Separating endogenous, exogenous, ecogenic, and epogenic component curves in developmental data. *Developmental Psychology*, 1970, *3*, 151–162.

Coan, R. W. Child personality and developmental psychology. In R. B. Cattell (Ed.), *Handbook of multivariate experimental psychology.* Chicago: Rand McNally, 1966.

Cohen, J. Multiple regression as a general data analytic system. *Psychological Bulletin*, 1968, *70*, 426–443.

Corballis, M. C., & Traub, R. E. Longitudinal factor analysis. *Psychometrika*, 1970, *35*, 79–98.

Cornelius, S. W. *Fluid-crystallized intelligence and differential aging: Longitudinal relations among primary abilities in late adulthood.* Unpublished dissertation, the Pennsylvania State University, 1980.

Cronbach, L. J. The two disciplines of scientific psychology. *American Psychologist*, 1957, *12*, 671–684.

Cronbach, L. J., & Furby, L. How should we measure "change"—or should we? *Psychological Bulletin*, 1970, *74*, 68–80.

Dixon, R. A., & Nesselroade, J. R. Pluralism and correlational analysis in developmental psychology: Historical commonalities. In R. M. Lerner (Ed.), *Developmental psychology: History and philosophy*. Hillsdale, N.J.: Lawrence Erlbaum Associates, 1983.

Eckensberger, L. H. Methodological issues of cross-cultural research in developmental psychology. In J. R. Nesselroade & H. W. Reese (Eds.), *Life-span developmental psychology: Methodological issues*. New York: Academic Press, 1973.

Elder, G. H., Jr., & Liker, J. K. *Hard times in women's lives: Historical influences across 40 years*. Unpublished manuscript, Cornell University, 1980.

Eysenck, H. J. Criterion analysis—an application of the hypothetico-deductive method to factor analysis. *Psychological Review*, 1950, *57*, 38–53.

Garrett, H. E. A developmental theory of intelligence. *American Psychologist*, 1946, *1*, 372–378.

Gorsuch, R. L. *Factor analysis*. Philadelphia: Saunders, 1974.

Guilford, J. P. *The nature of human intelligence*. New York: McGraw–Hill, 1967.

Guttman, L. Multiple group methods for common factor analysis: Their basis, computation, and interpretation. *Psychometrika*, 1952, *17*, 209–222.

Horn, J. L., & McArdle, J. J. Perspectives on mathematical/statistical model building (MASMOB) in research on aging. In L. W. Poon (Ed.), *Aging in the 1980s: Psychological Issues*. Washington, D.C.: American Psychological Association, 1980.

Humphreys, L. G. The organization of human abilities. *American Psychologist*, 1962, *17*, 475–483.

Hurley, J. R., & Cattell, R. B. The Procrustes program: Producing direct rotation to test a hypothesized factor structure. *Behavioral Science*, 1962, *7*, 258–262.

Jöreskog, K. G. Testing a simple structure hypothesis in factor analysis. *Psychometrika*, 1966, *31*, 165–178.

Jöreskog, K. G. A general method for estimating a linear structural equations system. In A. S. Goldberger & O. D. Duncan (Eds.), *Structural equation models in the social sciences*. New York: Seminar Press, 1973.

Jöreskog, K. G. Statistical estimation of structural models in longitudinal-developmental investigations. In J. R. Nesselroade & P. B. Baltes (Eds.), *Longitudinal research in the study of behavior and development*. New York: Academic Press, 1979.

Jöreskog, K. G., & Sörbom, D. Statistical models and methods for analysis of longitudinal data. In D. J. Aigner & A. S. Goldberger (Eds.), *Latent variables in socio–economic models*. Amsterdam: North Holland, 1977.

Jöreskog, K. G., & Sörbom, D. *EFAP–II Exploratory factor analysis program. A fortran IV program*. Chicago: International Educational Services, 1978.

Jöreskog, K. G., & Sörbom, D. The analysis of developmental data by structural equations. In H. Winsborough, O. D. Duncan, & P. B. Read (Eds.), *Cohort analysis in social research*. New York: Academic Press, 1982, in press.

Kenny, D. A. *Correlation and causality*. New York: Wiley, 1979.

Kohn, M. L., & Schooler, C. The reciprocal effects of the substantive complexity of work and intelligence flexibility: A longitudinal assessment. *The American Journal of Sociology*, 1978, *84*, 24–52.

Labouvie, E. W. Developmental causal structures of organism–environment interactions. *Human Development*, 1974, *17*, 444–452.

Labouvie, E. W. An extension of developmental models. A reply to Buss. *Psychological Bulletin*, 1975, *82*, 165–169.

Labouvie, E. W. Identity versus equivalence of psychological measures and constructs. In L. W. Poon (Ed.), *Aging in the 1980s: Psychological Issues*. Washington, D.C.: American Psychological Association, 1980.

Lerner, R. M., Skinner, E. A., & Sorrell, G. T. Methodological implications of contextual/dialectic theories of development. *Human Development*, 1980, *23*, 225–235.

Lienert, G. A., & Crott, H. W. Studies on the factor structure of intelligence in children, adolescents and adults. *Vita Humana*, 1964, *1*, 147–163.

McArdle, J. J. Causal modeling applied to psychonomic systems simulation. *Behavior Research Methods and Instrumentation*, 1980, *12*, 193–209.

Mosier, C. I. Determining a simple structure when loadings for certain tests are known. *Psychometrika*, 1939, *4*, 149–162.

Nesselroade, J. R. Application of multivariate strategies to problems of measuring and structuring long-term change. In L. R. Goulet & P. B. Baltes (Eds.), *Life-span developmental psychology: Theory and research*. New York: Academic Press, 1970.

Nesselroade, J. R. Issues in studying developmental change in adults from a multivariate perspective. In J. E. Birren & K. W. Schaie (Eds.), *The handbook of the psychology of aging*. New York: Van Nostrand Reinhold, 1977.

Nesselroade, J. R., & Bartsch, T. W. Multivariate experimental perspectives on the construct validity of the trait-state distinction. In R. B. Cattell & R. M. Dreger (Eds.), *Handbook of modern personality theory*. Washington, D.C.: Halstead Press, 1977.

Nesselroade, J. R., & Harkins, S. W. (Eds.). Methodological issues. In L. W. Poon (Ed.), *Aging in the 1980s: Psychological issues*. Washington, D.C.: American Psychological Association, 1980.

Nesselroade, J. R., Jacobs, A., & Pruchno, R. *Reliability vs. stability in the measurement of psychological states: An illustration with anxiety measures*. Unpublished manuscript, Max–Planck–Institute für Bildungsforschung, Berlin, 1981.

Nesselroade, J. R., Stigler, S., & Baltes, P. B. Regression toward the mean and the study of change. *Psychological Bulletin*, 1980, *88*, 622–637.

Reinert, G. Comparative factor analytic studies of intelligence throughout the human life-span. In L. R. Goulet & P. B. Baltes (Eds.), *Life-span developmental psychology: Theory and research*. New York: Academic Press, 1970.

Rogosa, D. Causal models in longitudinal research: Rationale, formulation, and interpretation. In J. R. Nesselroade & P. B. Baltes (Eds.), *Longitudinal research in the study of behavior and development*. New York: Academic Press, 1979.

Schoenemann, P. H. A generalized solution of the orthogonal procrustes problem. *Psychometrika*, 1966, *31*, 1–10.

Sörbom, D., & Jöreskog, K. G. COFAMM: Confirmatory factor analysis with model modification. Chicago: National Educational Resources, 1976.

Tucker, L. R. The objective definition of simple structure in linear factor analysis. *Psychometrika*, 1955, *20*, 209–225.

Wheaton, B., Muthèn, B., Alwin, D. F., & Summers, G. F. Assessing reliability and stability in panel models. In D. R. Heise (Ed.), *Sociological Methodology, 1977*. San Francisco, Calif.: Jossey–Bass, 1977.

Wittmann, W. *The lack of multivariate approaches in psychological research with special consideration of the interactionism controversy*. Unpublished manuscript, Psychology Department, University of Freiburg, FRG, 1981.

Wohlwill, J. F. *The study of behavioral development*. New York: Academic Press, 1973.

Wold, H. Ways and means of multidisciplinary studies. In *The search for absolute values in a changing world: Sixth International Conference on the Unity of the Science*. New York: The International Cultural Foundation, 1978.

V CLINICAL AND APPLIED PSYCHOLOGY

This final part includes chapters describing a representative selection of outstanding research projects oriented toward practical problems. The chapters are ordered roughly from least to most applied. As the least applied, Part V begins with chapters by Kietzman, Zubin, and Steinhauer describing research on psychopathology and by Downing and Rickels describing research on clinical psychopharmacology. The last and most outspokenly applied chapter is Edwards' on decision analysis for large organizations. Brengelmann's chapter on behavior therapy acknowledges closer ties to basic research than does Edwards', but it too is concerned with practical solutions—now. It is interesting to note that the primary professional attachments of most of these authors are to professional schools and research institutes rather than to traditional academic departments of psychology. Does this portend an increasing separation of applied from traditional psychology?

The Kietzman group offers, within the scientific tradition associated with Joseph Zubin, research on information processing in the mentally ill. These authors make clear their very general concern with perceptual and cognitive psychophysics, encompassing both normal and deviant behaviors from a basic, biopsychological perspective. They hope that better understanding of the etiologies of psychopathology will lead to better diagnosis, prognosis, and treatment.

Robert Downing and Karl Rickels, in their chapter on "nonspecific" psycho-pharmacological effects, describe two decades of research on factors such as the psychophysiological state of the individual and the history of his or her illness. Their scientific dream seems to envision a *differential* psychopharmacology. This recalls Eysenck's plea (in Chapter 13) for an experimental-correlational approach to biosocial personality research.

Johannes Brengelmann reviews his own program of research, analyzing experimentally the effects of behavior therapy on different types of clients. One is struck by the tremendous range of problems studied, including such diverse conditions as alcoholism and drug addiction, high blood pressure, smoking, overweight, stress, and anxiety. It is clear that behavior therapy has become an important part of the clinical scene in West Germany. Brengelmann gives us not only his own involvement in this development but also his hope for increasing application of the experimental-correlational approach to research. Although experimental psychologists are naturally sympathetic to applications of conditioning principles, we must be as critical in our evaluations of such applications as we have been in our evaluations of psychoanalytic and other therapies that did not come out of the experimental laboratory. For example, since receipt of Brengelmann's manuscript, an important study (Pendery, Maltzman & West, 1982)* has raised serious questions about the efficacy of behavioral therapy for teaching physically dependent alcoholics to be controlled drinkers. Out of 20 treated subjects, at best one maintained a long-term pattern of controlled drinking: the others continued to drink excessively with damaging consequences. This 10-year follow-up on supposedly successful treatment suggests that attempts to produce social drinkers may be extremely dangerous.

Ward Edwards, in his enthusiasm for applied decision analysis, throws out the gauntlet to the more traditional experimental psychology: What has it done for the solution of real-life problems? He believes that traditional experimental psychologists are ignoring the most interesting and important topics in their concern for "the generalized normal human mind." In his skepticism about the scientific enterprise, Edwards' arguments may be contrasted with those of Gergen (Chapter 3) about the limits of knowledge and of Parducci (Chapter 10) about the dangers of attempting to apply theories developed to explain the phenomena of laboratory experiments.

---

*Pendery, M. L., Maltzman, I. M., & West, L. J. Controlled drinking by alcoholics? New findings and a reevaluation of a major affirmative study. *Science,* 1982, *217,* 169–175.

19 Information Processing in Psychopathology

Mitchell L. Kietzman
*Queens College of the City University of New York
and
The New York State Psychiatric Institute*

Joseph Zubin

Stuart Steinhauer
*VA Medical Center, Highland Drive, Pittsburgh
and
The University of Pittsburgh Medical School, USA*

Over the centuries, clinical and phenomenological observations in psychopathology have created a literature that is fascinating but difficult to quantify scientifically. Because the deviations associated with psychopathology are not necessarily consistent across individuals, nor even within the same individual, conclusions based on this literature are not always dependable.

Beginning with the work of Kraepelin, systematic psychological and physiological experimentation has gradually spread to psychopathology. At first this approach was overshadowed by psychoanalysis, which reigned supreme after World War I. However, psychoanalysis was not amenable to experimentation and measurement, although attempts were made to investigate psychoanalysis experimentally (Sears, 1944). After World War II the emphasis in clinical psychology shifted to projective and cognitive techniques, but experimental approaches to psychopathology continued in the USA at the New York State Psychiatric Institute and the Worcester State Hospital in Massachusetts and in the UK at the Institute of Psychiatry. The few experimentally oriented psychopathologists readily seized on developments in experimental psychology, such as reaction-time measurement, sensory thresholds, constancy phenomena, sensory resolution (flicker), fatigue measures, and autokinetic effects. The clinic in turn challenged experimental psychologists with new avenues for investigation such as brain function in brain-damaged cases, retrograde amnesia, registration of memory, loss of familiarity (jamais vu), and false familiarity (déjà vu).

Through the interaction between clinic and laboratory, several clinical beliefs were eventually corrected or disproved. For example, early experimental evidence of perceptual distortions in schizophrenics had led to the assumption that their sensory thresholds differed from those of normals. New measurement techniques reopened the threshold question. It was found that sensory, perceptual, and cognitive behavior in such patients was not always deviant. Improved diagnosis and the introduction of signal-detection and forced-choice methods led to new understanding of sensory, perceptual, and cognitive functioning in the mentally ill. In recent years, the most promising development in experimental psychopathology has perhaps been the rapid rise of research in the field of information processing. The purpose of information processing, as applied to behavior in general and psychopathology in particular, is to understand how the senses transform external stimuli into responses. Common to all such processing approaches is an emphasis, either explicit or implicit, on the *temporal;* processing basically means change over time. Therefore, as used here, the term *processing* refers primarily to events that are measured in time.

By delineating the processing stages between stimulus and response, the components (processes or events) that occur at different stages can be investigated. Other *endogenous* components occur simultaneously (in parallel) with these stages. These parallel components, which are control processes such as attention, are related to or influence the different stages. Figure 19.1 illustrates in a highly simplified version one attempt to graphically portray some of the characteristics of visual information processing. Most investigations focus on one or a limited number of stages and controlling events in an effort to explore in detail the processes and events that occur between stimulus and response. It is assumed that such a systematic description can yield advances in understanding various problems in educational, psychological, psychopathological, and even philosophical areas of knowledge.

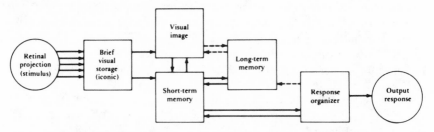

FIG. 19.1.   A typical visual information processing flow diagram, illustrating the inferred chain of events between the stimulus and the response (from Haber & Hershenson, 1980).

Several scientific models have been proposed to explain the chain of events between stimulus and response, but as yet there is no all encompassing model of information processing. This chapter considers such questions as: What is or might be the relationship between a systematic information-processing description of behavior and different types of psychopathology? And what are some of the primary needs and possible future directions of information-processing research, especially in relation to psychopathology?

Over 30 years ago Norbert Wiener (1948), the father of cybernetics, addressed these questions, although at the time the term *information processing* was not yet in vogue. In a remarkable chapter entitled "Cybernetics and Psychopathology," Wiener raised the possibility of understanding psychopathology by relating characteristics of computers to analogous human qualities, using an understanding of computer failure to explain human disorganization. Although cautious in his speculations about machine–human analogies, Wiener strongly believed that the principles of cybernetics potentially had important applications in psychopathology. Only recently have investigators begun to follow this lead.

Currently, the relationship between information processing and psychopathology remains almost exclusively an empirical one. A large number of empirically focused, data-oriented studies have been published comparing normal and behaviorally deviant populations. Such comparisons, by themselves, are of limited value. When compared to normals, patients usually display performance deficits. These can be explained as caused by lack of motivation, failure to understand instructions, inability to concentrate, etc. In short, patient performance may be worse because they perform poorly in general, not because of the specific deficit under investigation in a particular study. In recent years, this poor performance has come to be known as a *generalized deficit* (Chapman & Chapman, 1973). Thus, most empirical studies of this type tell us little that we do not already know (see a discussion in Kietzman, Spring, & Zubin, 1980).

Although there is no shortage of facts or data, the lack of a systematic framework relating psychopathology to information processing forces one to choose between the rashness of still tentative theory and the sterility of unexplained facts. In a recent assessment of event-related potential research, Sutton and Ruchkin (1981) remarked that too much effort has been devoted to compiling a *dictionary* rather than a *grammar* of results. A similar situation exists with information-processing research in the field of psychopathology. To construct such a framework, basic questions about information processing itself must first be asked: then, research aimed at answering these questions can be designed and carried out.

During the last few years, rapid and significant advances have been made in developing systematic models of information processing as applied to normal behavior and these have begun to be extended to psychopathology. In fact, chapters on information processing in several recent books (Kietzman et al., 1980; Magaro, 1980; Neale & Oltmanns, 1980; Schwartz, 1978) indicate such trends within the field. Generally, however, these treatments do not provide a step by step systematic analysis of psychopathology.

Visual Persistence

To illustrate systematic relationships between information processing and psychopathology we have selected the phenomenon of *visual persistence,* which is an early sensory component of visual perception. In visual perception there is a chain of events beginning with the impinging stimulus and leading to various sequential changes until the final response. One of the earliest components in this chain is visual persistence. There are several reasons for our choice of visual persistence as an example of information processing in psychopathology. First, it is the subject of a large amount of experimental research with normal subjects (Coltheart, 1980; Long, 1980). Second, there have been numerous recent studies of visual persistence in various patient populations such as the mentally retarded, as well as psychiatric and brain-damaged patients. Various techniques were used to study these diverse populations, and despite some diversity the results have been generally consistent, in that some groups deviate from normals and other patients in visual persistence. Such differences suggest deviation in the earliest stages of information processing.

Visual persistence refers to the fact that the effect of a visual stimulus continues beyond its physical offset. More technically, visual persistence can be defined as an early (initial) sensory stage of information processing that is characterized by high storage capacity and rapid decay.

Numerous techniques have been used to demonstrate visual persistence. For example, Eriksen and Collins (1967) presented two brief stimuli each consisting of a random pattern of dots separated by a brief interval of darkness. If the dark time between the stimuli was brief enough (e.g., 20 msec), the two stimuli fused to form a nonsense syllable. If the dark interval was lengthened, it became increasingly difficult to identify the syllable, and at a long (e.g., over 100 msec) dark interval the two dot patterns never were seen as a fused, single stimulus. The explanation for this perceptual phenomenon is that the visual persistence of the first stimulus continues and fuses with the perception of the second stimulus to produce the nonsense syllable, as long as the dark interval is within a critical period of persistence.

The phenomenon of visual persistence has been given a variety of names: visual information store, iconic storage, sensory storage, temporal integration or summation, stimulus persistence, immediate (sensory) memory, iconic persistence, iconic memory, and sensory registration. One cannot help but wonder if these names identify different phenomena. It may be that equating all these phenomena leads to an oversimplification. Recent reviews on the topic (Coltheart, 1980; Long, 1980) consider the possibility that different phenomena may have been incorrectly grouped as measures of a unitary visual persistence. Coltheart (1980) distinguishes the following three types of persistence: (1) *neural persistence* (the neural activity in the visual system evoked by the stimulus that continues after stimulus offset); (2) *visible or phenomenal persistence* (the stimulus continuing to be visible for some time after its offset); and (3) *informational persistence* (information about visual properties of the stimulus that continues to be available to an observer for some time after the stimulus offset). In a similar vein, Hawkins and Shulman (1979) propose two types of persistence, which they label Type I and Type II, whereas Long (1979a) subdivides Hawkin's and Shulman's Type II persistence and posits three types instead.

The reason for this multiplicity of terms and types is that research in the field utilizes a large number of experimental techniques and procedures. Long (1980) identifies five separate procedures, whereas Coltheart (1980) identifies seven procedures, some of which overlap with Long's. Extensive research on visual persistence in the last 20 years (since Sperling's 1960 monograph) has relied on all these techniques and procedures, and conclusions have been based upon results from all of them. Not surprisingly, some of the conclusions have been contradictory. Controversy has arisen about the exact nature of visual persistence, the manner in which various stimulus and subject parameters influence it, its physiological substrate, and its theoretical bases.

Clinical Implications.   Research on visual persistence, which began with laboratory studies of highly motivated and trained normal subjects, has begun to reach the clinic in two quite different ways. In the mid-1970s investigators began to measure visual persistence in psychiatric patients, primarily schizophrenics. Studies have been conducted by Saccuzzo and colleagues (Brody, Saccuzzo, & Braff, 1980; Miller, Saccuzzo, & Braff, 1979; Saccuzzo & Braff, 1981; Saccuzzo, Hirt, & Spencer, 1974; Saccuzzo & Miller, 1977; Saccuzzo & Schubert, 1981) and by Knight and co-workers (Knight, Sherer, Putchat, & Carter, 1978; Knight, Sherer, & Shapiro, 1977). Saccuzzo has focused primarily on the visual masking technique, whereas Knight has used the partial-report procedure (Knight et al., 1977) and the successive-field procedure (Knight et al., 1978). Both series of studies conclude that the visual persistence of at least some psychiatric patients differs from that of other patients and from normal subjects. Their general conclusions are that such dysfunctions indicate an impairment in the *earliest* stage of sensory information processing in these patients. Whether the impairment has to do with the duration of persistence, with slower processing, or some other factor remains a topic for current investigation.

The second line of visual persistence research with clinical implications is that being done with elderly subjects. This research has not yet reached the clinic, but it has an important potential application for the investigation of gerontologic and geriatric populations. Further, as Saccuzzo (1977) contends, there are many similarities between research with schizophrenic and with geriatric patients, so the problems and accomplishments of both fields complement each other.

Comparisons of the visual persistence of older and younger subjects have been undertaken by Walsh and his collaborators using visual masking (Walsh,

1976; Walsh & Thompson, 1978; Walsh, Williams, & Herzog, 1979) and by Kline and his colleagues using masking and successive-field techniques (Kline & Baffa, 1976, Kline & Birren, 1975; Kline & Orme–Rogers, 1978; Kline & Schieber, 1980; Kline & Szaftan, 1975). This research has led to the general conclusion that visual persistence *increases* with age, and this fact may help to explain some of the typical changes observed in senescence (see a general discussion by Botwinick, 1978). Walsh and Thompson (1978) reported shorter persistence for older subjects, but Kline and Schieber (1981), using the same technique, obtained the more usual finding of longer persistence for older subjects, thereby supporting the conclusion of increased persistence of stimuli in the senescent nervous system.

In summary, visual persistence, as an example of information processing, has been extensively investigated with normal populations, as well as with psychiatric and elderly populations. However, the potentially broad explanatory power of this approach may be limited by some of its complexities and difficulties. These difficulties are not unique to visual persistence research; rather, they represent the types of problems common to any attempt to use information-processing techniques in psychopathology. Some of these complexities are discussed below in detail in the hope of elucidating the problems encountered in applying information-processing procedures to study clinical subjects.

Basic Questions

Having summarized the empirical contributions of visual persistence research to psychopathology, we can now analyze these findings in more detail in terms of information processing. To do this, we need to trace the route that information processing takes between stimulus and response. This perhaps can be done best by asking and attempting to answer some *basic questions* about information processing and psychopathology, which can be formulated as follows: (1) Exactly which specific observed phenomenon is being investigated? (*specificity*); (2) What type of processing is taking place—energy processing or information processing? (*type*); (3) When, in the sequence between stimulus and response, is the particular component taking place? (*temporal position*); (4) Where in the central nervous system is the particular component of processing taking place? (*localization*). We deal with each of these questions in turn.[1]

---

[1]It is of interest to note that Titchener, in formulating his system of Structuralism (Heidbreder, 1933), also asked what he considered to be *basic questions* similar to those we ask with respect to information processing. Titchener's basic questions were: What? How? and Why?. His *what* and *how* questions described phenomena through analysis, whereas his *why* question led to explanation through synthesis. Although the meanings of his questions differ slightly from ours, the idea that his system was formulated by asking selected questions, similar to what we are asking, is an intriguing one. We replace Titchener's *why* question with two other questions, *where* and *when*, and we add, for reasons to be explained, an initial question as well, *which*?

1. Specificity of the Component.   The question of specificity reflects the fact that information-processing investigations always are focused on a selected phenomenon—a particular stage, process, or controlling event. No single study can encompass the entire chain of events between stimulus and response. For this report, visual persistence has been chosen as the specific component for study.

Although the specificity question seems simple and straightforward, answering it is not always easy. As mentioned previously, there are several terms that have been used to describe visual persistence, and a variety of techniques that are used to measure it. As a result, several types of persistence have to be distinguished.

Another aspect of the specificity question relates to the different characteristics of visual persistence being investigated. The variety of possible response measures makes it important to distinguish exactly what is being measured. For example, Knight et al. (1978) ask what might be meant by deficient iconic storage in schizophrenic patients. Is the icon inadequately formed? Is it abnormal in duration, smaller in its capacity to store information, or all of these? Is some other, as yet unnamed, characteristic of persistence different for patients? To date, research in visual persistence with psychiatric patients is relatively unsophisticated. The emphasis has been simply on determining whether patients from various diagnostic categories differ from each other and from normals.

2. Type of Processing.   In any given study exactly what is being processed—energy, information, or both? If both are involved (as they usually are), what is the relative importance of each. Answers to these questions can help clarify whether the processing under investigation is sensory, perceptual, or cognitive (Kietzman et al., 1980). Investigations in the sensory domain involve primarily energy processing, those in the cognitive domain involve primarily information processing, and those in the perceptual domain may fall into either category, some more influenced by manipulating energy, others by manipulating information.

To clarify the question about *what* is being processed, energy or information, consider the three types of visual persistence mentioned earlier: neural, phenomenal (visible), and informational (Coltheart, 1980). Each differs in the extent to which it depends on energy. In fact, one of the major distinctions between phenomenal and informational persistence in Coltheart's view is that the former can be manipulated (controlled) by energy changes (i.e., by variations in luminance and stimulus duration), whereas the latter seems invariant to energy manipulations. Thus, grouping persistence phenomena according to energy effects is an operational way of defining (and thereby categorizing) the various types of visual persistence.

Such distinctions among the types of persistence are essential when comparing patients with normals, because patients might differ in one type of persistence (e.g., phenomenal) but not in other types (e.g., informational). One approach would be to review the techniques used to measure visual persistence with patients and to classify them according to their susceptibility to energy manipulations. This has already been done in research with normal subjects; both the Coltheart (1980) and Long (1980) reviews emphasize the role that energy plays in the different techniques. Similarly, in research with elderly subjects, Walsh (1976) utilizes a distinction made by Turvey (1973) between peripheral and central visual masking effects. The distinction is based, in part, on whether energy influences the magnitude of masking. (This approach is discussed in detail later under the topic of *localization*.)

Finally, the "type of processing" may help clarify some of the confusion over the large number of terms and procedures found in visual persistence research. For example, Long (1980) seriously questions the use of the persistence-of-form technique (called "phenomenal continuity" by Coltheart, 1980) as a measure of persistence because with that technique increasing energy shortens rather than lengthens persistence. Two procedures used extensively in research with patients—the critical flicker frequency (CFF) threshold procedure, and the two-flash threshold procedure are classified by Long as persistence-of-form techniques. Both involve judgments that depend on the presence or absence of phenomenal continuity, (i.e., visible persistence). Research could clarify Long's contention that these are not actually measures of persistence because of their inverse relation to stimulus energy. For example, Nicotera, Berenhaus, Goldberg, Herskovic, and Kietzman (1977) measured both the CFF and the two-flash thresholds to the same subjects under comparable conditions. They found that increasing the stimulus intensity improved temporal resolution as measured by the CFF procedure, implying less persistence; the CFF rates increased as predicted by the Ferry–Porter law. However, increased stimulus intensity had *no* effect upon the two-flash threshold. Taken together, these results suggest that the two procedures may measure different phenomena and therefore are not comparable measures of visual persistence. Further, it suggests that even by Long's narrower definition of visual persistence, the two-flash threshold technique is an acceptable way of measuring it. Thus, the numerous two-flash threshold studies of psychiatric patients (Gruzelier & Venables, 1975) must be considered as part of the visual persistence literature.

3. Temporal Position of the Component.   The temporal position of visual persistence in the processing chain involves at least two aspects—ordinal location in time and other temporal characteristics such as latency and duration. In this report, the focus is on the ordinal position of visual persistence.

In visual persistence research with patients, there is general agreement that a dysfunction in persistence could indicate a very early processing impairment (Kline & Orme–Rogers, 1978; Saccuzzo & Braff, 1981). Several investigators have questioned whether the impairment is preiconic or posticonic or whether it reflects some difficulty in the icon processing itself (Spaulding, Rosenzweig, Huntzinger, Cromwell, Briggs, & Hayes, 1980).

4. Localization of the Component.   This question refers to the neuropsychological or psychophysiological locus of the component under consideration. This approach does not use actual psychophysiological measurement but employs selected behavioral measures that are particularly indicative of location in the nervous system.

Localization can be investigated in at least two ways: either in terms of *level* or of *laterality*. Because behavioral events have psychophysiological correlates *throughout* the nervous system, it is not possible, at least using only behavioral techniques, to obtain precise and clearly delimited answers to the localization question. Instead, the proposed strategies suggest more global answers. For example, the *level* approach distinguishes between peripheral and central levels of function. Peripheral level refers to psychophysiological correlates of behavior that develop relatively early and involve collateral rather than central (cortical) processing. In vision, for example, processes that can be explained largely by retinal phenomena, whether photochemical and/or neuroretinal, would be considered peripheral. In comparison, phenomena that obviously require higher cortical centers for processing can be considered central.

There are two ways, one methodological and one theoretical, in which this distinction between peripheral and central levels can be implemented. The methodological and most straightforward way to test for a distinction between the levels is with the dichoptic stimulation technique, in which corresponding retinal areas of the two eyes are stimulated by spatially separated but otherwise physically identical stimuli. By the use of prisms, the two stimuli (each seen by only one eye) are fused so that the subject sees only one composite stimulus and has no cues as to which part of that stimulus is associated with each eye. Because of the anatomy of the visual system, dichoptic stimulation results in effects that are necessarily retrochiasmal (i.e., at least at the level of the lateral geniculate) and therefore relatively more central. To determine whether a particular phenomenon is peripheral or central requires experiments that compare results of dichoptic stimulation with binocular (or monocular) stimulation. If results between the two (or three) conditions are highly similar, then the resulting effects are believed to be primarily central. If the results of dichoptic stimulation differ markedly from those of binocular stimulation, especially if the phenomenon (e.g., masking) is markedly reduced or eliminated, the phenomenon is considered more peripheral in locus. It should be noted, however, that Long (1979b) has recently challenged this interpretation of dichoptically obtained data.

Turvey (1973) has developed a theoretical model of visual information processing that is useful in identifying the level of a component. The model predicts different quantitative results for central and for peripheral visual masking. The two types of quantitative results are tested by relating the interstimulus interval to the energy or the duration of the target stimulus. In peripheral masking the product of the target stimulus energy (TE) and the critical interstimulus interval (the ISI, i.e., the minimum interval required to avoid masking) is a constant ($TE \times ISI = K_1$). In central masking, the target stimulus duration (TD) *plus* the critical interstimulus interval (ISI) is a constant ($TD + ISI = K_2$). To determine whether visual masking is peripheral or central, one merely decides which quantitative relation, the additive or multiplicative, best fits the data. Once again, this technique illustrates the importance of considering stimulus energy to obtain a better understanding of visual persistence.

Walsh (1976) used Turvey's (1973) dichoptic masking paradigms to explore how age affects visual masking. He found processing to be slower in older subjects than in younger ones. The data fit the additive relationship, implying central masking. Walsh (1976) pointed out that the different results obtained by other investigators might mean that they were investigating peripheral rather than central masking. In their investigations of schizophrenia, Saccuzzo and his co-workers (Saccuzzo et al., 1974; Saccuzzo & Miller, 1977) interpreted their data as indicating peripheral masking, but it is not known if they were in fact studying peripheral or central masking. It would be interesting to determine whether their data displayed the multiplicative relationship associated with peripheral masking in Turvey's model. Such distinctions and the methodology and theories associated with them illustrate the potential power of information-processing research in studying the elderly and psychiatric patients.

It also is possible to approach the localization question using the *laterality* procedure which involves a different strategy. Recent research indicates renewed interest in the possibility of asymmetric function (functional lateralization) of the two cerebral hemispheres (Kinsbourne, 1978; Milner, 1975). Evidence from clinical studies in neurologically lesioned or commissurectomized (split-brain) patients suggests that the left hemisphere is specialized primarily for analytic, sequential, and verbal processing, whereas the right is specialized mainly for holistic, spatial, and nonverbal processing. There is increasing evidence that hemispheric asymmetries play an important role in psychopathology (Walker & McGuire, 1982). In normal individuals and psychiatric patients without neurological problems, both hemispheres would be functioning simultaneously to some degree and such hemispheric specialization would be relative rather than absolute. Normally, stimuli project to both hemispheres and are processed by both hemispheres.

Investigating laterality of function is a complex matter. A number of organismic and experimental factors are known to modify the overly simple description of asymmetric functioning outlined previously. In behavioral vision studies the most common technique is to briefly present visual stimuli to the right or the left of a fixation target. Stimuli presented to the right of fixation (the right visual field) are known to project directly and initially to the left hemisphere, whereas stimuli presented to the left of fixation (the left visual field) project directly to the right hemisphere.

A laterality study of visual persistence (iconic recognition) with Korsakoff patients, alcoholic subjects, and normal controls has been reported by Oscar–Berman, Goodglass, and Cherlow (1973). Words and patterned target stimuli were presented monocularly to the lateral visual fields. The subjects were then tested in a backward visual masking paradigm in which the same (target) stimuli were used to determine the critical interstimulus interval needed to escape the masking effect in each lateral field. The critical interstimulus interval was shorter in the right visual field for both the words and the patterns, leading these investigators to conclude that the dominant hemisphere (the left hemisphere) is more efficient in the early (iconic) stage of processing.

Visual Persistence and Psychopathology: Illustrative Data

The emphasis of this discussion regarding problems in the application of information processing to psychopathology is limited to schizophrenia, which is the clinical group most studied in persistence research. Current research in visual persistence and psychopathology and our reservations about the conclusions drawn from such research are illustrated by considering a recently published study (Spaulding et al., 1980). This study of visual persistence (named *visual pattern integration* by Spaulding et al.) used the successive-field procedure introduced by Eriksen and Collins (1967) in work with normal subjects. Spaulding et al. compared the performance of schizophrenic and nonschizophrenic groups of patients and two groups of control subjects. The only significant difference observed was that schizophrenic patients performed more poorly than the college students, a typical generalized deficit type of outcome. The observed difference was, therefore, not interpreted by these investigators as reflecting a basic difference between schizophrenics and normals in icon processing, at least as measured by the successive-form procedure. The authors (Spaulding et al., 1980) conclude: ''At present, the abnormal psychology literature can only point to post-iconic processing as the first level of cognition at which deficits that have clear implications for later processing can be detected.''

From the preceding quotation, one might easily conclude that visual persistence is not impaired in schizophrenia. There are several reasons why we consider such a conclusion premature. First, several other studies using techniques and procedures regarded as measuring visual persistence have shown that schizophrenic patients do differ from other patients and from normals. For example, using a modified partial-report procedure, Knight et al. (1977) found that middle-inclusive and underinclusive schizophrenics were significantly inferior in iconic memory to an overinclusive schizophrenic group and a normal control group. In several studies using the visual masking technique, Saccuzzo and his co-workers found impaired masking in a variety of patient groups, including several schizophrenic groups. Saccuzzo and his colleagues concluded (Miller et al., 1979) that there is: "growing evidence of an early information disturbance in schizophrenia that is trait dependent and is not an artifact of nonspecific pathological disturbance."

Others have reported visual masking differences that seem related to schizophrenia. Steronko and Woods (1978) reported significant differences between nonpsychotic schizotypic individuals (college students whose MMPIs indicated schizophrenic tendencies) and other control groups, using a backward visual masking task. Mention has been made of two-flash threshold studies (Gruzelier & Venables, 1975), another procedure for measuring some aspect of visual persistence. In these studies certain types of schizophrenic patients displayed different patterns of correlation between the two-flash threshold and selected electrodermal autonomic measures that differed from those shown by other schizophrenic patients and by normal subjects.

Results of other investigations also suggest that early sensory processing may be different for some psychiatric patients. Collins, Kietzman, Sutton, and Shapiro (1978) reported differences in temporal integration (a type of persistence) as measured by the simple reaction times of schizophrenic and non-schizophrenic patients. Schizophrenics showed shorter durations of complete integration, implying less persistence. The outcome for this study was unique because it indicated that the schizophrenic patients were doing something that the normals could not do under the most optimal conditions. The "better performance" outcome is the strongest rebuttal to the ubiquitous generalized deficit problem, because it is impossible to attribute the superiority of patients (compared to the normals) as due to a generalized deficit.

Although repeated laboratory testing under apparently comparable conditions failed to replicate the original Collins et al. (1978) results (Berenhaus, Gottlieb, Mannuzza, & Kietzman, unpublished), data from a recent investigation of auditory temporal integration with patients are relevant to the issue of temporal integration in psychopathology. Using a detection threshold measure and comparing schizophrenics, depressives, and normal controls, Babkoff, Sutton, Zubin, and Har–Even (1980) reported that the slope of the auditory temporal integration curve differed for the three groups of subjects, with hallucinating schizophrenics showing the steepest slope. This auditory finding was related by Babkoff et al. (1980) to the visual temporal integration experiment by analyzing a previously unanalyzed set of Collins' reaction time data. Taken together, the results of both studies leave open the possibility that schizophrenics differ from normals in at least some aspects of temporal integration.

This brief summary of visual persistence suggests that some psychiatric patients display persistence differences. Thus, it is important to evaluate carefully the two studies that *did not* show patient–normal differences in persistence (Knight et al., 1978; Spaulding et al., 1980). Both investigations used a version of the Eriksen and Collins' (1967) successive-field technique. No differences were found between the various patient groups and the normal controls, leading these investigators to conclude that icon processing in schizophrenics is intact.

To help clarify why there are discrepancies in the persistence data of psychiatric patients, we first briefly consider research on visual persistence in the elderly. For some time researchers in that field have postulated that older people show increased persistence (Botwinick, 1978). Investigations of the elderly use many of the familiar persistence techniques such as masking (Kline & Birren, 1975; Kline & Szaftan, 1975; Walsh, 1976; Walsh & Thompson, 1978; Walsh et al., 1979) and successive fields (Kline & Baffa, 1976; Kline & Orme–Rogers, 1978). Presumably, this research with the elderly could be compared with similar schizophrenic research (Saccuzzo, 1977), but this does not seem to have happened. Thus, a study of schizophrenic patients (Spaulding et al., 1980) does not refer to an earlier persistence study of elderly subjects (Kline & Baffa, 1976) even though both used similar dot stimuli with the successive-field procedure. The importance of knowing about both areas of research is illustrated by following up on the Kline and Baffa study which failed to demonstrate a persistence difference between young and old subjects, presumably, the authors suggest, because the older subjects had difficulty in organizing the dot stimuli, thereby interfering with the attempt to assess persistence. However, in a subsequent experiment using line stimuli rather than dot stimuli, Kline and Orme–Rogers (1978) demonstrated significantly greater persistence and consequently superior visual performance for the older as compared to the younger subjects. This latter study has two important implications for schizophrenic research: (1) It demonstrates that the measurement of differences in persistence requires appropriate techniques; and (2) it illustrates that in some experiments patients can demonstrate a better performance, a result that overcomes the generalized-deficit argument, thereby considerably strengthening the final conclusions.

With respect to the existing persistence research with schizophrenics, the combined research of both Kline and Baffa (1976) and Kline and Orme–Rogers (1978) with the elderly reopens the question of whether some schizophrenic patients can be shown to differ in persistence if proper techniques are employed. In this regard, the Spaulding et al. (1980) experiment on schizophrenics might be repeated using line instead of dot stimuli.

Apparently, Knight et al. (1978) did the needed research. In their experiment they used line stimuli and still found no difference in persistence between normals and schizophrenics. However, the very fact that they obtained no difference between patients and normals is worthy of comment. The expected and usual finding in such research is that schizophrenic patients perform worse than normals, which can easily be attributed to the ubiquitous generalized deficit problem. In the Knight et al. experiment, why was no generalized deficit displayed by the patients? Were these patients only mildly ill? Did these patients actually differ in visual persistence (showed superior performance because of their longer persistence, as the elderly did in the Kline and Orme–Rogers study), but the difference was neutralized by a general deficit in their performance? Admittedly, this possibility is highly speculative, and yet the fact that several other studies using different techniques have shown patient impairments in visual persistence suggests that the successive-field technique as a tool for investigating visual persistence in psychopathology should not yet be eliminated. It would be interesting to do an experiment in which several tasks are included, some that measure persistence and some that do not. If the failure to demonstrate a difference in visual persistence (as in the Knight et al. study) is due to a balance between an actual persistence difference and a generalized deficit for the patients, then one might expect the persistence tasks to show little or no difference between the groups, whereas the other, nonpersistence tasks would show worsened performance by the patients due to their generalized deficit.

SUMMARY AND CONCLUSIONS

The purpose of this report was to survey the field of information processing with a view toward applying its methods, models, and data to psychopathology. Just as in the normative field of information processing, no overall framework has yet been developed for encompassing information-processing results with respect to psychopathology. Such a framework is sorely needed.

Information processing holds great promise for understanding psychopathology because it removes many obstacles that prevent progress in the field of psychopathology. These obstacles include such factors as the generalized deficit problem that characterizes most patient behavior and the well-known principle that the same response to given stimuli and stimulus situations may be arrived at by different routes. The last problem may result in a failure to detect differences even when they exist or may produce differences even when the underlying processes remain intact. Information processing, by attempting to track the actual processes in arriving at the response and by examining each of the components of the different processes, promises to provide a monitoring system capable of detecting deviations in the pathway from receptor to effector that now go undetected.

Another difficulty is the fact that the life experience of some patients is so essentially different from that of the normal controls that their information-processing characteristics may be modified in ways that do not occur in normals. (This may be an artifact due to life experience rather than an actual characteristic of schizophrenia.)

Differences introduced by life experience may be reduced by using research techniques with schizophrenics that are extremely simple and that allow as few subject-response options as possible. For this reason we have emphasized techniques that measure responses made within the first 1000 msec following stimulation (Zubin & Kietzman, 1966). Such immediate responses may be less dependent on speech and communicative ability, both of which may reflect some of the happenstance of life experience rather than a specific disorder.

As for the usefulness of information processing, it may enable patients to be classified more homogeneously by grouping them according to information-processing characteristics. This strategy could provide more objective criteria for diagnosis and for selecting better comparison groups in further experimentation. In addition, the monitoring of information processing may not only indicate where and how deviations occur but may also provide points of entry for therapeutic intervention. Such intervention could involve attempts to rectify deviations or provide ways to circumvent them. Furthermore, rehabilitation of disabled individuals may be undertaken more rationally if the actual "cause" of the difficulty (the deviation in processing) is identified.

Not all deviations in information processing necessarily lead to disordered behavior. However, some of these deviations may serve as markers for identifying individuals who under certain circumstances have a higher risk for developing episodes of psychopathology. Furthermore, some of these deviations may serve as earmarks of the beginning and end of episodes. These issues have been discussed elsewhere (Zubin & Steinhauer, 1981).

As for the future of information processing as a paradigm for research in psychopathology, it will depend on the trends in both fields. It is clear that information processing itself has captured the attention and imagination of cognitive psychologists in the 1980s. Much of the research is in the area of memory but it is starting to spread into the various other domains ranging across the cognitive, psychomotor, perceptual, sensory, and physiological areas. At present, the least developed approach is in the physiological domain. For the twenty-first century, our prediction is that the physiological response to stimuli will serve as a carrier wave, conveying sensory, perceptual, psychomotor, and conceptual information loads. Instead of speaking of the icon, we shall probably refer to a pattern of stimulation arising in a specific template of neurons that underlie the icon and that can be manipulated directly to lengthen its duration or shorten it or improve its interconnections with other neurophysiological mechanisms. Terms like *consciousness, will* (conation) and *memory* are still to be dealt with but primarily by philosophers, educators, therapists, and self-development specialists, whereas scientific psychology will deal with the physiological patterns underlying these concepts.

It is important at this juncture to enter a caveat that such progress can only take place if noninvasive methods are found for monitoring internal brain functioning. That this is likely to be the case for the twenty-first century is attested to by the fact that we can already trace many physiological processes engendered from the receptor up to the effector by electrophysiological techniques such as event related potentials. The difficulty at this time inheres in the fact that these electrophysiological tracings represent the confluence of more than one process, and it is currently difficult to distinguish these processes, one from another. However, the availability of techniques such as CAT scans, PET scans, cerebral blood flow (CBFs), magnetic approaches, and others yet to come should provide further possibilities for noninvasive monitoring of brain processes.

This reductionist approach does not mean that the *psyche* is to be ruled out. Quite the contrary, as much of the psyche as can be brought across the threshold of objectivity will constitute the domain of information-processing psychology. The remainder, which still defies objectification, will have to wait until adequate methods become available.

Whether psychology will tend in the direction of humanism by providing closer relations between scientific research and everyday-life problems or whether it will tend to become more abstracted from everyday life as the physical sciences tended to do is debatable. Our speculation is that psychology, like other basic sciences, will be removed further and further from the marketplace and from lay thinking and become more and more abstract, following the paradigm of physics and chemistry. Just as weight finally became abstracted from its concrete setting in daily life to an abstract *mass* measured by the ratio of force/acceleration, so will *intelligence* and *memory* become measured by their physiological substrates that have no apparent relationships to these concepts as conceived today. For example, Esyenck's attempt to utilize electrophysiological measures for assessing intelligence (Chapter 13) is the direction that the development of psychology might take. The contribution of scientific psychological discoveries to human affairs will continue in the same way that the physical sciences contribute to engineering.

As for psychopathology, it too will undergo a tremendous paradigmatic revolution. Instead of classifying individuals according to categories of disorder, they will be classified in accordance with their vulnerability to a disorder, even before an episode develops. This will be accomplished after specific markets for each disorder are discovered. By identifying the specific vulnerabilities of a person and noting the specific environmental contingencies that tend to elicit an episode of this disorder, an educational program for avoiding the triggering of episodes, even the initial episode, will become possible. Here again, the basic scientific markets for identifying the specific vulnerability and for determining the beginning and end of episodes will be drawn from the entire gamut of scientific models of etiology via the ecological, developmental, learning, genetic, internal–environmental, and neurophysiological models. The main thrust of the twenty-first century will be to describe as far as possible the interactions between the components of each of these models and their relation to the physiological correlates of behavior. The preventive work will fall largely into the hands of humanists and therapists, who will work side by side with the scientists. Thus, the twenty-first century will see the dawn of a new era in which scientific psychology, though becoming more abstract and removed from everyday life, will lay the basic foundation for preventing and ameliorating the disorders imposed on humankind by psychopathology.

ACKNOWLEDGMENTS

We wish to express our appreciation to K. Salzinger and P. J. Collins for their critical comments, to B. Bienstock for her helpful assistance in the preparation of this manuscript, and to T. Wicker for her typing assistance. Supported in part by a PSC/BHE Grant No. 13012 to Dr. Kietzman and by the U.S. Veterans Administration (Drs. Zubin and Steinhauer).

REFERENCES

Babkoff, H., Sutton, S., Zubin, J., & Har–Even, D. A comparison of psychiatric patients and normal controls on the integration of auditory stimuli. *Psychiatry Research,* 1980, *3,* 163–178.

Berenhaus, I., Gottlieb, M. D., Mannuzza, S., & Kietzman, M. L. *Unpublished observations.*

Botwinick, J. *Aging and behavior* (2nd ed.). New York: Springer, 1978.

Brody, D., Saccuzzo, D. P., & Braff, D. L. Information processing for masked and unmasked stimuli in schizophrenia and old age. *Journal of Abnormal Psychology,* 1980, *89,* 617–622.

Chapman, L. J., & Chapman, J. P. *Disordered thought in schizophrenia.* Englewood Cliffs, N.J.: Prentice–Hall, 1973.

Collins, P. J., Kietzman, M. L., Sutton, S., & Shapiro, E. Visual temporal integration in psychiatric patients. *Journal of Psychiatric Research,* 1978, *14,* 203–213.

Coltheart, M. Iconic memory and visible persistence. *Perception and Psychophysics,* 1980, *27,* 183–228.

Eriksen, C. W., & Collins, J. F. Some temporal characteristics of visual pattern perception. *Journal of Experimental Psychology,* 1967, *74,* 476–484.

Gruzelier, J. H., & Venables, P. H. Relations between two-flash discrimination and electrodermal activity re-examined in schizophrenics and normals. *Journal of Psychiatric Research,* 1975, *12,* 73–85.

Haber, R. N., & Hershenson, M. The psychology of visual perception (2nd ed.). New York: Holt, Rinehart, & Winston, 1980.

Hawkins, H. L., & Shulman, G. L. Two definitions of persistence in visual perception. *Perception & Psychophysics,* 1979, *25,* 348–350.

Heidbreder, E. *Seven psychologies.* New York: D. Appleton–Century, 1933.

Kietzman, M. L., Spring, B., & Zubin, J. Perception, cognition and attention. In H. I. Kaplan, A. M. Freedman, & B. W. Sadock (Eds.), *Comprehensive textbook of psychiatry/III.* Baltimore: Williams & Wilkins, 1980.

Kinsbourne, M. (Ed.). *Asymmetrical function of the brain.* New York: Cambridge University Press, 1978.

Kline, D. W., & Baffa, G. Differences in the sequential integration of form as a function of age and interstimulus interval. *Experimental Aging Research,* 1976, *2,* 333–343.

Kline, D. W., & Birren, S. E. Age differences in backward dichoptic masking. *Experimental Aging Research,* 1975, *1,* 17–25.

Kline, D. W., & Orme–Rogers, C. Examination of stimulus persistence as the basis for superior visual identification performance among older adults. *Journal of Gerontology,* 1978, *33,* 76–81.

Kline, D. W., & Schieber, F. J. *Visual persistence and temporal resolution.* Paper presented at Symposium on aging and human visual function. Sponsored by Committee on Vision, National Research Council, National Academy of Sciences, Washington, D.C. March 1980.

Kline, D. W., & Schieber, F. What are the age differences in visual sensory memory. *Journal of Gerontology,* 1981, *36,* 86–89.

Kline, D. W., & Szaftan, J. Age differences in backward monoptic visual noise masking. *Journal of Gerontology,* 1975, *30,* 307–311.

Knight, R., Sherer, M., Putchat, C., & Carter, G. A picture integration task for measuring iconic memory in schizophrenics. *Journal of Abnormal Psychology,* 1978, *87,* 314–321.

Knight, R., Sherer, M., & Shapiro, J. Iconic imagery in overinclusive and nonoverinclusive schizophrenics. *Journal of Abnormal Psychology,* 1977, *86,* 242–255.

Long, G. M. Comment on Hawkins and Shulman's Type I and Type II visual persistence. *Perception and Psychophysics,* 1979, *26,* 412–414. (a)

Long, G. M. The dichoptic viewing paradigm: Do the eyes have it? *Psychological Bulletin,* 1979, *86,* 391–403. (b)

Long, G. M. Iconic memory: A review and critique of the study of short-term visual storage. *Psychological Bulletin,* 1980, *88,* 785–820.

Magaro, P. A. *Cognition in schizophrenia and paranoia: The integration of cognitive processes.* Hillsdale, N.J. Lawrence Erlbaum Associates, 1980.

Miller, S., Saccuzzo, D., & Braff, D. L. Information processing deficits in remitted schizophrenics. *Journal of Abnormal Psychology,* 1979, *88,* 446–449.

Milner, B. (Ed.). *Hemispheric specialization and interaction.* Cambridge, Mass.: M.I.T. Press, 1975.

Neale, J. F., & Oltmanns, T. F. *Schizophrenia.* New York: Wiley, 1980.

Nicotera, N., Berenhaus, I., Goldberg, S., Herskovic, J., & Kietzman, M. L. Foveal two-flash and flicker-fusion thresholds as a function of pulse-luminance. *Bulletin of the Psychonomic Society,* 1977, *9,* 260.

Oscar-Berman, M., Goodglass, H., & Cherlow, D. G. Perceptual laterality and iconic recognition of visual materials by Korsakoff patients and normal adults. *Journal of Comparative and Physiological Psychology,* 1973, *82,* 316–321.

Saccuzzo, D. P. Bridges between schizophrenia and gerontology: Generalized or specific deficits? *Psychological Bulletin,* 1977, *84,* 595–600.

Saccuzzo, D. P., & Braff, D. L. Early information processing deficit in schizophrenia. *Archives of General Psychiatry,* 1981, *38,* 175–179.

Saccuzzo, D. P., Hirt, M., & Spencer, T. J. Backward masking as a measure of attention in schizophrenia. *Journal of Abnormal Psychology,* 1974, *83,* 512–522.

Saccuzzo, D. P., & Miller, S. Critical interstimulus interval in delusional schizophrenics and normals. *Journal of Abnormal Psychology,* 1977, *86,* 261–266.

Saccuzzo, D. P., & Schubert, D. L. Backward masking as a measure of slow processing in schizophrenia and spectrum disorders. *Journal of Abnormal Psychology,* 1981, *90,* 305–312.

Schwartz, S. Language and cognition in schizophrenia: A review and synthesis. In S. Schwartz (Ed.), *Language and cognition in schizophrenia.* Hillsdale, N.J.: Lawrence Erlbaum Associates, 1978.

Sears, R. R. Experimental analysis of psychoanalytic phenomena. In J. McV. Hunt (Ed.), *Personality and the behavior disorders.* New York, Ronald Press, 1944.

Spaulding, W., Rosenzweig, L., Huntzinger, R., Cromwell, R. L., Briggs, D., & Hayes, T. Visual pattern integration in psychiatric patients. *Journal of Abnormal Psychology,* 1980, *89,* 635–643.

Sperling, G. The information available in brief visual presentations. *Psychological Monographs,* 1960, *74,* (11, Whole No. 498).

Steronko, R. J., & Woods, D. J. Impairment in early stages of visual information processing in nonpsychotic schizotypic individuals. *Journal of Abnormal Psychology,* 1978, *87,* 481–490.

Sutton, S., & Ruchkin, D. S. *The late positive complex: Advances and new problems.* Paper presented at the Sixth Annual Conference on Event Related Slow Potentials of the Brain. Lake Forest, Ill., June 1981.

Turvey, M. T. On peripheral and central processes in vision: Inferences from an information processing analysis of masking with patterned stimuli. *Psychological Review,* 1973, *80,* 1–52.

Walker, E., & McGuire, M. Intra-and interhemispheric information-processing in schizophrenia. *Psychological Bulletin,* 1982, *92,* 701–725.

Walsh, D. A. Age differences in central perceptual processing: A dichoptic backward masking investigation. *Journal of Gerontology,* 1976, *31,* 178–185.

Walsh, D. A., & Thompson, L. W. Age differences in visual sensory memory. *Journal of Gerontology,* 1978, *33,* 383–387.

Walsh, D. A., Williams, M. V., & Herzog, C. K. Age-related differences in two stages of central perceptual processes: The effects of short duration targets and criterion differences. *Journal of Gerontology,* 1979, *34,* 234–241.

Wiener, N. *Cybernetics,* New York: Wiley, 1948.

Zubin, J., & Kietzman, M. L. A cross-cultural approach to classification and other mental disorders. In P. Hoch & J. Zubin (Eds.), *Psychopathology of schizophrenia.* New York: Grune & Stratton, 1966.

Zubin, J., & Steinhauer, S. How to break the logjam in schizophrenia: A look beyond genetics. *Journal of Nervous and Mental Disease,* 1981, *169,* 477–492.

20 Nonspecific Factors and Drug and Placebo Response in Psychiatry

Robert W. Downing

Karl Rickels
University of Pennsylvania, Philadelphia, USA

Introduction

For those who become involved in clinical trials conducted to assess the efficacy of psychotropic drugs, it very quickly becomes apparent that a broad range of factors other than the pharmacological properties of the drugs themselves affect or modify treatment. A double-blind, placebo-controlled drug trial can readily demonstrate that an anxiolytic as effective as chlordiazepoxide or diazepam induces a significantly greater amount of symptom ameliorization than does placebo in a group with specifiedly appropriate target symptomatology. However, the degree of symptom reduction varies greatly both in the group treated with an active agent and in the placebo group. Further, side effects are encountered more frequently in the active treatment group than in the control group. Still, the range of severity of the side effects of which drug-treated patients complain is considerable and the extent to which patients are able to tolerate or accept side effects at a given level of severity varies widely.

It is also the case that a far from negligible number of patients who receive inert placebo experience improvement and that a significant minority of them complain of medication-induced adverse effects. Finally, patients vary widely in the length of time they are willing to continue with both an active drug and a placebo treatment regimen and in the closeness with which they comply to prescribed medication dosage. Thus, even in a rigorously controlled clinical trial, and *a fortiori*, in day-to-day clinical practice, a substantial proportion of the variance in treatment response remains to be accounted for.

A body of research results accumulated over the past several decades demonstrates that a modest but significant proportion of this variance can be accounted for by what has come to be known as "nonspecific factors" (Downing & Rickels, 1978b, pp. 1419–1428; Rickels, 1968a, 1968b, 1978). Such factors have been typically defined as those potential influences upon response to drug treatment other than the pharmacological properties of the drugs themselves. Traditionally the content domain of nonspecific factors has been broad. It has encompassed such areas of investigational concern as the psychology and physiology of the individual patient, the nature of his or her social and material environments, the history of his or her illness and previous treatment, and the characteristics of the treating physician along with many other particulars of the current treatment situation. A schematic representation of such factors is given in Fig. 20.1.

We believe that among the factors that have motivated research effort in the area of nonspecific effects there are three that emerge as salient. The first of these

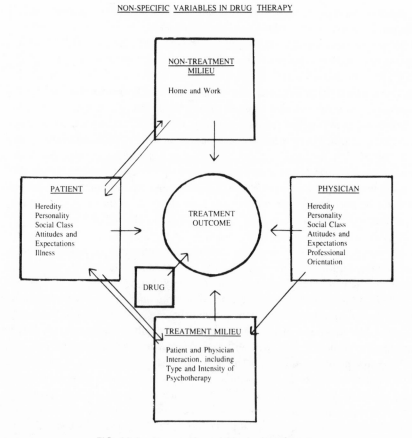

FIG. 20.1.   Nonspecific variables in drug therapy.

derives its provenance from clinical research and might be described as a need to take nonspecific factors into consideration by appropriate experimental design and proper statistical analysis to optimize the efficiency, accuracy, and precision of clinical drug trials. The second factor, although not completely distinct from the first, emphasizes a major goal of clinical practice: finding "the right drug for the right patient" (Klett & Moseley, 1965). The final factor might be regarded as elated to psychopharmacology and psychiatry as scientific disciplines. It has to do with furthering the understanding of the basic nature of the drug treatment process and perhaps the nature of psychopathology. It is with the work motivated by this last factor that the ensuing discussion is primarily concerned.

CLINICAL VERSUS RESEARCH ORIENTATION IN PSYCHOPHARMACOLOGY

In research intimately concerned with the outcome of clinical practice, ample opportunity is available for an active interplay between the needs and orientation of the practitioner and the needs and orientation of the researcher. Indeed this opportunity becomes necessity for those who are both practitioners and researchers. We now consider some salient facets of contrast between the clinical and the research orientation because they reflect a continuing dilemma for psychopharmacological research and for clinical research in general.

An essential part of the clinician's approach to his or her patient is an attempt to understand the patient in all of his or her particulars. Although the underlying processes are intuitive and implicit, the clinician has potentially available to him or her a great wealth of in-context information about the patient's current condition on which he or she can draw in formulating an approach to treatment. Further, he or she is able to concern himself or herself primarily with the variability and interplay of factors within the single patient with whom he or she is concerned at a particular point.

The understanding on which the researcher must rely is of a quite different nature. The amount of information with which he or she has to work is of necessity much more restricted and in many ways selective. He or she seeks a limited number of basic principles that apply with reasonable accuracy to all members of a reference group with inclusion criteria that it is his or her task to identify. As he or she deals with progressively more heterogeneous patient samples, he or she is confronted with progressively greater amounts of potential between-subject variability. This variability tends to blur, obscure, or qualify the effects produced by the circumscribed group of variables to which he or she is devoting attention.

This contrast between two types of understanding is of course neither new nor confined to psychiatry or psychopharmacology (Windelband, 1894). It seems of particular relevance in the present context not only because the nonspecific factors that may modify response to psychotropic agents are so numerous but also because it is so difficult to know which of the many potential nonspecific influences on treatment will actually emerge as most dominant for a given patient at a given juncture in his or her life and in a given treatment situation. Even when factors are validly identified that affect the treatment response of an individual patient or a restrictedly homogeneous patient group, such findings may not be readily generalizable to other individuals or groups.

Factors that emerge as exerting a statistically significant effect on the responses of a large heterogeneous group are likely to account for a small proportion of variance relative to the total variance present. The identification of such factors not only leaves much of the group's behavior yet to be explained but also is of little import for the conduct of treatment with an individual patient. Unless one is able to identify circumstances under which these findings modify the response of particular individuals, such findings are likely to thwart primary goals of both clinician and researcher.

We turn now to a consideration of the manner in which such issues have been reflected in research with nonspecific effects. Examples of substantive findings are confined to studies involving treatment with anxiolytic agents. Although nonspecific factors play a particularly large role in the treatment response of anxious patients, it should be emphasized that such effects modify response to all major types of psychotropic agents.

Work with Small, Homogeneous Groups

Chassan's (1979) advocacy of an "intensive design," an approach in which the single patient is treated alternately with two treatments or a treatment and control, has done much to call attention to this mode of research. Although statistical treatment of results is possible, information concerning the role of nonspecific factors obtained in the course of this procedure is useful in understanding the individual case but is difficult to generalize to an identifiable reference population.

The work of McNair, Fisher, and their colleagues provides a striking example of strong effects noted in small, homogeneous groups and of the employment of a modified intensive design in clarifying their nature. Having noted (Fisher & Fisher, 1963) that individuals with high scores on the Bass Scale (then thought to be a measure of acquiescence or need to please) respond strongly to placebo, they went on to explore the differential impact of this variable on response to diazepam and placebo on a post hoc basis (McNair, Kahn, Droppleman & Fisher, 1966, pp. 336–342; 1968, pp. 59–72). They found that by the end of a 2-week period patients with low Bass scores (LA) did significantly better on diazepam than on placebo, whereas patients with high Bass scores (HA)—now considered as possibly unthinking, noncritical individuals—responded very well to placebo but poorly to diazepam. A follow-up study revealed that the drug-acquiescence interaction persisted at least 4 months (McNair, Fisher, Sussman, Droppleman & Kahn, 1970). An intensive design was then employed utilizing only four HA–LA pairs of female patients seen by a single therapist to explore further the nature of this interaction. This design revealed that the HAs, in contrast to the LAs, failed to show a monotonic dose-response relationship for chlordiazepoxide, were extremely intolerant to the drug's side effects, and became progressively more tense while receiving it (McNair, Fisher, Kahn, & Droppleman, 1970). The originally observed interaction was replicated by Rickels (1968b) among general practice patients but not private psychiatric patients.

The impact of this acquiescence variable appears to emerge as both dramatic and replicable. However, in addition to issues concerned with the boundaries of its generalizability, one is confronted with the problem of specifying its precise nature. Is it essentially a tendency toward noncritical agreement, a more broadly shallow, unthinking cognitive style, or perhaps an inclination toward unqualified generalization? Further research is needed in which a range of marker variable is employed to delimit the relevant underlying construct.

The present authors studied the impact of several personality and physician factors in a group of uniformly low socioeconomic class, predominately black, female patients. Self-reported hostility (and particularly direct hostility) was found to be lower in side reactors than in nonside reactors (Downing & Rickels, 1967a). The effect was present in both minor tranquilizer- and placebo-treated patients but was stronger in the placebo group. Hostility level was more closely related to measures of presenting symptomatology (Downing, Rickels, & Horn, 1970a) and to a purported measure of directness of behavioral expression of affect in dropouts than in completers, and the former group was found to be more compliant than the latter (Downing, Rickels, & Horn, 1970b). It was also noted that dropouts came to the clinic with more critical attitudes than completers (Rickels & Anderson, 1967) and that they were more likely to be treated in a detached, impersonal way by their treating physicians (Howard, Rickels, Mock, Lipman, Covi, & Baumm, 1970). This body of findings seemed consonant with the view that, among this lower socioeconomic group, dropping out and the reporting of side effects represent an indirect expression of anger in patients with conflict about hostility expression.

More recent work (Downing & Rickels, 1980) has provided evidence that similar dynamics underlie the expression of complaints concerning side effects in middle-class patients. A closer analysis of the quality of conflict-generating hostility has improved the accuracy with which patients complaining of side effects can be identified. Conflict has emerged as linked to tendencies to behave irritably and to give overt expression to inner aggressive tendencies rather than to react with resentment to a world perceived as unfair.

Work with Large Heterogeneous Groups

The nature or character of results obtained from work dealing with large ($N \geq$ 100) samples of patients heterogeneous with regard to such factors as age, socioeconomic status, treatment setting, chronicity, and profile of secondary symptomatology is perhaps well revealed by an examination of a set of studies employing multiple regression techniques to investigate the relationship between nonspecific factors and treatment outcome. Multiple regression as a technique for data analysis was "discovered" by psychopharmacologists as a possibly useful technique for data analysis in the late 1960s. During the next several years, a small flood of studies appeared that attempted to identify characteristics of the patient, attributes of his or her illness and illness history, and particulars of the treatment process that would account for the large amounts of within treatment variance typical of psychotropic drug trials. (See Downing & Rickels, 1978b; Rickels, 1968a, 1968b; Uhlenhuth, Lipman, Rickels, Fisher, Covi, & Park, 1968; for examples).

Typically, these studies identified nonspecific predictors generalizable in principle to treatment populations but limited in utility and explanatory incisiveness by the small proportion of variance for which they accounted (usually less than 10% per predictor and less than 30% per predictor set). This was disappointing, but there were other aspects of the situation that combined disappointment with frustration. Predictors that defied interpretation were often identified at a high level of statistical significance. This might occur, usually as a result of multiple partialling effects (collinearity), when predictive impact was in a direction opposite to that expected. It might also result when the specific underlying dimension or dimensions of a "comprehensive" surface attribute (such as patient age or sex) could not be identified. If women improve more than men or if men improve more than women, is it because of distinct cultural experience, biological factors, distinctive treatment relationships, or any of a host of potentially relevant variables on which sex groups have not been closely matched? However, most disconcerting of all was the frequently encountered circumstance that a regression equation derived with data from one patient sample failed to generate a significant multiple R when applied to an apparently equivalent sample. Outcomes of this nature have tended to dampen enthusiasm and are, no doubt, one factor responsible for stemming the flow of research employing multiple regression.

We have made moderately heavy use of multiple regression procedures in our own research and have encountered problems of the sort described previously. We would like to describe a segment of results we have obtained recently (Downing & Rickels, 1978a) to suggest strategies for using the results of earlier exploratory work in forging a chain in which exploration and hypothesis testing form alternating sets of links.

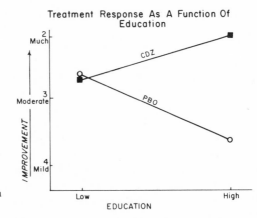

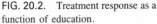

FIG. 20.2. Treatment response as a function of education.

A study was performed using 205 chlordiazepoxide (CDZ)- and 242 placebo (PBO)-treated primarily anxious neurotic outpatients in an effort to demonstrate the replicability of a set of nonspecific factor predictors. The patient sample was drawn from three treatment settings and heterogeneous with regard to demographic characteristics, illness history, secondary symptomatology, and particulars of the current treatment situation. A pool of 18 regressors sampling several relevant nonspecific factor domains was employed. Both the drug and placebo samples were divided into two equivalent halves so that cross-sample replicability could be assessed. Although shrinkage of multiple R's was considerable, significant predictability was obtained in cross-validation samples. We shall focus on several predictors, replicated across samples, which extended previous results and stimulated formulation of future studies.

Drug–placebo differences were greater among individuals with larger amounts of education (completion of high school–college). For less well-educated patients (grade school–partial high school) drug and placebo did not differ, the improvement of both treatment groups falling midway between that of the drug- and placebo-treated higher education groups (Fig. 20.2). These findings mirror results previously obtained with a vocabulary test (Rickels & Downing, 1965) and with Potency Factor scores for semantic differential ratings of "MY-SELF" (Downing & Rickels, 1967b). They suggest that a minor tranquilizer may be of particular benefit and placebo of lesser benefit to individuals of greater intellectual and personal adequacy.

Patients with severe *anxiety* and *somatization* respond most adequately to CDZ, whereas placebo response is unaffected by severity of these symptoms (Fig. 20.3). Patients with more severe *interpersonal* problems related to resentment and sensed inadequacy and patients with greater functional impairment resulting from *obsessive–compulsive* disturbance respond poorly to both drug and placebo. *Depression* has an adverse effect on response to CDZ, but its effect

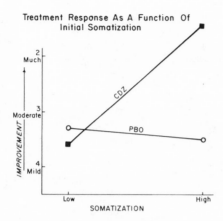

Treatment Response As A Function Of
Initial Somatization

FIG. 20.3.   Treatment response as a function of initial somatization.

upon response to placebo is more markedly adverse. It thus appears that the greatest "net" improvement is to be expected in patients whose anxiety and somatization are severe and for whom obsessive–compulsive symptomatology, depression, and social maladjustment play a subordinate role. Because insight-oriented psychotherapies claim effectiveness in treating adjustmental problems, because cognitive therapy has come to be regarded as an effective concomitant to antidepressant drugs, and because behavioral therapy is at least advocated as effective with obsessive–compulsive disturbance, the possibility of matching symptom profiles with a treatment of choice suggests itself.

Projects for formulating "mini-structures" or models of treatment response with explanatory and/or practical relevance thus suggest themselves for the several predictor domains reviewed here. Also needed, however, is a "meso-structure" to integrate models across predictor domains. The regression model utilized is, of course, linear with the weighted contribution from each regressor making its additive contribution to "net" improvement score predicted for a given patient. However, some configurations of scores across the variables serving as regressors are more common than others. For example, somatization tends to be more frequent among more highly than among less highly educated individuals. The application of a clustering algorithm to a set of replicable regressors might serve as a useful tool in classifying a heterogeneous sample into homogeneous subgroups. Subgroup membership might then provide a new set of predictors, and an attempt could be made to find additional predictors within subgroups.

Future Developments

It is perhaps easier to be specific in identifying developments in psychiatry, psychology, related social and biological sciences, and statistics likely to influence the directions of change in that area of psychopharmacology with which we have been concerned than it is to be specific about the changes themselves. We mention several developments of this nature.

The appearance of a new diagnostic system in the United States (DSM-III) (American Psychiatric Association, 1980) has led to a renewed awareness of the importance of diagnostic criteria that are objective, reliably applicable, and relevant for treatment. Although most of the approximately 230 diagnostic categories it contains are based upon purely descriptive criteria (Schulsinger, 1980), the structured interview schedules (SADS and SADS/L) developed by Spitzer, Endicott and their colleagues (Endicott & Spitzer, 1978) is promoting the collection of reliably assessed data concerning the symptomatology and illness history of large patient samples in a wide variety of research contexts.

At the same time, neurochemistry and neurophysiology have been making discoveries that may help to clarify biological substrata of anxiety and the neuronal mechanisms whereby benzodiazepines operate to lower anxiety. The recent observations that specific benzodiazepine receptors exist in certain parts of the brain is most exciting (Haefely, 1978; Tallman, Paul, Skolnick, & Gallagher, 1980), as this finding implies that endogenous ligands exist that, by binding to these receptors, exert calming and antianxiety effects. One may thus speculate that a patient's predisposition to anxiety may be related to the amount of endogenous ligands available to that patient.

On a related front, methods for determining plasma levels of a number of psychotropic drugs and their major metabolites permits a closer determination of effective dosages received by individual patients. Individual differences between administered dose and plasma level as well as between plasma level and treatment response may be useful in accounting for within-treatment variance and in elucidating mechanisms of drug action.

In psychology, heightened emphasis upon such themes as the following seem likely to influence the direction of future research: (1) need for a representative design that assures generalizability through sampling not only of subjects but of the situational units comprising their ecological environments (Brunswik, 1955; Tyler, 1981); and (2) concern with an approach to research that acknowledges the centrality of ongoing reciprocal transactions among the component entities of integrated systems (Bronfenbrenner, 1977; Pervin & Lewis, 1977). Research performed in accord with such orientations is facilitated by the availability of such techniques as multivariate analysis employing latent variables (Causal Modeling) (Bentler, 1980). Increasing requirements for analytical tools to investigate structural models that account for the patternings found in multivariate data sets can be expected to foster the development of quantitative techniques of greater flexibility and applicability.

A final trend that seems worthy of mention because of the profound impact it can be expected to have on research in the social and behavioral sciences is the growing explicitness with which exploratory data analysis is acknowledged (Leamer, 1978) and the proliferation of techniques and procedural manuals for its implementation (Belsley, Kuh, & Welsch, 1980; Tukey, 1977; Wainer & Thissen, 1981). Although the scientific establishment of facts requires that hypotheses be confirmed by replicable experimentation, there are many situations in the behavioral and social sciences where: (1) experimentation is not possible; (2) hypotheses are not confirmed, but data are available that might reveal the reason for hypothesis failure or that might suggest alternate hypotheses; and (3) the experimenter lacks hypotheses that he or she can entertain with any measure of confidence. Most investigators would agree with Leamer (1978) that the careful examination of data in such situations is imperative for the generation of new hypotheses that become subject to further assessment. Many may, however, be slow to give up the belief that this constitutes "second-class science" and reluctant to agree that such procedures should be regarded as "mining expeditions" rather than "fishing expeditions" (Leamer, 1978). Particularly when dealing with complex multivariate data sets, techniques that assist in the identification of patterns or that permit the identification of atypical or ill-behaved variables or subjects may be of vital importance in restructuring interpretations in the direction of testable hypotheses.

ACKNOWLEDGMENT

Preparation of this chapter was supported by USPHS Research Grant MH-08957 (Dr. Rickels) and USPHS Research Grant MH-30366 (Dr. Downing).

REFERENCES

American Psychiatric Association. *Diagnostic and statistical manual of mental disorders.* DSM-III Taskforce on Nomenclature and Statistics, American Psychiatric Association, Washington, D.C., 1980.

Belsley, D. A., Kuh, E., & Welsch, R. E. *Regression diagnostics: Identifying influential data and sources of collinearity.* New York: Wiley, 1980.

Bentler, F. M. Multivariate analysis with latent variables: Causal modeling. *Annual Review of Psychology,* 1980, *32,* 1–20.

Bronfenbrenner, U. Towards an experimental ecology of human development. *American Psychologist,* 1977, *32,* 513–531.

Brunswik, E. Representative design and probabilistic theory in a functional psychology. *Psychological Review,* 1955, *62,* 193–217.

Chassan, J. B. *Research design in clinical psychology and psychiatry.* New York: Irvington, 1979.

Downing, R. W., & Rickels, K. Self-report of hostility and the incidence of side reactions in neurotic outpatients treated with tranquilizing drugs and placebo. *Journal of Consulting and Clinical Psychology,* 1967, *31,* 71–76. (a)

Downing, R. W., & Rickels, K. Pre-treatment self estimates and clinical improvement with tranquilizer therapy. *Diseases of the Nervous System,* 1967, *28,* 671–674. (b)

Downing, R. W., & Rickels, K. Prediction of response to chlordiazepoxide and placebo in anxious outpatients: An attempt at replication. *Pharmakopsychiatrie, Neuro-Psychopharmakologie,* 1978, *11,* 207–219. (a)

Downing, R. W., & Rickels, K. Nonspecific factors and their interaction with psychological treatment in pharmacotherapy. In M. A. Lipton, A. DiMascio, & K. F. Killam (Eds.), *Psychopharmacology: A Generation of Progress*. New York: Raven Press, 1419–1428, 1978. (b)

Downing, R. W., & Rickels, K. Hostility conflict and reporting of side effects by psychiatric outpatients. *Psychological Reports*, 1980, *47*, 310–324.

Downing, R. W., Rickels, K., & Horn, N. L. Hostility conflict in neurotic patients who prematurely terminate drug treatment. *Journal of Nervous and Mental Disease*, 1970, *151*, 211–218. (a)

Downing, R. W., Rickels, K., & Horn, N. L. The role of compliance in the premature termination of neurotic outpatients in psychotropic drug treatments. *International Pharmacopsychiatry*, 1970, *4*, 53–58. (b)

Endicott, J., & Spitzer, R. A diagnostic interview: The schedule for affective disorders and schizophrenia. *Archives of General Psychiatry*, 1978, *35*, 837–844.

Fisher, S., & Fisher, R. L. Placebo response and acquiescence. *Psychopharmacologia (Berlin)*, 1963, *4*, 298–301.

Haefely, W. E. Central actions of benzodiazepines: General introduction. *British Journal of Psychiatry*, 1978, *133*, 231–238.

Howard, K., Rickels, K., Mock, J. E., Lipman, R. S., Covi, L., & Baumm, N. C. Therapeutic style and attrition rate from psychiatric drug treatment. *Journal of Nervous and Mental Disease*, 1970, *150*, 102–110.

Klett, C. J., & Moseley, E. C. The right drug for the right patient. *Journal of Consulting and Clinical Psychology*, 1965, *29*, 546–551.

Leamer, E. E. *Specification searches: Ad hoc inference with non-experimental data*. New York: Wiley, 1978.

McNair, D. M., Kahn, R. J., Droppleman, L. F., & Fisher, S. Compatibility, acquiescence and drug effects. In H. Brill, J. O. Cole, P. Deniker, H. Hippias, & P. B. Bradley (Eds.), *Neuropsychopharmacology*. Amsterdam: Excerpta Medica Foundation, 1966.

McNair, D. M., Kahn, R. J., Droppleman, L. F., & Fisher, S. Patient acquiescence and drug effects. In K. Rickels (Ed.), *Non-specific factors in drug therapy*. Springfield, Ill.: Charles C. Thomas, 1968.

McNair, D. M., Fisher, S., Kahn, R. J., & Droppleman, L. F. Drug–personality interaction in intensive outpatient treatment. *Archives of General Psychiatry*, 1970, *22*, 128–135.

McNair, D. M., Fisher, S., Sussman, C., Droppleman, L. F., & Kahn, R. J. Persistance of a drug-personality interaction in psychiatric outpatients. *Journal of Psychiatric Research*, 1970, *7*, 299–305.

Pervin, L. A., & Lewis, M. (Eds.). *Perspectives in interactional psychology*, New York: Plenum Press, 1977.

Rickels, K. (Ed.). *Non-specific factors in drug therapy*. Springfield, Ill.: Charles C. Thomas, 1968. (a)

Rickels, K. Antineurotic agents: Specific and non-specific effects. In D. H. Efron, J. O. Cole, J. Levine, J. R. Wittenborn (Eds.), *Psychopharmacology: A review of progress, 1957–1967*. Public Health Service Publication No. 1836, 231–247, 1968. (b)

Rickels, K. Use of antianxiety agents in anxious outpatients. *Paychopharmacology*, 1978, *58*, 1–17.

Rickels, K., & Anderson, F. L. Attrited and completed lower socioeconomic class clinical patients in psychiatric drug therapy. *Comprehensive Psychiatry*, 1967, *8*, 90–99.

Rickels, K., & Downing, R. Verbal ability (intelligence) and improvement in drug therapy of neurotic patients. *Journal of New Drugs*, 1965, *5*, 303–307.

Schulsinger, F. Biological psychiatry. *Annual Review of Psychology*, 1980, *31*, 583–606.

Tallman, J. F., Paul, S. M., Skolnick, P., & Gallagher, D. W. Receptors for the age of anxiety: Pharmacology of the benzodiazepines. *Science*, 1980, *207*, 274–281.

Tukey, J. W. *Exploratory data analysis*. Reading, Mass.: Addison-Wesley, 1977.

Tyler, L. E. More stately mansions, psychology extends its boundaries. *Annual Review of Psychology*, 1981, *32*, 1–20.

Uhlenhuth, E. H., Lipman, R. S., Rickels, K., Fisher, S., Covi, L. & Park, L. C. Predicting the relief of anxiety with meprobamate. *Archives of General Psychiatry*, 1968, *19*, 619–630.

Wainer, H., & Thissen, D. Graphical data analysis. *Annual Review of Psychology*, 1981, *32*, 191–241.

Windelband, W. *Geschichte und Naturwissenschaft*. Strassburg: Heitz, 1894.

21 New Approaches in Behavior Therapy Research

Johannes C. Brengelmann
Max-Planck-Institute of Psychiatry, Munich, West Germany

INTRODUCTION

Clinical psychology in Germany has a long history and a short past. Fifteen years ago systematic training and application regarding clinical psychology did not exist, certainly not on a scientific basis. The psychological scene was heavily influenced by depth-psychological speculation, antiscientific humanism, organic reductionism, holistic imprecision, divided Gestaltism, and lack of controlled clinical research. Even now universities are hardly in the position of producing clinical psychologists sufficiently in command of diagnostic and therapeutic procedures to be ready for general practice. On the other hand, society is in need of effective treatment and prevention programs for dependencies and chronic illness behavior, as well as psychiatric and educational problems, all of which contribute heavily toward mounting health costs.

This situation is sustained by a number of weak points characterizing the woes of clinical psychology. Psychologists are divided into academic and professional organizations with disparate interests. Professional organizations are deeply split concerning political issues. Continuous education is lacking, clinical psychologists are not licensed, and their work is dominated by medical doctors. Clinical psychologists have not been able to agree among themselves on major professional issues. Consequently, the psychologists are powerless in their negotiations with governments and public and private organizations.

Nevertheless, I predict a more positive future for clinical psychology in this country, particularly with regard to behavioral analysis and treatment. The predictions are based on developments that have occurred at the Max-Planck-Institute of Psychiatry, as well as in some other institutes during the last 12 to 15 years. To understand these developments, certain things should be noted.

Firstly, the terms *experimental treatment, behavior therapy,* or *behavior modification* are considered synonymous. We also sidestep hotly debated issues concerning the relationship between the psychotherapies. Reliable results produced by any therapy (e.g., psychoanalysis or nondirective therapy) are accepted and interpreted in our experimentally developed framework. Thus the term *experimental* is the denominator for all psychological analysis and treatment.

Secondly, our approach is distinctly inductive and empirical (i.e., we analyze the effectiveness of therapeutic procedures against agreed clinical criteria rather than testing "basic theoretical issues."

Thirdly, psychological research as defined is social in nature and has to demonstrate social and societal relevance. This means variation in task setting, investigation of transfer from the laboratory to the community, research in the field, evaluation, and cost/benefit analysis. It also entails willingness to train therapists and mediators and to inform the public where necessary.

Fourthly, the regard for determinants of behavioral disturbance and of treatment effects has accompanied our research almost from the beginning. Having grown up in personality research, we have used personality parameters as independent variables in treatment research, and this is more typical for Germany than for Anglo–American countries.

In sum, our research is method oriented, empirical, complex in nature, given to practical application, and correspondingly varied. A perfunctory review of about 500 relevant reports emanating from the Institute shows that we have been working therapeutically and preventatively in a number of areas such as smoking, overweight, alcoholism, drug addiction, adult psychiatry, neurology, child psychiatry, child psychology, psychophysiology, and behavior medicine. There are advantages and disadvantages to this research policy, but it broadly reflects the position of clinical psychology in this country. We are now presenting four selected aspects of work just indicated, dealing with broad-spectrum therapy, multicomponent analysis, large-scale application in prevention, and behavioral medicine.

BROAD-SPECTRUM THERAPY

Toward the end of the 1960s, our first controlled behavioral treatment research applied variants of electrical aversion to severe alcoholics with a fair success rate of about 30% abstinence after a year when compared with 7% obtained for a suitable control group (Vogler, Kraemer, Ferstl, & Brengelmann, 1971; Vogler, Ferstl, Kraemer, & Brengelmann, 1975). Subsequently, we decided that aversion therapy would not correct severe behavioral deficits existing in chronic alcoholics. We consequently changed to behavioral training and self-control procedures. Detailed treatment programs were specified containing the following major components: behavioral analysis, training in social skills, training in work and leisure time behavior, relaxation, self-control, contract management, and cooperation with self-help organizations.

Such a broad-spectrum treatment program of 20 weeks duration was applied with moderate success to 58 young alcoholics. Clients were allowed to choose between abstinence and controlled drinking as treatment goals, a procedure for which we were heavily attacked even years after. The stipulated treatment goals were achieved in 81% of the cases at the end of treatment and in 41% of the cases 12 months later (Vollmer & Kraemer, 1981).[1]

Another broad-spectrum program of 3- to 4-months duration, employing abstinence as the treatment goal, was applied to 89 female patients on an inpatient basis. One year follow-up showed that 48.3% of the patients were abstinent, 16.9% practiced controlled drinking, and 34.8% were considered to have relapsed. The corresponding data of a suitable control group drawn from the same state hospital were 26.7%, 11.6%, and 61.6%, respectively (Bräuninger & Hartung, 1983). This reflects a very significant improvement of behavioral therapy over standard treatment practiced in the same hospital or elsewhere.

These experiments were carried out in the early 1970s. The awareness that control groups form a *conditio sine qua non* was by no means generally accepted in this country, and there was widespread disbelief and opposition on the part of traditional therapists and treatment agencies against the new "mechanistic" approaches. However, further painstakingly documented and successful experiments have convinced insurance companies of the economic value of behavior therapy. As a result, one hospital with 175 beds and one ambulatory treatment center, both situated in Bavaria, are now supported by such companies on condition that behavior therapy is carried out. It took about 8 years from the first day of experimentation through the demonstration of positive results on to acceptance and practical implementation of behavioral treatment of alcoholism.

From the experimental point of view the broad-spectrum treatment approach is deficient in that it controls only for overall treatment effectiveness. However, this method has helped to establish practicable treatment procedures and to replace intuitive estimation of treatment effectiveness by controlled measurement of outcome. This trend is hardly going to be reversed in the future.

A similar development has occurred with regard to the treatment of drug abuse in young people. The first treatment program was designed to include a withdrawal and a rehabilitation program totaling 8-months duration and was followed by 5-months aftercare, as well as by a 2-year follow-up (De Jong & Bühringer, 1978). The target behaviors and associated treatments were as shown in Table 21.1.

The broad-spectrum character of this program is easily noted. The most important drug behaviors and alternative behaviors were selected and treatments specified for each. Treatment manuals were prepared for the withdrawal, re-

---

[1]See Introduction to Part V, page 290, for warning by editors on dangers of controlled-drinking treatment for physically-dependent alcoholics.

habilitation, and aftercare periods, and a handbook of self-help procedures was written. Manuals were made available for therapists, patients, and cotherapists or mediators in the natural environment. On the basis of a 2-year follow-up, 32% of all 89 patients including dropouts were treated successfully, the success criteria being freedom from drug taking, social integration with nonusers, and continued work and/or occupational training. For clients who completed the entire treatment program the success rate increased to 80%. These results are shown in Table 21.2.

The completion of treatment and the compliance with treatment prescriptions appear to be most potent determinants of maintenance of therapeutic success during follow-up. This was observed in a number of heterogeneous treatment experiments. Moreover, compliance with treatment and good initial progress in treatment are good predictors of final success within a therapy program. A number of other determinants was investigated, both behavioral and cognitive. Some of these appear to generalize to various treatment modalities, but most others not. The knowledge about these determinants will improve future treatment.

In view of the increasing number of drug addicts, the rising proportion of addicts treated, and the substitution of jail sentence for treatment, the need for psychological intervention is growing. For this reason, an ambulant treatment program was developed that met with similar success.

TABLE 21.1
Target Behaviors and Associated Treatments of Drug Addiction (De Jong & Bühringer, 1978)

Target Behavior	Kind of Treatment
1. *Drug behavior*	Coverant control
	Thought stopping
	Training to refuse drug offers (role playing)
	Response prevention
	Organizational structuring of rehabilitation center
2. *Leisure time behavior*	Hierarchical organized reinforcement program
3. *Working behavior*	Token economy
4. *Social behavior*	Assertiveness training program
	Training of communication skills
5. *Self-organization*	Contract management
	Role playing of critical situations with authorities
6. *Problem solving and decision making*	Instruction and exercises in conducting behavioral analyses for themselves
	Training in decision making

TABLE 21.2
Success Rates of Behavior Therapy of Young Drug Addicts (De Jong & Bühringer, 1978)

Follow-Up	Total Group		Completers		Dropouts	
	1 Year	*2 Years*	*1 Year*	*2 Years*	*1 Year*	*2 Years*
Drug-free	37%	32%	80%	80%	25%	19%
Relapsed	28%	21%	5%	10%	33%	21%
Other treatment or jailed	21%	23%	10%	5%	23%	28%
Not traceable	11%	18%	0%	0%	17%	26%
Died	2%	4%	5%	5%	1%	4%
N	89%	89%	21%	21%	68%	68%

The willingness to include the social field and societal demands into clinical research is shown by the fact that 1 year after the initiation of the first experiment in 1972 a federally supported program for documentation, evaluation, and improvement of stationary and ambulant drug treatment programs was instituted. Between 1973 and 1978 about 60 such centers cooperated in this project carried out by one research group on drug addiction. Today there are still 30 cooperating centers. Continued education in drug treatment has been offered since 1975 to about 80 therapists stemming from more than 50 institutions. This may serve as evidence for the fact that the much discussed researcher–clinician concept of the clinical psychologist is practicable and that society is willing to accept psychological services under research conditions.

MULTICOMPONENT ANALYSIS AS USED IN THE TREATMENT FOR SMOKING

In the preceding section we have argued that broad-spectrum approaches improve the success rate of treatment fairly rapidly. However, this can be valid only for programs based on effective components, which are transparent to the client and do not overburden him. The famous 5-day plan against smoking, for example, represents a highly complex program built on facets that cannot be expected to be useful on behavioral grounds. Its effect on smoking is, indeed, comparable to that of a placebo response.

There has always been an urgent need for multicomponent analysis, but the experimental literature yields little in this direction, possibly because of the expense involved. When in 1970 the Federal Government entrusted us to develop an effective and widely applicable antismoking program, the literature declared all forms of treatment practiced to be equally effective. This superstition is still

TABLE 21.3
Nine Conditions for the Treatment of Smoking (N = 355, 256 males and 99 females)

Treatment	N Clients	Follow-Up at 59 Weeks Reduction of Cigarettes Smoked (%)
Control	30	16, 8
Placebo	26	
Medical (lobeline)	27	20, 8
Psychotherapy (nondirective)	40	
Covert sensitization	45	
Negative practice	48	29, 3
Electric aversion	41	
Self-control	46	
Self-control + electrical aversion	52	35, 6
Total N	355	

widely spread, and forms a most formidable obstruction to the scientific development of therapies. We decided, therefore, to investigate the nine forms of treatment shown in Table 21.3. In addition, three more experiments were formed and are referred to in the text (Brengelmann, 1979a, 1979b).

Firstly, the three conditions Placebo, Lobeline, and Psychotherapy are effective in reducing smoking during the first half of the 6-weeks training course. Thereafter, steadily increasing relapse is observed despite continuing treatment. This is the reason why we term these treatments *unspecific.* All other procedures are behavioral and demonstrate continuous improvement for as long as treatment lasts, although this is also followed by relapse. There are no significant differences between the three aversion therapies or between the two self-control methods. However, Self-control fares considerably better than Aversion, and all behavior therapies are superior to the unspecific therapies. The gist of this pattern of results is that considerable differences exist between kinds of treatments and that most of these differences would not have been observed using the traditional before–after design. Therefore, it is mandatory to regard treatments as exerting specific influences and to investigate their process characteristics.

Our *second* point concerns the effects of complexity or intensity of treatment. In the experiment just quoted the self-control method employed no more than gradually increasing stimulus control by means of a set of behavioral prescriptions, as well as daily monitoring of the number of cigarettes smoked. In two subsequent experiments a contract management procedure and a positive reinforcement procedure, by means of which money deposited before treatment could be earned back, were added to form a modestly complex and highly transparent self-control program. The effectiveness of treatment increased considerably. Thus, intensity of treatment is an important issue, at least when behavioral procedures are used.

The *third* point concerns the role of the therapist, which is rated very highly in this country by psychotherapists. In the first experiment the effects due to therapists were experimentally controlled, because therapists were rotated to treatment groups after subjects had been assigned at random to these groups. In the second experiment two psychologists and a psychology student widely differing in therapeutic expertise produced no significantly different treatment effects by means of the self-control procedure employed. In the third experiment the same treatment prescriptions used in group sessions were also mailed to other clients with whom no direct personal contact was ever established. Whether treated by mail or by therapist, the results were comparable. It is concluded that the significant treatment effects obtained are produced by procedural specifications rather than by the therapist. We believe that the quality of these specifications determines the results rather than the therapist's attributes.

Our *fourth* and last point refers to the as yet unsolved problem of relapse. Over the years the effectiveness of antismoking procedures has improved in various quarters, but the relapse rate is still high. The four main classes of determinants of relapse may be the following:

1. It is known that the rate of smoking varies according to environmental conditions such as continued exposure to negative health consequences, as is the case with doctors and certain patients. Here the smoking rate decreases, whereas it increases under other conditions such as social approval.

2. Personality trait factors of various kinds did not correlate significantly with smoking. However, there are a number of specific smoking factors that correlate at the 0.1% level ($N = 355$) with rate of smoking during long-term follow-up (59 weeks after treatment). These are:

Relaxation during smoking	(0.51)
Need to smoke under stress	(0.49)
Situational smoking (e.g., in bed)	(0.46)
Faithfulness to one brand	(0.43)
Multiple use of tobaccos	(0.31)
Knowledge of health danger	(0.29)

The first two factors refer to situational stress, the second two to situational determinants without emotional envolvement. Because the correlation coeffi-

SELF-CONTROL (SC) APPLIED TO SMOKING

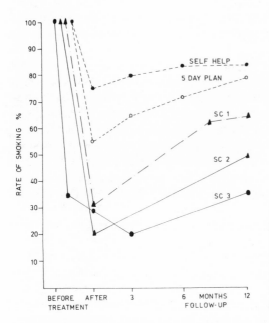

FIG. 21.1.   Percentage reduction of number of cigarettes smoked. Self-control (SC) appears to be most efficacious. Intensification of treatment (SC1 to SC2) and repetition of treatment (SC3) tend to improve short-term and long-term treatment effects.

cients are sizable, it is suggested that differential treatments need to be fitted to the smoking types. The observation that "knowledge of health danger" correlates positively with smoking is revealing of so-called cognitive dissonance. The more people smoke, the more they know that smoking is going to be dangerous to them. Another factor concerning the knowledge that smoking causes cancer also correlates at the 1% level with smoking. This supports the view of many scientists that cognitive health education is not effective in changing the smoking habit. We use such evidence to demand utilization of behavioral procedures in health education.

3. Two motivational state measures correlated highly with smoking, as follows:

Expectation of treatment success (-0.69)

Stimulation by smoking (craving) (0.48).

The first factor signifies satisfaction with treatment success and, maybe more importantly, compliance with treatment rules that guarantee success. Positive reinforcement of compliance and aversion therapy of craving seem to be treatments of choice to combat relapse.

4. In yet another mail order experiment we have repeated the most efficient self-control program three times with 4-week interval between Treatment 1 to

Treatment 2 and Treatment 2 to Treatment 3, so that overlearning took place. This overlearning appeared to be particularly effective for long-term maintenance of results (Fig. 21.1; Brengelmann 1979b). Curiously enough, overlearning and distributed learning, as practiced here, are hardly used elsewhere.

Finally I want to underline the fact that the Federal Government has accepted the self-control program against smoking. It is now being used in the public evening schools (*Volkshochschulen*) all over the country. The government has assessed the effectiveness of the program after transfer to these schools, with satisfactory results. Equally satisfying is the thought that a public body has begun to analyze critically its own creations.

LARGE-SCALE APPLICATION IN PREVENTION

Many health risk factors are located in the behavioral field. Because behavioral risks are widely distributed in the general population, large-scale application of psychological intervention is asked for. We have already reported on the feasibility of treating smoking through the mail. A similar attempt was made for the reduction of overweight.

In the first experiment, it was shown that treatment by mail is as effective as group treatment by means of the same self-control procedure (Ferstl, Jockusch, & Brengelmann, 1975). Both groups reduced their weight by about 7½ kg during 12 weeks of intervention, and 52% of the subjects maintained their reduced weight for 2 years. In a second experiment, treatment duration was increased to 24 weeks and mean weight loss was 10 kg (Richter, 1975). This may mean that treatment duration increases effectiveness but also that distributed practice might have achieved superior results.

We were then interested in testing the use of television for weight reduction. This program was also supported by the Federal Government, as were many others. Four groups of 300 subjects each were subjected to mail-order and television treatment, as well as to a no-treatment condition. Seven TV treatments were broadcasted during a period of 6 months. Mail-order and TV treatment followed the same concept. Of the subjects, 36% were male and 64% female. Overweight was 12.5 kg above the normal and 22.5 kg above the ideal weight. The results expressed in terms of weight loss were as follows (Ferstl et al., 1977):

Control group	1.1 kg
Television group	2.5 kg
Mail-order group	7.5kg
Television and mail-order groups combined	8.6 kg

Mail-order treatment proved as effective as in previous experiments. TV treatment added no significant weight loss neither to the Mail-Order nor to the Control condition. However, it was interesting to see that 10 subjects who volunteered to appear in the TV broadcast lost more than double the weight than the Mail-Order group. This is surely the result of social reinforcement and may suggest that the possibilities of treatment through television have not been exhausted. The interest of the public was certainly great. The program was watched by 12 million people, 32,000 volunteered for the mail-order treatment, and 100,000 for the combined Mail-Order/TV treatment. It is obviously easier to arouse interest than to change eating behavior permanently.

FROM BEHAVIORAL PSYCHIATRY TO BEHAVIORAL MEDICINE

As in other countries, behavior therapy began to establish itself first in psychiaary. The main treatment targets were child psychiatric problems, including autism, and adult psychiatric problems such as phobia, anxiety, and obsessive compulsion. More recently, several groups have concentrated on the treatment of anorexia nervosa and reactive depression. There are also several service centers where behavior therapy is applied to a wide variety of problems in both individual and group treatment. Nevertheless, the progress for psychologists participating in this development is rather slow.

For several years, psychologists have shown interest in applying their expertise to medical problems. Two experimental examples may be quoted, one using the broad-spectrum approach for the treatment of essential hypertension and the other a more analytical approach in the treatment of chronic medical illness.

The experiment on hypertension that was carried out by my co-worker, Maass, employed the following three treatment groups (Brengelmann, 1979a):

1. Standard group: Reduction of food intake to 1200 calories plus daily one diuretic (moduretic) ($N = 22$)

2. Beta-blocker: Standard treatment plus beta-blocker medication at the discretion of the doctor ($N = 13$)

3. Behavior therapy: Standard treatment and behavioral treatment for smoking, overweight, lack of exercise, anxiety, stress, and compliance ($N = 33$)

All patients were hospitalized and randomly allotted to treatment. During 5 weeks of treatment in a hospital, systolic blood pressure dropped significantly from about 170 to below 140 and diastolic blood pressure dropped from over 100 to somewhat above 85. There were no significant differences between the groups during this treatment phase. After discharge, family doctors returned information on blood pressure and medication. With every 3 months of follow-up systematic and significant differences began to appear and became stronger in time. For all groups, blood pressure values increased slowly but steadily. However, the increase was largest for the Standard group and smallest for the Behavior Therapy group, leaving the Beta-Blocker group in between. These results are shown in Fig. 21.2.

The pattern of medication by the family doctors appears to be of interest too. After 1 year, the Beta-Blocker group remained at a high level of strong hypotensive medication. These were given in 85% of the cases. The respective figures were 46% for the Standard group and 21% for the Behavior Therapy group. The conclusion is drawn that Behavior Therapy reduces both high blood pressure and medication in a relative sense. Although it cannot be said at this time which treatment component is responsible for this, results of this kind raise serious interest at least with a number of heart specialists.

The second experiment, conducted by my co-workers Niebel, Saalfeld, and Sonderegger, dealt with chronic medical patients who also presented serious psychological problems (Brengelmann, 1980). As a first step, these problems were collected in intensive interviews. The list of 1000 items was given again in a standardized fashion and factor analyzed. After further cross-validation, the 12 resulting stable factors were used as criteria for treatment effectiveness and were applied four times: before and after treatment and at two points of follow-up (1 and 4 months after discharge). Four of these represented internal psychological reactions to stress, whereas five dealt with manifest behavior. Treatment took place in nine sessions distributed over 3 weeks, each group session lasting for $1\frac{1}{2}$ hour. There were four treatment groups, as follows:

1. Asymptomatic treatment (AST): This is a comprehensive program concentrating exclusively on training positive, alternative behaviors in groups. No problems were discussed ($N = 23$).

2. Anxiety management training (AMT): The program was formally similar to AST but directed at reducing negative thoughts, feelings, or behaviors ($N = 23$).

3. Autogenic training (AuTr): Patients received an intensive somatic treatment program plus relaxation treatment ($N = 13$).

4. Clinical routine (CliR): Patients received only a somatic treatment program (balneology, massage, physiological treatment, medication, $N = 13$).

The results are given in Table 21.4. These results are as clear as we would like to see them more often. AST produces the most positive changes, followed by AMT, and that with regard to both reaction classes, internal and behavioral. AST is relatively more successful with regard to the behavioral aspects and AMT with regard to the internal reactions. The conclusions would be: (1) that positive reinforcement of alternative, individually tailored behavior trained in groups is

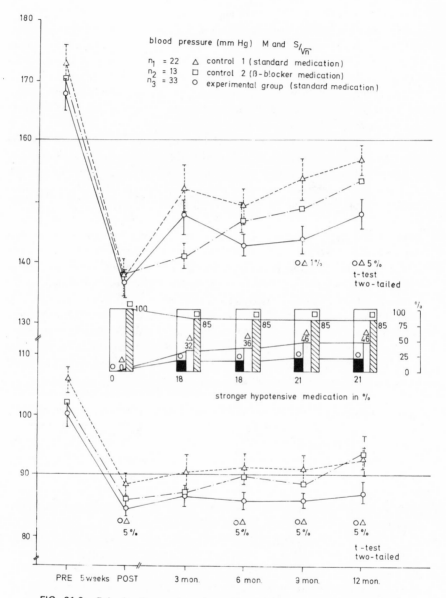

FIG. 21.2. Behavior therapy (experimental group) helps in controlling high blood pressure and in reducing hypotensive medication.

TABLE 21.4
Positive Psychological Changes Induced by Four Therapies[a]

	AST			AMT			AuTr		KliR	
	Post	FU1	FU2	Post	FU1	FU2	Post	FU2	Post	FU2
Internal reactions to stress										
1. Sleep and bodily reactions	+	+++	+++	+	++	+	-	+	-	-
2. Anxiety relating to aging and death	+	++	++	+	++	+++	-	-	-	-
3. Negative self-evaluation	+	+++	+++	-	+	+	-	-	-	-
4. Depressiveness	-	+++	+++	-	+	+	-	-	-	-
Stress behavior										
5. Social stress at work	++	+++	+++	-	-	+	-	-	-	-
6. Assertiveness	+++	+++	++	-	-	-	-	-	-	-
7. Enjoyment of nature	++	+++	++	-	-	-	-	-	-	-
8. Social enjoyment	+++	+++	-	++	-	++	-	-	-	-
9. Work overload	+	+++	+++	+	+	-	-	-	-	-

[a]Behavioral: AST = Asymptomatic therapy
AMT = anxiety management training
post = change from *pre* to *post*,
FU1 = follow-up 1 (1 month),
FU2 = follow-up 2 (4 months).

medical: AuTr = autogenic training
CliR = clinical routine
+5%, ++1%, ++0, 10.7%;
- = no specific change.

the treatment of choice in general; (2) that AMT is useful, particularly with internal stress reactions, as might be expected; and (3) that the traditional methods of treatment show no discernible effect, neither immediately after the 4 weeks of stationary treatment nor during the following months.

Similar results were obtained with regard to general life criteria depicting positive and negative feeling states, as well as limitations in daily activities. Moreover, behavior therapies markedly reduced the amount of medication prescribed. The use of tranquilizers was strongly reduced by AMT, and AST significantly reduced the intake of barbiturates.

Because 5 million Germans are estimated to avail themselves each year of the services of clinics of the kind we are dealing with and because about 30% to 50% of these patients would benefit from behavioral therapy, the problem for psychologists states itself: stronger participation in medical therapy.

EXPECTATIONS FOR THE FUTURE

There is a long tradition of clinical psychology in the sense that basic researchers, such as Ebbinghaus, have worked on problems that would now be considered clinical. Sparse clinical work and unsystematic training has been observed to exist at universities, particularly since the end of World War II. But the early experimental roots are not recognizable to any large extent in the postwar development. Some of the developments since then have been described on the basis of which nearer-term and long-term predictions of 5 and 20 years, respectively, can be made.

Behavior therapy as defined represents *the* scientific development in clinical work. To be sure, there are changes in speculative thought in prescientific clinical psychology, but they are merely thoughts. They always go back to the same sources while seeking new applications, and they make no serious attempt to check on the truth of their tenets. Behavior therapy, on the other hand, uses the most modern scientific methodology available at a time and accepts purposeful changes on the basis of agreed criteria of success. This methodological expertise combined with ever improving technological advance in research design and data analysis is the strength of modern clinical psychology. If there is one long-term change to be expected, then it will be the continuous development of the scientific approach, which is not going to reverse itself.

One development that has already begun and is going to continue is the increased differentiation of behavior–analytical and therapeutic technology leading to more specific fitting of treatment to problem. This is evident in the increase of multicomponent analysis and of comparative work, meaning comparison between treatment components known to be effective and not between traditional rough classes such as psychoanalysis and behavior therapy. This increase in treatment technology carries a highly important positive asset frequently overlooked and not easily moved into awareness, namely the demonstrated fact that treatment research leads to immediately applicable procedures. As shown, this often means also the necessity to revamp the whole treatment organization and indeed the total administrative and physical environment, including the architecture.

Since the beginning of the scientific era of clinical psychology in Germany, therapists of various persuasions have immediately grasped that speculation is the strength of psychoanalysis and practical technology, that of behavior therapy. This now forms a definite trend as a recent investigation of the nonmedical psychotherapeutic services in the BRD, carried out at the Max-Planck-Institute of Psychiatry, shows (Wittchen & Fichter, 1980). After 15 years of existence, counting the years generously, behavior therapy is practiced by 44% of the therapists, verbal therapy (*Gesprächstherapie,* a very unfortunate expression) by 37%, and psychoanalysis by 19% of all therapists. However, verbal therapists express desire for continued education in behavior therapy in 88% of the time. This trend is going to be active for the near and longer terms. As we all know, it parallels a development taking place in the United States. As a researcher I may be happy about this ecclecticistic trend for want of anything better, but I am unhappy about the therapeutic polypragmasia involved. A treatment cannot be improved by mixing a good natural wine with sugar water, as we have maintained earlier on. It is for that reason that the much belabored integration between traditional and modern psychotherapies should not take place before traditional techniques are tested and adapted. This will present a great problem for the rest of the century. On the one hand, psychologists who have diagnosed and treated according to traditional ways of thinking can hardly be expected to relinquish their ingrained behavior in favor of an incompatible new approach. On the other hand, present-day university education in scientific clinical psychology is wanting. There will be no scientifically based clinical psychology on a broad basis at the turn of the century.

We have taken pains to demonstrate that research in daily application is not only compatible but indeed very much desired. I am not only referring to research in the field as usually understood but also to compound research whereby psychologists working in institutions as well as those in private practice join scientists to test and improve therapies as used in daily work. It is going to be difficult to convince many or most that this can be done and that this approach will be most important for strengthening the knowledge and prestige of the clinical psychologist, which he or she sorely needs. The first compound research of this kind is already on the drawing board and the next 5 years will show progress. How it will fare in the long run is difficult to say. This depends solely on the continued availability of individuals who are willing and capable to organize such research and carry it out. Unfortunately, psychology has not been very active in producing such organizers.

The format of applied clinical work has changed considerably during the last decade as regards two points: (1) Formerly, psychologists were mostly occupied with diagnostic work that presented little consequence for treatment. This has already changed to much greater emphasis on treatment. Diagnostic work by means of traditional tests will continue to be reduced in the measure as behavior analysis and therapy expand during the rest of the century. It will be increasingly recognized that therapy is the main asset of the practicing psychologist. (2) Individual therapy will always be used for more seriously disturbed patients and in initial stages of treatment, but group treatment will steadily continue to gain in importance for reasons of both economy and therapeutic effectiveness.

A number of new beginnings will be made already during the next 5 years, depending on the speed with which scientific clinical psychology develops and asserts itself. The seeds for this are already sown. Psychologists will move ahead broadly in the area of behavioral medicine, particularly in clinical settings. Medical psychology as presently practiced at the universities will be heavily influenced by this movement. This new branch of medicine has been ailing since its inception because it is conservative and divided in its approach. It is still lacking the unitary theoretical and practical foundation that behavioral psychology can offer. Also in private practice psychologists will begin to cooperate with medical specialists, particularly internists, although in a hesitating fashion. Furthermore, psychological practitioners are going to realize that there are tasks to be fulfilled in the general area of public health, which are mostly taken care of by medical doctors, sociologists, or social educators. I also predict that clinical psychologists will begin to interest themselves in the area of industrial psychology during the next 5 years. They will introduce health measures already developed; they will begin to hold behavioral training courses for managers; they will also commence to apply principles of behavior to the management of industrial organizations. This field is wide open to behavioral applications with assured success, but clinical psychologists have not identified themselves with behavioral applications in industry. Finally, I would not be surprised if the concept of behavioral theology with its pastoral applications were discussed systematically in the near future. I can imagine churches working together closely with behavioral psychologists because they become more and more involved in everyday human behavior, particularly in the social area. Clergy has long known that the realization of metaphysical goals in the human soul has to pass through the diversity of behavior and its deviations. Exact knowledge of behavioral principles is, therefore, necessary to render this service effective. It is actually surprising that theologists, having recognized the need of psychological services, have turned to psychoanalysis for help rather than to behavioral psychology.

Toward the end I would like to busy myself with health care and delivery research. In the area of the addictions, treatment or prevention programs have been developed and followed up in many counseling centers across the country. Programs were fully documented and continued education was developed in stages. In another instance a community-based program concerning behavioral health risk factors with regard to cardiovascular diseases has been set up in five places near a major North German city. Preventive measures against addictions are being set up in a Central German country. Such programs are comprehensive in nature. They include planning, specification, documentation, implementation, supervision, and education. This is a fine example as to how behavioral technology can be applied to problems of the community also from the organizational point of view. Psychologists have to muster all their expertise to design and to execute experimental and quasi-experimental health measures on a broad basis. Further developments are to be expected in this area and also in theoretical respects. Cost/benefit analysis, decision theory, and systems theory will require further elaboration and application in the future. If the economy of the country will bear its health costs, care and delivery research will be intensified. By 1985 a comprehensive system of trend indicators for addictions will be available and will be helpful in the overall planning of health measures. A similar development will take place as to the prevention of cardiovascular diseases, although at a slower pace. The planning, supervision, and evaluation of health care measures will be paralleled by intensified continuing education of psychologists, and more psychological positions will become available in this area.

REFERENCES

Bräuninger, H., & Hartung, O. Planung, Organisation und Durchführung eines verhaltenstherapeutisch orientierten stationären Behandlungsprogramms für suchtkranke Frauen. In J. C. Brengelmann (Ed.), *Neue Therapien des Alkoholismus*. München: G. Röttger, 1983.

Brengelmann, J. C. La médecine comportementale. *Psychologie Médicale*, 1979, *11*, 2335–2349. (a)

Brengelmann, J. C. Selbstkontrolle als wirksamste und wirtschaftlichste Methode der Raucherentwöhnung. *Suchtgefahren*, 1979, *5*, 194–204. (b)

Brengelmann, J. C. (Ed.). *Entwicklung der Verhaltenstherapie in der Praxis*. München: G. Röttger, 1980.

Brengelmann, J. C., & Sedlmayr, E. (mit Terfloth, I., & Schwarze-Bindhardt, U.). *Experimente zur Behandlung des Rauchens. Schriftenreihe des Bundesministeriums für Jugend, Familie und Gesundheit*, Bd. 35. Stuttgart: Kohlhammer, 1973.

BZgA. *Wirksamkeitskontrolle von Raucherentwöhnungskursen in Volkshochschulen und anderen Einrichtungen der Erwachsenenbildung*. Köln: Bundeszentrale für gesundheitliche Aufklärung, 1981.

De Jong, R., & Bühringer, G. (Eds.). *Ein verhaltenstherapeutisches Stufenprogramm zur stationären Behandlung von Drogenabhängigen*. München: G. Röttger, 1978.

Ferstl, R., Jockusch, U., & Brengelmann, J. C. Die verhaltenstherapeutische Behandlung des Übergewichts. *Internationales Journal für Gesundheitserziehung*, 1975, *18*, 119–136.

Ferstl, R., Henrich, G., Richter, M., Bühringer, G., & Brengelmann, J. C. Die Beeinflussung des Übergewichts: *Bericht über ein Projekt zur begleitenden Untersuchung über die Wirksamkeit der ZDF-Sendereihe gegen das Übergewicht*. München: G. Röttger, 1977.

Richter, M. *Die Behandlung des Übergewichts mit Hilfe der Selbstkontrollmethode*. München: Bericht des Instituts für Therapieforschung (IFT) an die Bundeszentrale für gesundheitliche Aufklärung in Köln. 1975.

Vogler, R. E., Kraemer, S., Ferstl, R., & Brengelmann, J. C. Aversion conditioning with severe alcoholics. *Proceedings of the Third Annual Congress of the European Behavior Therpy Association*, 1971, 227–232.

Vogler, R. E., Ferstl, R., Kraemer, S., & Brengelmann, J. C. Electrical aversion conditioning of alcoholics: One year follow-up. *Journal of Behavior Therapy and Experimental Psychiatry*, 1975, *6*, 171–173.

Vollmer, H., & Kraemer, S. (Eds.). *Ambulante Behandlung des Alkoholismus: Erfahrungen aus der verhaltenstherapeutischen Arbeit mit jungen Alkoholabhängigen.* München: G. Röttger, 1981.

Wittchen, H. U., & Fichter, M. *Psychotherapie in der Bundesrepublik. Materalien und Analysen zur psychosozialen und psychotherapeutischen Versorgung.* Weinheim, Basel: Beltz, 1980.

22 Decision Analysis: A Nonpsychological Psychotechnology

Ward Edwards
University of Southern California, Los Angeles, USA

The rich tradition of scientific psychology in Germany, so well-illustrated and so well-served by Professor Lienert, has both basic and applied dimensions. Because we are discussing fundamental or basic research, I plan to focus on a specific class of applications.

The intellectual origin of these applications would be labeled *psychophysics,* if the originators were psychologists. But most of them were not, and, indeed, I suspect that the majority of the fathers of the field would find the word psychophysics unfamiliar and anomalous.

The field I plan to discuss is *decision analysis.* Its history lies in statistics and particularly in statistical decision theory, in economics, and perhaps a bit in psychology in more recent years. I have reviewed that history in various publications (Edwards, 1954, 1961) and shall not do so again here. The actual development of the ideas that underlie the application occurred during the 1960s (Raiffa, 1968), and the accumulation of instances of successful applications waited until the 1970s. Now, in the 1980s, I find the demand for decision analysts greater than the demand for psychometricians—and I believe that their potential for impact on society is much greater as well.

WHAT IS A DECISION ANALYSIS?

A decision analysis is a set of essentially clinical procedures, many of them to some degree mathematical in content but all based on human judgments of various kinds, that can aid individuals or groups confronted with a situation in which action of some kind must be taken, but the appropriate action is either

341

unclear or controversial or both. Its major consumer so far has been the American government, with the German government and various businesses in the United States, Germany, the United Kingdom, and other countries close behind. I anticipate rapid expansion of its use to other governments and firms.

How does it work? It consists of a fairly well-defined set of steps, typically implemented by a group of senior officials from the client organization (sometimes but not always including the President, Minister, or other labeled decision maker) in interaction over a period of days or weeks with one or more expert consultants, drawn either from consulting firms or from university faculties. The following discussion assumes the full-time efforts of all concerned in an environment quite free from distractions. If that is not the case, you should multiply my time estimates by a factor of 10 to 100, depending on just how much attention the decision analyst can obtain from his or her clients.

The first step is simply to discuss the decision problem as the client representatives see it. This serves both to make sure that they recognize the inevitable disparities among their various views and to inform the analyst(s) about the nature of the problem and the language relevant to it. This step normally consumes not less than 4 nor more than 8 hours.

The next step is to formalize the problem somewhat. Formalization at this stage consists of two tasks. The first is to specify, in some reasonable degree of detail, the decision options available; that is, what the decision-making group can do. The second is to specify, again in reasonable detail, what the possible outcomes of each of these options might be and upon what events not under the control of the decision-making organization those outcomes depend. Because a great deal of discussion of both topics has gone on already, this step also can usually be completed during the first full day.

After a hard day's work, a few after-dark libations, and a good night's sleep, all assemble the following morning, review the structure of the decision problem that they have arrived at—and, typically, are aghast at what they find. This distress leads to an urgent and typically effective attempt to redefine or restructure options so that they make more sense. It may happen that, in the course of this creative process, a new option occurs to someone that so obviously solves the problem that no further work is necessary. More often, the problem is still alive and well; the new options do not work magic on it; they merely make more sense than did the old ones.

At this point the analyst starts playing a much more active role than has hitherto been the case. By now, he or she knows rather well what the problem is, what the options are, and what the values bearing on those options are. The latter topic is now the major concern. To evaluate options or, more precisely, to evaluate the various outcomes to which options may lead, it is necessary to know both what values are important to the decision-making group and how important each value is relative to the others. The technical tool usually used to assess such questions is called *multiattribute utility measurement* (Edwards, 1971, 1977;

Keeney & Raiffa, 1976; Raiffa, 1968). Its first step is the evolution of a value tree—a hierarchy expressing what values are important to this particular problem and organizing them into a structure that typically ranges from general but unmeasurable to specific and measurable. The development of a value tree is usually a recursive process, both because discussion changes people's minds about how it should be structured and because the values included in it should: (1) be important to the decision makers; and (2) be able to discriminate among options. Any value that fails to pass both tests is a candidate for summary deletion from the value tree. Any value that, having not arisen at first, is later suggested for inclusion and that passes these two tests is a candidate for addition to that tree—too often requiring some reorganization of its structure. This process becomes even more complicated if, as I am currently doing in my own research, one tries to use value trees as a device for promoting conflict resolution in highly politicized social conflicts, such as school busing in Los Angeles, selection of sites for dams in Arizona, or nuclear power versus other energy sources almost anywhere.

Formally, the function of multiattribute utility measurement is to evaluate outcomes. These outcomes will ordinarily depend not only on the option chosen but also on events not under the decision maker's control. Even if such events are controlled by a hostile opponent, they are often called *chance events* and are usually represented as having probabilities of occurrence. A decision tree consists of a set of available options, each followed by a set of chance events to which it can lead, which are in turn followed by new (or old) options made available by the sequence so far, and so on in an alternating sequence of choices and chance events. Decision trees have a problem: They tend to become unmanageably large ("a bushy mess," in decision-analytic slang) very quickly. To manage bushy messes, one chops off each branch somewhere. The tip of the branch at the point at which it is chopped off is called an *outcome*. The utility of an outcome is simply a representation of the attractiveness of the unimaginably complex sequence of future acts and events that one would need to consider if one had not chopped the tree at that point. A particularly convenient and quite common place to do such chopping is immediately after the decision now under consideration. This amounts to treating that decision as though its outcome were certain; if so, the utility of the action is identical with the utility of its outcome. The most common cases in which one does not do this arise if an option under consideration has acquisition of more information as one of its elements.

This completes my discussion of structuring; I turn to measurements next.

Once one has a value tree, the next step in multiattribute utility analysis is to weight its values explicitly. I always use additive aggregation rules and consequently insist that within each set of values compared with one another the values should sum to 1. Figure 22.1 shows a typical value tree, obtained at one stage of the evaluation of Arizona dam sites on which I have been working recently. Note the weights, obtained from one participant. I should emphasize that this is not the

FIG. 22.1. An example of a value tree.

- A — Environmental Impacts (.55)
  - AA — Cultural (.07)
    - AAA — Historic Sites Flooded (.40)
    - AAB — Prehistoric Sites Flooded (.60)
  - AB — Biological (.34)
    - ABA — Threatened & Endangered Species (.32)
    - ABB — Terrestrial Habitat (.33)
    - ABC — Aquatic Habitat (.32)
    - ABD — Special Use & Management Areas (.04)
  - AC — Geological (.08)
    - ACA — Prime Farmland (.50)
    - ACB — Mineral Resources (.50)
  - AD — Visual Quality (.08)
  - AE — Noise (.03)
  - AF — Air Quality (.06)
  - AG — Water Quality (.34)
- B — Social Impacts (.27)
  - BA — Indian Relocation (.69)
  - BB — Non-Indian Relocation (.14)
  - BC — Individual-related Flooding Problems (.00)
  - BD — Recreation (.17)
    - BDA — Lakes (.29)
    - BDB — Streams (.71)
- C — Economic Impacts (.18)
  - CA — Benefits (.25)
    - CAA — Water Supply Regulation (.22)
    - CAB — Flood Control Benefits (.56)
    - CAC — Development Opportunities (.22)
  - CB — Costs (.75)
    - CBA — Reimbursable Costs (.50)
    - CBB — Non-reimbursable Costs (.50)

final version of the value tree with which we worked, and these weights do not represent the views of one of the actual decision makers.

The next question is: How well does the object of evaluation serve each of the lowest-level values in the tree? This question can often be answered by means of a measurement, a model, or some fairly objective source of information. If objective information is unattainable, or if (as often happens) the decision-making group concludes that judgments would be just as good and much quicker, cheaper, and more relevant, judgments are used.

The final step is to use the tree structure, the single-dimension utilities or, as I prefer to call them, location measures, and the weights to aggregate upward through the tree. If the aggregate value of the outcomes, or, if we are assuming certainty, of the option, a single number, is desired, the aggregation will be all the way to the top. If some less-sweeping aggregation is preferable, as usually is the case, aggregation can proceed to some less-than-top but still abstract level; the amount of aggregation appropriate to the problem is a matter for the discretion of the decision-making group.

The final step in a decision analysis is presumably a decision. Sometimes it turns out that a decision has been made along the way, perhaps without even recognition of that fact by the decision-making group. If not, the information bearing on the decision is now assembled for that group in an extremely orderly way. Indeed, the obvious recommendation is to take the action with the highest utility or expected utility. Although decision-making groups do not always do that, they must, of course, be in a position to justify their choice if it is different.

Computer hardware and software can be very helpful to this process, though it is not computationally demanding and can if necessary be carried out on the back of a (quite large) envelope. One of the most useful functions of computer decision aids is that they provide an audit trail for the decision; that is, they spell out in detail the issues considered in the course of making the decision, the weighting applied to each, and the rationale for the action ultimately chosen. Sophisticated decision analysis programs facilitate both the execution of the various steps I have listed and the development of this audit trail.

Lest all this sound unduly formidable, I should make clear that the methods I have described are part of a procedure called *decision conferencing,* carried out by various organizations and individuals but probably originated at Decisions and Designs, Inc., a Washington consulting firm. A decision conferencing session typically takes 2 days, costs in the $5000 region (not counting the time and efforts of the decision makers themselves), and is most often used to make commercial decisions in the multimillion dollar range.

For other kinds of problems, other adaptations of the same ideas are appropriate. Most governmental decision analyses take longer and involve much more value conflict. Among other things, this implies the importance both of more participants and of more extensive documentation.

THE RESEARCH AND DEVELOPMENT PROBLEMS OF
DECISION ANALYSIS

As a technology, decision analysis is up and running. Some very sophisticated books have been written about it (Keeney & Raiffa, 1976; Raiffa & Schlaifer, 1961; Schlaifer, 1969). More important, it is in widespread and successful use. Still, it needs both research and development of various kinds.

Perhaps the most pressing research need for decision analysis, as for most clinical procedures, is validation. Decision analysts, just like clinical psychologists and psychiatrists, are accustomed to justifying their actions (and fees) on the basis of the perfectly correct assertion that the customer: (1) was happy with the result; and (2) came back. These two criteria are obviously necessary for success in any clinical discipline. But I have great difficulty in differentiating between their use to justify those clinical disciplines of which I approve and those, like palmistry, of which I disapprove. The dyed-in-the-wool mathematically oriented decision analysts, of whom I am not one, will also justify their procedures on the basis of the axioms from which they are derived. You want to be coherent both in your beliefs and in the relations between your beliefs, your values, and your actions, don't you? Only conformity to the axiomatic structure of decision analysis can guarantee such coherence.

I find the coherence argument not much more satisfactory than the customer satisfaction argument. Whereas I admire coherence as an intellectual virtue, I would much rather be occasionally and incoherently wise than consistently foolish.

If the majority of decision analysts were psychologists trained in psychophysics and psychometrics, the picture would be quite different. First, they would recognize that the clinical procedure I have described includes a number of different steps and that the reliability and validity of each is a separate topic of study. Second, they would recognize that what must be validated is method, not result. And third, they would take the problem seriously enough to build both validation studies and follow-ups into their programs of professional activities.

Our laboratory at the University of Southern California has been much concerned recently with one aspect of the validation problem: that of validating the weights obtained in multiattribute utility elicitation procedures. We have completed three studies of this kind. I summarize two briefly. One used the laboratory procedure of multiple-cue probability learning. We put subjects through a training session in which they were expected to learn a set of weights on the basis of outcome feedback and found that they were in fact quite well able to report the weights with adequate accuracy afterward. Moreover, the techniques used for eliciting weights, though they differed greatly in difficulty, produced rather comparable results.

A much more interesting study used experienced credit officers of a major California bank as subjects. Most banks in the United States, including this one, base decisions about whether or not you can have a credit card, and if so, what your credit limit should be, on a credit-scoring model calculated from a discriminant analysis. The form of that model, of course, is exactly the weighted average form of an additive multiattribute utility function. Bank credit officers are exceedingly familiar with the model; they use it every day. So we set out to recover its parameters from them, using various elicitation techniques. Our major findings were two. First, the bank officers did an excellent job of reproducing the results of the discriminant analysis model. Second, any method was just about as good as any other for obtaining the necessary judgments of weights, as long as the method was not holistic. Methods that obtained holistic judgments of applications and then attempted to recover weights by computational procedures such as regression were clearly inferior to methods in which the respondents judged weights more or less directly.

An obvious criticism of the study is that the officers, knowing the model well, may simply have been reproducing it for us. The obvious solution to that problem is to use a model that they are not familiar with—that is, a new one. We had a lucky break. It turned out that the bank decided to develop a credit-scoring model for much larger loans. We expect during the next few months to study how well its loan officers do at reproducing the parameters of this model, which they do not know. Our best guess is that the picture will not be greatly different from that found in the previous study.

Three studies have only scratched the surface of the validation problem. Much more needs to be done. In particular, someone more brilliant than I needs to figure out the answer to two questions: What does it mean to say that a decision structure, such as a value tree, is valid? And how can one determine whether a particular elicitation method for value trees is or is not valid?

A second kind of research need has to do with the front end of decision analysis. Once we know the relevant structures, the process is rather straightforward. But eliciting options, value trees, and decision trees is by no means straightforward, and there is considerable reason to believe that different analysts might obtain different results when performing that particular elicitation task. How can the structuring part of decision analysis be turned from art into science? In spite of various recent papers on the topic, I think the fair answer is that no one has any very good ideas.

Although I could go on for some time listing various kinds of research questions, the basically technological ones I have just presented are enough for my present purpose.

INCOMPATIBILITIES BETWEEN SCIENTIFIC
PSYCHOLOGY AND DECISION ANALYSIS

The title of this chapter implies that in my opinion decision analysis is a psychotechnology that should have grown out of psychophysics. The reason why is obvious. Decision analysis depends on four kinds of activities. The first, structuring the problem, is common to most human endeavors but certainly is frequently encountered in the practice of clinical psychology. The second, elicitation of values, is really a part of structuring. The third, elicitation of numbers for weights, location measures, and probabilities, is obviously straight psychophysics, applied to nonsensory quantities. The fourth, aggregation and decision, is a mathematical process that anyone can do.

Why, then, did decision analysis not grow out of psychophysics? I believe there are two reasons, both firmly rooted in the nature of the scientific psychological enterprise as it has been most commonly conceived.

The first of these roots is the definition of the object of psychological study as the "generalized normal adult human mind." That definition, I believe, originated with Wundt and was transplanted to American soil by various of Wundt's students, especially Titchener. We honor it to this day, as a few minutes spent reading any current issue of the *Journal of Experimental Psychology* will confirm.

I have never met a generalized normal adult human mind, and doubt that I ever will. The specific normal adult human beings that I have met vary from one another enormously, both in their abilities and in their interests. That variation is, of course, another time-honored topic of psychological study. But the linkage between study of individual differences and study of generalized processes has always been weak. The students of individual differences have typically had practical purposes in mind—notably personnel selection. They have sometimes found the tasks that process-oriented psychological researchers use in their experiments very useful as bases for selection. But only a pioneering few have tried to build process theories around study of each variability. And, whereas I applaud the enterprise, I have learned little from its results. J. P. Guilford found, many years ago, that human intellectual performance has more than 60 dimensions. I feel confident that if Guilford had been able to continue his search, the number of dimensions he found and named would be much greater by now. If human intellectual performance has 60, or perhaps 600, dimensions, I don't really want to know, because I would have no idea what to do with the knowledge. We too often overlook the point that the purpose of a theory is only secondarily to be right. Its primary purpose is to help us think about the facts on which it bears.

To most process-oriented theoreticians, individual differences have been a nuisance, to be eliminated from data by averaging if possible.

As long as the central topic of study for process-oriented psychologists was sensory or perceptual processes, this neglect of individual differences was relatively unimportant, because these happen to be areas of human performance in which individual differences are not large. Individual differences in ability to perform rote memorization tasks are quite large, and the history of psychological study of rote memory has been as extensive as that of psychological study of sensation and perception. I have always been astonished at the ability of workers in this field to spend the afternoon correcting proofs of their latest paper about the severe limits on human ability to process and remember information, and that evening spend 3 hours listening to actors performing a play by Shakespeare, without ever noticing an incongruity. But that incongruity has characterized psychology for longer than I can remember.

Nowadays, of course, the hot topics are all concerned with human intellectual performance—or information processing, as we are more likely to call it. And the study of human information processing raises a second issue in addition to that of wide individual variability. It is, of course, the issue of use of tools. The topic of intuitive ability to perform arithmetic is not prominent in psychological literature. I am reasonably confident that a number of consistent and reproducible deviations from optimal arithmetical performance would be easy to find in such a program of research. But no one would care, and so the research does not get done. The reason why is simple: The tools for doing arithmetic correctly are so widely known and easily available that the intuitive processes that might lead to errors in arithmetical performance are just not interesting. I contrast that with the very extensive recent literature on human errors of various kinds in working with probabilities. The tools for making probabilistic calculations correctly are equally well defined but much less widely known to nonexperts. Consequently, the intuitive errors of these nonexperts are extensively studied, and labels such as the representativeness bias, the availability bias, conservatism, and the like, intended to explain the systematic errors found, are part of the conceptual baggage of every process theorist. When probability theory is routinely taught in high schools, as algebra is now, I imagine that these labels will vanish from our theoretical vocabulary. Meanwhile, our lack of interest in what people can accomplish using tools has made us less useful than we might otherwise be in the development of psychotechnologies that depend for their effectiveness on the use of intellectual tools, as decision analysis does.

I should pause for a moment to exempt the field of engineering psychology, or human factors engineering, or ergonomics, from the preceding discussion about tools. That field, of course, has been consistently concerned with the design of tools so that men and women can use them effectively. Until quite recently, however, not much engineering psychological effort has gone into the design of intellectual tools. Nowadays, as the person–computer interface becomes more and more important, it seems likely that engineering psychological work on that interface will develop–but it has been surprisingly slow to emerge so far, as anyone who has ever used a remote computer terminal would be only too eager to testify.

The second reason why decision analysis did not grow out of psychophysics, or even out of psychology, is a habit of psychological thought. Psychologists insist on the meaningfulness of the distinction between normative and descriptive models of behavior and insist that psychology's proper business is with descriptive, not normative, models. This habit of thought relates closely to my discussion of tools aforementioned. Most intellectual tools (though not all) are designed to facilitate implementation of normative models, such as arithmetic, the grammar and syntax of language, and such complex ones as dynamic programming. Indeed, the fancier normative models can scarcely be used without tools and so have little status as normative models of human intellectual performance. This is somewhat surprising. Scheduling is a frequent and important human intellectual activity—but little research has been done on the degree of resemblance between the result of human intuitive scheduling and the output of optimal scheduling algorithms.

To my mind, a normative model is simply a model of how thinking ought to be done when it is important that it be done well—as it often is. And, whenever normative models are used, they are therefore also models of how thinking *is* done. If we, as psychologists, would like our models to be applicable to important as well as unimportant activities, and perhaps even to important as well as unimportant people, we should be willing to accept the idea that those models must, at a minimum, be able to accommodate correctness as well as error, skill as well as bias, and aided as well as unaided intellectual processes.

WHAT MIGHT PSYCHOLOGY BE ABOUT IN 20 YEARS?

From the point of view that this chapter has taken, many psychologists, and in particular many cognitive psychologists, have been hampered in the task of serving the society that supports them by outworn and no-longer-useful definitions of what psychology is about. Let us suppose, obviously contrary to fact, that: (1) this argument has been convincing to you—indeed, so convincing that you set out in a missionary spirit to persuade the next generation of cognitive psychologists to view their tasks, and the tasks of psychological theory in general, in a different light; and (2) that you succeed in persuading so many of our colleagues that the changes in definition for which I am calling in fact come to pass. What would the result be, in 20 years of so?

First, we would need a new definition of our role. I find the most stimulating approach to that definition in thinking about the workplace and the tasks that people perform in it. Increasingly these are intellectual tasks. Virtually invariably, they are performed with tools; this manuscript is being typed into a cathode-ray tube display that communicates with a word processor in USC's central computer. That does not make it any different from or any better than what I might have produced using a quill pen—but it does require of me a substantial set of skills, of which typing is by far the most trivial, for using these powerful and convenient tools.

Consider a definition of cognitive psychology that specifies its basic business as that of providing human beings who have cognitive tasks to perform with the knowledges and skills needed to perform them. First note that this definition is not exactly in conflict with the one we use today. To the degree that we can successfully provide the performers of cognitive tasks with the knowledges and skills they need, we can predict both how they will go about performing their tasks and how successful that performance will be.

What will we, the cognitive psychologists, need to be able to do in order to do our jobs? First, we must understand the cognitive tasks that show up in the workplace. Because they are myriad, and we cannot hope to deal with them all in detail, we shall have to understand them at a generic level. This is, of course, a familiar requirement for intellectual activities of many kinds. Arithmetic deals with a host of tasks by means of a four-cell task taxonomy: The cell labels are addition, subtraction, multiplication, and division. Because that taxonomy is a bit too simple for some complex arithmetical tasks, we have expanded it slightly; the name for the expansion is *algebra*.

We have a relatively similar example in the task taxonomy that underlies decision analysis. It is quite simple; I took you through it in some detail a few minutes ago. It is incomplete, as are both arithmetic and algebra. It is expandable and, indeed, expands almost daily, as we develop better formal understanding of elements of it that now seem artistic rather than procedural. I offer that as an example of the most important function that cognitive psychologists of the future will need to perform. It is by no means the only example. Scientists interested in language have been performing a relatively similar taxonomic task for quite some time now, with considerable success. Many other fields of intellectual endeavor are probably ripe for similar attacks. I am especially intrigued with the idea that tasks requiring interactions among people may be ready for taxonomic thought. Can we, for example, do a good taxonomic job of describing the subtasks that go into the task of persuasion? I cannot—and yet the obvious success that advertisers have in persuading people implies that a great deal of knowledge about the process exists in relatively unsystematic form. An easier still-untouched area ready for taxonomic thought is what we often call *creative thinking*. I know of at least two subtopics within that aggregate label that are obviously ready for systematic analysis and study because that systematic analysis and study is already under way. One is hypothesis invention—the task of inventing relatively simple explanations of complex sets of symptoms or phenomena. The other is action invention—the task of figuring out, in some situation requiring that some task must be accomplished, what available actions may meet the need.

Taxonomy, though a necessary first step, is never enough. The obvious next step is to figure out how the tasks identified in the taxonomy should be performed. Typically, this will mean the development of algorithms for performing these tasks. We have not traditionally thought of algorithm development as psychologist's work. But it obviously is. Indeed, as the students of artificial intelligence keep reminding us, any rule of thought that cannot be expressed in algorithmic form is suspect as too vague or incomplete to be considered a rule of thought. The best way by far of demonstrating that a rule can be expressed in algorithmic form is to write the algorithm. And the recent developments in computer technology come reasonably close to assuring us that most of the algorithms that we manage to write we can also implement.

Given that we can specify the taxonomy of tasks to be performed, sufficiently abstractly and economically so that it is not endlessly long, and given that we can specify and implement algorithms for performing these tasks, what roles do the human beings have? Taking decision analysis or arithmetic as our model of the answer to this question, human beings have several roles. First, they must specify the goals of the intellectual endeavor. Second, they must specify the inputs and indeed, in many cases, must provide them by means of direct judgment. And, third, they must evaluate the output. This is plenty for human beings to do, even in a fully algorithmicized intellectual environment. However, I do not expect that a fully algorithmicized intellectual environment will exist by the year 2000, or even 2050. So we shall continue to find human beings being asked to do the intellectual tasks that are still harshly resistant to formal analysis—just as they do today. To take only one example, I venture the speculation that we shall develop algorithms capable of producing simple prose, such as instructions about how to get from here to there within a city using public transportation, long before we shall develop algorithms capable of editing that prose into gracefulness, high grammatical quality, and simplicity. Indeed, I would speculate that an algorithm capable of performing the simple task of proofreading is a long way away. What we are quite likely to find instead is partial algorithmicization—exactly what we find in the autopilots of airplanes today. Sophisticated autopilots can fly planes much better than pilots can under most conditions. But that ceases to be true in some kinds of emergencies, and even in some kinds of routine operations. In such partial automation of intellectual work, the boundaries between what may best be automated and what should be left to the human being constantly change, as we develop higher and higher levels of skill in automating elements of the total task. I would expect exactly the same evolution to occur in the performance of intellectual tasks as well. If we, the cognitive psychologists, are to be participants in this process, we shall have a steady succession of new tasks to do, as new partial automations lead to new requirements for interfaces among people, algorithms, and the computers that implement them.

Piecemeal versions of all the tasks I have been describing as the responsibilities of cognitive psychologists already go on. The field of flight, especially space flight, offers the best as well as some of the most glamorous examples. The manned spacecraft program has so far represented our highest achievement, in two different senses, in blending algorithms with human skills to make the most of both. I suppose that much of this chapter can be considered a plea that the strategy that worked so well in that brilliant effort be applied more generally in defining the role of cognitive psychology, as it relates to human beings working on intellectual tasks.

I can find only three things to complain about in the vision of the future of cognitive psychology with which I have just entertained myself. The first is that our research will be much less convenient, primarily because we shall have to concern ourselves both with real tasks, often difficult to simulate in psychological laboratories, and with real and expert performers of those tasks, both hard to obtain and expensive. Too bad; no one ever promised that, as knowledge grows and topics become more complex, we could forever conduct easily manageable experiments on college student subjects without becoming fearful of triviality. The second is that generalizations of great depth and insight are likely to emerge only rarely from such a program. This, although indeed too bad, does not seem to me to differ much from what any outside observer would say about psychology as it is today. The third is that the concept of the generalized normal adult human mind would, in the program I am advocating, vanish from view as a definition of our subject matter. If that is a complaint, it is someone else's complaint; for me, the demise of that concept is an inducement to rejoice.

ACKNOWLEDGMENT

Preparation of this chapter was sponsored by the Defense Advanced Projects Agency (DoD), ARPA Order No. 4089, under Contract No. MDA903-81-C-0203 issued by Department of Army, Defense Supply Service–Washington, Washington, D.C. 20310.

REFERENCES

Edwards, W. The theory of decision making. *Psychological Bulletin,* 1954, *51,* 380–417.

Edwards, W. Behavioral decision theory. In P. R. Farnsworth (Ed.), *Annual review of psychology* (Vol. 12). Palo Alto, Calif.: Annual Reviews, 1961.

Edwards, W. Social utilities. *The Engineering Economist,* 1971, *6,* 119–129.

Edwards, W. How to use multiattribute utility measurement for social decision making. *IEEE Transactions on Systems, Man and Cybernetics,* 1977, *7,* 326–340.

Keeney, R. L., & Raiffa, H. *Decisions with multiple objectives: Preferences and value tradeoffs.* New York: Wiley, 1976.

Raiffa, H. *Decision analysis: Introductory lectures on choices under uncertainty.* Reading, Mass.: Addison–Wesley, 1968.

Raiffa, H., & Schlaifer, R. *Applied statistical decision theory.* Boston: Harvard University, 1961.

Schlaifer, R. *Analysis of decisions under uncertainty.* New York: McGraw–Hill, 1969.

Epilogue:
The Future of Experimental
Psychology—Toward the Year
2000

Viktor Sarris
University of Frankfurt a. M., West Germany

Allen Parducci
University of California, Los Angeles, USA

Each of the contributors to this volume was asked to speculate about the future of psychology and particularly about the changes that might be expected in psychology during the next twenty years. It is perhaps a testimonial to the perilous nature of our times and to the self-doubts characteristic of contemporary psychology that none of these prognostications are given with much assurance. Rather, one finds in the separate chapters accounts of the changes that the contributors *hope* will come. Many of these hopes are expressed with respect to particular research projects, and the reader can find them in the separate chapters. What we are attempting in this EPILOGUE is a summary of the contributors' grander hopes and expectations for psychology in general.

With a few notable exceptions, the contributors to this volume favor the development of approaches that are more rigorously experimental: *Psychology should become more solidly scientific.* However, this "hard-science" orientation takes a number of different directions. One direction leads toward a psychology that would be more biological in character, with closer ties to the neurosciences. But even among those pointing in this general direction, there are distinct differences in route. Where some look to pharmacological developments, others urge an increased concern with genetic factors. Biopsychologically-oriented hopes for the future are often expressed in the context of clinical problems, personality, and the concern with individual differences.

Another direction toward the future gives the traditional experimental approach an increased role in areas of psychology where it has had less influence. The desire for a more rigorous science is not seen as precluding development of these "softer" areas. Increased use of quasi-experimental designs is one way. A number of contributors propose new, "tough-minded" approaches. For example, causal modeling is urged as a means of eliminating alternative interpretations of correlational data.

Although humanistic concerns in psychology get little representation in this experimentally-oriented collection, a number of contributors express hope for a rapprochement between scientific and humanistic psychology. Some who urge this direction stick with traditional experimental methods but want these to be adapted so as to have greater ecological validity. This is to be accomplished by a more representative sampling of the environmental conditions to which the researchers want to generalize. Others emphasize greater concern with individual differences and also greater concern with interactions between organismic and environmental factors. Several contributors argue for a more direct development of practical applications. This is perhaps one of the more central points of contention, with others evincing skepticism about the likelihood of finding practical solutions to important problems. Some even argue that attempts to apply psychology are likely to fail—or that, in any event, applications of psychology are not the proper concern of laboratory scientists.

On the one hand, there is a refreshing absence of superficial salesmanship for the potential wonders of applied psychology. On the other hand, there is a corresponding absence of promises of impending theoretical integration. Doubts are even expressed about the discovery of general cognitive principles. Increased specialization of theoretical models and also of professional activities is predicted if not also desired by many contributors.

There is also the belief that future research will reflect the development of new methods and techniques. This in itself might be interpreted as a recognition that contemporary methods of research are inadequate for the problems at hand. More optimistically, it might be interpreted as a belief that in view of past developments new, greatly improved methods will be found.

Perhaps the broadest generalization that might be used to characterize the tone of the various contributions to this volume is the absence of stridency and a general reluctance to indulge in the puffery and exaggerated promises that have too often dominated even the most experimentally-oriented areas. As a field, psychology seems to have arrived at a more modest appreciation of what it has accomplished and what it can reasonably be expected to accomplish. Psychologists have learned that many of their grandest "theories" are *not even wrong,* that the looseness of many of psychology's most important concepts precludes the substantive predictions that permit a theory with empirical import to be tested. Psychologists seem also to have a more general appreciation of the difficulties of their science, of the enormous problems presented by the natural confounding of relevant conditions. The difficulties in the way of any attempt to unify the diverse fields of psychology are also generally recognized. As a young science, psychology can look to the history of older sciences, like physics and chemistry, which were not without their own problems of unification.

The prescriptions of radical behaviorism and the notion that a black-box approach to the relationships between stimuli and responses would yield genuine understanding no longer find much support. Many contemporary psychologists, like most of the contributors to this volume, are interested in problems that cannot be reduced to such simple formulations. There is a new freedom from the old constraints. But the new freedom does not guarantee new success, and this is generally appreciated. Are the problems of psychology simply too difficult?

The reader can have found in this volume few signs of despair or disenchantment with the *science* of psychology. If its successes have not met the grandiose expectations of earlier epochs, the present state of experimental psychology seems to be one of lowered expectations and a more realistic concern with the art of the possible. Along with this goes an enduring faith in science and a concern that this faith should stand up to the antiintellectualism of our times.

> *When considering knowledge in general as something carrying value and dignity there are, however, differences between its different kinds as to the degree of their certainty, on the one hand, and their significance and interest on the other. As to both advantages we must rank the soul on the top. One gets the impression that the study of soul may contribute to the advancement of such research, particularly to the understanding of nature. After all, the soul is something like the principle of whole life. . . . To get an adequate idea of the nature of soul belongs to the most difficult of tasks.*[1]

> Aristotle (ca. 330 B.C.)

---

[1]Translated by Viktor Sarris from Aristotle's *Peri Psyches*, §1 of first section.

Author Index

Italics denote pages with bibliographic information.

A

Abramson, L. Y., 33, *41*, 243, *250*, 256, *265*
Acito, F., 270, *284*
Alba, J. W., 97, *101*
Alberts, J. R., 91, *102*
Allport, G. W., 211, *232*, 256, *265*
Alwin, D. F., 279, *287*
Amsel, A., 66, 68, *68*, *69*, 91, *101*
Ananiev, B. G., 129, *134*
Anderson, F. L., 315, *321*
Anderson, N. H., 3, 7, *13*
Anderson, R. D., 270, *284*
Anderson, S. M., 263, *266*
Anohkin, P. K., 90, *101*
Ardila, R., 44, 45, 47, 48, 51, 52, 53, *54*, *55*
Atkinson, J. W., 235, 238, 239, 240, 241, 242, 245, 246, *250*, *251*
Atkinson, R. C., 165, *175*
Attig, M. S., 97, *101*
Austin, J. L., 27, *41*

B

Babkoff, H., 302, *307*
Baffa, G., 296, 303, *307*

Baltes, P. B., 267, 273, 274, 276, 277, 279, 280, 284, *285*, *287*
Bandura, A., 36, *41*
Barclay, A. G., 12, *14*, 53, *56*
Barker, R. G., 23, *25*, 211, 228, *232*
Barkóci, I., 74, *85*
Barlow, D. H., 45, *55*
Barry, W. M., 190, *193*
Bartsch, T. W., 279, *287*
Bauman, Z., 38, *41*
Baumm, N. C., 315, *321*
Beauchamp, G. K., 141, 146, *149*
Beauchamp, K. L., 45, *55*
Beck, E. C., 190, *195*
Beebe-Center, J. G., 136, *148*
Belous, V. V., 202, *208*
Belsley, D. A., 320, *320*
Bem, D. J., 256, *265*
Bentham, J., 142, *148*
Bentler, F. M., 319, *320*
Bentler, P. M., 267, 274, 276, 280, 283, 284, *285*
Berenhaus, I., 302, *307*
Berkowitz, L., 48, *55*
Bever, T. G., 168, *176*
Bickman, L., 11, *13*

359

Birch, D. A., 235, 239, 240, 241, 242, 245, 250, 251
Birdsall, T. G., 3, 14
Birnbaum, M. H., 137, 138, 148
Birren, S. E., 296, 303, 307
Bitterman, M. E., 62, 63, 64, 66, 67, 68, 69
Blancheteau, M., 153, 163
Blankenship, V., 240, 243, 246, 247, 248, 249, 251
Blass, E. M., 91, 101
Block, J. H., 229, 232
Bluth, G. L., 173, 176
Bohus, B., 100, 101
Boies, S. W., 113, 126
Bongort, K., 242, 245, 250, 251
Boring, E. G., 1, 13
Botwinick, J., 296, 303, 307
Bouguer, P. P., 17, 25
Bowers, K. S., 216, 232
Braff, D. L., 295, 298, 302, 307, 308
Braginsky, B. M., 44, 55
Braginsky, D. D., 44, 55
Brand, D. M., 173, 176
Bransford, J. D., 112, 124
Bräuninger, H., 325, 339
Brengelmann, J. C., 324, 328, 331, 332, 333, 339
Brickman, P., 136, 148
Briggs, D., 299, 301, 302, 303, 308
Brody, D., 295, 307
Bronfenbrenner, U., 319, 320
Broverman, D. M., 190, 195
Bruce, R. L., 45, 55
Bruno, J. P., 91, 101
Brunswik, E., 9, 21, 319, 13, 25, 320
Bühler, K., 4, 13
Bühringer, G., 325, 326, 327, 339
Burt, C. L., 272, 278, 285
Buss, A. H., 203, 208
Buss, A. R., 268, 285

C

Calfee, R. C., 44, 55, 138, 149
Campbell, B. A., 90, 91, 101
Campbell, D. T., 8, 13, 47, 55, 136, 148, 276, 285
Capaldi, E. J., 76, 85
Carter, G., 295, 297, 308
Cartwright, D., 28, 41, 240, 251
Cattell, R. B., 45, 55, 190, 193, 211, 232, 268, 269, 270, 271, 276, 278, 285, 286

Chalke, F. C. R., 190, 193
Chapman, J. P., 293, 307
Chapman, L. J., 293, 307
Chassan, J. B., 314, 320
Cheatle, M. D., 91, 102
Cherlow, D. G., 301, 308
Chess, S., 203, 209
Comer, P. A., 153, 163
Conrad, K., 199, 208
Craik, F. I. M., 117, 124
Christoph, G., 66, 69
Clark, E. V., 168, 176
Clark, H. H., 168, 176
Clark, L. H., 3, 13
Coan, R. W., 268, 285
Cohen, J., 284, 285
Cohen, N. J., 95, 101
Collingwood, R. G., 33, 41
Collins, J. F., 294, 303, 307
Collins, P. J., 302, 307
Coltheart, M., 294, 295, 297, 298, 307
Cook, S. W., 12, 14, 53, 56
Cook, T. D., 47, 55
Corkin, S., 95, 102
Cornelius, S. W., 267, 277, 281, 282, 283, 285
Corning, W. C., 61, 69
Costanzo, P. R., 37, 42
Coulter, X., 90, 101
Couvillon, P. A., 62, 63, 69
Covi, L., 315, 316, 321, 322
Crespi, L. P., 66, 69
Crombie, A. C., 18, 25
Cromwell, R. L., 299, 301, 302, 303, 308
Cronbach, L. J., 8, 9, 13, 179, 193, 237, 251, 276, 279, 285, 286
Crott, H. W., 272, 278, 287
Cunningham, C. L., 63, 69

D

Dashiell, J. F., 74, 77, 85
Davidson, L. P., 138, 149
Dean, P., 119, 124
DeJong, R., 325, 326, 327, 339
Dempster, F. N., 115, 124
Deutsch, J. A., 82, 83, 85
deVilliers, P. A., 241, 251
Diaz-Guerrero, R., 44, 55
Dickinson, A., 65, 69
Diener, E., 217, 233
Di Loreto, A. O., 188, 193

Dixon, R. A., 268, *286*
Downing, R. W., 312, 315, 316, 317, *320, 321*
Droppleman, L. F., 314, 315, *321*
Duhem, P., 29, *41*
Dunér, A., 227, *233*
Durlach, P. J., 63, *69*, 78, *86*
Dustman, R. E., 190, *195*
Dyal, J. A., 61, *69*
D'Zurilla, T. J., 217, *232*

E

Ebbinghaus, H., 64, *69*
Eckensberger, L. H., 278, *286*
Edwards, W., 235, 341, 342, *251, 353*
Eisenbeiser, T., 245, 246, *251*
Ekehammar, B., 216, 224, 225, *232, 233*
Elder, G. H., Jr., 281, *286*
Eliasz, A., 199, 205, *208*
Elkin, E. H., 154, *163*
Elliott, M. H., 66, *69*
Endicott, J., 319, *321*
Endler, N. S., 8, *13*, 213, 216, 217, 227, *232, 233*, 242, 243, *251*
Engledow, J. L., 270, *284*
Enright, M., 94, *102*
Epstein, S., 216, *232*
Ericsson, K. A., 95, *101*, 113, *124*
Eriksen, C. W., 294, 303, *307*
Ertl, J. P., 190, *193*
Estes, W. K., 3, 8, 13, 20, *25*
Eysenck, H. J., 5, 8, *13*, 179, 180, 181, 182, 183, 185, 188, 189, 191, 192, *194*, 200, 201, 203, *208*, 269, 270, *286*

F

Fagan, J. W., 94, *102*
Farquhar, J., 259, *265*
Feather, N. T., 235, 238, 246, *250*
Ferstl, R., 324, 331, *339, 340*
Festinger, L., 240, *251*, 255, *265*
Feyerabend, P. K., 30, 32, *41*
Fichter, M., 337, *340*
Fisher, R. A., 19, *25*
Fisher, R. L., 314, *321*
Fisher, S., 314, 315, *321*
Fiske, D. W., 205, *208*
Flagg, S. F., 72, *86*
Fowler, C. A., 114, *124*
Fowler, H., 76, *85*, 100, *101*

Fraisse, P., 44, 47, *55*, 129, *134*, 151, 153, 154, 155, 156, 157, 158, 159, 160, *162, 163*
Franks, J. J., 112, *124*
vonFrisch, K., 61, *69*
Frith, C., 183, *194*
Fulker, D. W., 181, *194*
Furby, L., 279, *286*

G

Gadamer, H. G., 38, *41*
Galanter, E. H., 111, *125*
Gallagher, D. W., 319, *321*
Gallop, G., 242, *251*
Garrett, H. E., 272, 278, *286*
Gauld, A., 38, *41*
Gelade, G., 113, *126*
Gergen, K. J., 32, 33, 38, 39, *41*
Germana, J., 44, *55*
Gerzén, M., 216, *233*
Giddens, A., 38, *42*
Gilford, R. M., 160, *163*
Glass, G. V., 5, *14*, 19, 22, *25, 26*
Goldberg, S., 298, *308*
Goldfried, M. R., 217, *232*
Golubeva, E. A., 201, *208*
Gonzalez, R. C., 66, 67, *69*
Goodglass, H., 301, *308*
Gottlieb, M. D., 302, *307*
Graesser, A. C. H., 119, 120, 121, 122, *124, 125*
Gray, J. A., 200, 201, *208*
Griffin, M., 97, *101*
Gross, L. P., 247, *251*
Gruzelier, J. H., 298, 302, *307*
Guilford, J. P., 270, *286*
Guttman, L., 269, *286*

H

Haber, R. N., 292, *307*
Haefely, W. E., 319, *321*
Hall, W. G., 91, *101, 102*
Halmiová, O., 132, *134*
Hamilton, W., 115, *124*
Hammond, K. R., 213, *232*
Hanson, N. R., 30, *42*
Har-Even, D., 302, *307*
Harkins, S. W., 276, *287*
Haroutunian, V., 91, *101*
Hartshorne, H., 216, *232*

Hartung, O., 325, *339*
Hasher, L., 96, 97, *101*
Hawkins, H. L., 295, *307*
Hayes, T., 299, 301, 302, 303, *308*
Hearst, E., 46, 66, *55, 69*
Hebb, D. O., 205, *208*
Heckhausen, H., 235, 238, 240, 244, *251*
Heffler, B., 228, *233*
Heidbreder, E., 296, *307*
Heider, F., 256, *265*
Heineken, E., 44, *55*
Helson, H., 135, *148*
Hemple, C. G., 142, *148*
Hendrickson, A. E., 190, *194*
Hendrickson, D. E., 190, *194*
Herrnstein, R. J., 241, *251*
Hersen, M., 45, *55*
Hershenson, M., 292, *307*
Herskovic, J., 298, *308*
Herzog, C. K., 296, 303, *309*
Hilgard, E. R., 95, *101*
Hindle, B., 17, *26*
Hindle, H. M., 17, *26*
Hirt, M., 295, 300, *308*
Hjelle, L. A., 198, *208*
Hofstatter, P. R., 4, *13*
Hokanson, J. E., 249, *251*
Holzkamp, K., 9, *13*, 254, *265*
Honig, W. K., 76, *85*, 100, *101*
Horn, G., 68, *69*
Horn, J. L., 190, *195*, 268, 274, 280, *286*
Horn, N. L., 315, *321*
Hovland, C. I., 256, *265*
Howard, K., 315, *321*
Howarth, E., 183, *194*
Hull, C. L., 3, *13*, 60, 66, *69*, 74, 80, 81, 82, 83, *85*, 240, *251*
Hulse, S. H., 76, *85*, 100, *101*
Humphreys, L. G., 276, *286*
Hunt, E. B., 8, *13*
Hunt, J. McV., 227, *232*
Huntzinger, R., 299, 301, 302, 303, *308*
Hurley, J. R., 269, *286*

I

Intraub, H., 114, *124*
Ivanov-Smolensky, A. G., 200, *208*

J

Jacobs, A., 279, *287*
James, W., 19, *26*

Janis, I. L., 256, *265*
Jockusch, V., 331, *339*
Johanson, I. B., 91, *102*
John, E. R., 114, *126*
Jöreskog, K. G., 270, 274, 276, 280, *286, 287*
Juola, J. F., 160, *163*

K

Kabat, L., 263, *266*
Kahn, R. J., 314, 315, *321*
Kahneman, D., 257, *266*
Kantor, J. R., 211, *232*
Kardos, L., 78, 82, *85*
Karlin, J. E., 157, *163*
Karpicke, J., 66, *69*
Kassou, A., 153, *163*
Kaufman, E. L., 122, *124*
Keeney, R. L., 343, 346, *353*
Kelley, H. H., 256, *265*
Kenny, D. A., 273, *286*
Kenny, J. T., 91, *101*
Kent, R. N., 217, *232*
Kiesler, C. A., 12, *14*, 53, *56*
Kietzman, M. L., 293, 297, 298, 302, 305, *307, 308, 309*
Kinsbourne, M., 300, *307*
Kintsch, W., 65, *69*, 166, 167, 168, 171, 172, 174, *176*
Klett, C. J., 313, *321*
Kline, D. W., 296, 298, 303, *307, 308*
Kling, J. W., 44, 47, *55*
Knapp, D., 123, *124*
Knight, R., 295, 297, 301, 302, 303, *308*
Knobel, S., 145, *149*
Koch, S., 3, 12, *13, 14*, 28, 42, 53, *56*
Köhler, W., 114, *124*
Kohn, M. L., 281, *286*
Kolers, P. A., 95, *102*
Konorski, J., 66, *69*
Kováč, D., 129, 130, 131, *134*
Kraemer, S., 324, 325, *339, 340*
Krasnogorsky, N. P., 200, *208*
Krauth, J., 228, *232*
Krawsky, G., 153, *163*
Kretschmer, E., 199, *208*
Kruta, V., 17, *26*
Kuh, E., 320, *320*
Kuhl, J., 238, 243, 244, 245, 246, *251*
Kuhn, T. S., 30, *42*, 54, *55*

L

Labouvie, E. W., 268, 276, 278, *286*
Lacey, O. L., 153, *163*
Lauterbach, W., 45, *55*
Lazarus, R. S., 115, *124*
Leamer, E. E., 319, 320, *321*
Leeper, R., 81, 82, 83, *86*
Leith, G. O., 185, 186, 187, *194*
Leon, M., 91, *102*
Leontev, A. N., 198, 202, *209*
Lerner, R. M., 268, *286*
Levey, A., 201, *208*
Lewin, K., 129, *134*, 211, *232*, 239, *251*, 254, *266*
Lewis, J., 8, *13*
Lewis, M., 319, *321*
Lienert, G. A., 128, *134*, 228, *232*, 272, 278, *287*
Ligon, E. M., 155, *163*
Liker, J. K., 281, *286*
Lindquist, E. F., 19, *26*
Lindsley, D. B., 190, *194*
Linsenmeier, J., 263, *266*
Lipman, R. S., 315, 316, *321*, *322*
Lomov, B. F., 130, *134*
Long, G. M., 294, 295, 298, 299, *308*
Lord, M. W., 122, *124*
Lowes, G., 67, *69*
Lucas, D., 94, *102*
Lunneborg, C., 8, *13*
Luria, A. R., 94, *102*

M

Macaulay, J., 48, *55*
Maccoby, N., 259, *265*
Mackintosh, N. J., 63, 65, *69*, 72, *86*
Maddi, S. R., 205, *208*
Magaro, P. A., 293, *308*
Magnusson, D., 212, 213, 215, 216, 217, 220, 221, 224, 225, 226, 227, 228, *232*, *233*, 242, 243, *251*
Maltzman, I. M., 290, *290*
Mandler, G., 110, 112, 116, 117, 118, 119, 120, 121, 122, 123, *124*, *125*
Mangan, G. L., 179, *194*, 200, *209*
Mannuzza, S., 302, *307*
Marcel, A. S., 110, 112, 113, 114, 116, *125*
Mardberg, B., 228, *233*
Mariotte, E., 17, *26*
Marsh, H. W., 145, *148*

Marshall, L. M., 138, *149*
Martin, L. T., 91, *102*
Maslach, C., 259, 265, *266*
Maslow, A. H., 6, *13*
Matheson, D. W., 45, *55*
Matysiak, J., 205, 206, *209*
May, M. A., 216, *232*
May, W. H., 115, *125*
McArdle, J. J., 268, 274, 280, *286*, *287*
McClelland, J. L., 112, *125*
McCord, R. R., 185, *194*
McGaw, B., 22, *25*
McGinnies, E., 153, *163*
McGuire, M., 300, *309*
McLean, P. D., 180, *195*
McMurray, G., 154, *163*
McNair, D. M., 314, 315, *321*
Meehl, P. E., 4, *13*
Meischner, W., 17, *26*
Meltzer, R. H., 118, 119, *125*
Menzel, R., 61, *69*
Merlin, V. S., 200, 202, *209*
Mervis, C., 112, *126*
Meyer, B. J. F., 173, *176*
Milgram, S., 48, *55*
Miller, G. A., 111, 115, 117, *125*
Miller, J. R., 168, 171, 172, 174, *176*
Miller, R. R., 76, *86*, 100, *102*
Miller, S., 295, 300, 302, *308*
Milner, B., 95, *102*, 300, *308*
Miron, M. S., 115, *125*
Mischel, W., 8, *13*, 216, 217, 220, *233*, 242, *251*
Mock, J. E., 315, *321*
Mohr, J. P., 95, *102*
Moseley, E. C., 313, *321*
Mosier, C. I., 269, *287*
Mueller, C. W., 98, *102*
Murphy, G., 46, *55*, 211, *233*
Murphy, L. B., 46, *55*
Murray, H. A., 211, *233*
Muthèn, B., 279, *287*

N

Nagy, Z. M., 91, *102*
Natsoulas, T., 110, *125*
Neale, J. F., 293, *308*
Nebylitsyn, V. D., 199, 200, 201, *209*
Nesselroade, J. R., 267, 268, 273, 274, 276, 277, 279, 280, 284, *285*, *286*, *287*

Newcomb, T. M., 46, *55*
Newell, A., 28, *42,* 166, *176*
Nisbett, R. E., 95, *102*, 257, *266*
Norman, D. A., 110, 111, 116, *125*
Nyman, B., 216, *233*

O

O'Connor, K., 189, *195*
Oláh, A., 220, *233*
Oltmanns, T. F., 293, *308*
Orme-Rogers, C., 296, 298, 303, *307*
Ortony, A., 111, 112, *126*
Osborne, R. T., 190, *195*
Oscar-Berman, M., 301, *308*
Osgood, C. E., 19, *26*, 115, *125*
Ovsiankina, M., 236, *251*

P

Parducci, A., 44, *55,* 136, 138, 141, 143, 144, 145, 146, *148, 149*
Park, L. C., 316, *322*
Parker, R. E., 114, *125*
Parsons, P., 93, *103*
Patterson, K. E., 118, 119, *125*
Paul, S. M., 319, *321*
Pavlov, I. P., 61, *69,* 201, 205, *209*
Pendery, M. L., 290, *290*
Perrett, L. P., 141, *149*
Pert, A., 67, *69*
Pervin, L. A., 213, 227, 229, *233,* 319, *321*
Peterson, G., 66, *69*
Peters, H., 44, *55*
Petrinovich, L., 9, *13,* 22, *26*
Piaget, J., 44, 47, *55*
Pierce, J. R., 157, *163*
Pitcoff, K., 67, *69*
Plum, A., 190, *195*
Polomin, R., 203, *208*
Pongratz, L. J., 18, *26*
Posner, M. I., 113, 116, *126*
Postman, L., 79, *86,* 256, *265*
Potts, A., 67, *69*
Pribram, H. H., 240, 247, *251*
Pribram, K., 111, *125*
Price, L. H., 242, *250*
Pruchno, R., 279, *287*
Putchat, C., 295, 297, *308*

Q, R

Quine, W. V., 29, *42*

Riegel, K. F., 12, *14*
Radics, L., 78, *85*
Radl, S., 260, *266*
Raiffa, H., 341, 343, 346, *353*
Raynor, J. O., 238, *251*
Reese, H. W., 273, 274, 276, 284, *285*
Reese, T. W., 122, *124*
Reinert, G., 272, 278, *287*
Rescorla, R. A., 63, *69,* 78, *86*
Reuman, D., 242, *251*
Rhodes, I. E., 190, *195*
Richter, M., 331, *339*
Rickels, K., 312, 315, 316, 317, *320, 321, 322*
Riegel, K. F., 53, *56*
Riggs, L. A., 45, 47, *55*
Rips, L. J., 166, *176*
Riskey, D. R., 141, 146, *149*
Robinson, D. N., 17, *26*
Rogosa, D., 274, 276, 280, 281, 282, *287*
Romanes, G. J., 59, *69*
Rorer, L. G., 12, *14,* 53, *56*
Rosch, E., 112, *126*
Rosenblatt, J. S., 91, *102*
Rosenstein, A. J., 227, *232*
Rosenzweig, L., 299, 301, 302, 303, *308*
Ross, L., 257, *266*
Rovee-Collier, C. K., 94, *102*
Ruchkin, D. S., 293, *308*
Rudy, J. W., 91, *102*
Ruggiero, F. T., 72, *86*
Ruisel, I., 132, *134*
Rumelhart, D. E., 111, 112, *125, 126*
Russalov, V. D., 201, *209*
Russel, I. S., 71, *86*
Russell, B., 27, *42*

S

Sidman, M., 95, *102*
Sidowski, J. B., 45, *56*
Simon, A. J., 95, *101*
Simon, H., 113, *124*
Simon, H. A., 166, 167, *176*
Sipos, I., 132, *134*
Skinner, B. F., 247, *252*
Skinner, E. A., 268, *286*
Skolnick, P., 319, *321*
Slade, R., 114, *124*
Smirnov, S., 159, *163*
Smith, E. E., 166, *176*
Smith, M. B., 12, *14,* 53, *56*
Smith, M. L., 5, *14,* 22, *25, 26*

Smith, P., 263, *266*
Smith, R. E., 217, *233*
Snyder, C. R. R., 113, 116, *126*
Sörbom, D., 270, 274, *286, 287*
Sorrell, G. T., 268, *286*
Spaulding, W., 299, 301, 302, 303, *308*
Spear, N. E., 76, *86*, 91, 93, 98, 100, *101, 102, 103*
Spence, K. W., 64, *69*, 200, *209*
Spencer, T. J., 295, 300, *308*
Sperling, G., 295, *308*
Sperling, S., 12, *14*, 53, *56*
Spielberger, C. D., 227, *233*
Spiro, A., 277, *285*
Spitzer, R., 319, *321*
Spring, B., 293, 297, *307*
Squire, L. R., 95, *101*
Stagner, R., 211, *233*
Stanley, J. C., 8, *13*, 276, *285*
Stanton, M., 68, *69*
Stattin, H., 217, 221, 226, *233*
Stehouwer, D. J., 91, *101*
Steinhauer, S., 305, *309*
Stelmack, R. M., 182, *195*
Steinert, P. A., 93, *103*
Stern, W., 7, *14*
Sternberg, S., 160, *163, 166, 176*
Steronko, R. J., 302, *308*
Stevens, S. S., 20, *26*, 45, *56*
Stigler, S., 280, *287*
Stoddard, L. T., 95, *102*
Stoloff, M., 91, *101*
Strelau, J., 200, 204, *209*
Sullivan, M. W., 94, *102*
Summers, G. F., 279, *287*
Sussman, C., 315, *321*
Sutton, S., 293, 302, *307, 309*
Swets, J. A., 3, *14*
Symons, J. R., 184, *195*
Szaftan, J., 296, 303, *308*

T

Tallman, J. F., 319, *321*
Tanner, W. P., 3, *14*
Tassinary, L., 114, *124*
Taylor, C., 38, *42*
Teasdale, J. D., 33, *41*, 243, *250*, 256, *265*
Teicher, M. H., 91, *101*
Teplov, B. M., 199, 200, 201, 205, *209*
Teuber, H. L., 95, *102*
Thatcher, R. W., 114, *126*

Thissen, D., 320, *322*
Thomas, A., 203, *209*
Thomas, C., 145, *149*
Thompson, L. W., 296, 303, *309*
Thomson, D. A., 79, *86*
Thorndike, E. L., 59, *70*
Tinbergen, N., 23, *26*
Tolman, E. C., 3, *14*, 65, *70*, 75, *86*, 211, *233*
Treisman, A. M., 113, *126*
Triandis, H. C., 53, *56*
Trown, E. A., 186, *194*
Tucker, L. R., 269, *287*
Tukey, J. W., 320, *321*
Tulving, E., 79, *86*, 95, *102*, 117, *124*
Turver, M. T., 298, 299, 300, *309*
Tversky, A., 257, *266*
Tweney, R. D., 18, *26*
Tyler, L. E., 319, *322*

U

Uhlenhuth, E. H., 316, *322*
Underwood, B. J., 22, *26*, 45, 47, *56*, 96, *103*

V

vanDijk, T. A., 166, 167, 168, *176*
Venables, P. H., 298, 302, *307*
Vipond, D., 174, *176*
Volkmann, J., 122, *124*
Vogel, W., 190, *195*
Vogler, R. E., 324, *339, 340*
Vollmer, H., 325, *340*

W

Wachtel, P., 211, *233*
Wagner, A. R., 63, *69*
Wainer, H., 320, *322*
Wakefield, J. A., 185, *194*
Walker, E., 300, *309*
Walsh, D. A., 295, 296, 298, 300, 303, *309*
Warden, C. J., 79, *86*
Warrington, E. K., 94, *103*, 115, *126*
Watson, J. B., 3, *14*
Weiß, M., 243, *251*
Weiner, B., 238, 244, *252*
Weisen, A., 184, *195*
Weiskrantz, L., 94, 95, *103*
Welsch, R. E., 320, *320*

Wertheimer, M., 12, *14,* 23, *26,* 53, *56*
West, L. J., 290, *290*
Westland, G., 44, *56*
Wheaton, B., 279, *287*
Wiener, N., 293, *309*
Williams, D. R., 65, *70*
Williams, M. V., 296, 303, *309*
Willis, S. L., 277, *285*
Willows, A. O. D., 61, *69*
Wilson, G. D., 182, *194*
Wilson, T. D., 95, *102*
Winch, P., 33, 38, *42*
Windelband, W., 313, *322*
Wittchen, H. V., 337, *340*
Witte, R. S., 65, *69*
Wittgenstein, L., 2, *14,* 39, *42*
Wittmann, W., 271, *287*
Wohlwill, J. F., 268, *287*
Wold, H., 274, *287*

Wolford, G., 114, *124*
Wood, P., 259, *265*
Woods, D. J., 302, *308*
Woodworth, R. S., 18, 19, 20, *26,* 128, *134*
Wright, H. F., 23, *25*
Wundt, W., 199, *209*

Y, Z

Yarbrough, J. C., 172, *176*
Zacks, R. T., 96, *101*
Zeigarnik, B., 236, *252*
Zetterblom, G., 227, *233*
Ziegler, D. J., 198, *208*
Zimbardo, P. G., 255, 258, 260, 263, 265, *266*
Zubin, J., 293, 297, 302, 305, *307, 309*
Zuckerman, M., 203, *209*

Subject Index

A

Adaptation-level theory, 135–138
Alcoholism (*see also* Behavioral therapy)
  dangers of controlled-drinking approach, 290
  treatment, 324–325
Algorithms, 351–353
Anchoring (*see* Category ratings)
Anti-intellectualism, 5–6
Applied psychology
  clinical, 291–339
  decision analysis, 341–353
  separation from academic psychology, 289
  social, 258–259, 268
Artificial intelligence, 351–353 (*see also* Cognitive psychology)
Attribution theory, 255
Autonymy, 254

B

Behavioral therapies
  effectiveness, 324–325, 329, 331, 333
    comparisons, 332–336
    placebo effects, 329
    relapse rate, 327, 329–331
  future of, 336–339
  goals of, 325–326

problems treated
  alcoholism, 290, 324–325
  chronic medical patients, 331–336, 338–339
  drug abuse, 325–327
  hypertension, 332–333
  overweight, 331–332
  smoking, 327, 332–333
reinforcements, 328–330, 332–333
types of treatment
  aversion therapy, 324, 328, 330
  broad spectrum therapy, 324–327, 332
  by mail and TV, 331–332
  self-control procedures, 324–326, 328–331
Behaviorism
  cognitivism vs., 6–7, 105, 109, 165, 357
  history, 3, 109

C

Category ratings (*see* Adaptation level, Range-Frequency theory)
  anchoring of, 145
  non-monotonic scales, 146
  number of categories, 144
  open scales, 145
Causal modeling, 267, 274–284
Childrearing, 48–51

Cognitive dissonance, 255–257, 260, 330
Cognitive psychology
    artificial intelligence and, 351–353
    behaviorism vs., 3, 6–7, 75, 105, 109, 128
    hardware vs. software, 7
    history, 3–4, 124, 128, 349
    social, 253–265
Communication, electronic, 263 (*see also* Computers)
Computers, 21, 127 (*see also* Artificial intelligence)
    in decision analysis, 345, 349, 352
Conditioning (*see also* Learning)
    classical
        in honeybees, 61–63
    instrumental, 64–69, 77, 80–84
        habit family hierarchy, 74
        place learning, 73–85
Consciousness
    chunking and clustering, 116–121, 169
    constructive approaches, 112–115, 167
    focal dimensions, 119–120
    limitations of, 115–123
    physiological basis for, 305
    processes and functions, 110–111, 113, 117, 123
    schemas, 105, 111–112
Consumatory effects, 246–249
Cross-cultural research, 48–51, 226

D

Decision analysis, 341–353
    probability learning, 346
    psychophysics and, 341, 347–349
Developmental psychology
    research in, 48–51, 267–284
Discriminant analysis model, 347

E

Ecological validity (*see* Validity, ecological; Experimental design, representative)
Educational psychology, 143–144, 184–188
Environment, taxonomy of, 229–230
Evolution, 66–68
Experimental design (*see also* Experimental methods)
    correlations vs., 8–9
    functional measurement, 7
    micro vs. macro-analysis, 133–4, 167, 169
    non-traditional methods, 178

organismic factors, 8, 131, 179
    person/situation designs, 217–220
    practical applications vs., 10
    quasi-experimental, 47–51, 226
    representative design, 9–10, 228
Experimental methods, 43–46 (*see also* Experimental design)
Experimental psychology
    exploratory methods vs., 268–273
    hard vs. soft areas, 4–5
    naive model for, 1–2
    progress in, 2–3, 13, 28
    substantive failure, 2–3, 110
Experiments
    theories ancillary to, 41
    vivify theories, 40

F

Factor analysis, 267–270
Falsifiability (*see* Theories)
Forgetting and recall, 132–133 (*see also* Memory)
Functional measurement, 7
Future, expectations for, 21, 53–54, 98, 355–357
    behavioral therapy, 336–339
    correlation and experimentation, 23
    exploratory research, 229, 319–320
    information processing and psychopathology, 305
    less applied, 306
    nomothetic and ideographic, 24–25, 134, 227–228, 348
    representative design, 319
    wishes for, 355–357

G

Gerontology, 282–284
Group dynamics, 254–256

H

History of psychology, 17–21
    clinical, 323
    cognition and computers, 21
    experimental method, 18, 147–148
    funding of research, 20
    psychopathology, approaches to, 291–293
    statistics, 19
Humanistic concerns, 356

I

Individual differences
  extrovert vs. introvert, 180–183
  in effects of drugs, 313–319
  functional measurement, 7
  genetics of, 177, 181
  inertial motivation, 245
  in memory, 162
  organismic factors, 8, 131, 179–180
  in psychotherapy, 188
  in temperament, 179
Information processing, 76, 151, 162 (*see also*
  Cognitive psychology)
Intelligence, 166, 177, 306
  artificial, 351–353
  cortical arousal and, 189–193
Interfunctional context and research, 130–131

J

Judgmental relativity, 135–149

L

Learned helplessness, 243, 256
Learning (*see also* Conditioning; Memory)
  evolutionary divergence, 66–68
  vertibrate vs. invertibrate, 60–64

M

Mathematical models, 3, 45, 165
Measurement model, 274–276
Memory
  factors affecting
    duration, 153–157
    motivation, 88–89
    neuropeptides, 100
    ontogenetic, 90–94
    physiological, 162
    recall and reminiscence, 183
    subitizing in, 122–123
  stages in
    encoding, 155–160
    retrieval, 78–79, 118–119, 160, 166
    visual, 73, 80–84 (*see also* Vision, per-
      sistence in)
  types of (*see also* Vision, persistence in)
    long-term, 162, 292
    short-term, 113, 165, 192

Memory, in animals, 71–85 (*see also*
  Conditioning)
  difference from humans, 80
Memory, pathology of
  alcohol and, 98–100
  amnesias, 94–96
  dissociations, 94–97
Methods (*see* Experimental methods; Experimental design)
Miniature systems, 3, 165
Motivation
  achievement motivation, 238
  anxiety-provoking situations, 220–227
  cognitive approach, 235–249
  memory and learning, 88–89
  neurobiological research, 240
  neuropeptides and, 100
Multivariate correlational methods, 268 ff.,
  276–278

N

Normative models, 350

P

Paradigms, 128, 156, 182, 227–230
Personality
  determinants of, 197–208
    physiological bases, 197–203
  research, 211–237
  situation by person interactions, 212–216
  stability of, 220
  temperament, 197–199, 204–209
  trait/situation models, 215–217
Persuasive communications, 255–256
Philosophy
  positivist-empiricist, 27–31
    loss of confidence in, 29–31
Problem solving, 166
Psychoanalysis, 336–338
Psychobiology
  and intelligence, 189–193
  and memory, 87–101
  and personality, 198–209
Psychology as a field
  applied vs. basic, 10–12
  hard vs. soft, 4–5
  heterogeneity of, 9, 12
  international comparisons, 51–53
  unification of, 177, 356–357

Psychopathology
  experimentally induced, 263
  information processing in, 291–309
  of memory (see Memory, pathology of)
  social types, 260–263, 265
Psychopharmacology
  clinical vs. research approach, 313
    double-blind design, 311
    placebo effects, 311, 314–315
  diagnostic categories, 319
  multiple regression procedures, 316
  psychotropic agents, 311, 314, 316, 319
Psychotherapy, 188 (see also Behavioral
    therapy)

R

Range-frequency theory, 138–144
  and anchoring, 145
Rating scales (see Category ratings)
Reading, 151, 157, 166
  readability formulas, 172, 175
  retention, 175
  text propositions, 169
Reinforcement (see also Conditioning,
    instrumental)
  principle of, 28, 143–144
Regulative theory of behavior, 204–208
Relativism
  in perception and judgment, 135–149
Reward (see Conditioning, instrumental)

S

Schemas
  in consciousness, 105, 111–112
  perceptual, 132
Schizophrenia, 301–304
Shyness, 259–260

Smoking, treatment of, 327, 332–333
Social comparison theory, 260
Social controls, 257
Social psychology, 46–47, 253–266
Stanford prison experiment, 258
Stimulus processing coefficient, 205
Structural modeling (see Causal modeling)
Subjective reality, 253, 258

T

Theories
  convergence of methods and purposes,
    271–272
  experiments as vivification of, 40
  falsifiability, 31–37, 105–106, 168, 356
  promoting values, 39–40

U

Utilities, measurement of, 342–346

V

Validity
  ecological, 9–10, 128
    domain representativeness, 276–278
    sampling of situations, 228
    simplicity vs., 10
Values (see Philosophy; Decision Analysis;
    Utilities)
Vision
  information processing in, 292–309
  masking, 295, 297, 299 ff.
  persistence in (see also Memory, visual),
    294–309
    impairment in clinical patients, 295
    peripheral vs central, 299–301
    schizophrenics, 301–304

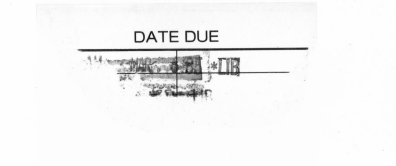